David Welch is Professor of Modern History and Director of the Centre for the Study of War, Propaganda and Society at the University of Kent. His publications include *Propaganda, Power and Persuasion: From the First World War to WikiLeaks*, *War and the Media: The Changing Context of Reportage and Propaganda, 1900–2003* and *Propaganda and the German Cinema, 1933–1945* (all I.B.Tauris). He co-curated the 2013 exhibition at the British Library and authored the accompanying book: *Propaganda, Power and Persuasion*.

'This is the most important book about German information policy, including censorship, 1914–18, ever written. David Welch has written brilliantly about the uses of propaganda by Germany in World War I to instruct, uplift and control domestic opinion in a time of total war.'

David Culbert
Professor of History, Louisiana State University

'... [the book] throws fresh light not only on the propaganda history of the Great War, but also on why the German people were able and willing to sustain their support for their government's war effort. David Welch has made yet another significant contribution to the history of the twentieth century – the people's century, the century of total war and of the communications revolution.'

Philip M. Taylor (1954–2010)
Professor of International Communications,
University of Leeds

'... its contribution to the growing historiography of the First World War and its social, cultural and intellectual impact is clear. This book will appeal to general readers in European history as well as specialists in German history or the First World War and is now among the important works dealing with the origins of propaganda as a factor in modern politics.'

Vejas Liulevicius
Journal of Modern History

'... [an] extraordinarily wide-ranging, intelligent and authoritative study ... an outstanding piece of historical scholarship. Throughout the book, Welch sustains a complex and subtle analysis that provides his readers with an entirely new understanding of both the devastating German experience of the First World War on the home front and the ill-considered domestic policies that were, to such a large extent, responsible for their experience.'

Nicholas Reeves
Historical Journal of Film, Radio and Television

GERMANY AND PROPAGANDA IN WORLD WAR I
Pacifism, Mobilization and Total War

DAVID WELCH

New paperback edition published in 2014 by I.B.Tauris & Co Ltd
6 Salem Road, London W2 4BU
175 Fifth Avenue, New York NY 10010
www.ibtauris.com

Distributed in the United States and Canada Exclusively by Palgrave Macmillan
175 Fifth Avenue, New York NY 10010

First published in hardback in 2000 by The Athlone Press

Copyright © 2000, 2014, David Welch

The right of David Welch to be identified as the author of this work has been asserted by the author in accordance with the Copyright, Designs and Patents Act 1988.

All rights reserved. Except for brief quotations in a review, this book, or any part thereof, may not be reproduced, stored in or introduced into a retrieval system, or transmitted, in any form or by any means, electronic, mechanical, photocopying, recording or otherwise, without the prior written permission of the publisher.

Every attempt has been made to gain permission for the use of the images in this book. Any omissions will be rectified in future editions.

ISBN: 978 1 78076 827 4
eISBN: 978 0 85773 611 6

A full CIP record for this book is available from the British Library
A full CIP record is available from the Library of Congress

Library of Congress Catalog Card Number: available

Printed and bound by Page Bros, Norwich

Contents

List of Illustrations, Map and Tables		vi
Acknowledgements		x
Preface to the New Edition		xi
	Introduction	1
1	Days of Decision: Germany on the Eve of War	9
2	The Mobilization of the Masses	22
3	War Aims	61
4	The Crucible of War	80
5	Dissenting Voices: Pacifism, Feminist Ferment and the Women's Movement	141
6	War Aims Again	168
7	Civilians 'Fall-In'	204
8	Defeat and Revolution	231
	Conclusion: 'The Sins of Omission'	260
Notes		269
Bibliography		343
Index		363

List of Illustrations, Map and Tables

FIGURES

1 German reserves on the way to the Western Front, August 1914. Chalked on the side of the carriage is the confident boast: 'Excursion to Paris, See you again on the Boulevard'. 6
2 Enthusiastic crowd in the Odeon Platz, Munich, 2 August 1914. Among the crowd can be seen the young Adolf Hitler. 17
3 General war fever, August 1914. 18
4 A postcard depicting Reuters, the London-based news agency, as 'the lying toad' disseminating propaganda to the allied capitals in London and Paris. 31
5 The organization of official propaganda, 1914–16. 44
6 'We Barbarians!' Louis Oppenheim's 1916 poster claiming that Germany has fewer illiterates, spends more on education, prints more books, has a better social security system, and has more Nobel prize winning scientists than Britain and France. 50
7 A sketch taken from a military journal showing the inside and outside of the mobile cinemas that were touring the frontline showing propaganda films to soldiers (*Mitteilungen betr. Kriegsaufklärung*, October 1917). 58
8 A postcard of Lord Grey ('War Monger and Mass Murderer'). The devil confides that 'even *I* can learn from this man!'. 63
9 'Who is Militaristic?' A German poster that compares favourably Germany's past military record with those of Britain and France. 65
10 The Kaiserin saying farewell to some nursing sisters about to leave for the front with the hospital train in the background. 81
11 'There is Enough Aluminium, Copper, Brass, Nickel, Zinc in the Country. Hand it in – the Army Needs It!' Louis Oppenheim, 1917. 86

List of Illustrations, Map and Tables vii

12 A poster that compares favourably the combined national income of Germany to that of Britain. 87
13 The unveiling of the colossal wooden statue of Hindenburg in the Siegeshalle in Berlin, 4 September 1915. 92
14 'Subscribe to War Loans. Times are Hard, But Victory is Certain.' Bruno Paul's 1917 poster of Hindenburg as the national figurehead. 93
15 (a) A recruitment poster urging: 'German Women – Work in the Home Army!' The female munition worker produces the 'potato masher' grenade for the soldier. 106

   (b) a photograph of female munition workers making shells. 106

   (c) The Krupps armaments works in Essen. 107
16 A poster and postcard; 'Where is Food Need Greatest?' The chart shows what the populations in Germany, England, France and Russia could buy at the end of the third year of war for 1 mark. Using the examples of bread, potatoes and sugar, the chart reveals that Germans could purchase considerably more of all three. 116
17 An anti-British poster 'He is the Guilty'. 124
18 A Berlin ration card allowing for 2 kilograms of bread. 125
19 Poster of a nationwide campaign encouraging adults and children to collect acorns, beechnuts, dried fruit peel, etc., and deliver them to designated collection points. 126
20 Four examples of unrestricted submarine warfare. 137

   (a) 'Subscribe to War Loans and Help in the U-Boat War Against England'. 137

   (b) 'U-Boats are Out!' Hans Rudi Erdt's famous poster. 137

   (c) An agitational cartoon from the right-wing satirical magazine, *Kladderadatsch*, of the unrestricted submarine warfare against England launched in February 1917. 138

   (d) U-Boat calendar claiming that unrestricted submarine warfare will eventually force Britain to seek a peace settlement. 139
21 A *Simplicissmus* cartoon attacking German pacifists: 'Once again they tried to bury the hatchet of war in the barrel of ink. Unfortunately it was too big on this occasion.' 23 November 1915. 149
22 'Collect Combed-Out Women's Hair! Our Industry Needs it for Drive Belts.' This campaign in Magdeburg was organized by the German Red Cross and the poster designer, Jupp

Wiertz, employed a crucifix-like image for the campaign – presumably to symbolize the sacrifice that was being made by women.	164
23 'Help Us Win! Subscribe to the War Loans.' Fritz Erler's 1917 haunting poster for the Sixth War Loan.	214
24 The organization for 'patriotic instruction'.	217
25 'Through Work to Victory! Through Victory to Peace!' A symbolic handshake between the fighting front and the home front. Alexander Cay, 1917.	218
26 'This is the Way to Peace – the Enemy Wills it So! Therefore Subscribe to the War Loans!' Lucian Bernhard's powerful poster of the mailed gauntlet for the Seventh War Loan.	221
27 Another variation of the Teutonic knight – brandishing sword and shield but wearing a First World War steel helmet. Poster for the Seventh War Loan.	222
28 'Subscribe to War Loans. Help those who watch-over your Happiness.' An archetypal German family from the Nibelungen legend.	223
29 A dramatic poster for the Seventh War Loan depicts President Wilson as a warlike dragon.	224
30 Gerd Paul's dramatic poster for the Seventh War Loan depicting a Siegfried-like warrior beating a cowering British lion with the caption: 'The last blows are necessary for final victory. Subscribe to the War Loan'.	225
31 A German hospital ward on Christmas day.	226
32 Erich Gruner's wood-cut poster: 'Thanks. Offering from the Kaiser and the Nation to the Army and Navy. Christmas Gifts for 1917'.	227
33 A still from the final scene of *Der Knute entflohen (Escaping from Tyranny)*. Walter (Carl Richard) having heroically escaped from a Russian POW camp returns home to his parents proudly displaying the iron cross.	228
34 Two examples of British propaganda leaflets intended to drive a wedge between the Kaiser and his people:	241
(a) One of the most famous leaflets showing the Kaiser and his six sons in full military regalia, all unscathed by war: 'One family which has not lost a single member'.	241

(b)	Hindenburg warns the Kaiser that the people are buckling under their burdens. The Kaiser replies: 'Why are they groaning? WE feel no hardship!'.	242
35	Karl Sigrist's poster for the Eighth War Loan with the dove of peace and the German eagle.	244
36	'German Women, Work for Victory!' A 1918 recruitment poster urging women to contribute to victory by working in the munitions factories.	245
37	An extraordinarily simple but powerful poster advertising a 'Day of sacrifice' (1917).	248
38	Ludwig Hohlwein's moving 1918 poster 'Ludendorff Fund for Disabled Veterans'.	250
39	'Heroes Back From the Front! Your Country Greets You!' The small child, the symbol of Munich, welcomes returning soldiers back from the front as heroes (Walter Ditz).	251
40	The Kaiser's visit to Kiel, October 1918.	255
41	Mutiny of the Fleet in Wilhelmshaven, November 1918.	256
42	Demonstrations in Berlin, 9 November 1918.	257
43	Front page of the SPD newspaper, *Vorwärts*, 9 November 1918, announcing the abdication of the Kaiser. The brief statement is signed by Chancellor Prince Max von Baden who has ordered the armed forces not to use their weapons: 'No shots will be fired!'.	258

MAP

1	The Schlieffen Plan.	5

TABLES

1	*Food rations as a percentage of peacetime consumption, 1916–18*	128
2	*Average daily meat consumption in grams per head, by groups*	130
3	*Index of child mortality (1913 = 100)*	131
4	*Strikes and lock-outs in Germany 1913–19 (based on Reich statistics)*	310

Acknowledgements

This book has taken more than a decade in the researching and writing. During that time a number of archives have moved from east to west in the aftermath of German unification. I have been greatly helped by the archivists of the Politisches Archiv des Auswärtigen Amts, Bonn; the Staatsarchiv, Bremen; the Staatsarchiv, Hamburg; the Bayerische Hauptstaatsarchiv, Munich; the Generallandesarchiv, Karlsruhe; the Institut für Wissenschaftlichen Film, Göttingen; the Staatsarchiv, Potsdam; the Bundesarchiv, Koblenz (now all transferred to Berlin); the Bundesarchiv Militärchiv, Freiburg; the Heeresarchiv and the Hauptstaatsarchiv, Stuttgart; the Imperial War Museum and the Public Record Office, London.

It is with great pleasure that I acknowledge the immeasurable help I have received from friends and colleagues in completing this work. In particular I would like to thank Professors Richard Evans, Dick Geary and Christine Bolt for reading individual chapters and a special word of thanks to Professor Arthur Marwick for his constructive comments on the manuscript. I also owe a debt of thanks to Professors David Culbert and Philip Taylor. The shortcomings that remain are, of course, my responsibility alone. I am indebted to the British Academy and the Deutscher Akademischer Austauschdienst for funding the orginal research for the book. However, this book would not have been written without the loving support and acerbic comments of my wife Anne, and the indulgence of our two children Christopher and Lizzie. To them I owe a very special debt of gratitude.

Preface to the New Edition

This book was originally published in 2000 and was the first work to fully examine German society during the First World War and the interaction between politics, propaganda and public opinion. It has still to be superseded and remains the only work on the subject in English.

The First World War made greater demands on the material and human resources of the nations involved than any previous conflict. The war still holds a unique position as the benchmark against which the heroism, brutality and futility of modern industrialized warfare has come to be measured. In 'total war' it was no longer sufficient simply to organise industry or to mobilize manpower in order to carry a modern state through a long war. Of course it would prove to be a war of intense industrial competition and scientific innovation; the manufacture of arms and munitions became critically important. But equally important was the need to engage the will and support of whole nations. To this end, once the war erupted, the belligerents rapidly began publishing accounts of how it had been caused. They did so because the attribution of responsibility for starting the war was the key element in the propaganda battle. Propaganda was directed towards the home population to illicit support for the war, towards neutral countries as a means of influence, and towards the enemy as a weapon. The First World War was the first war in which the mass media played a significant part in disseminating news from the fighting front to the home front, as well as being the first war to target systematically produced government propaganda at the general public. In order to encourage all citizens to contribute to the war effort, both the home and fighting fronts needed to be persuaded of the importance of their collective effort to securing ultimate victory.

So for the first time belligerent governments were required to mobilize entire civilian populations into 'fighting communities'. Like Britain, Germany on the eve of war was beset by numerous internal tensions. When Britain declared war on Germany, a 'State of Siege' was announced, placing the Prussian military hierarchy in charge of the country, and the normally competing social and political groupings resolved to work for victory by means of a political truce (*Burgfrieden*). In Germany, in particular then, the war seemed (initially at least) to create a new sense of solidarity in which class antagonisms were transcended by a 'national community' (*Volksgemeinschaft*). This proved a fruitful theme in German propaganda. The belief that the war was foisted upon Germany as a result of enemy encirclement – principally in the shape of the Franco–Russian Entente – persuaded most sections of the community (with the exception of pacifists) to put aside their differences. However, maintaining the *Burgfrieden* depended on a swift victory. As the conflict dragged on, tensions resurfaced. Eventually the German imperial authorities' failure to respond to genuine grievances and demands for political reform stretched the political truce beyond bearable limits and, by the end of 1917, it had lost its credibility as a unifying theme.

The centenary of the outbreak of World War I has resulted in a plethora of new works on the conflict, and many more will follow as various landmark anniversaries are commemorated. The literature continues to be dominated by the origins of the conflict and by debate over which nation was largely responsible for starting the war. Apportioning blame has become part of the ritual of denouncing Germany[1]. However, most of these new books continue to ignore the significance of propaganda in mobilizing support for the war and sustaining civilian and fighting populations throughout the four years of the increasingly bloody conflict.

This work reaffirms that German society was a highly complex hybrid of competing groups and interests and that to compare the Kaiser's war aims in 1914 with those of Hitler's in 1939 (as some British military historians have attempted to do) is far too simplistic. Far from being a ruthless dictator, the Kaiser constantly prevaricated and his political leadership was weak. Wilhelm II was no Hitler.

Drawing on a wide range of sources – from posters, newspapers, journals, film, parliamentary debates, police and military reports and private papers – I have attempted to show that, contrary to received opinion, the German government had developed a sophisticated notion of propaganda and its reception by different publics, and had established a network of monitoring stations to provide feedback on the 'pulse of the people'. It is my contention that the eventual moral collapse of Germany was due less to the failure to disseminate propaganda than to the inability of the military authorities and the Kaiser to reinforce this propaganda, and to acknowledge the importance of public opinion in forging an effective link between leadership and the people in conditions of 'total war'. Those in power were unable and unwilling to reform German society along the lines demanded by public opinion. This book is the story of the ultimate failure of German propaganda to convince the nation as a whole that ultimate victory was possible. As such, I believe, it provides important insights into the German experience of the Great War.

David Welch
Canterbury, 2014

Introduction

The history of the First World War has been dominated by the debate on its origins and by accounts of its development on the military, political and diplomatic fronts.[1] Few works have tackled the history of the war and its impact on German society.[2] This book sets out to redress the balance by analysing the interaction between imperial propaganda and the responses of different social groups in Germany both to each other and to the impact of total war.

One of the most significant lessons to be learnt from the experience of the First World War was that public opinion could no longer be ignored as a determining factor in the formulation of government policies. Unlike previous wars, the Great War was the first 'total war' in which whole nations, and not just professional armies, were locked in mortal combat. The war served to increase the level of popular interest and participation in the affairs of state. The gap between the soldiers at the front and the civilians at home was narrowed substantially in that the entire resources of the state — military, economic and psychological — had to be mobilized. In 'total war', which requires civilians to participate in the war effort, morale came to be recognized as a significant military factor, and propaganda began to emerge as the principal instrument of control over public opinion and an essential weapon in the national arsenal.

Adolf Hitler, writing in *Mein Kampf*, was scathing in his condemnation of German war propaganda and declared that Germany had failed to recognize propaganda as a weapon of the first order.[3] But the German government had, in fact, from an early stage in the war — certainly earlier than the Allies — developed a sophisticated notion of propaganda and its reception by different publics, and had established a national network of monitoring stations to provide feedback on the 'pulse of the people'. It is the contention of this book that the moral collapse of Germany was due less to the failure to disseminate propaganda than to the inability of the military authorities and the Kaiser to reinforce this propaganda by responding positively to public opinion thus forging an effective link between the leadership and the people. The government had constructed the means to read the mood of the people, but failed to act upon what it read! The Prussian ruling elite had been warned to take heed of Goethe's words: 'The revolution from below is always due to the sins of omission of those above.' Their contempt for the ordinary people and their failure to recognize the need for domestic political reforms were major factors in undermining civilian morale.

Three major problems hampered German war propaganda. Firstly, it was tied too intimately to German success on the battlefield; secondly, under the State of Siege of 1914 the Commanding Generals of the twenty-four corps districts took control of the means of communications but failed to appreciate the critical mood of the home front; and lastly not all groups in Germany were prepared unconditionally to suffer food and social deprivations without concomitant political and social reform. The Third Supreme Command of Hindenburg and Ludendorff viewed the public as an inert mass, and failed to appreciate that public opinion could (and will) assert itself. At the root of the *Burgfrieden* (political truce) of 1914 lay the notion of a short, defensive war. However, under the leadership of Hindenburg and Ludendorff, and a compliant Kaiser, that notion was transformed into a war of conquest with vast annexations and indemnities. No amount of propaganda could explain away the fundamental change in the nature of the war, from a defensive conflict to one culminating in a *Siegfrieden* (peace through victory).

The book reflects my interest in propaganda. It is not intended to be the definitive account of the German home front during the Great War; that is still to be written. This is essentially a narrative history, explicitly focusing on the interaction between propaganda and public opinion in total war. I have not adopted a model of analysis in the manner, for example, of a class model in the Weberian, ideal-typical fashion. Rather, I have attempted to provide an analysis *in toto* of German society at war and the manner in which propaganda became (arguably for the first time) an essential weapon in the political arsenal and an intrinsic part of the war effort. The interaction of propaganda and public opinion, therefore, can only be understood in the wider context of the everyday experiences of the home front, and, to a lesser extent, the fighting front.

To achieve this, I have adopted a consciously schematic approach that does not follow a strict chronological order. The concept of the *Burgfrieden* is crucial to understanding the nature of imperial war propaganda and provides the fulcrum upon which it developed. Chapter 1 sketches conditions in Germany in the years leading up to August 1914 and the manner in which the 'spirit of 1914' facilitated the manufacturing of the *Burgfrieden* into an ideological instrument to keep disintegrating social factions under control. By 1916, it had become largely an 'empty slogan' employed by conservative and military leaders to maintain the *status quo*. Chapter 2 details the first attempts to mobilize the means of communications for government propaganda. Inevitably, censorship came to be seen as an important weapon in controlling the flow of information. War aims that could justify the *Burgfrieden* were a crucial factor in persuading the whole population to 'fall-in' and contribute to the German war effort (Chapter 3). Intrinsic to the success of the *Burgfrieden* was the propaganda *leitmotiv* of a short, defensive war. The slogan '*Feinde ringsum!*' ('enemies on all sides of us') encouraged the suspension of class conflict and regional hostilities rife in German society, in order to defeat hostile European powers intent on encircling Germany. The image of the enemy, and particularly the English (the Germans rarely used the term 'British') and the Russians, was an important emotional rallying call guaranteed to whip up xenophobic hatred. The notion of a justified war of defence also rationalized the Schlieffen Plan, a military strategy based upon the premise that Germany would have to fight both France and Russia in any future war. The plan contemplated a 'knockout blow' in the west against France before turning to Russia. The success of the plan depended on the ability of the German army to move through neutral Belgium at great speed in order to surprise France (Figure 1). Russia's decision to mobilize its troops on 30 July 1914 provided the 'trigger' that set in motion the Schlieffen Plan and the German decision to attack France (in the process violating Belgian neutrality), because it was felt that any delay might undermine Schlieffen's military strategy (see Map 1). Belgium's justified refusal to allow safe passage for the German army through its territory led to Britain declaring war on Germany on 4 August (under a guarantee that Britain had given to Belgium in 1839), thus precipitating a general European war.[4]

The invasion of neutral Belgium and the violation of international law placed imperial German propaganda on the defensive. To Allied claims of Prussian barbarism, the German response was an incredulous 'Wir Barbaren?' that went on to detail German cultural achievements over the centuries (Figure 6). Such a defence became a familiar *leitmotiv* in German propaganda, but one of which the home front, not surprisingly, tired as food shortages began to take effect, from 1915 onwards.

It is important to stress that the complex relationship between propaganda and public opinion should be viewed in the broader economic and political context within which it operates. Propaganda in the modern state is not some adjunct, artificially bolted on to the machinery of politics; it is an essential part of the whole political process. E.H. Carr has reminded us that: 'power over opinion is therefore not less essential for political purposes than military and economic power, and has always been associated with them. The art of persuasion has always been a necessary part of the equipment of a political leader.'[5]

Chapter 4 ('The Crucible of War') examines the extraordinary pressures that total war imposed on the institutions and value systems of the major imperial powers. The imperative need to finance industrialized warfare on a global scale resulted in the Enabling Act in August 1914 that established the creation of war bonds which were to be the chief source of revenue for the German war effort. Propaganda, in particular posters, was the most important means of persuading the public to subscribe to war loans as an act of patriotism. Total war forced Germany to restructure its economy and led to the introduction of the Hindenburg Programme and the Auxiliary Service Law, both of which had profound ramifications for the labour force. By 1915, there were food shortages and the so-called 'turnip winter' of 1916–17 led to food riots, declining health standards, hoarding, a flourishing black market, and, ultimately, a reappraisal of German war aims. From the outset of the conflict a few brave, dissenting voices refused to accept the inevitability of a European war. Such groups, often led by women, formed a minority voice; it is a voice, nonetheless, that deserves to be heard and this forms the basis of Chapter 5. These pacifists and feminists remained largely inured to the blandishments of jingoistic propaganda.

Having analysed the economic and social conditions experienced by the home front, I return to the central theme of the book – the relationship between propaganda and public opinion. The final two years of the war were a period that witnessed the rise of the right-wing Fatherland Party and the historical split in the great German Social Democratic movement. Official propaganda continued, however, to insist that a *Siegfrieden* was assured provided the people remained resolute behind their leaders.

The 'silent dictatorship' of Hindenburg and Ludendorff and the declining popularity of the Kaiser are examined critically. Wilhelm II and Hindenburg remained contemptuous of propaganda and the need to mobilize opinion. Ludendorff, on the other hand, was convinced of the power of propaganda. The 'patriotic instruction' programme that he launched in the autumn of 1917 was intended to counter the people's negative perceptions of the war. It was also the last desperate attempt on the part of the ruling elites to preempt a feared 'revolution from below'. The punitive peace treaty with Bolshevik Russia imposed by the Germans at Brest-Litovsk represented the last propaganda coup for the government.

My analysis is not restricted to the dissemination of propaganda themes, but extends to how public opinion responded to the various campaigns. To this end, I have incorporated an array of historical sources that includes posters, postcards, leaflets, the cinema, the press and the monthly public opinion reports compiled by the Deputy Commanding Generals (*Monatsberichten*).

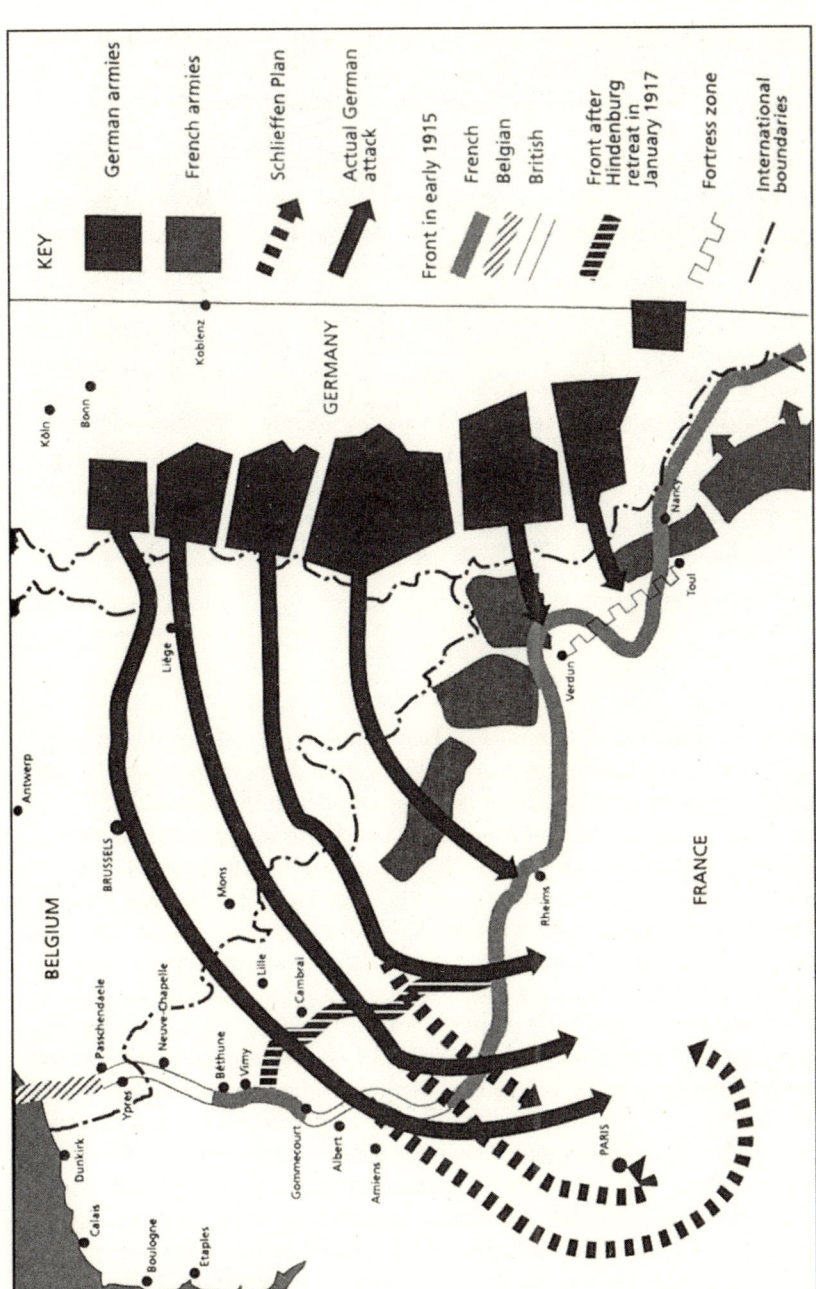

Map 1 The Schlieffen Plan.

Figure 1 German reserves on the way to the Western Front, August 1914. Chalked on the side of the carriage is the confident boast: 'Excursion to Paris, See you again on the Boulevard'.

The copious 'feedback' received in Berlin and Munich from the twenty-four district corps together with police reports and those from the *Büro für Sozialpolitik*, provide evidence of popular attitudes to the regime. The cinema came of age as a result of the First World War and emerged from the conflict as *the* medium of the first half of the twentieth century. The German authorities were rather slow to see the advantages of such a medium for propaganda and entertainment purposes. Nevertheless, film was used to disseminate official slogans and campaigns, such as the war bond drive, and the newsreels presented the drama (but not the suffering) of the fighting front to the civilian population. These moving images of the war had an extraordinarily powerful impact on the home front. I have also leaned heavily on the diversity of the German press to convey the manner in which public opinion was moulded. Remarkably, the press was allowed to report, uncensored, some of the most acrimonious Reichstag debates. Although censorship had been introduced in 1914 under the State of Siege, the press, and particularly the socialist press, continued to debate war aims and political reforms. It was enjoined by forces of the right and various organs of the government, that labelled all criticism of the Wilhelmine State acts of subversion. The ensuing debate, often truncated by military censorship, nevertheless proved of seminal importance for the continuation of the war and, in the long term, for democracy in Germany.

I have argued in this book that propaganda played an important role in the history of the First World War by influencing public opinion which emerged from the conflict with an enhanced role in modern political life. The war also revealed how easily public opinion could be duped and cynically manipulated. There are, however, limits to what propaganda alone can achieve. General Ludendorff called unsuccessfully for an Imperial Propaganda Ministry along the lines of the British model, in the belief that more centralized control would guarantee propaganda success. In spite of what the Nazis claimed after the Great War, imperial propaganda did not fail; it may not have been as cynically constructed as British propaganda, but it suited the German people. The duration of the conflict, the Allied blockade, food shortages and the failure to introduce social and political reforms eventually wore down the German people. It is a measure of the effectiveness of the propaganda machinery – which appealed to traditional German values of obedience, duty and patriotism – that a consensus (of sorts) was maintained for so long. The eventual collapse of morale in 1918 was due not to the authorities' failure to disseminate skilful propaganda, but to the fact that they refused to heed the German people's wishes for political and economic reforms to compensate for the hardship and sacrifices endured over four years. Only in the final year of the war did morale manifestly break down. One cause of this, ironically, was British and Bolshevik propaganda aimed at undermining the solidarity of the German working class and polarizing the Social Democratic movement.

The sudden announcement that Germany was to sue for an armistice in October 1918 came as a great shock to a population that had, after Brest-Litovsk and the Ludendorff Offensive, been encouraged to believe that a victorious end to the war was near. The humiliating nature of the peace terms – negotiated by discredited politicians, not the military – was to perpetuate the myth of the 'stab-in-the-back' legend (*Dolchstosslegende*) and was also to have a profound effect on the way in which post-war Germany would come to view propaganda. The discrepancy between jingoistic imperial propaganda and the reality of defeat and Versailles invoked distrust and a re-examination of traditional loyalties. In Britain, public reaction to war propaganda was to associate the term with lies and falsehood. The Ministry of Information was immediately disbanded once the conflict had ended. The British government regarded propaganda as politically dangerous and even morally unacceptable in peace time. In Germany, on the other hand, a right-wing, nationalist consensus developed around the *Dolchstosslegende* that imbued the skilful employment of propaganda with almost mystical power. It is therefore not surprising to discover that when the Nazis came to power in 1933, one of the first government departments to be established was the Ministry for Popular Enlightenment and Propaganda.

1
Days of Decision
Germany on the Eve of War

'War, war, the people have risen – it is as though they were not there at all before and now all at once, they are immense and touching.'

Kurt Riezler

THE POLITICAL BACKGROUND

The First World War revealed the structural weaknesses and contradictions within German society. The causes of these problems had long been present but were exposed by the exigencies of total war which required the full mobilization of human and material resources and the support of all groups participating in the war effort.

For decades German administrations had engineered a successful social, imperialist foreign policy in order to deflect deep-seated domestic antagonisms abroad. The fundamental cause of these tensions can be traced to Germany's political development during the course of the nineteenth century which contrasted sharply with other Western democracies. Moreover although Germany's industrialization took off later than other leading industrialized nations it proved to be more rapid and uneven. On the eve of the Great War Germany was thus plagued with divisions which could not be overcome without radical change and democratization. However, by 1914, efforts to solve these issues had reached a point of stagnation. In order to understand better these tensions it is necessary to say something about the nature of German unification and to trace briefly the country's political development during the late nineteenth century.

Historians have argued that the root cause of Germany's internal problems lay in the failure of the Frankfurt Parliament in 1848 to achieve a popular revolution that would destroy the old power basis of Prussia and Austria and create a new liberal parliamentary framework for national unity.[1] This failure of political will resulted in an anachronistic political and social system dominated by Prussia and arousing deep hostility among the masses. When unification grafted the autocratic Prussian political system onto a German society in 1871 under the manipulatory skills of Otto von Bismarck, the attainment of national unity was nevertheless greeted with widespread enthusiasm and pride. After all imperial Germany had its virtues; under Bismarck's leadership it had realized the dream of unification; spectacular economic gains were being made; it boasted an efficient and incorruptible administration with a substantially independent judiciary; its social welfare legislation was the most advanced in Europe; and German scholarship was the envy of the civilized world.

By integrating traditional beliefs with increasingly jingoistic nationalist emotions, the Hohenzollern Empire miraculously upheld its legitimacy. The expanding industrial bourgeoisie proved particularly susceptible and even embraced it with enthusiasm. The financial and upper-middle classes were prepared to submit to the continuing political dominance of the Prussian rural aristocracy in return for a form of state capitalism promoting their own economic interests, while the rapidly expanding working class was 'integrated' into the system, partly because it would not risk revolutionary violence to overthrow a benevolent state dispensing the most advanced social security system in Europe, and partly because its political and economic organizations developed largely into non-revolutionary interest associations whose members on the whole accepted passive roles in the system.[2] The peasantry, not surprisingly, fearful of the consequences of industrialization and bound by traditionally strong economic ties to the ruling aristocracy, passively accepted these new political orientations.

Nevertheless despite attempts to fuse Prussian hegemony with a modern integral nationalism in the form of a thinly disguised autocracy, the Hohenzollern Empire was founded upon numerous contradictions and compromises which would later prove disastrous. Measured against the great aims of 1848/9, the 'unity from above' associated with the founding of the imperial empire represented a defeat for middle-class parliamentary liberalism.

The Bismarckian system gave Germany a Reichstag (national parliament) elected by democratic manhood suffrage. Next to the Kaiser it was supposedly the second most important institution. However, although it would develop into a fairly accurate barometer of German political opinion, its political influence was limited to the area of legislation. Characteristic of the Reich was the 'government over the parties' and the restriction of the people's representation to a position in which it was only able to express a non-binding opinion on political questions. In Germany the prize of political power was permanently denied to the Reichstag and to parliamentary politicians. The Constitution of 1871 guaranteed the Chancellor a position of power unrestricted either by Parliament or the political parties. Responsible only to the Kaiser, it was the Chancellor who decided policy outlines and appointed and dismissed state secretaries. He also chaired the sessions of the *Bundesrat* (Federal Council), which was formally the highest government institution of the empire and the legislative organ of the federal states. Prussia controlled a majority of votes in the *Bundesrat* and the policy of the Reich was dominated by the Prussian Cabinet. The Prussian *Landtag* (parliament) was elected on a three-class voting system, whereby voting power was proportionate to a man's tax contribution. This political anachronism ensured the predominance of the landed aristocracy, the Junkers, together with wealthy merchants and industrialists, and socially conservative groups. It produced a parliament whose composition manifestly failed to reflect the rapid industrialization and urbanization of Germany. These groups determinedly resisted attempts by the Reichstag (elected on a one man one vote basis) to change their privileged position, and as long as they could preserve the constitutional arrangement with its divided parliaments, they were able to block all serious attempts at constitutional reforms.[3]

Moreover the Junker influence had deeply permeated the military and bureaucratic elites, both of whom viewed the advance of parliamentary government as a challenge to their own prerogatives and a threat to the *status quo*. The officer-corps in particular, because of its prejudices and narrow social recruitment, became increasingly isolated from large sections of the population who were committed to a liberal, democratic and relatively antimilitarist political system.[4] The resulting cleavage between the privileged few and the rest of society was largely responsible for perpetuating social and political divisions in Wilhelmine Germany up until the outbreak of the First World War.

In contrast with its political progress, the pace of Germany's economic development had rapidly transformed the country from a mainly rural society to a modern industrial nation. According to Gerald Feldman the belated unification and the speed of its industrialization created a traumatic and artificial break with the past:

> Germany became a mass society before she overcame her feudal past and before the liberal-individualistic period of early capitalism had created those institutions of self-government and ideas of liberty which make possible the existence of a mass society capable of organising for the collective defense of their interests as free men.[5]

In the short term only the dynamic growth of Germany into the greatest European industrial state prevented the eruption of smouldering tensions. But paradoxically the very economic forces unleashed by Germany's unification under Prussia would expose the economic vulnerability of the antiquated ruling class. Not even pragmatic alliances between the Junkers and the big industrialists ('rye and iron') could preserve their predominance in an age of industrialization and universal suffrage. Protective tariffs, repression of the labour movement and benevolent social legislation all failed to overcome the intensified social divisions of Germany.

The traditional ruling elites increasingly began to doubt their ability to govern effectively under the conditions of mass politics. After Kaiser Wilhelm's dismissal of Bismarck in 1890 a new course was to be steered. At home there was to be reconciliation with the emerging Social Democrats and abroad a more aggressive foreign policy designed to win for Germany world power status. The year 1895 heralded the start of a new period of economic prosperity and rapid technical development for German industry. The expansion of the chemical and electrical industries in particular led to a second wave of industrialization. Nevertheless, thinly veiled attempts at reconciliation by the Kaiser were resisted by the Social Democrats under August Bebel's leadership. The question 'revolution or reform?' was passionately debated by Social Democrats. Although they were formally committed to a Marxist, republican ideology, full employment, rising real incomes and the subsequent 'secondary integration' of the working class into German society cast serious doubts on Marx's theories of impoverishment and revolution. Under the leadership of spokesmen like Georg von Vollmar and Eduard Bernstein, the Social Democrats, with the support of trade unions, became increasingly reformist in practice and nationalist in outlook. Nonetheless, they were still denounced by the Kaiser as 'enemies of the state', 'who do not deserve the name of Germans and must be rooted out'.[6] Despite this the SPD continued to gain support. In the 1912 elections, after a series of major strikes, one out of every three Germans voted for a socialist candidate. The rise of the SPD and the Progressive Party and the subsequent decline of the old parties threw German political life into turmoil.

The liberal middle class felt it was in danger of being crushed between agricultural and industrial interests on the one hand and the workers on the other. In particular the National Liberals under the leadership of first Johannes Miquel and later Ernst Bassermann were constantly urged to form a 'collective movement' to prevent any further strengthening of the Social Democrats' position. On the defensive in domestic political affairs, middle class forces pursued a line of aggressive, imperialist, power politics. The outward expression of this *Weltpolitik* was the expanding naval programme of Admiral Tirpitz and the agitational foreign policy of the *Alldeutsche Verband* (Pan-German Association), the *Flottenverein* (Navy League) and other *Agitationsverbände* disseminating nationalist and anti-Semitic ideas.[7] According to

Fritz Fischer this energetic foreign policy was designed to strengthen the endangered *status quo*:

> Large scale industry and the Junker, the army, dominated by a conservative ethos, and the civil service, ideologically and socially all interwoven in terms of their members' social background, became the specific and reliable supporters of an 'idea of the state' which viewed world policy and national power politics essentially as a means of dissipating social tensions at home by campaigns abroad.[8]

But did conservative and militarist groups unleash a war deliberately to preserve their position and to avoid reform?

Fischer and more recently John Röhl have argued that the German people were being prepared for an impending war as early as December 1912 after the famous secret 'Council of War' meeting between the Kaiser and his military advisers behind Chancellor Bethmann Hollweg's back.[9] Hans-Ulrich Wehler, however, has warned of the danger of viewing the period as 'a dead straight, one-way street down which imperial policy consciously proceeded for years in advance towards the Great War'.[10] Critics of the Fischer thesis stress the defensive character of the political decisions made in Germany at the time, arguing that the growing tendency in government circles to consider a preventive war does not necessarily prove that Germany was deliberately preparing and planning a major war.[11]

Nevertheless in the decade before 1914, it is possible to trace a fatalism which, fostered by imperialistic enthusiasm, began to see a European war as inevitable. Writing in 1911, even Bethmann Hollweg appeared to support the idea that the German people were 'in need of a war'.[12] The aristocratic and bourgeois classes in particular accepted a forthcoming war as a necessary expedient that would put back the clock in domestic politics and provide the ultimate means of implementing a successful *Weltpolitik*. Writers like Fischer and Klaus Wernecke have demonstrated that a carefully orchestrated anti-Russian campaign was constructed during this period in order to justify Germany's aggressive intentions.[13] The subsequent anti-Russian hysteria generated by this vociferous campaign proved fatal. In the days following the murder of Archduke Franz Ferdinand in Sarajevo, events seemed to overtake the Reich leadership as fatalistic attitudes began to paralyse politicians and military alike. As Wolfgang Mommsen has observed: 'The widespread assumption that war would come sooner or later, whatever particular policies might be pursued, had, in the final analysis, the effect of a "self-fulfilling prophecy".'[14]

THE 'SPIRIT OF 1914': GERMANY AND THE OUTBREAK OF WAR

Those sectors of the ruling class who felt most threatened by the socialist challenge undoubtedly looked upon the outbreak of the First World War as a possible answer in the Bismarckian tradition, to Germany's internal problems.[15] As German society rallied behind the war effort and a *Burgfrieden* (literally, 'fortress truce', but in practice, a 'political truce') was proclaimed, the war appeared to demonstrate the soundness of this belief. Provided the Kaiser could deliver the promised swift victory, political quiescence seemed assured.[16] For many socialists, however, the possibility of a European war had been inconceivable, believing as they did that governments would not risk undermining the *status quo* by subjecting the system to revolutionary strains. Yet the declaration of war against Russia on 1 August aroused, initially at least, widespread enthusiasm with only a minority warning of the dangers. By ending domestic political strife in the *Burgfrieden* the nation was apparently united behind the banner of a fully justified war of self-defence. Even the Social Democrats voted in favour of war credits. In August 1914 therefore it seemed that the war had created a new sense of solidarity in which class antagonisms were transcended by some entirely fictitious 'national community' (*Volksgemeinschaft*).

The illusion that the war would be a short one was not uniquely German, but it partly explains the attitude and behaviour of different social and political groups to the announcement of hostilities. The initial enthusiasm aroused by the war (and not *for* the war), the emergence of the *Volksstaat*, and the apparent *volte face* of the Social Democrats can all be traced to this belief that the war would be quickly and gloriously concluded. The events leading up to and including the fateful month of August reveal a curious mixture of rising nationalism, superficial harmony and hatred of Tsarist Russia, but also a nervousness and uncertainty as the shock of war began to sink in.

The failure of diplomacy to resolve the Balkan crisis ushered in mounting tension and jingoism in all the major European cities. In Germany events were reaching a climax. On 25 July 1914 Austria–Hungary severed diplomatic relations with Serbia which it alleged had been responsible for the assassination of Archduke Ferdinand and his consort. That evening in Berlin crowds gathered outside the Reichstag and the Austro-Hungarian embassy and began burning Serbian flags. Describing these events the socialist newspaper *Vorwärts* reported that the crowds consisted mainly of young people.[17] Meanwhile the Kaiser, apparently unaware of the growing seriousness of the situation, was still enjoying a cruise in the Norwegian fjords. His hasty return to Potsdam on 27 July was greeted by the usual enthusiastic crowds, only this time patriotically singing 'Deutschland, Deutschland, über Alles'. Equally revealing was the response of ordinary bank depositors who reacted to the worsening diplomatic situation by withdrawing savings and gold. Food prices were also rising as anxious citizens, fearful of shortages, began hoarding provisions. Within a few days, as stock exchange values plunged, some municipal banks actually suspended dealings and in the provinces paper money was invariably refused altogether.[18]

By 31 July Germany was gripped by war fever and hysteria with rumours abounding. A *Kriegsgefahrzustand*, or 'condition of state of war' was proclaimed and Germany demanded that Russia should cease mobilizing within 12 hours. The afternoon special newspaper editions announced that the Kaiser had decreed a State of Siege throughout Germany. Later that day he and his family appeared before a huge crowd on the balcony of the Imperial Palace in Berlin. In what was virtually an announcement of war he regretted, apparently more in sorrow than anger, that: 'The sword is being forced into my hand. . . . This war will demand of us enormous sacrifices in life and money, but we shall show our foes what it is to provoke Germany.'[19] Even at this late hour *Vorwärts* prepared a sober edition pleading for sanity and a just compromise. Its editorial entitled 'Europe's Hour of Destiny' courageously drew a distinction between the true wishes of the ordinary people and the machinations of governments and concluded: 'If, nevertheless, the hideous spectre should become reality, if the bloody torrent of a war of nations should sweep over Europe – one thing is sure; Social Democracy bears no responsibility for the coming events.'[20] During the night of the 31st and the following day, people waited anxiously for the ensuing moves. On 1 August the anticipated order for mobilization was given, signed by the Emperor and Bethmann Hollweg, and to take effect the next day. At 7.10 p.m. Germany declared war on Russia, the Kaiser proclaiming the news from his balcony to a large crowd in Berlin.[21]

On the day that mobilization was announced the Imperial Law of the State of Siege came into operation in each of the twenty-four army corps districts into which the Reich had been divided (with the exception of Bavaria where special laws existed). The law according to Article 68 of the Imperial Constitution was based on the Prussian Law of Siege of 4 June 1851. It stated that 'if the public safety of federal territory is endangered, the Kaiser may declare any part of the same to be in a state of war'.[22] As they were solely responsible to the Emperor the military commanders were now largely independent of the civil government and parliamentary bodies. Acting in the name of the Kaiser this law even empowered them to suspend fundamental civil liberties such as freedom of speech, freedom of assembly and freedom of association. Henceforth these liberties were subject to the capricious whims of the military authorities, and, as we shall see later, they eagerly seized upon this as a weapon to be used against political opponents at home. The excessive powers given to the military commanders were further complicated by the fact that the army corps districts did not always coincide with the administrative provinces. As each of the twenty-four army corps possessed autonomous control of their local authorities and often interpreted their new powers differently, this led to unsolicited and overzealous interference in the civil bureaucracy and to an overall failure to coordinate national policy making. Such conditions did not augur well for preparing the German people for the ordeal of a long and total war.

However, on 1 August 1914, the population did not seriously question the declaration of the State of Siege. Gradually though, as the war dragged relentlessly on, the arbitrary nature of excessive military interference in internal affairs began to test the nation's solidarity and led to growing resentment and criticism from all shades of the political divide.[23] But in the period of mobilization immediately after the declaration of war against Russia the mood of the population fluctuated dramatically, reflecting the general uncertainty. James Gerard, the American Ambassador, noted the excitement of large crowds in Berlin 'parading the streets singing *"Deutschland über Alles,"* and demanding war'.[24] Similar demonstrations clamouring for war took place in Leipzig, and were described by one historian who witnessed the scenes as 'a soaring religious sentiment... the ascent of a whole people to the heights'.[25] A young Adolf Hitler is captured in a photograph of the cheering crowd that gathered in the Odeon Platz in Munich on 2 August (see Figure 2). He wrote later that he was 'carried away by the enthusiasm of the moment and I sank down upon my knees and thanked Heaven out of the fullness of my heart for the favour of having been permitted to live in such a time'.[26] Set against this apparent overwhelming sense of euphoric national unity (largely recorded in the large cities) were the anti-war demonstrations that took place all over Germany. Such demonstrations, often organized by women, were censored and rarely appeared in the press. We should, therefore, be careful of generalizations about 'popular belligerence' and 'unanimity of enthusiasm' that have framed subsequent historical writings on the subject and not be misled by those, largely male, avant-garde intellectuals and artists who wished to escape from 'materialism' and the boredom of civil life and tended to glorify war and the so-called 'spirit of 1914'. The rhetoric of unity and popular support for the war had been shrewdly constructed by government propaganda during the crisis, which had convinced large sections of the population that Germany was fighting a defensive war against the aggression of Tsarist Russia and its Western allies. Nevertheless, for those who were prepared to distance themselves from the propaganda construct, there existed alongside

Figure 2 Enthusiastic crowd in the Odeon Platz, Munich, 2 August 1914. Among the crowd can be seen the young Adolf Hitler.

the military bands, the patriotic songs and the parades, a sombre, melancholic mood that spoke of resignation rather than euphoria. Peter Hanssen, a Reichstag Deputy from Schleswig-Holstein, recorded vividly the mobilization scenes on his way south to Berlin and the oppressed atmosphere in the capital: 'People were standing close together on the sidewalks of Unter den Linden to catch a glimpse of the Kaiser.... But there was no rejoicing, no enthusiasm; over all hung that same heavy, sad, and depressed atmosphere.'[27]

The departure of soldiers for the front at first undoubtedly created enthusiasm and provided a much needed emotional release from the mounting tensions of previous weeks (see Figure 3). Princess Blücher, an Englishwoman married to a German nobleman, noted that the whole life of Germany was moving to the tune of *Die Wacht am Rhein*, just as the soldiers marched to the rhythm of its refrain.[28] But as the effervescence of the demonstrations quickly subsided, patriotic duty towards the Fatherland, and not glory, was emphasized.[29] The war theology of the various churches, disseminated through countless pamphlets and sermons, self-righteously proclaimed the justness of Germany's cause with regret that Russia's provocation should make the war inevitable. As well as the main religious organizations – Protestants, Catholics, Jews – other representative groups including big business, trade unions, women and students, all pledged their support for total mobilization.[30] Even the Jesuits, whose movements had been restricted since 1872 under the

Figure 3 General war fever, August 1914.

Exceptional Laws, appealed to the new military authorities to allow them to participate in the war effort.[31] Behind the calls for national unity lay a social romanticism which visualized longstanding class conflicts being eliminated and replaced by an idealized 'fighting community' imbued with military values. Typical of the intelligentsia's response was that of the economist, Emil Lederer. Employing Ferdinand Tönnies' terminology he announced in 1914 that, 'We can say that on the day of mobilization the *society* which existed until then was transformed into a *community.*'[32]

The belief in such a community spirit was cemented on 4 August, shortly after Britain declared war on Germany. A ceremonial session of the Reichstag was held in the White Hall of the Imperial Palace where the Kaiser, wearing an army uniform, outlined Germany's war aims in a speech from the throne. Reaffirming Germany's obligation to defend her ally, he stressed that the war was not one of conquest, but to maintain the nation's economic and political position. After reading his speech he handed the manuscript to the Chancellor and continued freely in a raised voice: 'From this day on, I recognise no parties, but only Germans. If the party leaders agree with me on this matter, I invite them to step forward and confirm this with a handshake.'[33] To wild applause the leaders of the competing parties stepped forward and extended their hands: the so-called *Burgfrieden*, or 'spirit of 1914' had entered into war mythology. Later that day the Social Democrats voted for war credits. During the session the Chancellor, Bethmann Hollweg, took the opportunity to justify Germany's violation of Belgian territory ('we will atone for this injustice') and to accuse Russia and France of aggression. 'We are drawing the sword only in defence of a righteous cause,' he claimed. 'Russia has set the torch to the house.... France has already violated the peace.... We are therefore acting in self-defence... Germany's great hour of trial has come. Our army is in the field. Our navy is ready for battle. Behind them stands a united people.' (Wild applause.) Next, Hugo Haase, the SPD leader, read a brief declaration to the effect that the party would vote for war credits. Explaining this decision he said that although the SPD had always opposed imperialism, 'Russian despotism was threatening the freedom of the German people' and 'in this hour of danger we will not leave the Fatherland in the lurch'.[34] The announcement was received with endless applause. The Chancellor then stood up and concluded: 'Whatever we have in store, we may well believe that August 4, 1914, will, for all time, remain one of Germany's greatest days!'

Opponents of German militarism were thus disarmed and temporarily silenced by the feelings of solidarity of the first months of the war. Service for the Fatherland was extolled in songs and poems and skilfully exploited by the German press.[35] The playwright Frank Wedekind, for example, an old opponent of German militarism, declared at a patriotic rally in Munich on 18 September 1914: 'The unity of German Social Democracy with the Imperial High Command is the loyal brotherhood of arms!'[36] However, the Social Democrats had not simply agreed to support war credits, they had also agreed to an Enabling Act which gave the *Bundesrat* the power to enact emergency economic legislation without the consent of the Reichstag. Three years earlier at an International Labour Conference in London the same party had stated that they 'were ready to oppose any declaration of war, whatever the grounds may be'.[37] The reasons for the sudden change of policy by the SPD are complex and intrinsically linked to the exaggerated expectations aroused by the ambivalent *Burgfrieden*. The party was not simply overwhelmed by the emotional and hysterical atmosphere of August 1914 as is often said. The real significance of the *Burgfrieden* and the Kaiser's declaration that 'I recognise no parties, but only Germans', was that it appealed to different groups for different reasons. Socialists believed that it offered the possibility of reconciliation and subsequent political reforms. For many SPD leaders these expectations had a crucial bearing on their decision to support the 'political truce'.[38] However, in conservative circles the *Burgfrieden* symbolised something quite different and became increasingly a means of strengthening the *status quo* by throttling discussion and preventing initiatives aimed at reforming the system.[39] For Pan Germans the 'spirit of 1914' was intrinsically linked to establishing an organic *Volksgemeinschaft* (people's community) whereby Germans recognized their common ethnic identity (and, more sinisterly, their racial superiority).[40] For the vast mass of ordinary citizens the 'truce' provided a sense of solidarity that the leadership and the people were united in fighting a defensive war out of encirclement. So long as the *Burgfrieden* was adhered to these different interpretations could be reconciled within the emerging *Volksstaat*.

Another problem facing the SPD was that they had no coherent policy to implement should war break out. Its leaders therefore feared massive repression if they resisted the call to arms. Having spent so long building up their organizations and affiliated trade unions, they were reluctant to risk their achievements in defence of a position apparently out of key with the feelings of their own membership, and the country as a whole. Two left-wing Socialist Deputies, Max König and Wilhelm Dittmann, who were travelling from Dortmund to Berlin to attend the Reichstag session noted, during the course of their journey, the strength of feeling among ordinary SPD supporters. Implored at every station 'not to be stingy in voting for money', these remonstrations made a profound impression on König, who later was moved to write that had the party voted against the war credits popular resentment would have 'swept the socialist organization clean away'.[41] Moreover the war was initially seen by the left as a defensive war against its arch-enemy, Tsarist Russia. The problem for the Social Democrats in taking this line was that even the most reactionary groups were now saying they opposed the Tsar because of his tyranny.[42] Despite suspicions of these new political bedfellows, the SPD leadership believed nevertheless that by supporting the war effort they were not only legitimizing and integrating Social Democracy into the mainstream of political life, but also ending the isolation of the working class which for decades had been ostracized by government and society.

Two days after the historic vote for the first war credits the Kaiser and Kaiserin issued separate proclamations to the German people. In a special message to the women of Germany, the Empress called upon them to 'lighten the struggle for our husbands, sons, and brothers'. The Kaiser spoke of the 'hostility from the East and West', and ended with a plea for unity: 'Never has Germany been subdued when it was united. Forward with God, who will be with us as He was with our ancestors!'[43]

There can be little doubt that there existed a general euphoria in these early weeks of war – albeit not as widespread, or on the scale that subsequent historical works have claimed. No amount of government propaganda or middle-class jingoistic literature could have artificially manufactured such an emotional patriotic consensus. It was to be short lived, but while it lasted it genuinely transcended class barriers.[44] Berlin's Police Commissioner noted: 'Our sources who have considerable contact with the workers' groups who just a short time ago were organizing protests and supporting the Internationale are now bursting with boundless patriotism.'[45] The attitude of the ruling class was summed up by Kurt Riezler, adviser to Bethmann Hollweg, who wrote in his diary: 'War, war, the people have risen – it is as though they were not there at all before and now all at once, they are immense and touching.'[46]

At first the outbreak of war appeared to provide a solution to the major political and economic problems that had been confronting imperial Germany for over two decades. However, these hopes were soon to be disappointed: the *Burgfrieden* could not survive a long war, just as the reconciliation of class tensions was dependent on a swift military victory. In reality the superficial harmony of 1914 was a far cry from the 'national community' (*Volksgemeinschaft*) invoked by the *Burgfrieden*, even though, as we shall discover in the next chapter, the vocabulary of 'political truce' would gain considerable influence throughout the first year of the war. By the end of 1916 these hopes had all but disintegrated.

2
The Mobilization of the Masses

'In the beginning was the Lie'

Goethe (*Faust*)

The First World War made greater demands on the material and human resources of the nations involved than any previous conflict. It was no longer sufficient simply to organize industry or to mobilize manpower in order to carry a modern state through a long war. Of course it would prove to be a war of intense industrial competition and scientific innovation; the manufacture of arms and munitions became critically important. But equally important was the need to engage the will and support of whole nations. For the first time belligerent governments were required to mobilize entire civilian populations into 'fighting communities'. Consequently all governments were faced with the urgent task of justifying their entry into the war to their own people. In Germany the necessity for the imperial government to generate popular support in the first phase of the war was largely superfluous. The immediate emotional impact of the announcement of war led to a sense of unity and togetherness on the part of the German people, which invariably manifested itself in a hysterical hatred of the 'outsider' or enemy.

The German government on the outbreak of war at once surrendered to the local army commanders extensive political powers over civil administration. General mobilization was accompanied by the proclamation of the Prussian Law of Siege which gave sole responsibility for 'public safety' to the Deputy Commanding Generals in each of the twenty-four army corps districts.

The vagueness of this law not only allowed the army to wrestle responsibility and power from the Reichstag but significantly it marked the beginning of military interference in all aspects of internal affairs for the duration of the war. The growing political power of the German military extended far beyond the Prussian War Ministry which they, and not civilians, controlled. At the same time, a Bavarian State of War Law transferred authority to local Deputy Commanding Generals, subject to the supervision of the War Ministry in Munich. The elitist background and anachronistic values of the German officer corps and their belief in the primacy of 'militarism' over political considerations meant that they were largely ill-prepared and ill-suited for taking control of internal affairs. As all matters concerning the war effort were considered to be within their domain, the military also assumed responsibility for manipulating public opinion by means of propaganda and censorship. From the beginning their overriding fear was that the soldiers' morale could be undermined by the home front. Wartime measures that affected the civilian population were invariably taken with the troops' welfare uppermost in mind. The army leadership's contempt for politics and for civilian bureaucrats, together with their suspicion of the masses whom they perceived as a threat, resulted in a crucial failure to understand or trust the home front and led inevitably to a widening polarization of views about the nature of the war and how it should be conducted. This was somewhat ironic, for in many ways the army saw itself as *the* integrating force in German society. Indeed, in its leaders' desire for stability they were even prepared to support, for example, trade union demands for political and economic reforms.[1] In return they wished to conduct the war removed from all criticism and would not tolerate any form of parliamentary control. As such they were not prepared to allow politicians or political parties to participate in the decision-making process. Even Chancellor Bethmann Hollweg was removed from office when his differences with the High Command became irreconcilable. It is in this context that we see the major failure of the Kaiser – his inability and unwillingness to use the monarchy to provide the necessary unifying force between conflicting interest groups. One of the major contentions of this book is that the eventual collapse of Germany was due less to the authorities' failure to disseminate nationalist propaganda (as right-wing apologists would later claim) than to the inability of the military command and the monarchy to reinforce this propaganda by acknowledging the importance of public opinion in forging an effective link between leadership and people. It was not simply a question of the military clique's reluctance to establish the machinery for manipulating public opinion; rather they failed to take the trouble to understand the psychology of the German people. Indeed, their own reactionary attitudes and fears prevented them from recognizing propaganda's *real* potential as an integrating force to be used positively. However, this would emerge later. In 1914 the public's ignorance concerning the Law of Siege and the extent to which the army (a 'collection of tyrannies') had now become the arbiter of the nation's civil and domestic life had yet to be fully recognized.

THE ORGANIZATION OF OFFICIAL PROPAGANDA

The first impression that emerges from the study of propaganda in the Great War is one of generally uncoordinated improvisation. By the end of the conflict, however, propaganda would, for the first time, be elevated to the position of a branch of government. It is ironic (in the light of later criticisms) that of all the belligerents, Germany had been the only power to pay serious attention to propaganda before 1914. For some years and with considerable thoroughness, imperial Germany had been attempting to influence popular and official opinion in foreign countries. Therefore, when war broke out in August 1914 it had a distinct initial advantage over the propaganda of the Allied governments. Germany had been developing a semi-official propaganda network through her embassies, legations, consular offices and branches of German banks and shipping companies – all of which acted as agents for the dissemination of literature favourable to the Fatherland.

After the proclamation of hostilities and the unprovoked invasion of Belgium, German propaganda was immediately directed towards spreading in neutral countries the German version of the causes of the war, and the hostile intentions of its enemies. One of the first propaganda agencies set up to influence neutral opinion was the so-called Erzberger, Office, named after its director Matthias Erzberger a leading figure of the Zentrum Party (Catholic Centre Party). It was set up under the auspices of the Navy Ministry and worked in close collaboration with the Foreign Office.[2] Erzberger's first task was to coordinate the work of foreign propaganda, for after the outbreak of war, official and semi-official propaganda agencies had proliferated. In October 1914, there were some twenty-seven such agencies. Erzberger was instrumental in establishing a central coordinating body, the Central Office for the Foreign Service (*Zentralstelle für Auslandsdienst*), attached to the Foreign Office and under the direction of the former ambassador to Tokyo, Baron von Mumm. Its main function seems to have been to analyse the general war situation and to issue propaganda directives and distribute its own literature, but it was never totally successful in reducing the chaos.

The Wolff Telegraph Bureau, which was subsidized by the German government, also attempted to feed a steady stream of pro-German news into international channels. However, its effectiveness was limited by the fact that under a pre-war agreement with Reuters and Havas, Wolff was responsible only for Germany, its colonies, Austro-Hungary and Scandinavia. At the very outset of hostilities, one of the first major acts taken by Great Britain to undermine the German propaganda effort was to cut the undersea cables between Germany and America (the Emden–New York cable line). Thus, all news from Germany, with the exception of wireless reports, had to proceed via London, the cable centre of the world. The result was that Germany's wireless transmitter at Nauen became its sole means of telegraphic communication with the world outside Europe. To offset this catastrophe, Germany made great strides in wireless telegraphy during the war. A special agency, the Uberseedienst Transozean GmbH, was set up to disseminate a wide variety of propaganda and to protect the Reich's interests abroad. The Nauen station, the most powerful transmitting station in the world, reaching as far afield as Persia and Mexico, gradually developed into an efficient and skilful distributor of propaganda. It turned out war news 24 hours a day, and while it was not always blatantly pro-German, it constantly emphasized German victories and the superiority of German culture and the German way of life.[3]

From the first, Transozean utilized its large pecuniary resources by either acquiring control of neutral newspapers or launching new ones. Most notable was *Germania* covering South America and in association with Ostasiatische Lloyd, it founded *The War* and a Chinese edition of *Deutsche Zeitung*. The *Continental Korrespondenz* was published in English, Spanish and Portuguese and was designed to furnish the neutral press with ready-made copy. Numerous polyglot periodicals and leaflets were also distributed.[4] Furthermore a huge propaganda campaign was launched in the United States of America spearheaded by the *Staats-Zeitung* in New York.[5]

The semi-official *Presse-Abteilung zur Beeinflussung der Neutralen* was responsible for the *War Chronicle* in German, English, French, Spanish and Dutch, and *Die Toekomat* published in Holland in Dutch. This organization was also responsible for a propagandistic comic paper printed in Spain (*La guasa internacional*). The *Hamburger Fremdenblatt* with its *Welt im Bild* published in twelve languages and the *Hamburger Nachrichten* with Spanish and Portuguese editions were the first German newspapers to recognize the importance of propaganda directed at neutral countries. But despite all attempts to supervise their work in neutral, allied, and enemy countries, German propaganda remained generally uncoordinated and heavy-handed. The chief themes of foreign propaganda were to give an exaggerated impression of the military successes achieved by Germany in the war; to influence neutral opinion; to show the dissensions that existed between the Entente powers due to their divergent war aims; and to encourage nationalist and revolutionary movements within the British and Russian empires. These campaigns were used in an attempt to control neutral opinion, and the object seems to have been to impress, even at the risk of intimidating, rather than to persuade. Because the Supreme Command remained wedded to an expansionist programme, this made it difficult to appeal to groups like the Poles, Finns and the revolutionary Russians. Nevertheless, it was undoubtedly concerned to win over neutrals and proclaim its support for self determination of national groups, freedom of the seas, etc. It is not the purpose of this work to gauge the success or otherwise of German propaganda abroad. There is evidence to suggest that, by emphasizing common interests and the certainty of a German victory, Germany was able to control opinion and encourage her allies in Austro-Hungary, Bulgaria and Turkey. However, despite elaborate explanations justifying its military actions, German propaganda failed (with one or two notable exceptions) to prevent the majority of neutral opinion from remaining sharply anti-German, as it had been since the invasion of Belgium.[6]

Clearly, in the initial stages of the war, Germany was more conscious of the need to influence neutral countries than its enemies. After the violation of Belgian sovereignty, neutral opinion quickly crystallized against Germany. Therefore unlike Britain and France, German propaganda was immediately thrown on the defensive and subsequently there was a greater need to explain her war aims and to justify her position. The manner in which the war started also forced the government and the military authorities to take energetic measures to control public opinion at home. The initial measures taken reveal again that Germany was ahead in this respect, although partly as a result of the *Burgfrieden*, it tended to concentrate on establishing propaganda agencies for operations abroad. Nevertheless, during the first year of the war, numerous bodies were set up and guidelines laid down in order to mobilize opinion within Germany. Despite the self-congratulatory nature of British propagandists and the criticisms of German nationalists after the war, Germany was better prepared and more willing to manipulate and manage news and opinions than her enemies.

The military offensive that Germany had undertaken (and the hostile reaction which greeted it) had persuaded it that morale at home mattered a great deal and that total warfare could not be confined to the military sphere. Even Lord Northcliffe, who was later to become British Director of Propaganda to Enemy Countries, acknowledged that Germany had taken the initiative in stimulating the interest of the public in the war. As early as November 1914 he wrote in a letter to Asquith: 'I find that whereas there is in Germany immense enthusiasm for the war, there exists in many parts of this country apathy, ignorance, or ridiculous optimism.'[7] Northcliffe contrasted the position in Germany and in Britain. In Germany a xenophobia was being whipped up by the work of photographers, artists, war correspondents, posters and the new medium of the cinema, whereas the British people were offered 'nothing but casualty lists'.[8] Such propaganda was also being reinforced by the actual military successes of the German armies in the first year of the war, which suggested a rapid victory.

The major concern of the German government was to maintain the *Burgfrieden* by uniting the 'fighting people' at home behind their troops fighting abroad, in support of the objectives for which it had gone to war. From the beginning then, policy makers were significantly influenced in their political decisions by considerations of propaganda and public opinion. It was felt absolutely crucial to link the domestic 'political truce' with the notion of a defensive war. In many ways the propaganda of World War I was pre-eminently a propaganda of war aims. This was particularly the case in Germany after the invasion of Belgium and the early military successes. However, the mobilization of the masses was looked upon essentially as a negative task. The military groups tended initially to resent the claims of the new weapon of propaganda as a slur on their own abilities. Their instinctive reaction was to restrict or forbid discussion of war aims by means of censorship and coercion.[9] Nevertheless in order to build on the foundations of the *Burgfrieden* it was also necessary to stress the positive aspects of Germany's new found unity. This meant concentrating on certain themes that reinforced the official view that Germany was waging a war of self-defence against the aggressive encircling Entente. The main topics stressed in home propaganda were the superiority of German military organization and the certainty of a swift victory; the need for fortitude (*Durchhalten*) and unity, and the historic mission of German culture in the face of the image and ways of the enemy. Not surprisingly, the desire for national expansion which was associated with influential Pan-German groups was played down in the first year of the war. To disseminate these themes the military authorities called upon the resources of the individual media. The way they were employed and the degree of control and censorship exercised depended largely on how important they were considered for the programmes of 'patriotic instruction' (see Chapter 7).

However, we need first to return to the origins of the war to discover the true explanation for Germany's relative preparedness. Because Germany was immediately forced onto the defensive, she was required to explain her war aims not only to neutrals but also to the German people. In Chapter 1 I showed that although the announcement of war was greeted with considerable enthusiasm, there were still deep divisions and anxieties within German society despite the spontaneous demonstrations of patriotism. The *Burgfrieden* did not symbolize the end of these divisions; rather it was an act of faith on the part of the nation and represented reserved support of a just war and a swift victory.

The German authorities' attempts to construct a propaganda machinery to explain war aims and maintain morale reveal their concern and their recognition of the need for an enduring consensus. Contingency plans for coordinating such measures had already been formulated in July 1914 when the Prussian War Ministry issued instructions that were to be carried out in the event of war. Their overriding fear was that the demands of war might exacerbate internal divisions in different parts of the country, especially among national minorities seeking substantial gains. Accordingly they confirmed that the military commanders would be given full powers under the Prussian Law of the State of Siege of 1851 to take whatever measures they felt necessary in their respective districts.[10] Chancellor Bethmann Hollweg immediately attempted to persuade Falkenhayn, the Prussian War Minister, that such a declaration could have 'disastrous consequences for the solidarity and strength of patriotic feeling, and that any possible military advantages would not compensate for the harm that could be caused in the area of politics or ideals'.[11] The military retorted that as plans for mobilization had already been based on the declaration of the State of Siege, it was too late to change them now. Although this was intended to facilitate the coordination of the war effort, in practice it led to individual military commanders arbitrarily suspending different sections of the Constitution. Eventually in December 1916, the War Minister was given the title of 'Supreme Military Commander' (*Obermilitärbefehlshaber*) and with it the power to coordinate the measures taken by the military commanders but not to issue orders to them. Only in the last days of the Reich would the War Minister be given the authority to issue such orders.

In order to appreciate the complex manner in which the German Empire was administered, it is imperative to have some understanding of the role of the Prussian War Ministry in defining social and economic policies. But having said that, the most important and certainly the largest formation within the General Headquarters (*Grosse Hauptquartier* – GHQ) was the High Command (*Oberste Heeresleitung* – OHL). The General Headquarters was so immense that it needed eleven railway trains to transport it from one theatre of war to another. The Kaiser as 'Supreme Warlord' was formally its head, although under the provisions of the Imperial Constitution, the Chief of the Prussian General Staff was responsible for giving operational orders for the entire German army, and as such was given the new title of Chief of the General Staff of the Field Army. The important task of providing a link between the OHL and the government in Berlin was undertaken by representatives of the Chancellor and the Foreign Office who were allocated staff and a department within the OHL.[12] The OHL was divided into various divisions. Section I was the largest division and was responsible for operational planning, and played little part in political matters. Section II, under the ambitious leadership of Colonel Bauer, would eventually assume an important role in the militarization and control of the German economy under the Auxiliary Labour Law (see Chapter 4). However, it was Section IIIb, the News Section (*Nachrichtungabteilung*), that was responsible for the military management of all questions dealing with censorship, public opinion and propaganda. The head of Section IIIb for the entire war was the rather mysterious figure of Major (later Lieutenant-Colonel) Walter Nicolai.

Section IIIb had been set up in 1870/1 when it developed out of Section B of the Third (French) Section of the General Headquarters. It was at first charged to gather news of the enemy, but not to print it. Up until 1904 Section IIIb consisted mainly of a few officers responsible for protecting the French news gathering service. It was expanded to include Russia after the Russo-Japanese War of 1905. The navy possessed its own news-gathering service dealing specifically with the movements of the English fleet. Indeed, this division was maintained even during the First World War, although the army High Command recognized its drawbacks. At the outbreak of war, Section IIIb was responsible for the collection of intelligence reports from abroad and for counter-espionage at home. However, as the war progressed, and the strains within German society became more acute, Section IIIb increasingly concerned itself with political and economic analyses. Eventually it developed into one of the most important sections within the OHL, dealing mainly with censorship and establishing guidelines for propaganda.

Given the antiquated organizational structure of the German army, it is perhaps surprising to discover that Section IIIb responded to the demands of war with considerable efficiency (though with little imagination or flexibility). It attempted to solve the problem of coordinating propaganda through the *Zivilversorgungsschein* – penetrating civil society with military values. Such reactionary ideas were bound, in a society undergoing profound structural changes, to cause further polarizations of opinions. And they did. However, in 1914, the nation was held together by a rare agreement that existed within the OHL on the objectives to be pursued regarding the civilian population. Quite simply these objectives were to maintain the *Burgfrieden*, and to prevent criticism of Germany's war aims, which in practice meant suppressing the radical left.

The most pressing concern in August 1914 was to prevent the fragile 'political truce' from collapsing. As the organizational structure for the co-ordination and dissemination of propaganda had yet to be established, the OHL was more concerned with establishing general principles and guidelines. Thus on 13 August, the Chief of the General Staff of the Field Army issued a proclamation to the various government ministries and the General Commanders stressing the importance of safeguarding the *Burgfrieden* at all costs. Signed by Moltke's First Quartermaster General, Hermann von Stein (later to become Minister for War), the document emphasized that the 'favourable attitude of the parties and the press towards the war is of great importance to the OHL', and warned that any attempts to undermine this unity would be 'energetically suppressed'.[13]

CENSORSHIP AND THE PRESS

The outbreak of war saw the establishment of censorship in all the belligerent countries. Most nations considered it vital from the point of view of national security to control the means of communication. And of all the means available none was more highly regarded (or suspected, depending on one's political allegiances) than the press. It was invariably argued that a rigid censorship was necessary to prevent the enemy from securing valuable information. In Germany, the justification for tight censorship was the upholding of the *Burgfrieden* and a fear that newspapers might publish sensitive military information. There was little in this fear, for the only wire service in Germany was the 'official' Wolff Telegraph Bureau (WTB) established in 1871 with a government guarantee that it would deal exclusively with all official news. In return, Wolff agreed that all 'sensitive material' would first be cleared with the Foreign Office. Thus when war broke out, WTB became the German newspapers' sole source of official war news.[14] (See Figure 4.)

The most striking features of the German press on the eve of the war were its decentralization, its commercialism and its size. Although a product of nineteenth-century liberalism, the popular press, far from being a source of conflict, must be viewed as a force for stability and integration within German society. A tradition of government management of news had been established under Bismarck and Wilhelm II. Between 1878 and 1890, for example, over 155 journals and 1,200 other publications had been banned under anti-socialist legislation. The press was not regarded as an independent check on government in the political process, or even as the conscience of the political parties. It was used instead as an instrument of sectionalist propaganda to champion specific causes. Generally it encouraged acceptance of the social system and frequently propagated nationalist and even imperialist ideals. By remaining sectarian in its appeal and outlook and by avoiding contentious issues, the press served as an agent of the *status quo*.

The proliferation of German newspapers in the last decades of the nineteenth century was due to a number of factors associated with Germany's industrial revolution. The unification of Germany was followed by the consolidation of the political parties, growing urbanization, universal education and an expanding economy. In 1866 there were approximately 1,500 newspapers, of which 300 were dailies. By 1900, this figure had increased to 3,500 and by 1914 the number of newspapers had risen above 4,000, with a total circulation of between 5,000 and 6,000 million copies.[15] Great Britain by comparison possessed only 2,400 newspapers; and while Germany could boast of almost 2,000 dailies, France had fewer than 500.[16]

Figure 4 A postcard depicting Reuters, the London-based news agency, as 'the lying toad' disseminating propaganda to the allied capitals in London and Paris.

Another important feature of the German press during this period was the discovery that newspapers could be profitable commercial enterprises. Therefore along with the 'quality' press, the end of the nineteenth century saw the growth of what later became the mass circulation press. Based on the example of the 'penny press' in Britain, the German *Generalanzeiger*, as this new type of paper was called, flourished largely in the form of provincial and local papers catering for the tastes of the mass reading public. By keeping subscription rates low through extensive advertising and by successfully giving the public what they wanted, the *Generalanzeiger* proliferated, making up nearly half of the newspapers established between 1871 and 1914.[17] The formula was invariably the same; it offered human interest stories, entertainment and news, and often provided extra inducements by way of insurance policies at discount rates. These papers professed a non-political editorial policy though in practice many eventually drifted into specific political allegiances. The *Berliner Lokalanzeiger*, for example which was founded in 1883 by August Scherl, claimed political neutrality but was blatantly conservative in outlook. In 1898 Leopold Ullstein set up the *Berliner Morgenpost* styled on the *Generalanzeiger* but with firm political opinions. The ensuing circulation battle between Scherl and Ullstein resulted in the incorporation of more enlightened editorial comment. By February 1914 the *Morgenpost* had a circulation of 400,000, compared with the 250,000 of the *Lokalanzeiger*.

While the *Generalanzeiger* were becoming politically conscious and more commercialized, the prestigious papers such as the *Frankfurter Zeitung* (founded in 1856 by Leopold Sonnemann) and the *Berliner Tageblatt* (set up in 1871 by Rudolf Mosse), were gaining international reputations for their quality and liberal outlook. Of the overtly political press, the *Norddeutsche Allgemeine Zeitung* (1862), although nominally independent, eventually became an official government daily mouthpiece. By 1894 the Social Democratic Party, despite anti-socialist legislation resulting in fines and imprisonments, could claim 75 newspapers. The central organ of the party was *Vorwärts*, a successful daily which set the example for socialist newspapers throughout Europe. It was particularly admired in Britain, where the socialist press had been slower to get off the ground.[18]

Conservative elites in Germany possessed a deeply entrenched hostility towards commercialization. By the turn of the century a large portion of the newspaper market was concentrated in the hands of three publishers, Ullstein, Scherl and Mosse. The consolidation of commercial interests with the advent of the mass circulation press, led to the growth of publishing houses, newspaper chains and advertising agencies. For many conservatives the publishing world of Mosse and the Ullsteins, with their liberal notions of gradual political reform, represented the corrupting influence of big business, and Jewish big business at that. Traditionally the German press had an educational role which in practice meant that a newspaper was not simply expected to inform but to instruct as well. It was feared that commercial considerations and gimmicks might result in declining standards. Even the *Generalanzeiger* had a seriousness that would have been inconceivable in a Northcliffe or Hearst paper. Nevertheless, the lingering contempt among sections of the ruling elite for the growing commercialism of the German press and their distrust of the motives of the press barons, provides one of the explanations for the immediate imposition of press censorship in August 1914.

Even though most German newspapers supported the *Burgfrieden* and the national cause once the war had started, neither the government nor the military had much confidence in them. The public's thirst for news about the war caused the circulation figures to soar and many papers doubled their daily printings. The government immediately imposed direct controls on the press, creating what one journalist referred to as 'a state of siege on truth'.[19] In addition to controlling news at source, the government also relied on a plethora of regulations issued nationally by the General Staff and regionally by local military commanders. Military policy towards the press, or 'news management', was again the responsibility of Major Nicolai's Section IIIb of the OHL. The Law of the State of Siege had specifically suspended 'the right to express opinion freely by word, print or picture', only in areas directly endangered by the fighting. However, this was quickly applied to the whole country. The military in particular were more or less united in believing that journalists would be unable to distinguish between sensitive and harmless information. They therefore wanted laws passed forbidding the publication of military information, thereby removing their own actions from public criticism. On the same day as the announcement of the State of Siege, Chancellor Bethmann Hollweg issued instructions to the press containing 26 comprehensive prohibitions intended to prevent information that had not been passed by the military censor from being printed.[20]

A day later on 1 August in a secret memorandum sent to every publisher in the Reich, the military authorities outlined with typical thoroughness the guiding principles for the reporting of military information should war break out.[21] The press, they said, must first of all be conscious of their 'heavy responsibility and the consequences of their reports'. The welfare of the Fatherland demanded strict discretion in all matters concerning the High Command. For this reason the press would 'give thanks to the war leadership' for providing guidelines to 'protect the Fatherland'. Tact and insight was required but the Press Bureau of the General Staff would assist the legitimate demands of the nation for news by issuing reports 'as often as possible' to the Military Commanders to pass on to the publishers in their respective districts. Even the act of censorship itself was to be suppressed. Instead the newspapers should 'patriotically educate' the nation of the need for secrecy and remind it of its duty. However, they warned ominously:

> By refraining unselfishly from publishing military reports it will spare the military and naval authorities the necessity of taking legal action, the strictest enforcement of which in cases of violation of this prohibition is demanded in the interests of the state.

As far as the press was concerned 'tact and insight' were of little value in such a military straightjacket. Any possibility of a constructive press policy had been destroyed even before the announcement of war. Ironic then that on 2 August the Chief of the General Staff von Moltke remarked that a close relationship between the war leadership and the press was essential as the press 'was an indispensable means of waging war'.[22] A few days later on 10 August a special Press Service was set up under the control of Section IIIb in order to establish clearly defined areas of responsibility between different ministries and to facilitate as efficiently as possible the management of military information.[23] Since the 3 August representatives of the press had been briefed daily by an officer from Section IIIb in the Reichstag. These briefings were to continue and the Foreign Office expanded its section issuing reports (*Referate*) on the domestic and foreign political and economic situation. At these briefings the press were informed of the plans of the General Staff and a principle was quickly established that: 'we will not always be able to reveal everything, but what we will say will be true'.

The effect of these measures was not lost on the press, and the socialist press in particular. *Vorwärts* published a muted editorial protest on 1 August:

> The orders issued by the military authorities force restrictions upon us and threaten the existence of our paper.... We take for granted that the members of our Party, because of their training and their loyalty to their convictions, will understand the restraint forced upon us and will remain faithful to us in these trying days.[24]

The military, on the other hand, were concerned that newspapers were still printing military news. On 8 August in a statement issued through the Wolff Telegraph Bureau (WTB) to all publishers, General von Kessel, the Chief Commander in the Marken (the military district which included Berlin), reminded the press, 'for the last time ... the printing of news regarding military affairs is prohibited ... unless the censorship has made an exception'. Editors were warned in no uncertain terms that 'from now on measures of force will be resorted to against the transgressors. Public warnings have not been lacking'. Emphasizing the government's determination to apply coercive measures to recalcitrant editors, the same communiqué announced that the *Tägliche Rundschau für Schlesien und Posen* had been suppressed for publishing military news 'in spite of repeated general warnings'.[25]

The following day *Vorwärts* informed its readers that the paper 'was limited in its freedom of action. It is extremely difficult for the editors of a socialist labour paper to combine the duty of protecting the interests of the labouring class with the task of conforming with the regulations of the military authorities'.[26] Clearly *Vorwärts* felt that support for the German war effort did not preclude it from discussing social and economic conditions at home. Towards the end of the month the military censor actually asked the paper to write more enthusiastically about the war[27], and a few days later, the War Minister von Falkenhayn, rescinded a ban imposed on revolutionary and

Social Democratic literature dating back to 1894, providing 'it was published after 31 August 1914... and did nothing to endanger the spirit of loyalty in the army'.[28] By the middle of September the fragility of the *Burgfrieden* was already beginning to show as news of military victories became less frequent. Writing in his diary on 11 September, Reichstag Deputy Hanssen noted the quickly changing mood of Berliners:

> Spirits are not so jubilant... reports from the battlefield are not so stimulating.... The High Command has already pampered the morale of those at home. At least one victory a day is demanded. When that fails, general apathy is evident. Street life is approaching normal. The war spirit is passing into the background because of the desire for amusement. One sees many women dressed in black and many unemployed. A poor, undernourished, suffering family, consisting of the father and four daughters, was standing on the Potsdamer Platz, selling homemade wooden swords. The swords were painted green, and written on them in large red letters were these words: 'Each shot – a Russian.' Brutality is on the increase.[29]

Worried that increasing indiscretions by the socialist press might inflame such a situation, von Kessel issued an order on 27 September suppressing *Vorwärts*. After pleas from Hugo Haase and Richard Fischer, both Reichstag Deputies and members of the editorial board, the order was lifted three days later with the stipulation that any reference to 'class hatred and class struggle' was to be avoided in future.[30] Even the bourgeois press did not escape the wrath of the censor. On 1 December 1914 the Finance Committee of the Reichstag met to appropriate five billion marks for the continuance of the war. Bethmann Hollweg opened the session by emphasizing the brilliant feats performed by the German troops but stressing the need to save in case the war lasted longer than expected: 'We must tighten up our belts in time if we are going to hold out.' (*Durchhalten*) Reporting on the speech the oldest and stylistically most conservative newspaper, the *Vossische Zeitung*, stated that the Chancellor had urged the German people to 'tighten up the hunger-belt before it is too late'. The government immediately ordered the suppression of the paper and the Finance Committee issued a statement condemning the account as false, pointing out the difference between a 'girth' and a 'hunger-belt'.[31]

The enormous discretionary powers vested in the Deputy Commanding Generals inevitably led to complaints from the press of unevenhandedness. The position was further complicated by the fact that certain army corps districts interpreted the Law on the State of Siege in different ways. The VIII Army Corps in the Cologne and Koblenz area, for example, whilst retaining control over the censorship of newspapers in their large urban conurbations, delegated such powers to the Landrat in the remaining areas of the administrative district.[32] Such discretionary powers placed the press in an invidious position as they were never completely sure how their military overlords would respond to their reports. As early as 28 August the Secretary of State, von Jagow, in a telegram to the Foreign Office, conceded that some military censors were being overzealous and inconsistent and called for the two sides to reach some form of agreement.[33] Bethmann Hollweg even hinted that the powers of the Deputy Commanding Generals might have to be brought more into line with the wishes of the Imperial Chancellor.[34] The government on the one hand considered that newspapers needed to be contained, yet they had no wish to alienate the press or in any way disturb the *Burgfrieden*. As a result of an official complaint made by the German Publishers' Association (*Verein Deutscher Zeitungsverleger*) that some military censors were actually suppressing news that had been officially cleared, the General Staff were forced to admit that there was indeed a lack of uniformity in the handling of press censorship.[35] In October Section IIIb informed the Imperial Naval Office that the 'unfortunate' tone taken by the military censors and their eagerness to employ 'sharp' measures against newspapers was resulting in general bad feeling. It even went so far as to claim that the authorities' lacked sufficient knowledge of the newspaper world and that a concerted approach to censorship was required. The General Staff supported the idea first put forward by the German Publishers' Association of a Supreme Censorship Office (*Oberzensurstelle*) to coordinate this work, although for different reasons.[36] The publishers hoped it would act as a court of appeal and undermine the power of their provincial military overlords. The OHL saw it as a way of increasing their own position over the Deputy Commanding Generals and a means of providing much needed guidance and coordination. The organizational structure was agreed in December and the *Oberzensurstelle* began operating in earnest in February 1915.[37]

However, before the Supreme Censorship Office could begin functioning a crisis arose in November which required the direct intervention of the Chancellor. For some time the military authorities had been concerned that press criticism was undermining morale and that a new clamp down was needed. This led to some absurd decisions being implemented. For example in early November a North Schleswig paper was suppressed for 'scarcely mentioning the birthday of the Empress' and for giving the impression that the University of Copenhagen 'is a local university'. Banning the paper for a week the Deputy Commander commented: '...one can see that the whole race is painfully and deplorably lacking in patriotism'.[38] Two days later on 9 November the Commanding Generals received new instructions from the War Ministry on tougher new measures to be taken against newspapers or individuals criticizing the government.[39] When the press got hold of this document, which was leaked to MPs, a storm of protests erupted over what was feared to be the enthusiastic enforcement of preventive censorship making public criticism virtually impossible. On 30 November Bethmann Hollweg was forced to hold a press conference in the Reichstag to explain the government's position and to defuse the situation. His statement was read out by von Mumm. The Chancellor, it said, recognized the constraints now imposed upon the press but assured them that no plans were being made to introduce preventive censorship for all news and reports. Articles dealing with political matters would not be first vetted by the Foreign Office. The 'instructions' issued by the OHL on the command of the Kaiser were 'merely guidelines'. However, the Chancellor hoped that as the press were a party to the *Burgfrieden* they would abide by these guidelines which had been instigated *'by the imperative need for the Reich to be united against enemy countries'*. Once peace negotiations had been entered into then 'the voices of public opinion will and must be once more fully heard'.[40] The proclamation concluded by saying that the Chancellor's statement was not intended to precipitate further discussion on the subject.

This fooled no one. In early December Reichstag Deputies renewed their attack on censorship and called for the repeal of the Exceptional Laws. Adolf Gröber of the Centre Party opened the debate by quoting the words of the Kaiser: 'I recognise no parties'. Referring to the position of the Jesuits, Gröber pointed out that the government gratefully accepts their services as army chaplains, in civil capacities, and in the service of the Imperial Navy, but refuses to abolish the Jesuit Law, 'which places members of the order outside the protection of the law and the courts'. The next speaker, Dr Andreas Blunck of the Liberal Party, claimed that had the government been in touch with public opinion they would have recognized the call to abolish these hated laws. This was followed by two bitter attacks on censorship by the SDP leader, Hugo Haase and the Liberal Dr Müller-Meiningen, both of whom condemned the encroachments of the censorship. Concern in the Reichstag was that there had been no political checks on the Commanding Generals, although here politicians had to be careful that their complaints were not construed as an attack on the principle of military security. Replying for the government, Dr Clemens Delbrück, Prussian Minister of the Interior,[41] claimed that it had in fact avoided enforcing the Exceptional Laws, but conceded that censors had often made mistakes. Adding that this 'was unfortunate since all the party papers seem to be patriotic', but warning that 'censorship could not be avoided'. It was during the course of his speech that Delbrück made the significant but fateful announcement that 'the magnitude of the times, the unity of the people, and the enormous sacrifices which the preservation of this unity requires, must lead to a new orientation (*Neuorientierung*) of our domestic policy'.[42] The failure of the imperial government to carry out these promised reforms was destined to play a crucial role in its eventual downfall (see Chapter 6). On 10 December Section IIIb called to the attention of the Deputy Commanding Generals the mistakes that had been made and the role of censorship in the war effort. They pointed out that the people had a right to share in the excitement of the war for it was never envisaged that all news and observations about the war should be suppressed. 'Censorship should only seek to prevent exaggeration, distortion, and lack of judgement... which could either arouse false hopes at home or provide encouragement to the enemy.'[43] 1914, then, drew to a close with the questions of political reforms, war aims and censorship very much in the air.

One of the first tasks facing the newly created Supreme Censorship Office (*Oberzensurstelle*) was to clarify the legal position of the press and the enforcement of pre-censorship (*Präventivzensur*). Immediately on publication, publishers of all material subject to press inspection had, since the beginning of the war, to present a copy to the local police authorities who had been delegated these independent powers by the Military Commanders. This led to so many complaints that by February 1915 the Prussian Minister of the Interior von Loebbel was forced to advise the police that 'preventive censorship should generally be applied only to military articles'.[44] Nevertheless, in reply to a query from the XVII Army Corps, the *Oberzensurstelle* confirmed in a letter of 12 February 1915 that under the Law of Siege, freedom of the press was suspended for the duration of the war and therefore it was legally possible to apply pre-censorship to both military *and* domestic news.[45] Nothing was more guaranteed to incur the hostility of the press than the demand that all 'unofficial' news must first be submitted to the censors before publication. However, two weeks later von Moltke wrote to the Military Commanders in an attempt to defuse the situation and to widen the discussion on relations between the military authorities and the press. He pointed out that bearing in mind the recent criticisms of press censorship in the Reichstag, simply banning guilty newspapers was not the only solution. He suggested instead that it might be wiser to scale down the disciplinary measures and rely more on warnings and 'enlightened' education. To support his argument he made four points: (1) banning a newspaper affects the innocent readership as much as the guilty editorial board, and attracts considerable undesirable publicity abroad; (2) infringements of the censorship regulations are not normally the result of malice; (3) banning a paper does not rectify the damage already done; and (4) a stronger call to the responsibility and feelings of honour of the press will probably bring about the desired response better than repressive measures. Moltke believed that the press for their part would see this as an act of faith and would seek to repay the renunciation of repressive measures with more editorial consideration for the position of the military.[46] To some extent Moltke found support from the Kaiser who in August issued a Cabinet order to the War Ministry that the handling of press censorship needed improving. The King believed this could only be achieved through greater centralization and called upon the War Ministry and the OHL to extend the *Oberzensurstelle*.[47] Accordingly in September extensive plans were drawn up to establish the War Press Office (*Kriegspresseamt* – KPA).

THE WAR PRESS OFFICE (*KRIEGSPRESSEAMT*)

As a result of the enlargement of the *Oberzensurstelle*, ordered by the Kaiser, the *Kriegspresseamt* (KPA) was established in Berlin in October 1915 under the direct control of the OHL and Major Nicolai's Section IIIb. Its first head was Major Erhard Deutelmoser (who would be dismissed by Hindenburg and Ludendorff in 1916 when they were appointed to lead the OHL). The plans setting out its responsibilities were extraordinarily detailed but three major tasks stand out:[48]

1. To facilitate co-operation between the OHL and the civilian authorities with regard to the press.
2. To provide as much controlled information as possible to the various authorities and to the press.
3. To establish and supervise the uniform application of the censorship.

The KPA was divided into the Information Office (Major Hosse), the Supreme Censorship Office (von Olberg) and the Office for Foreign Affairs (von Herwarth), each with clearly defined responsibilities but with the overriding aim of providing a centralized source of information, propaganda and censorship, both for home and abroad. As the contradictions within German society became more and more acute under the stress of war, the KPA came to play an increasingly important role countering internal unrest.

It was hoped that the Information Office in particular would establish a well oiled chain of command ranging down from the OHL, via the civilian and military authorities to the press. It had the crucial task of disseminating propaganda and manipulating public opinion according to the intentions of the High Command. In order to facilitate this function the Information Office was organised into three sections:

Section Ia: To observe the German press and report on it.
Section Ib: The answering of questions and the releasing of news to officials and to the press.
Section Ic: The administration of the archives and the library. These were to be built 'as quickly as possible' so as to guarantee a 'swift and constructive approach not only to the contemporary situation but to all the important military, political, and economic questions'.

Section Ia consisted of six *Referate* (reporting bodies) dealing with German political parties, a *Referate* for Austro-Hungary, and an editorial office. The *Referate* were expected to prepare short extracts from the papers, magazines, leaflets, books, etc., given to them to work on. The editorial office would then compile these into concise reports. Furthermore a daily survey of the morning and evening papers would be undertaken and at the end of the week a more comprehensive weekly survey (*Wochenübersicht*) produced. They were also expected to brief the OHL about forthcoming events of interest and the current state of civilian morale. Many of these reports were passed on to Section Ib to be released to the press.

Section Ib received information, reports and directives from every available source. The foreign office of the KPA sent news from abroad; the Supreme Censorship Office issued directives of new measures taken, reports of Reichstag sittings were received in full, and journalists were encouraged to file individual reports. The news material collected was then fed back to the OHL and to other offices designated by them. It was used in particular to brief the censorship authorities on the military and political situation in the hope that such information would help them to arrive at balanced judgements. Finally, Section Ib provided a carefully controlled forum in which the press could pose questions to the military and the KPA would issue public or confidential statements depending on the situation. In order to supply the press with as much military information as they required, the KPA published three periodicals: *Deutsche Kriegsnachrichten, Nachrichten der Auslandspresse* and *Deutsche Kriegswochenschau*. For expediency the daily army reports (*Heeresberichte*) were given at 11 a.m. for the evening papers. By October 1916 the KPA decided to add an evening update to this briefing and a summary of both reports was sent over the WTB wire.[49] In an effort to satisfy a public clamouring for more news, regular 'press discussions' (*Pressebesprechungen*) between a committee of journalists (headed by Georg Bernhard, editor of the influential *Vossiche Zeitung* and director of the Ullstein publishing house) and officials from all the ministries (chaired by Major Schweitzer), were held in the Reichstag two or three times weekly. Such 'discussions' were nominally independent of the KPA, although they were of course closely studied by Section Ia. The new system functioned quite efficiently from the military point of view and one can detect, at least until 1917, a growing sense of purpose articulated through increasing coordination. This was to change in 1917.

The reorganization of the *Oberzensurstelle* into the KPA was undertaken so that censorship could be administered 'with justice and uniformity'. However, according to the plans setting out the new organisation, this 'justice' had to be tempered by the imperative needs to (1) maintain the *Burgfrieden* and public faith in the government and High Command; and (2) avoid providing the enemy with useful military, political or economic information. Under its reorganization, the Supreme Censorship Office was to consist of five specialist departments covering the General Staff, War Ministry, the Imperial Navy, the Colonial Office and domestic policy. Its functions were to establish general directives, to encourage widespread acceptance of its policies, and to arbitrate in disputes where mistakes had been made. However, only the head of the KPA (not the chief of the *Oberzensurstelle*) could approve major changes to existing censorship regulations.[50]

The High Command expected that the establishment of the KPA together with the centralization of censorship, would greatly help to improve relations between the press and the censor. It did not, and was bitterly attacked by both press and parliament as yet one more effort by the military authorities to monopolize the channels of opinion reaching the public through the press. Nevertheless in November 1915 the KPA met representatives of the *Reichsverband der deutschen Presse* and the *Verein Deutscher Zeitungsverleger* in a further attempt to construct an 'efficient and positive censorship programme in a spirit of co-operation'. They praised and thanked the press for 'their honourable contribution to the war effort', but complained that confidential information was still finding its way into enemy newspapers. Deutelmoser, the head of the KPA, was particularly concerned that the press should avoid using 'semi-official' headlines and reporting war bulletins in a sensational manner. In order to assist the press wade through the plethora of censorship regulations more quickly, the *Oberzensurstelle* optimistically provided a reference catalogue with a card index of all censorship measures currently in force. In a rather obvious attempt to stress their sincerity the KPA also reaffirmed that the *Oberzensurstelle* would willingly investigate all complaints made against local censorship offices.[51] The press for their part was not convinced.

Nevertheless, fifteen months after the outbreak of war the basis for a centrally guided and controlled press and for the coordination of propaganda in general had been set up. The creation of the War Press Office had not only given the OHL direct control over censorship, but it had strengthened its position at the expense of the War Ministry. Licking its wounds, the War Ministry struggled to retain its independence by accepting a restrained role setting up committee meetings, dealing with strikes and monitoring the movements of the political parties, especially the minority radical groups. Although it is difficult to gauge the success of the War Press Office, it did provide a much needed centralized source of news and censorship, and if anything, appeared to deal more effectively with internal dissent than did its counterparts in Britain and France – at least until the final year of the war. As the war progressed and public opinion began to polarize over Germany's war aims, the KPA played an increasingly important role as vehicle for maintaining the *status quo*. Through the KPA, information was controlled at source by preventive censorship, nationally by means of directives sanctioned by the OHL and regionally by the Deputy Commanding Generals. The prestige of the OHL normally guaranteed that local military commanders would follow its guidelines. Suppression ranged across military reverses, war aims, food shortages, peace demonstrations, strikes, casualty lists and notices of deaths, and military and industrial technology. Indeed, any information likely to demoralize the troops or the home front was censored. It has been suggested that the all-embracing nature of military censorship led the German press to lose touch with public opinion.[52] To some extent this was true; as one newspaper tended to offer the same censored news as another, its credibility in the eyes of the reading public gradually began to be eroded. Moreover the censorship regulations were so deliberately complex and time-consuming that editors simply complied by dutifully printing only official news distributed through the Wolff Telegraph Bureau.

However uniform the news, the 'state of siege on truth' was not as constricted as is often supposed. Germans could read accounts in the neutral press which were published in Germany, and most surprising of all, German newspapers were allowed to print enemy army reports, provided they were published in full. Criticisms levelled against the government in the Reichstag were also carried by the papers. The debate about Germany's war aims, for example, provided, as we shall see in the next chapter, a striking example of the ability of the press to reflect accurately the divisions that existed in Germany. Such a debate, with its bitter attack on censorship, would have been inconceivable in Britain or France. Moreover, censorship was not severe enough to prevent numerous indiscretions by the German socialist and even bourgeois press. One explanation for this is that while Moltke was Chief of the General Staff and Deutelmoser head of the KPA, both showed considerable restraint in the face of growing press and parliamentary criticism of political interference by the military. Even Nicolai as chief of Section IIIb was prepared to play a relatively low keyed role in political matters. This was to change with the appointment of Hindenburg and Ludendorff to the OHL in August 1916. Both were populist figures conscious of the need to manipulate public opinion and determined to use the mystical prestige of the OHL in pursuit of their own political ambitions and the further militarization of German society. Deutelmoser was removed as head of the KPA for being too sympathetic to Chancellor Bethmann Hollweg, and replaced by the more compliant Major Stotten. Once Deutelmoser was out of the way, Ludendorff could pursue his personal campaign for an even more rigorous suppression of the press and a demand for a Ministry of Propaganda to coordinate a massive propaganda exercise of patriotic 'enlightenment'.

But more of this later. By the beginning of 1916, the main channels of imperial propaganda organized by the OHL are those depicted in Figure 5.

CINEMA AND SOCIETY IN IMPERIAL GERMANY

By the end of the nineteenth century, the major advances made by the economy had created in Germany a mass urban population that enjoyed increasing leisure time with the necessary disposable income to demand more and more amusement and diversion.[53] Such demand, as we have seen, led directly to the growth of the popular press. It also resulted in arguably the first true mass entertainment medium, the popular cinema. By the outbreak of the War in 1914, the cinema had become *the* entertainment medium of the masses. It is therefore surprising to discover that the German authorities were rather slow to manipulate the medium systematically for their propaganda purposes. It would take the war and the need to sustain civilian morale to persuade the governing elite in imperial Germany of its importance and subsequently to bring about a fundamental shift in official policy towards the cinema. By 1918, military opinion had swung to such an extent that many experts (including Ludendorff) were clearly exaggerating the cinema's importance as an instrument of psychological warfare.

The basic structure of the German film industry was established before the outbreak of the Great War. In the decade leading up to 1905 the film industry centred around the roving tent shows (*Wanderkinos*) travelling the countryside with local carnivals and fairs. As film distribution improved, permanent cinemas situated in the larger cities began to replace the itinerant fairground exhibitor at a staggering pace as ambitious entrepreneurs clamoured for the easy profits that were to be made. Estimates on the number of cinemas in pre-war Germany vary widely but by the outbreak of war there were over 2,500 cinemas spread throughout the country.[54] Most of the major urban conurbations could boast over 30 cinemas that could seat, on average, between 200 to 300 patrons.[55]

The proliferation of cinemas was matched by increasing cinema attendance. In 1913, a survey conducted in Mannheim, for example, showed that one third of the population visited the cinema at least once a week, and most attended even more often.[56] By 1914 it is estimated that daily film attendance for the nation as a whole was one and half million.[57] The new cinema audience was made up of the lower strata of society consisting mainly of the industrial proletariat. Since 1890, the German economy had grown fast enough to allow a moderate growth in buying power. In the decade before 1914, the average working day decreased while the average annual earnings

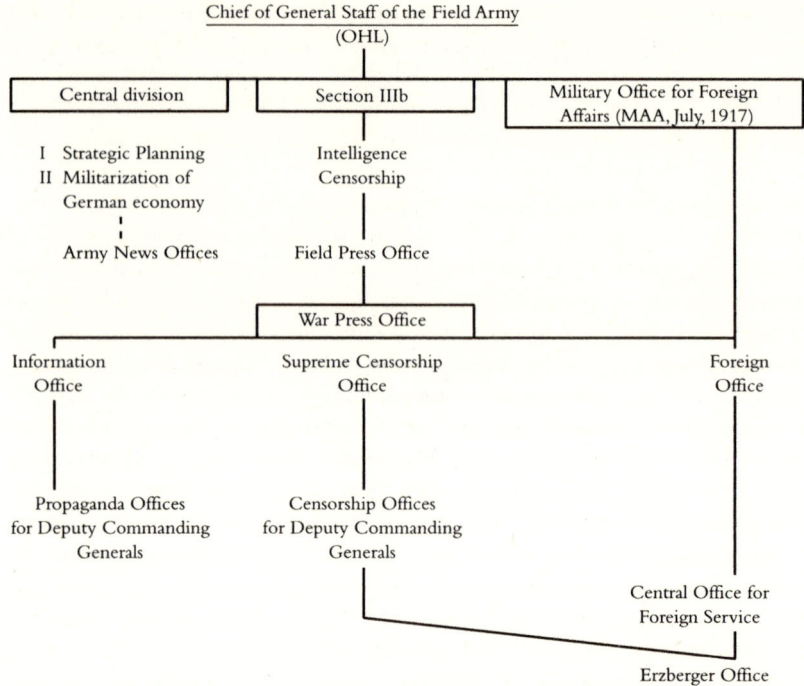

Figure 5 The organization of official propaganda, 1914–16.

of industrial workers rose continually (albeit slower than in the period 1890 to 1900). Between 1900 and 1913, real wages increased by 13 per cent enabling the average industrial worker to save 1 per cent of his income and spend 4 per cent on what Jürgen Kocka termed 'psychic and social needs'.[58] The shortening of the working day together with a larger disposable income led to a demand on the part of the proletariat for more working-class entertainment. Barred from the traditional forms of middle-class entertainment, such as the legitimate theatre and concert halls, the lower classes began to spend more time and money in the cinemas which rapidly served as an art substitute for such a semi-literate public. The undemanding nature of silent films together with their novelty value and the low cost of admission only enhanced the appeal of the cinema theatres, which quickly gained a reputation for attracting individuals of ill repute and for uninhibited and raucous behaviour.

The social composition of early cinema audiences, together with the highly sensationalist and violent films that were being shown, led to a growing concern about the nature of this new entertainment medium on the part of the guardians of public morality. In 1905, associations made up largely of teachers, religious groups and cultural societies formed a cinema reform movement (*Kinoreformbewegung*) which immediately denounced the cinema as a subversive and corrupting influence on the nation's morals. Justifying their position, they argued that because of film's reliance on sensational visual images, unlike for example, the traditional theatre, the cinema exerted a much more sustained impact on the impressionable and semi-literate lower classes, and on youth in particular.[59] The *Kinoreformbewegung* eventually grew into a political pressure group, the Cinematic Reform Party (*Kinematographische Reformpartei*) demanding tighter censorship and more control over the type of films that were being made and distributed. They also campaigned for the production of more educational and cultural films, arguing that such films would not only raise the standing of the film industry but would act as a means of introducing the lower social classes to aspects of 'higher culture'.

The most popular films in pre-war Germany were the so-called 'junk-films' (*Schundfilme*), which, with their flimsy plots with obvious sexual and violent overtones were similar to the equally popular pulp fiction pamphlets that sold in such vast quantities.[60] Official concern about these films embraced not only the spiritual damage that they were thought to inflict but also a growing fear that such behaviour was being imitated. To this end, pressure groups like the Cinematic Reform Party and the Dürer League were finding increasingly vociferous support from many judicial and political figures who began blaming these 'junk-films' for the growing crime rate and juvenile delinquency. Such fears were far more tangible than abstract debates about film as a valid art form, for since 1890, the crime rate had risen alarmingly, and by 1914 stood 20 per cent above the figure for the late 1880s.[61] Film censorship developed then out of a pragmatic concern for law and order and as a means of protecting the legitimate theatre. The first steps were taken in Berlin in 1906 when the police imposed upon cinema theatres the same preventive censorship to which any theatrical performance had been subject since 1851. Henceforth, films could only be shown in public if they had obtained the advanced approval of the Berlin Chief of Police who retained the power to ban films thought objectionable.[62] Although not all the major cities would impose such strict censorship as Berlin, the procedure adopted in the capital naturally influenced the rest of Germany. Most local authorities were content to supervise more closely the film programmes and in particular to restrict the entry of children and adolescents who were not accompanied by adults. Not surprisingly, such a haphazard handling of film censorship led to considerable local variations where a film could be banned in one district yet shown in the next.

Despite protests from cinema theatre owners that pre-censorship caused expensive delays, it was gradually accepted that more uniform standards for film censorship were needed and that the cinema could not be regulated by old laws designed for the fairgrounds or legitimate theatre. In 1911, Brunswick began centralizing its censorship procedures, and it was followed by the Bavarian Interior Ministry in January 1912 which set up a central board of film censors in Munich to examine every film shown in Bavaria.[63]

In July, the Prussian Ministry of the Interior issued two decrees that eventually led to the establishment of a Film Censorship Office (*Filmprüfungsamt*). Films were now automatically censored immediately after their production and, if approved, granted a certificate which was valid throughout Prussia.[64] The censors had the power to remove offensive scenes, or to restrict screenings of a particular film to adult audiences if it were deemed inappropriate for children's matinees. The Berlin film censors were mostly concerned with film material likely to undermine moral standards or endanger public order. Once passed by the Berlin censors, a film was unlikely to be rejected by other states. In March, 1914, after a concerted and energetic campaign by various interests groups, Württemberg not only set up its own film censorship office in Stuttgart, but went even further than Prussia by enacting the most stringent and comprehensive films laws to date.[65]

At the same time, the imperial government, under pressure particularly from the theatrical lobby, introduced into the Reichstag a draft film censorship law (*Reichslichtspielgesetz*) covering the whole of Germany and designed to restrict the number of permitted cinemas in each locality and to establish a commercial code that would regulate trading standards.[66] The legitimate theatre felt justifiably threatened by the proliferation of cinemas and for some years organized opposition to the cinema had been undertaken by groups such as the Guild of German Stage Employees and the League of German Playwrights. In the immediate pre-war years, theatre owners actually tried to prevent their actors from working in the newly constructed film studios at Tempelhof and Neubabelsberg. Furthermore, in 1913, an entertainment tax on cinema receipts ranging from 5 to 20 per cent was introduced, resulting in the closure of some cinemas. The use made of the cinema tax varied from one municipality to another; in Barmen, for example, it was used to subsidize the city's legitimate theatre which was thought to have suffered from unfair competition from the cinema.[67] Despite a well organized countercampaign on the part of cinema distributors and theatre owners protesting at further restrictions, the drafting of the government's *Reichslichtspielgesetz* in February 1914, was seen as a major victory for the self-appointed guardians of public morality and represented a serious blow to a cinema industry that was attempting to come to terms with changing public demands for more sophisticated forms of entertainment. However, the bill, which almost certainly would have been approved by the Reichstag, lapsed on the outbreak of war. It would not be resubmitted until 1917, by which time political divisions and war weariness spelt its death knell. Nevertheless, by the outbreak of war in August 1914, cinemas in Germany were more tightly regulated than in any other European country, and every major city could boast of a central state film censor's office. Such measures would greatly facilitate the mobilization of the medium for propaganda purposes during the ensuing conflict.

War and imperial film propaganda, 1914–16
The First World War gave the German cinema its great opportunity and as cinema audiences continued to increase the government gradually began to appreciate the possibilities of the cinema for influencing morale and public opinion. However, on the eve of war few believed that film was a suitable medium for the dissemination of propaganda.[68] Initially the military authorities feared that it could disrupt the established social order and immediately sought to impose even more restrictions. Accordingly on 11 August 1914, cinemas and musical halls were warned that unless their programmes reflected the 'seriousness of the time' and the 'patriotic mood of the nation', then films would be confiscated and entertainment premises closed.[69] On the other hand, General von Kessel, the Chief Commander in the Marks, reminded theatre and cinema proprietors that it was simply counterproductive to exaggerate the certainty of a German victory by means of cheap and boastful pronouncements from the stage.[70] Towards the end of 1914 concern for the moral welfare of cinema and theatre audiences led the Berlin censor, for example, to ban a number of films and plays on the grounds that they were liable to 'inflict spiritual and moral damage'.[71] Humorous films in particular were viewed by the authorities as frivolous indulgences that could be tolerated only within certain limits and only provided 'the Fatherland, the military, and the uniform were not ridiculed'.[72] This prompted one member of the German Committee of Stage Associates to complain that the censor was taking humour too seriously! The writer, Dr Hans Günther, argued that in grave times, laughter was a 'wholesome, liberating experience that should not be construed as being disrespectful to the state'.[73] Nevertheless, the Prussian War Minister went so far as to blame superficial foreign films that had been imported into the country for poisoning 'the nation's healthy instincts', and suggested that the German film industry should, instead, produce 'serious' films that reflected the true feelings of the Fatherland.[74] A group of cinema owners had already issued an *Aufruf zur nationalen Selbsthilfe*, calling upon their colleagues not to exhibit foreign films, and in September 1914, the police authorities began confiscating foreign films.[75]

The government responded first by imposing a ban on the importation of all new foreign films, and in January 1915, a decree by the War Ministry issued through the local military commanders informed the cinema industry that in future only films likely to 'uphold morale and promote patriotism for the Fatherland' would be passed by the censor. All so-called 'trash' films (including the detective genre that had proved so popular with pre-war audiences) that were not in keeping with 'the gravity of the present times' were to be banned, and failure to comply with these measures would lead to cinema closures.[76] This represented the first official evaluation of commercial films from both a political and artistic viewpoint. The response of the cinema industry was to produce a series of melodramatic *kitsch* films known as the 'field-grey' genre, as the action invariably centred on the heroism of German soldiers. Included in this genre were films with titles such as: *How Max Won the Iron Cross; On the Field of Honour; Miss Field Grey; I Know No Parties; and Christmas Bells*. Freed from the burden of foreign competition and encouraged by the government to produce indigenous works, the film industry began to attract directors and actors from the legitimate theatre. Such collaboration resulted in rare films like *Der Golem* (1915) and *Homunculus* (1916) which foreshadowed the fantastic themes and sets to be found in the expressionist films of the Weimar period.

The awakened nationalism of 1914 turned not only against foreign films but against foreign culture in general. The pressure of patriotic opinion resulted in the elimination of foreign elements from most forms of entertainment. The historic mission of German high culture formed one of the government's main propaganda platforms. Foreign *Unkultur* was portrayed as the antithesis of German civilization and its cultural achievements. Posters and postcards in particular, proclaimed the superiority of German culture and were skilfully exploited to channel patriotic emotions such as courage or hatred. Postcards showed the first foreign prisoners of war being escorted in German cities, while others printed slogans such as: *Jeder Tritt ein Britt* ('for every step, a Brit'); *Jeder Stoss ein Franzos* ('for every blow, a Frenchy'); *Jeder Schuss ein Russ* ('for every shot, a Russki'). From the very outset of the war, Germany seized upon the poster as one of the most powerful and speedy means of influencing popular opinion.[77] Posters were used in numerous campaigns ranging from requests for war loans, recruiting, information about food and fuel substitutes, calls for greater industrial effort, and a series entitled 'Wir Barbaren!' (We Barbarians!) which compared favourably the cultural achievements of Germany to those of Britain and France (see Figure 6). A more light-hearted example of this national self-consciousness can be gauged from the outcry that greeted a circular by the Syndicat de la Parfumerie française that was printed in the German press which claimed that Eau de Cologne was really a French invention. One journalist even demanded that all French scent and soaps on sale in Germany should be immediately destroyed and citizens encouraged to use only German toilet products![78]

Despite its new found ideological chauvinism, the cinema continued to attract criticism and hostility from sections of the established order. Discussions on what was regarded as the low moral level of the cinema figured prominently in Reichstag debates. In March 1915, for example, Deputy Marx of the Centre Party stressed the importance of the cinema as a means of maintaining wartime solidarity. However, while he welcomed the 'cleansing' of foreign elements from the industry he warned that frivolity and permissiveness were already creeping back into commercial films and urged the government to become even more vigilant. Replying for the government, Loebbel, the Minister of Interior, assured the House that the government had no intention of relaxing the stringent controls over the cinema industry and expressed the hope that the exigencies of war might bring about a lasting improvement in public morality.[79] Towards the end of 1915, as the *Burgfrieden* began to break down, fears were expressed in the Reichstag that popular films were exacerbating class tensions by portraying the social behaviour of the upper classes in a negative and misleading manner. One Deputy warned that stereotyped images of the 'idle rich' could well lead to resentment and envy among the lower classes.[80] In a later sitting, von Mumm argued that such films 'were no friend of the German art' and served only to 'debase our people'.[81]

However, the major concern both inside and outside the Reichstag was that with fathers being conscripted and more and more mothers contributing to the war effort, children would spend increasing time in cinemas watching escapist trivia without parental control. As early as March 1915 therefore, police authorities issued instructions that cinemas would be closely watched to make sure that banned films were not shown to children.[82] Furthermore, singing and declamatory shows were forbidden during matinee performances when children might be present, and in the evenings, cinema theatres were not allowed to remain open after 11 p.m.[83] These measures were prompted by the dramatic rise in juvenile crime during the first year of the war. Figures taken from Stuttgart, for example, for the period 1914–15, revealed a 100 per cent increase in crimes carried out by juveniles, mostly consisting of theft and damage to property. In Bremen, the Senate immediately banned juveniles under 18 years of age from visiting public houses, coffee houses or confectionary establishments (*Konditoreien*) after 8 pm, nor were they allowed to attend music halls or even vocal and declamatory recitals which 'are devoid of a higher scientific or artistic interest'.[84]

After numerous complaints from religious leaders and other civic groups and working on the premise that the 'youth of today are easily excited by

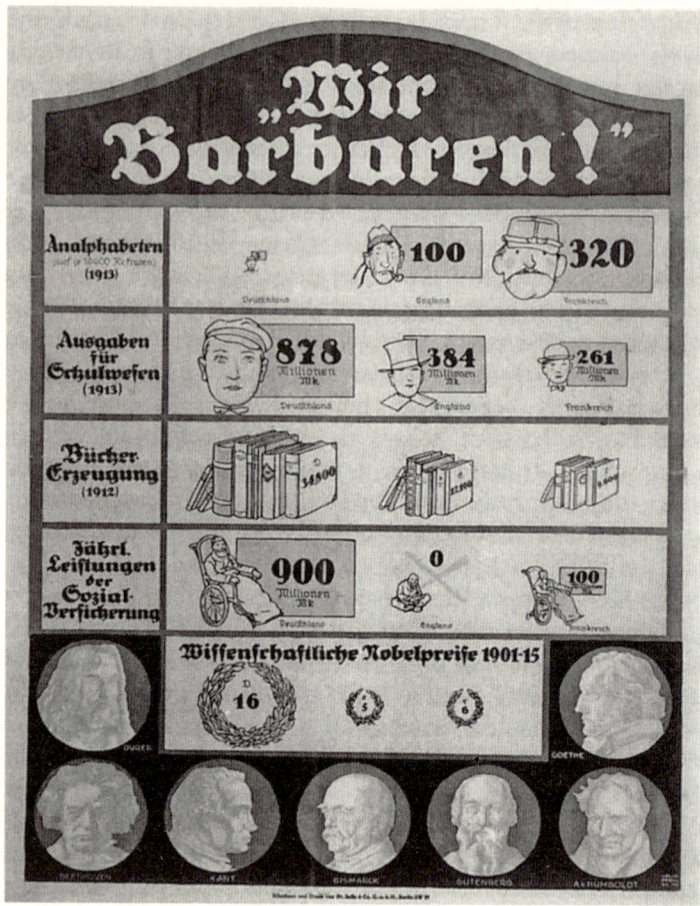

Figure 6 'We Barbarians!' Louis Oppenheim's 1916 poster.

the sensationalist and criminal action they see in films', the local military authorities launched in July 1916 a two-pronged attack on the commercial cinema industry. First of all they considerably tightened-up their supervision of films regarded as suitable for children. Secondly, they attacked the excesses of commercialism and in particular the ubiquitously provocative film posters that many conservatives believed were even more lurid than the films themselves and which, it was claimed, unscrupulously manipulated children. In what formed part of a wider clamp-down on commercial exploitation, the authorities now imposed stringent restrictions on the size of film posters, where they could be displayed, and what could and could not be advertised.[85]

Such measures were generally welcomed in official circles. In the Reichstag, Dr Stresemann (National Liberal Party) announced that specialist committees had been formed to establish guidelines for the distribution of literature and films designed for children.[86] However, there were parliamentarians who argued that the claims made against the commercial cinema were largely unsubstantiated. Gustav Noske of the SDP, for example, persuasively argued that the authorities should concentrate on the positive aspects offered by film. To do this, he suggested, the government needed to apply a fairer system of censorship similar to the one governing the legitimate theatre. Noske criticized the *Kriegspresseamt* for failing to control the prejudices of local military commanders and called for a more enlightened and uniform policy of censorship.[87]

Such a reversal of policy was in fact only a year away. Despite the hostility and all the restrictions imposed, the war had revealed the immense power of film as a means of influencing public opinion and providing relaxation. Eventually the government was forced to recognize that the commercial cinema would not be suppressed but could be used to bolster morale. Thus towards the end of 1916, the War Ministry began secretly commissioning a number of private companies to produce propaganda feature films for home consumption. In January 1917 the High Command not only introduced censorship of films for export in an attempt to control the image of Germany abroad, but it also set up its own organization, the Photographic and Film Office (Bufa) whose role was to coordinate the wartime activities of the German film industry. Throughout 1917 General Ludendorff had been stressing the importance of film as a propaganda medium and calling for the industry to be centralized. As a result of Ludendorff's 'suggestions', a new umbrella organization financed jointly by the state and private industry was founded on 18 December 1917 and became known as *Universum-Film-Aktiengesellschaft* (Ufa). Ufa's contribution to the ailing war effort will be discussed in Chapter 7.

The war newsreel
In many ways the wartime experiences of the newsreel companies were similar to those encountered by the producers of popular films. Nevertheless, despite the military's resistance to the medium of film and their enduring reluctance to allow film reporting of the theatres of war, the German authorities did show a greater awareness of the possibilities offered by newsreels for disseminating military information and for promoting propaganda themes.[88]

There were no German newsreels before 1913. Like commercial film production the industry was dominated by the French, and in particular its leading film company, *Pathé Frères*, which had been founded as early as 1896.

However, just before the outbreak of war, *Eiko-Woche* was formed as a result of the collaboration between the press magnate August Scherl (owner of the *Berliner Lokal-Anzeiger* and *Die Woche*) and Dürener Rohlfilmindustrie Kino-Film GmbH, Scherl advertised *Eiko-Woche* as 'the living reportage of the *Berliner Lokal-Anzeiger*' and soon began to support the public's growing interest in cinema by publishing the film magazine *Kinematograph*.[89] By September 1914, all French film companies had been closed down, and seven newsreels were now exhibited within Germany. As well as *Eiko-Woche*, the others included: *Hubertus-Kriegswoche, Nordisk authentische Weltkriegsberichte, Kinokop-Woche, Kriegsberichte der National-Film-GmbH, Münchener Neuigkeiten* and *Messter-Woche*. Of these, *Eiko-Woche* and *Messter-Woche* were the most important, and the only ones to be distributed in neutral countries.

Despite the proliferation of newsreel companies, the industry still suffered from lack of investment. The German army had neither the expertise nor the equipment at its disposal, and it was left to the enthusiasm and pioneering work of film producers like Oskar Messter to seize the opportunity offered by the war. Messter recognized that the first primitive war newsreels were a source of enormous interest to all sections of the population including the middle class who had previously looked upon cinema-going with disdain, and his *Messter-Woche* was financed entirely from the family engineering business.[90] Messter immediately offered his services to the war effort, and was appointed to the Press Office of Section IIIb of the OHL under Major Schweitzer, where he was commissioned to draw up a licensing system for the filming of military reports from the front. Out of 64 applicants only four companies, Messter-Film GmbH, Eiko-Film GmbH, Express-Film of Freiburg and Martin Kopp of Munich, were granted a licence.[91] In order to obtain these permits the companies had to satisfy a set of guidelines devised by Messter and the OHL. First of all the newsreel companies had to be German owned and managed, 'patriotically minded', and possess the necessary capital and German equipment. Each company had to submit the names of two cameramen who were 'trustworthy and German' and who would operate under strict military supervision. In order to rationalize their limited resources the licensed companies were allocated areas so that Messter covered the Western Front, Eiko the Eastern Front and East Prussia, and Express Film the Southern Front. Martin Kopp's *Kinokop-Woche* appears to have been given a freer hand, although it is clear from the content of the war newsreels that the companies must have exchanged their film material.[92]

The suspicion in the film world that Messter had abused his position by becoming the mouthpiece of the OHL was confirmed when *Messter Film-GmbH*, whose management had taken up positions within Section IIIb, issued the following officially sounding announcement to all rival companies on 14 October 1914 in the trade magazine *Kinematograph*:

> Notification concerning authentic war films! May we courteously point out that from now on film shots from the theatres of war can only be taken with the express permission of the General Staff. Such films can only be hired under the conditions set out by the OHL and are loaned for a limited period. We herewith make this known to all.[93]

Some days before this announcement, Messter released the first officially approved war newsreel. For some time Oskar Messter had been preparing a newsreel film diary entitled 'Documents of the World War' (*Dokumente zum Weltkrieg*) whose name he changed to Messter-Woche on 1 October 1914. Using his famous trade mark, the globe with the film strip, the intention was to produce fortnightly newsreels (later increased to a weekly report). The first *Messter-Woche* was exhibited on 9 October and showed among other things, pictures from the fighting area in Damnau in East Prussia and shots of refugees returning to homes and churches destroyed by the Russians. On the home front, Princess August Wilhelm is shown attending a cinema performance in aid of wounded soldiers in the Palast-Theater am Zoo in Berlin.[94] *Messter-Woche No. 2*, released on 16 October, was the first newsreel to be approved and stamped by the War Ministry under the new licensing system. It ran for almost 10 minutes and its eclectic but somewhat 'safe' format set the tone for all other newsreels during the first part of the war. Nevertheless, it was received rapturously by a public eager for as much information about the war as possible. The following is a breakdown of its contents as it was shown to cinema audiences:

Messter-Woche No. 2, 16 October 1914:

1. A bridge at Friedland destroyed by the Russians.
2. Insterburg: the hotel in which Prince Nikoljewitsch and General Rennenkampf of the Russian High Command had set up their headquarters.
3. Russian prisoners of war.
4. A view of the French fortification at Longwy; the ironworks after they had been captured by German troops. Not a single building destroyed, because the inhabitants had welcomed the victorious German troops.
5. Longwy from the German offensive.
6. Shots of a number of houses in Longwy destroyed by fleeing French troops. Close-up of an occupant trapped in a shelled house waiting to be rescued by the Germans.

7. A churchyard whose walls had been used by the French as a fortification.
8. Prince Joachim, the youngest son of the Kaiser, eagerly waiting to return to his unit after recovering from wounds received at the battlefront.
9. Departure of a column of army trucks bound for the front.
10. Shots of 'brave' wounded soldiers 'on the road to recovery'.
11. Reformed units returning 'voluntarily' to the front.[95]

Despite the elaborate qualifications that Messter had devised, the General Staff remained suspicious of film and continued to refuse cameramen access to military operations, especially at the battle front. Censorship quickly became a source of friction. In December 1914, *Kinematograph* criticized the inhibited quality and scope of the war newsreels, and called for the relaxation of censorship and for more cameramen to be allowed to film in the theatres of war.[96] The film world hoped that by joining the OHL, Messter would be able to secure concessions from the military authorities. However, in the first few years of the war the military remained adamant, content simply to encourage newsreels that showed harmless marching scenes, military trains, scenes of mass gatherings, etc. In short, events that were commonly taking place all over Germany.

In order to overcome such restrictions, the newsreel companies resorted increasingly to fake battle scenes and the depiction of everyday life of the sappers, laughing and joking at their base camps. The lack of authentic shots from the battlefront was initially accepted by cinema audiences without complaint. This was due mainly to film's novelty value and also to the fact that these staged battles, although pedestrian by today's standards, proved relatively exciting and stirred the imagination of film audiences. *Messter-Woche* newsreels in particular, soon established a set format, with its distinctive trade mark and its organizational pattern. Produced fortnightly, they contained 10–15 subjects, each of 150–170 metres of film, lasting approximately 12 minutes. Early war newsreels concentrated almost exclusively on the Western and Eastern Fronts at the expense of the home front. Occasionally, the Kaiser and his family visiting wounded soldiers or inspecting a factory would appear in the newsreels, but generally it was felt unnecessary, at this stage of the war, to show the participation of civilians in the war effort. After all, these film reports were intended primarily for the home front, and civilians were eager to see what life was like at the fighting front. A typical example of how the newsreels reported the war during this period can be found in *Messter-Woche No. 44*, released in November 1915. It shows German troops on the Western Front, mainly in the Belgian sector:

Messter-Woche No. 44, November 1915:

1. German soldiers relieved from the front lines laugh, joke and wrestle together at a farm.
2. A line of soldiers in full kit, smiling and waving to the camera, marches out of barracks to the trenches.
3. A boiler–distiller provides fresh water.
4. A steamroller with locals assisting repairs a road, possibly near Brussels.
5. German officers fraternize with locals at the chateau in which they have been billeted. They are shown playing with local children, persuading them to pose for the camera.
6. The grave of a French soldier is tended and decorated by a German medical orderly. It reads: 'here lies an unknown French warrior'.
7. A piece of British 15-inch shell, which is marked as having fallen one metre from the local church, is exhibited.
8. German soldiers are seen using sewing machines for sandbag-making.
9. A mine crater exploded by the enemy is fortified by the Germans.
10. Prince Rupert of Bavaria talks to soldiers close to the front.
11. A guard in a front-line trench sees danger through a trench periscope and the troops man the fire-step (probably staged).
12. A training exercise for an attack, supported by hand-grenades.[97]

New technical devices like the cartoon and the use of animated maps to illustrate troop movements were also used to enhance the presentation of the events taking place and to convey the impression that the audience was being taken as close as possible to the battlefront. Towards the end of 1915 film cameramen were occasionally allowed to film a report from the front, although never of military manoeuvres or the actual fighting.[98] It was felt that 'calm was the first duty of the citizen' and that while those at home could be shown pictures of their fathers and sons in the reserve lines, they should not be subjected to the true horror of the fighting which could prove disturbing and consequently undermine morale. As the public became more discerning of what was genuine or not, newsreel companies increasingly resorted to advertising their reports as being 'filmed right on the front line'. Such newsreels were rare indeed, and most continued to play down the bloody nature of the war and concentrated instead on romanticizing the everyday life of soldiers well away from the fighting front. In 1916, when a specially compiled newsreel *Von der Front* was shown to the troops, the idealized picture it conveyed was greeted with roars of derisive laughter.[99] Clearly it did not square with the audience's own experiences.

While the German soldiers at the front found such newsreels amusing the British were more impressed. Throughout 1915, the film industry in Britain, together with the press, had been asking why nothing had been done officially by the government to counteract, by means of film, the effect of the German cinema campaign in neutral countries. *The Cinema*, for example, in an important article entitled 'The Kaiser's Cinema Campaign: Wake Up, England!', claimed that Germany had developed 'a practical monopoly of the cinema as a means of instructing public opinion'. In its editorial addressed to Sir Edward Grey, it argued that of all the means of propaganda, 'the camera was the most vivid, the most convincing, and the most difficult to detect in error', and yet Britain was lagging far behind Germany's 'exhaustive arrangements for the instruction by means of the cinema, of its own public, and those of neutral countries'. Writing in the *Daily Mail*, Dr Distin-Maddick spelt out what this meant:

> The supreme War Lord (the Kaiser) keeps his people plentifully supplied with the constant changing of films and photographs of the war, assisted by lecturers, so that every German subject and child is taught what war means, and how their own flesh and blood are fighting for their country.[100]

By the summer of 1915 British Ambassadors abroad were reiterating the point. Spring Rice, the Ambassador in America, drew attention to the widespread circulation of German films, arguing, '... their effect must be very great considering the popularity of the cinematograph shows and the mentality of their patron.'[101]

Messter in the meantime had been discussing ways of showing his newsreels in Austro-Hungary and the Balkans. In 1915 he had begun negotiations with *Sascha-Filmgesellschaft* of Vienna. As a result, on 4 April 1916, *Sascha-Messter-Woche* was established, distributing 'Sascha-Messter War-Reports' throughout Central Europe, the Balkans and South America.[102] In August 1916, a concerned Messter temporarily separated himself from Section IIIb by submitting a report to the General Staff on 'the importance of film as a political weapon', in which he argued that a centrally planned and co-ordinated official film campaign to promote Germany's war aims was now essential. He substantiated his claim by estimating the number of people who had seen the *Messter-Woche* since its inception. According to Messter, the numbers for Germany and Austria totalled over 15.5 million, Sweden 1.26 million, Turkey 1.75 million, Hungary 1.2 million, Romania 1.8 million, Spain 1 million, Argentina 2.3 million, and the United States a staggering 6 million![103] Although the centralization of the German film industry was still some way off, in October 1916, the military transferred film reporting to a new organization, the *Militärische Film und Photostelle* and began co-ordinating its work with that of the News Section of the Foreign Office

(*Nachrichtenabteilung des Auswärtigen Amtes*) which was responsible for countering foreign propaganda in neutral countries.[104]

German businessmen were also responding to the investment opportunities offered by the cinema. On 19 November 1916, Alfred Hugenberg, then chairman of Krupps and later press baron and owner of Ufa, set up the most important civilian company, the German Cinematographic Company (*Deutsche Lichtbild Gesellschaft*) or Deulig, with the intention of producing and distributing films publicizing German industry and culture.[105] Almost immediately, Deulig established a subsidiary company, Balkan-Orient GmbH, to provide films for the Balkans and the orient. The OHL initially supported Deulig by instructing local censors to pass their films without objections.[106] Gradually, however, the conflict between Deulig's commercial interests and the political demands made by the OHL led to irreconcilable differences and the realization on the part of the military that they would have to amalgamate all their film departments into one organization. Therefore on 30 January 1917 the OHL set up a purely military institution, the Photographic and Film Office (*Bild- und Filmamt*), or Bufa, under the control of the *Militärische Stelle des Auswärtigen Amtes* (MAA). According to its statute, Bufa's task clearly extended far beyond the making of purely military films. Conscious of the need to counter enemy propaganda abroad and to bolster flagging public morale at home. Bufa's task was to refashion the whole of the German film industry into a fighting propaganda machine that would make a vital contribution to the war effort.[107] Thus Bufa was responsible for collecting all visual materials, sending their own cameramen to the front to film battles, and producing short newsreels and documentaries about the participation being made by both the home front and the armed forces. By 1917, the notion of the home front playing its part in the war alongside the fighting front was (at last) widely accepted. Newsreels, for example, showed the work being undertaken by women in the armaments factories, and the importance of the 'Hindenburg-Programme' to the war effort. Bufa was to document this for future generations. The General Staff had also begun to appreciate the value of film entertainment as a means of relaxation for troops, and Bufa was responsible for setting up the *Fieldkinos* and supplying film programmes to over 900 such soldiers' cinemas that had been established in the reserve lines. (See Figure 7.)

In August 1917 at a meeting in Munich between the War Press Office and 'Enlightenment Directors' who were employed to monitor propaganda output and public feedback, the initial reaction to the first Bufa films was unfavourable. Shots of the front were considered artificial and too sentimental and it was recommended that such films should not be shown to

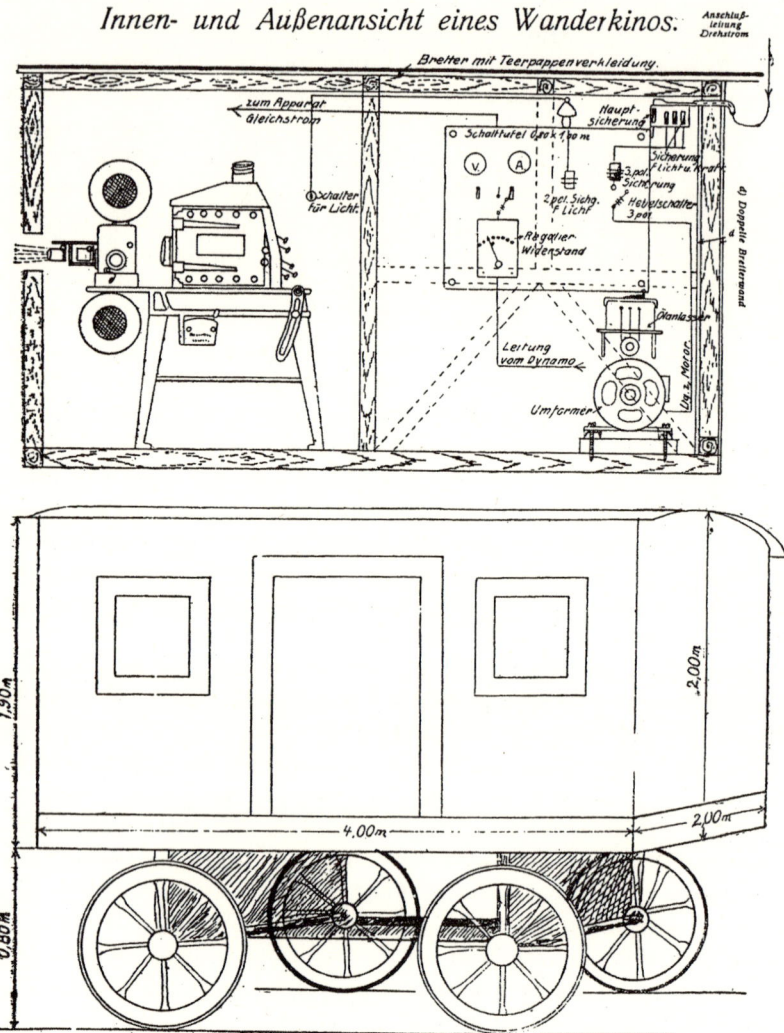

Figure 7 A sketch taken from a military journal showing the inside and outside of the mobile cinemas that were touring the front-line showing propaganda films to soldiers (*Mitteilungen betr. Kriegsaufklärung*, October 1917).

the troops.[108] A petition by Munich cinema owners in the Autumn of 1917 complained of the 'same old scenes of falling grenades, trenches, desolate terrain and prisoners etc'.[109] A few months after the creation of Bufa, the imperial government secretly established the *Universum-Film-Aktiengesellschaft* (Ufa), with the intention of producing and distributing patriotic feature films in the same way that Bufa supervised newsreels and war documentaries. Although Ufa was the realization of a centralized and carefully coordinated German film industry, it was, in fact, established too late to make a major contribution to the war effort.[110]

At the beginning of the war, the government was largely poorly equipped and ill-prepared to conduct a propaganda campaign through the medium of film. The early wartime controls of the film industry and the harsh censorship of films reflected the hostility of the ruling elites towards the cinema. Although during the course of the war the middle class began to take the cinema more seriously, it remained what it had been before, the opiate of the working masses.[111] Nevertheless, by the end of the war the cinema had emerged not simply as a means of mass entertainment, but as a widely accepted art form, anchored in German culture and with its respectability firmly enhanced. The combination of exciting, escapist, feature films together with the first crude newsreels depicting German military successes proved irresistible – for a number of reasons. During the exhilaration of the first months of the war the public's demand for glimpses of total war was insatiable. However, once the German advance had been halted, audiences looked increasingly to the cinema for shelter and warmth and to the films for entertainment. Between 1914 and 1917 the number of German cinemas increased by 28 per cent, from 2,446 to 3,130.[112] The First World War also placed the German film industry on a firm financial footing. In 1914, film production in German was dominated by France and Denmark, and only 15 per cent of all feature films exhibited in Germany were of German origin.[113] The war forced the German market to produce its own films and consequently German film companies increased five-fold from 25 in 1914 to 130 in 1918 and the number of distributors doubled.[114] Initially the OHL largely failed to recognize the public's increasing interest in film. Gradually, however, the need to sustain civilian morale and to disseminate German war aims effectively (both at home and in neutral countries), forced the military to turn to film propaganda as the most important means, together with the press, of mobilizing opinion. On 4 July 1917, in a celebrated letter to the War Ministry, Ludendorff underlined the importance of film as a propaganda medium for such purposes:

> The war has shown the overwhelming power of the image and the film as a medium for education and influence. . . . For the rest of the war the film

will continue to play an immensely significant role as a medium of political and military influence. It is therefore essential to ensure, if the war is to be brought to a successful conclusion, that film be used to its maximum effect wherever possible.[115]

The First World War brought about momentous changes in all aspects of German life, and none more so than in the breaking down of authoritarian attitudes towards the urban masses and a grudging recognition of their importance to the war effort. During the Second Reich, as in all the belligerent states, the governing elite was forced to recognize that victory demanded not only military and economic preparedness, but equally importantly, the mobilization and participation of the entire civilian population. In order to sustain the *Burgfrieden* and public support for Germany's war aims, the imperial government – more specifically, the military cliques – sought to organize and direct nationalist passions by means of a systematic manipulation of the mass media. Generally this took the form of a bludgeoning censorship supported in some cases by crude coercion. In the second half of the war, in response to the alarming deterioration of the population's morale, the government set up a national network of observation stations in an attempt to monitor public opinion (see Chapter 6). Government action and directives were to be reported but not critically debated. Moreover the extent and arbitrary nature of censorship only exacerbated tensions and led, in many cases, to a re-examination of loyalties to traditional institutions and values. The film industry, for example, responded to repressive censorship and the hostility of the legitimate theatre and survived the war to become *the* popular entertainment medium of the first half of the twentieth century. Similarly, the degree of censorship actually forced the press to re-examine their editorial and news content. Gradually, as circulation figures began to soar, the press came to realize the *political* importance of newspapers. The public's insatiable thirst for news spelt the death of the old amusement only papers. The impact of war on German society, therefore, produced positive as well as negative consequences. As the early crude form of censorship gave way to more constructive and organized propaganda, national unity could not be indefinitely maintained by propaganda alone. Nevertheless, the need for a well-oiled and coordinated propaganda machine proved all the more imperative as German interest groups divided into hostile camps on two pressing issues; war aims and internal reforms.

3
War Aims

'This war is a war of holding out (*Durchhalten*)'.
(*Kölnische Zeitung*, 3 October 1915)

The mobilization of the masses and the gradual transformation of the war from being effectively a war of limited aims into one of total victory required a consensus that would symbolize a unity of will and purpose. The *Burgfrieden* was intended to reflect widespread support for Germany's war aims. The war was portrayed initially as a short defensive campaign with promises of a rapid victory. Traditional interpretations of German policies have suggested that as these promises failed to materialize, the question of war aims reappeared and the German nation divided into two warring camps; on the one hand the supporters of national self-sufficiency who argued the case for self-defence, on the other the imperialists of the Pan-German stamp. It was Fritz Fischer who substituted the conventional pattern of two polarized camps, one annexationist, the other moderate, with the thesis of 'fundamental unanimity of will' according to which the entire nation was united in working for the aggrandizement of German power and regarded this as the true object of the war.[1] Fischer claimed that differences of attitude and variations of opinion were of minor significance in the face of an overwhelming obsession shared by all the influential groups and classes with world power.[2] Leaving aside the question of how far German war aims were foreshadowed in the policies of the pre-war years, to accuse sections of the population of having lent temporary support to the invasion of Belgium is not to find the entire nation guilty of possessing a monolithic will to world power.

HATRED OF THE ENEMY

Like all the belligerents, Germany in the months following the outbreak of war was gripped by a jingoistic wave of hysteria that sought release through an intense hatred of the enemy. Indeed one of the first tasks of the newly created propaganda agencies was to whip up enthusiasm for the war and to heighten patriotism by means of stereotyped images of the enemy: Russian despotism, French aggression and hatred of England and freedom of the seas were cited by the government as fully justifying their actions to obtain for the German empire equality of status with the other great world powers. The hatred of the enemy theme aimed also to utilize the widespread agreement on defence that embraced all groups. Therefore the concepts of freedom of the seas and British expansionism provided a useful ploy to ensure agreement (or at least to minimize open dissent) and to obscure Germany's war aims. *'Gott strafe England!'* and *'Wir haben nur einen Hass – England'*, sang the Germans and newspapers were fond of quoting from Ernst Lissauer's 'Hymn of Hate':

> Hate by water and hate by land;
> Hate by heart and hate of the hand;
> We love as one and hate as one;
> We have but one enemy alone – England.

According to James Gerard, the American Ambassador to Germany, the phrase '*Gott strafe England!*' seemed to be all over Germany:

> It was printed on stamps to be affixed to the back of letters like our Red Cross stamps. I even found my German servant in the Embassy affixing these stamps to the back of all letters, official and otherwise, that were sent out.... Paper money was stamped with the words '*Gott strafe England!*' 'und America' being often added as the war progressed.'[3]

The *Kölnische Zeitung*, the main organ of the government (after the *Norddeutsche Allgemeine Zeitung*), and the mouthpiece of the German Foreign Office, referred to England's actions as 'the greatest conspiracy in the history of the world.' A particularly vitriolic field postcard sold in aid of the Red Cross showed a cartoon of Sir Edward Grey (the British Foreign Secretary), as 'Warmonger and Mass-Murderer' standing next to the Devil who admits that even he could learn from this 'young man!'. (See Figure 8.) A curious development of the hate of all things foreign was the hunt led by the Police Chief of Berlin, von Jagow (a cousin of the Foreign Minister), for foreign words. Once it had been decided that all words of foreign origin must be expunged from the German language, the Hotel Bristol, for example, on the Unter den Linden, disappeared and the Hotel Westminster, on the same street, became Lindenhof. Commenting on this Gerard observed:

> There is a large hotel called 'The Cumberland', with a pastry department over which there was a sign, the French word, 'Confiserie'. The management was compelled to take this down, but the hotel was allowed to retain

Figure 8 A postcard of Lord Grey ('War Monger and Mass Murderer').

the name of 'Cumberland', because the father-in-law of the Kaiser's only daughter is the Duke of Cumberland. The word 'chauffeur' was eliminated, and there were many discussions as to what should be substituted. Many declared for *'kraftwagenführer'*, or 'power wagon driver'. But finally the word was Germanised as *'schauffoer'*.[4]

Not surprisingly in the light of such intense nationalism, Germany proved particularly prone to spy scares. In August 1914, a Deputy of the Reichstag noted somewhat sardonically:

> The Gods alone know how many 'spies' have been beaten and imprisoned today! The mobilised reserve officers do not get by unmolested. They have in many instances become fat and round during peace-time and perhaps their bad-looking uniforms account for the mistakes in identity. It is commonly believed that spies go round dressed like Prussian officers.[5]

The so-called mobilization psychoses led to a flood of rumours that spies had permeated every aspect of German society. The susceptibility of the population to spy mania could often lead to spontaneous acts of violence. The civil authorities were concerned that law and order should be maintained and that the police should withstand such pressure. In Stuttgart, for example, policemen were issued with the following instructions:

> Policemen! The inhabitants are starting to go crazy! The streets are filled with old people of both sexes engaged in undignified activities. Everyone suspects his neighbour of being a Russian or French spy and assumes it is their duty to beat him and the policeman, who might try to help that person, to a pulp. . . . One gets the impression of being in an insane asylum. Policemen, stay cold-blooded, remain men instead of women, don't have the wind put into you and keep your eyes open, like you are obliged to.[6]

To inspire additional hatred against the enemy, the German government also employed atrocity propaganda – although arguably not on the scale used by the Allies. According to one German writer though, the atrocity propaganda was quite systematically organized:

> The Russians were accused above all of cutting the arms and legs off the men, the breasts off the women. The French and Belgians were accused of gouging out eyes. There were variations and combinations. But the *leitmotiv* remained always the same: in the east, hacking and cutting, in the west, gouging'.[7]

The German press (with the honourable exception of *Vorwärts*) certainly emphasised atrocities but it was largely tempered by a public recognition that the papers were paying the Allies back in their own currency. Nevertheless, an English woman in Bavaria at the outbreak of war, noted the similarities between the German press and French and British newspapers:

> The propaganda in the papers bore a strong resemblance to the propaganda I afterwards read in French and English newspapers. Atrocities, atrocities and always more atrocities – tales of Belgian women haunting the scenes of fighting, and gouging out wounded Germans' eyes; harmless German soldiers resting and being killed by hidden peasants; Belgian children trained to torture wounded soldiers – all the old, old stories hashed up once more, but so dinned into the public's ears that the Allies loomed in most people's eyes as horrible, blood-soaked, sadistic savages. In fact very much the same sort of savages that were being created in English and French minds, and labelled Boches and Huns.[8]

Figure 9 'Who is Militaristic?' A German poster that compares favourably Germany's past military record with those of Britain and France.

Almost all forms of communication were immediately put to use circulating atrocity stories. Cartoons in magazines like *Simplicissimus* and *Kladderadatsch* illustrated accusations of enemy atrocity and made much of Russian bestiality and the use of coloured troops by the Entente.[9] The Germans invariably pursued two lines: while denying charges against themselves, they brought forward cases in which their enemies were alleged to have violated the laws of War. German journalists in particular used historical as well as biological arguments to 'prove' enemy atrocities. In September 1914 an officially inspired article in the *Norddeutsche Allgemeine Zeitung*, described alleged Belgian and French atrocities as a part of a deliberate programme of provocation 'typical of the "Hun-nature" of the French'. Referring to the 'gruesome, bestial evidence' of French atrocities committed during the war of 1871, the writer concluded that such recurrences were only to be expected from these nations.[10] The case against an inferior and barbarous Russia was even easier to make. As with the French, the Germans brought similar charges to those levelled against themselves. In May 1915, for example, the *Münchner Neueste Nachrichten* quoted an official source which claimed that by the cemetery of Neuville the French placed prisoners in front of their line to cover their operations:

This is not the first time that our military authorities have found themselves obliged to stigmatise the barbaric methods of warfare used by our adversaries. Already in November the Siberian Army Corps, during the great Russian offensive in Poland, drove the inhabitants of the country before itself as a screen, and only a few weeks ago the officers of the Russian staff in Galicia gave an actual official notification to the Austro-Hungarian forces in front of them, that they were about to place before themselves in the firing line 1,500 Jews, with their wives and children...[11]

The other line taken by German authorities was to treat all the charges of atrocities brought against them as malicious inventions. Catholic priests in particular vehemently refuted atrocity claims. In Cologne, for example, during the first year of the war, Roman Catholic priests formed a *'Pax Gesellschaft'* in which a Reverend Bernhard Duhr collected official denials and published them in *Der Lügengeist im Volkerkrieg*. Earlier, in September, sixty German Catholics had signed a memorandum to the Cardinals in Rome, declaring: 'The German army wages war, not against the people of another country, but only against the armed forces themselves.'[12] (See Figure 9.) Similarly, ninety-three scholars, writers, scientists and artists (including Karl Lamprecht, Max Planck, Gerhart Hauptmann and Max Reinhardt) signed a manifesto *'Es ist nicht war!'* ('It is not true!') that categorically denied German atrocities and counter-charged the Belgian population of carrying out atrocities in the West and the Russians for crimes committed against Germans in the East.[13] However, the Bryce Report of May 1915 which claimed that the Germans had engaged in systematic practices of atrocity, proved a severe blow to Germany's international reputation and called for refutation and a bitter counter-attack recounting the sins of British imperialism.[14] British mistreatment of the Irish, Indians, Egyptians and Boers in particular was given special attention in the German press and with a series of pamphlets aimed at exposing England's atrocity-strewn past.[15] There was also the situation in the African colonies where the Allies were invading German soil and allegedly mistreating German civilians. In January 1915, the *Norddeutsche Allgemeine Zeitung* reported that German civilians were being forced to work in Africa without sun helmets and that several had already died from such brutal treatment. Most humiliating of all was that German workers were being supervised by black natives.[16] The *Frankfurter Zeitung* described the occupation of German New Guinea by Australian troops. An English missionary who had worked for many years in the capital, Rabaul, betrayed the way to the wireless telegraph station. When the English missionary was remonstrated with, for having given such a poor return for German hospitality, he revenged himself by accusing the Germans to the English Commandant in Rabaul.

The Commandant then took six German prisoners and had them whipped in public. A German who attempted to escape this indignity by cutting his veins, was prevented, and, after being bandaged, was punished with thirty lashes. The paper made the point that the sentence was carried out by Australian soldiers whose ancestors had been sent to Sydney as convicts: 'This Australian brutality is a pendant to the rest of the Colonial warfare of the English.'[17]

A few months after the publication of the Bryce Report another great outcry was raised in the German press over the alleged murder of the crew of a German U-boat by HMS 'Baralong' under the cover of an American flag. The brutal massacre of a dozen members of a German submarine crew by English sailors in flagrant disregard for the rules of war, lent itself nicely to exploitation for atrocity propaganda, especially coming so soon after the worldwide condemnation of Germany following the sinking of the 'Lusitania' in May.[18] The 'Baralong' incident took place on 19 August 1915, but was not reported until October when the German embassy released evidence to the American press. The outcry in the German press continued unabated for the rest of the war, and 'Baralong' came to symbolize for many Germans associations of extreme British brutality. 'The English soul is barbarous', claimed Baron von Reventlow, in what was a typical response to the 'Baralong atrocity', 'it is no exception, but the normal outcome of the Anglo-Saxon soul, and is on a par with other barbarous acts committed by Englishmen'.[19]

The German authorities were only too willing to publicize 'facts' of enemy atrocities and undoubtedly they convinced the German people. However, in the battle for neutral opinion the Germans lost some of their offensive force by having constantly to defend themselves against charges of atrocity. This propaganda of hate had certain definitive objectives; it was used to stiffen the fighting spirit of soldiers and civilians, help raise war loans, encourage enlistment, justify breaches of international law, and in the case of Germany to obscure official war aims. But as the promised swift military victory failed to materialize even hate or atrocity propaganda could not circumvent the increasing demand to clarify imperial war aims.

ANNEXATIONISTS VS DEFENCE

The mobilization of German resources for total war revealed again, just as pre-war German politics had done, the conflicting interest groups which had dominated German society. The military authorities, had, by and large, overestimated the enthusiasm of the working class for the war. However, this was not immediately apparent as these tensions were partially obscured by the *Burgfrieden*. The chief objectives of the OHL regarding the civilian population were to maintain the *Burgfrieden* and to subvert any discussion of Germany's war aims, which in practice meant suppressing the radical left. But as the war dragged on, these aims increasingly began to conflict with each other. The new found unity of August 1914 had been established very much on the basis of a limited agreement over the defensive nature of Germany's war aims. Clearly in total war where it is necessary to mobilize all national resources including public opinion, it is imperative for governments to maintain the support of their people. It is perhaps understandable, then, that having secured the *Burgfrieden*, the imperial government should wish to restrict discussion of war aims less such a debate should lead to a damaging internal conflict.

Recognizing the fragility of the *Burgfrieden*, the government and the military immediately took measures to ensure its continuance. On 28 August 1914, the Secretary of State, von Jagow, agreed with the General Staff that newspapers were not to discuss the question of Germany's war aims and in particular, the future fate of Belgium.[20] Any doubts about the public's resolve to wage war were not permitted as this might undermine the impression of unity and energy that German propaganda was trying to convey at this time. Instead, political parties, interest groups, and the mass media were to stress that a German victory would result in freedom for oppressed peoples from Russian despotism and from English world hegemony.[21] However, the demand for such a discussion would simply not go away. The invasion of Belgium and France had revealed that Germany's military objectives were not consistent with her professed aims of defence. Therefore it became increasingly difficult for propaganda to sustain the link between the domestic *Burgfrieden* and the notion of a defensive war.

In many ways the propaganda of World War I was pre-eminently a propaganda of war aims. It has been said that war aims determine the nature of the relationship between the policy makers and the propagandist. Policy makers are responsible for ensuring that propaganda reflects and supports the nation's war aims, while it is the task of the propagandist to gain maximum publicity for such aims.[22] In imperial Germany the tasks of the propagandist were further complicated not simply because of the military's exaggerated belief in the degree of widespread support for the war, but also because, at an official level, two conflicting views about the nature of the war began to emerge that had profound implications for the future of German society. By 1915 as both the forces of the Right and the Left became increasingly frustrated at the failure of the promised swift victory, the question of war aims polarized society into two camps: those supporting a war of self defence and those demanding total victory with annexations. The military and certain political groupings wished to remove strategy and war objectives from political or civilian interference. However, as the war dragged on, the support for a compromise peace increased and with it a recognition that responsibility for securing such a peace could not be left to either the military or indeed to a government which was not responsible to parliament. These were not simply marginal differences of opinion about how the war should be conducted, as Fritz Fischer has consistently maintained. Such opinions were fundamental to different visions of German society, which in turn resurrected the subject of political reforms that had been temporarily obscured by the *Burgfrieden*. The war aims debate, therefore, was structured very much along class lines and increasingly was used to further political aims.' The annexationists and traditional power-elites saw total victory as a means of staving off radical political changes and maintaining the *status quo*; whereas those who supported a defensive war eventually came to see a negotiated peace as a necessary condition for a new political reorientation.

The first year of war had resulted in the fateful battle of the Marne which stemmed the German advance on Paris. German victories against Russia continued in the east, notably Hindenburg's victory at Tannenberg in August 1914. During October, Antwerp fell; but in the naval engagement off the Falklands Islands, the Germans suffered defeat in December 1914. On 1 March 1915, the British declared a virtual blockade of the German coast; and in the spring of 1915 the Allies' Dardanelles campaign proved a failure. One by one, Turkey, Italy, Bulgaria and Greece joined the conflict.

In Germany the euphoria of the early months of the war had long given way to widespread cynicism and feelings of foreboding. In 1915 when the first casualty figures began to be known, Rosa Luxemburg noted:

> Gone is the first mad delirium. Gone are the patriotic demonstrations.... the show is over. The curtain has fallen on trains filled with reservists, as they pull out amidst the exuberant cries of enthusiastic young girls. No longer do we see laughing faces, smiling cheerfully from the train windows to a war-mad population... quietly... the public with drawn faces go about its daily task.[23]

In the second year of the war, Germans were concerned with bread shortages, a new orientation at home, and Reichstag Deputies continued to denounce the excesses of military censorship. However, throughout 1915 Germany was consumed with the question of war aims. As propaganda and prophecy tried to obscure or explain war aims it was clear that the ordinary citizen felt unsure about the purpose of the war – other than one of defence. The two extremes, the annexationists and the left-wing socialists knew what they wanted, even if the government remained either silent or ambiguous on the question. During 1915 both groups intensified their activities and began to increase in size. Thus, by the end of the year the competing claims of the two groups resulted in a well organized annexationist movement confronted by an increasingly significant opposition movement.[24]

Meanwhile, the Chancellor, Bethmann Hollweg, attempted with his 'policy of the diagonal' to steer a middle course and to achieve a liberal compromise which intimated that there might be annexations *and* internal reforms. Bethmann's equivocal attitude to war aims, his desire to be 'all things to all men' was doomed to failure and led eventually not only to his own fall but to the dismissal of Falkenhayn, the Chief of the General Staff, to be replaced by Hindenburg and Ludendorff, the popular heroes of Tannenberg. Much has been written about Bethmann Hollweg's role during the war, moving as he did from his annexationist September programme of 1914 to one of offering olive branches by means of certain well-publicized 'feelers' for peace.[25] In his pursuit of a conciliatory course at home and abroad, Bethmann believed he could find a diagonal line, as he often put it, between extreme political factions to achieve national unity and restore the *Burgfrieden*.[26] In practice this meant a defensive war, subduing the Pan-German chauvinists who he believed were preventing a separate peace with Russia, and courting the socialists and liberals by playing down the issue of war aims. Such a strategy not only failed, but in the process, deeply antagonized political groupings on both sides. The bitter squabbles of opposing groups like Dietrich Schäfer's Independent Committee for a German Peace (*Unabhängige Ausschuss für einen deutschen Frieden*) and the more moderate German National Committee (*Deutsche Nationalausschuss*), which broke into the open in 1916, were symptomatic of the deep-seated nature of these divisions.[27]

Ironically it was the Chancellor himself who was largely responsible for heightening the war aims debate. After the outbreak of war his initial response was to employ censorship in the name of the *Burgfrieden* to impose a strict silence on the question of Germany's war aims.[28] However, on 2 December 1914, he informed the Reichstag that the real cause of the war was Britain's insistence on a balance of power policy that perpetuated British domination. Russian Pan-Slavism and the French 'revanche' policy were contributory factors.[29] Bethmann's next official statement on Germany's war aims came eight months later on 19 August 1915 when he addressed the Reichstag on the Polish question. In the intervening period, a combination of factors including a growing resentment over the excesses of military censorship coupled with Bethmann's equivocal attitude prompted newspapers and opposing political groups to press for a more open discussion about war aims. As Gerald Feldman noted: 'Both sides employed Bethmann's vague statements to prove that the government supported their policies, and yet everyone complained, not without justification, that nobody knew what Germany was fighting for.'[30]

The ambiguous nature surrounding the question of war aims affected the Social Democrats more than most. SPD politicians in particular were placed in a difficult position. On the one hand they had supported the *Burgfrieden* and had no wish to appear unpatriotic (especially after the spate of early military victories) and yet they were concerned about the nature of the war and the attempts by the censors to muzzle them. The dilemma facing the Party was well summed up by SPD Deputy Wolfgang Heine in a much publicized speech to an enthusiastic audience in Stuttgart in February 1915:

> Today I would like to speak about Germany's future and Social Democracy. I agree with the Chancellor when he said that the aim of the war is to be a free people. A prerequisite to our becoming a free people is peace and Social Democracy is the party which represents peace among nations.... We are not 'rah-rah' patriots. It is not in the German character to be chauvinistic. We are simply defending our Fatherland, our economic life, our existence, our German civilisation, the independence and integrity of the Reich.
>
> In this we must not weaken our resolve. As the Chancellor has said, we must continue to hold out. We do not intend to crush the world but rather to secure a lasting and honourable peace.... However, it is not appropriate to demand peace at this time.... If we want peace, then we must, for the time being, trust German arms, the German generals, the German people, and the men who are performing miracles at the front. Today the army is the nation and the nation the army. (*Applause*)... Let us put our trust in the Emperor's love for peace and his determination to achieve it. Therefore today's proclamation printed in all the newspapers and clearly bearing the imprint of the Chancellor, warning the public not to discuss the conditions of peace at the present time is important. We support this proclamation. From our point of view this is not a war of conquest. In attempting to secure an honourable peace, Social Democracy supports the Kaiser and the Chancellor...[31]

The SPD's real fear was that a defensive war (which they supported) was in danger of turning into one of uninhibited conquest and that none of the territorial gains would eventually be surrendered by Germany. These fears were fuelled by increasingly vociferous annexationist propaganda which began to appear in the press and in countless pamphlets apparently unencumbered by the censorship laws and the Chancellor's recent proclamation not to discuss peace terms. *Vorwärts* felt compelled to complain about such unequal treatment and the failure of the authorities to prevent the flood of annexationist literature.³² Indeed the socialist party organ even went so far as to suggest that an 'intoxicating imperialism was sweeping through all bourgeois classes'.³³ Such protests went unheeded for in April, Dr Paasche the Vice-President of the Reichstag, made an emotional speech entitled 'The War of Freedom Against England' in which he claimed to be speaking for the whole nation: 'We must not speak of the conditions of peace but should stress that in the heart of every German there lives the wish that enemy territory conquered with the effusion of so much German blood shall not be given up...'. Rather ominously for those who were concerned to reach a negotiated peace, he concluded his speech by demanding that: *'The pen must never again ruin what the sword has gained'* (my italics).³⁴

Talk of peace brought a swift and concerted response from the annexationist camp. The military victories of 1914–15 called forth vast plans of annexation and domination from a variety of right-wing groups. The Junker and commercial classes supported by the German Colonial Society and the powerful Navy and Army Leagues were clearly bent upon annexations. In May they were supported by the Six Economic Associations who in a massive petition to the Chancellor demanded a colonial empire that would incorporate Belgium, the French channel coast and inland coal territories, and extensive agricultural territory in Russia.³⁵ Within a few weeks the university professors produced a manifesto under the guise of preserving German civilization and culture which expressed annexationist views with considerable clarity.³⁶ It was in response to the annexationists' plans and also the sinking of the Lusitania that socialists and some Progressives demanded a debate on war aims, and, as a result, such a debate took place in the Reichstag on 28 and 29 May 1915. During the Friday debate, Bethmann Hollweg attacked Italy for denouncing the Triple Alliance following the secret Treaty of London in April and again reaffirmed Germany's defensive intentions. The debate of the 29th, however, revealed the sharp divisions that existed between sections of the SPD (concerned at the territorial expansion of the German empire) and the Conservative Party already determined on annexations 'as a measure of defense'.³⁷

Friedrich Ebert, the Social Democrat's party secretary, opened the debate by promising 'our whole-hearted support in prosecuting the war, in view of the new menace from Italy'. But he went on to urge that 'we desire a peace not embittered by any fresh conquests or annexations'. Graf von Westarp for the Conservatives objected to Ebert's remarks and declared that Germany 'must not shrink after its victory from advancing its frontiers'. Eugen Schiffer, speaking on behalf of the National-Liberals group, expressed himself in agreement with the Conservatives at which point Karl Liebknecht, who in

March had voted against the Second War Loan, caused a storm of protests by shouting 'Capitalist interests!' After calling Liebknecht to order, the debate was concluded by Philipp Scheidemann (SPD) who protested against the motion of von Westarp that there should be no discussion of international questions in the House. Scheidemann argued that the Chancellor was wrong to endorse the Conservative view and reminded him of the Kaiser's speech from the throne at the outbreak of hostilities: 'We are waging no war of conquest.' Scheidemann, a former Vice-President of the Reichstag, added:

> We (Social Democrats) stand for this principle. As soon as our security is achieved or our adversaries disposed to negotiate, peace can, as a matter of course, be concluded. Our people's best wall of defence is, apart from its resolute spirit, the possibility of our living permanently in the future at peace with our neighbours.[38]

The Social Democrats within the Reichstag were not entirely alone in their opposition to further annexations (more will be said of this in Chapters 5 and 6). As early as October 1914, the New Fatherland Alliance (*Bund Neues Vaterland*) had opposed annexations. Also many Progressives were undecided. In August a Reichstag 'Fraktion' of the Progressive People's Party issued an ambiguous declaration that the time had not yet come for the formulation of a definite programme for the ending of the war, but that the Party is 'opposed to a fundamental rejection of territorial conquests as it is to boundless annexation plans....'.[39] By and large, though, the Progressives accepted the need for annexations in order to maintain Germany's security and a future peace. They simply failed to agree on the type and extent of annexations that were necessary to achieve these goals. However, the weeks that followed the lively debate in the Reichstag on 29 May revealed the deep divisions of opinion within the Social Democratic Party, culminating in the suspension of *Vorwärts* and witnessing the manifest splits within the socialist camp.

The first serious indication of such a split occurred on 9 June when a number of prominent Social Democrats appealed to the committee of the party warning them against continuing the 'Policy of 4 August', i.e. the policy which voted the war budget and supported the 'political truce'. Within a few days the radical *Vossische Zeitung* collected over 200 signatures from the party's rank-and-file demanding socialist action against annexations.[40] This led to the publication in the *Leipziger Volkszeitung* of the famous manifesto 'The Demand of the Hour' (*Das Gebot der Stunde*).[41] Signed by Bernstein, Kautsky and the Chairman of the Party, Hugo Haase, the manifesto disassociated the authors publicly from the policy of the majority and called for an immediate peace. The manifesto pointed to the enormous sacrifice that had been made by all the nations involved and the growing evidence for a lasting peace:

> while the ruling circles hesitate to fulfil this longing for peace, thousands and thousands look to Social Democracy which was once considered to be the party of peace and expect from it the word of delivery.... As the plans of conquest have become public knowledge, Social Democracy has gained full freedom to make clear in the most expert fashion it opposition point of view. The present situation makes this freedom a duty...[42]

A few days later the government suspended the *Leipziger Volkszeitung* for publishing the manifesto, and on 22 June a vote of protest from ten other members of the Social Democratic Party Committee against the action of Haase, Bernstein and Kautsky was published in *Vorwärts*: 'there was not the least occasion,' they asserted, 'for such a *pronunciamento*.'[43]

The circular of 9 June and the publication of *Das Gebot der Stunde* caused enormous excitement in the German press, with the Social Democratic press itself divided. In view of the agitation coming from the pacifist wing, the official committee of the party felt compelled to show that they were doing everything possible in the pursuit of peace. To this end, they produced their own manifesto entitled 'Social Democracy and Peace' (*Sozialdemokratie und Frieden*) in *Vorwärts* of 26 June. While not going as far as the Haase group, it protested strongly against annexations: 'The people want no annexations, the people want peace'.[44] For breaching the government order forbidding the discussion of war aims, *Vorwärts* was suspended for five days.[45]

With the SPD's official organ suspended, the nationalist press now eagerly offered a platform to vocal elements within the Social Democratic Party who opposed these pacifist tendencies and who were prepared to support the moderate side of socialism. A Baden Social Democrat, Wilhelm Kolb produced a pamphlet entitled 'Socialism at the Crossroads' (*Die Sozialdemokratie am Scheidewege*), which was widely reported and argued that the Social Democracy of the future should aim at reforming, not abolishing, the institutions of the capitalist state.[46] Another Social Democrat, Dr Albert Südekum raised the old National-Liberal argument that Social Democracy strengthens the reaction, by pointing out the dangers of the policy represented by the Haase 'Fraktion', 'Social-Democrats,' he argued, 'constitute the main body upon which the Chancellor has to rely for defeating the annexationist politicians. If the party is driven into opposition to the government, the government will be forced to surrender to the annexationists.' Another theme that the nationalist press seized upon at this time was the idea that life in the trenches would convert the Social Democratic rank-and-file to militant nationalism. The *Kölnische Zeitung* confidently anticipated such a conversion:

> The insight of those few, who have looked deeply into the development of the modern world powers and recognised the significance of *Weltpolitik* for the working classes, will be reinforced by the personal experiences of those innumerable Social-Democrat comrades, who have gone through the hard school of war, and have learnt there, how far humanity still is from realising the old ideal of Cobden, 'Peace and goodwill among nations,' and how valuable our military organisation is... From no German mouth will the cry 'Down with your arms!' come...[47]

These were not simply minor differences of opinion. They were the manifestations of new groupings taking place within the Social Democratic Party and as such they were of considerable interest to the press in general. The *Berliner Tageblatt*, the most popular newspaper in Germany, attempted to analyse these 'new groupings' (*Ungruppierung*) by distinguishing four groups in the party:

1. The Liebknecht Group, which continues to reproach the leaders of the Party with betraying their past and to declare that the war is a war of conquest.
2. The second group (Bernstein, Haase, Kautsky) differs from the first, not so much in the essence of its views, but in the way in which they are postulated. Haase, as the official Chairman of the Party is obliged to put forward his individual views in such a way as not to imperil Party unity.
3. The main group of the party, the 'block of August 4', does not deny the imperialist nature of the war. It is concerned to make a speedy peace possible, but it regards as a pre-requisite that a similar attitude should be taken up in enemy countries as well. And it lays stress on the imperialist tendencies in England and Russia.
4. Finally there is the group called the 'annexationists'. They do not associate themselves with the Conservative and National-Liberal annexationists, but they do believe that the present frontiers of Germany cannot be regarded as determined for all time...[48]

In the light of such widespread and damaging press coverage of internal splits, the Committee of the SPD held a meeting in Berlin on 30 June and 1 July to end speculation about party dissensions. All 41 local committees were represented. It passed a resolution approving the action of the directorate of the party, which included the following passage: 'The publication of the appeal "The Requirement of the Hour", by Comrade Haase – especially since it was done without first ascertaining the views of the Directorate and of the Parliamentary Group – is not in accord with the duties of the Chairman of the Party.'[49] This, of course, represented a vote of no confidence in Haase's leadership, a feeling that was echoed by individual SPD Deputies.[50] It was left to *Vorwärts*, when it reappeared on 2 July, to plead for tolerance and some latitude of opinion within the party.[51] As a result, the paper, which was sympathetic to the Haase group, became embroiled in a long running public controversy with the party directorate which it published in subsequent editions throughout the month of July.

On the 31 July, the Kaiser made his second proclamation to the people in which he repeated that conquest was not Germany's aim, but stressed that peace must guarantee military, political and economic security and fulfil the conditions for 'the unhindered development of our activities at home and on the free seas'.[52] On 19 August the fifth war session of the Reichstag was opened with a speech by the Chancellor in which he took up the Kaiser's ambiguous reference to 'guarantees' for the future development of Germany. The aim in the east was couched in broad terms of 'freedom for great and small nations' with special emphasis on the Polish problem.[53] His vague references to Poland led some newspapers to make enquiries about the Polish question. However, they were firmly reminded that any public discussion of Germany's war aims was forbidden and that included the fate of Poland. According to the authorities such a discussion would only arouse party antagonisms.[54] Nevertheless, the ambiguity was recognized by all groups. The Socialists and Progressives stressed the dual need to free Poland from the Russian yoke and to protect the Balkan states from Russian aggression, while the Conservatives and National Liberals hoped that Germany's national interests would be given as much importance as the demands of the Poles.[55] Eventually, on 20 August, the House voted for the Third War Credit of 10 billion marks, but not without further strains to the *Bürgfrieden*. Prior to the vote at a party committee meeting 36 socialist Deputies had indicated that they would oppose the government, but at the end of the debate Liebknecht alone voted against; three changed their minds and the remaining 32 withdrew from the Chamber at the time of the vote (including Haase, Bernstein and Ledebour). Nevertheless, because the SPD were unable to get from the government a clear statement of their war aims, they decided to publish in *Vorwärts* 'Five Socialist Principles' which as a Party they considered essential to a satisfactory peace:

1. No cession of German territory
2. Security for the commercial development of Germany
3. No weakening or the destruction of Austria–Hungary or Turkey

4. No annexations of non-German territory by Germany
5. A perpetual international Court of Arbitration[56]

Vorwärts' protest that they were not permitted to publish the full contents of the party's peace programme was taken up in the Reichstag a few days later by socialist Deputy Edmund Fischer who contrasted the unequal treatment meted out to different political parties:

> We, Social-Democrats, in contrast to the bourgeois parties, are not allowed to speak about war aims even in gatherings of our members behind closed doors. Public meetings about food questions are not tolerated at all. Addresses require the authorisation of the police, and manuscripts must be handed in at least seven days beforehand. It depends upon the arbitrary choice of the police whether any public declaration is permitted or not. It is we, the Social-Democratic bodies, who have to put up with continued measures of this kind... As to the war aims, the Bassermanns, the Stresemanns, and the Furhmanns etc., may print anything they like; *Vorwärts* on the other hand is forbidden to do so, for the reason, of course, that it opposes the demand for annexations![57]

The censored publication of the socialist's peace programme together with Fischer's powerful speech in the Reichstag moved the *Frankfurter Zeitung* to call for greater freedom by suggesting that the conditions which justified the State of Siege at the beginning of the war no longer existed.[58] Talk of peace programmes and greater freedom of expression brought an immediate response from the annexationist camp. On the day that news of the fall of Brest-Litovsk was announced, the *Kölnische Zeitung's* leading article was a review by the historian Hermann Oncken of a book on 'The Working Class in New Germany' (*Die Arbeitschaft im neuen Deutschland*) which, according to Oncken, proved that annexations would fulfil the workers' ambitions and act as a great creator of wealth. Ending his article by openly glorifying war, the historian wrote: 'The great destroyer, War, will this time also become the Creator of new life, such as it has always shown itself to be in the great crises of history.'

> So, of yore as since, by the sword was consummated
>   That glorious thing which history beheld,
> And every great thing which will ever be brought to pass,
>   To the sword in the end it owes its success.[59]

On 28 September, the German Conservative Party announced its war aims. Referring to Brest-Litovsk as an 'unparalleled achievement', it claimed that a lasting peace could only be assured by destroying Russian domination in the east, and the defeat of England, 'who has brought about the war and who will never cease to threaten our position in the world and our future development'.[60] The nervousness of the annexationists in the face of radical and socialist opposition was betrayed by the German Imperialist Party, who in October demanded that the Reichstag ('mangy sheep in the flock') be dissolved and replaced by an imperial council for the discussion of the terms of peace.[61] Throughout October and November the imperialist views of the Six Economic Associations continued to be given widespread coverage in the newspapers. Clearly alarmed as early as September by the escalating debate about war aims, the General Staff attempted to set out even firmer guidelines restricting publications and debate.[62] Under these new 'clarifications', *Vorwärts* reported on 3 October that socialists belonging to the pacifist wing of the party in Essen and Dusseldorf within the Seventh Army Corps and who signed the appeal to the Directorate of 9 June had been warned by the police that they would be arrested for the duration of the war should they attempt to make speeches or circulate any printed matter dealing with war aims.[63] A few weeks later the press were widely condemning the Minister of the Interior, von Loebbel, for secretly attempting to control the direction of the press with new guidelines (the so-called 'Loebbel Circular'). Nevertheless, the right-wing press continued to deny that there was a widespread desire for peace in Germany. Typical was the editorial from the *Vossische Zeitung* of 14 November which argued that talk of peace was 'ridiculous':

> is there anyone who believes that, *Just at the moment* when we are about to open new roads of attack, we are really in a hurry to conclude a peace, whereby England would remain our unvanquished enemy? There is no German who has any other thought but this: he who after this war is going to remain our enemy must be rendered harmless.'[64]

Before the sixth session of the Reichstag was due to begin on 30 November, *Vorwärts* saw an opportunity to counter these annexationist claims by asking the German government in the light of a recent statement made in Britain what they would consider to be acceptable terms for peace. In a leading article entitled 'Free Speech!', *Vorwärts* demanded that if the government was unwilling to respond to British overtures then it must concede the right of doing so to public opinion:

> If it feels that it cannot loosen its control over public meeting and discussions in the press, then a start must be made in the Reichstag... with firm statements about Alsace-Lorraine, Belgium, Northern France etc.,.... It is not enough to go on repeating 'holding-out' (*Durchhalten*).[65]

As a result the Social Democrats agreed to present an interpellation in the Reichstag concerning Germany's war aims. On 9 December the 'angel of peace' in the form of Philipp Scheidemann asked the Chancellor what the prospects for peace were. Bethmann Hollweg replied: 'If our enemies come with peace offers which are compatible with the dignity and security of Germany, then we are ready to discuss terms. We do not wish to be responsible for continuing the miseries of war.'[66] The Chancellor appeared to be indicating government sympathy with the minority opposition parties. It was not the Chancellor alone, however, who was implicated but also the High Command and influential Pan-German groups who believed that Germany's greatness depended on military conquest and whose attitude on war aims was annexationist. Such views would prevail and ultimately force Bethmann Hollweg to resign in July 1917. In the meantime the German opposition recognized that in view of the struggle between the Chancellor and the High Command they could expect precious little from the government.

On 20 December 1915 the Reichstag eventually voted for the war credits but not without 20 socialist Deputies breaking party discipline and voting against while 24 more left the chamber before the vote was taken. Therefore despite the Chancellor's placatory remarks, 1915 came to a close with the Reichstag sharply divided on the question of war aims and peace proposals. The year had revealed the gradual disintegration of the *Burgfrieden* and the fear of another winter of war was expressed by all classes.[67] As the question of war aims continued to divide the annexationists and non-annexationists into increasingly hostile camps, the majority of Germans were more concerned with coming to terms with the mounting hardships and tragic losses of war, content to allow the Pan-Germans to play at redrawing the map of Europe. Writing in his diary, the Reichstag Deputy, Hans Peter Hanssen noted: 'People are facing the new year with thoughts of tears, blood, and misery.'[68]

4
The Crucible of War

THE ECONOMIC IMPACT OF TOTAL WAR

Restructuring and financing the war economy
The Great War severely disrupted economic life in all the major belligerent nations. Economic disruption was not simply confined to the normal financial dealings associated with overseas trade, banking and foreign exchange. In Germany, for example, where universal conscription was introduced, a drain on the labour force was immediately sustained as a result of mobilization. Within a few days of the outbreak of war, some five million Germans had been conscripted into the armed forces. This in turn, left many families deprived of bread-winning husbands, fathers and sons. (See Figure 10.)

For the imperial German government, the first task was to muster German resources for a massive war drive. Urgent steps were taken to control the economy and the labour force and the distribution of food production. The impact of the war on the German economy was therefore similar to that in the other nations involved in the conflict. Extensive state intervention resulted in industrial rationalization, the recruitment of young and female workers, while a combination of food shortages and inflation led to a deterioration in workers' standard of living. In Germany, however, partly as a result of the pre-war strength of the Social Democratic movement and the failure of the authorities to make adequate political concessions to social democracy, the war transformed and intensified economic and political grievances into a more critical analysis of the intractability of German economic and political structures. The *Burgfrieden* and its subsequent disintegration resulted not only in the polarization of German society but for many it strengthened their commitment to Marxism and militant tactics. Ironically this would result in the fatal split in the SPD and would have the most severe ramifications for the Social Democratic movement.

From the outset German leaders had allowed only for a lightning victory and to a large degree this determined the way in which the war was to be financed. Gerald Feldman in his masterly work on the wartime German economy argued convincingly that economic mobilization was determined not by objective considerations of national interest but rather by conflicts

Figure 10 The Kaiserin saying farewell to some nursing sisters about to leave for the front with the hospital train in the background.

within the ruling military–bureaucratic elite which was unwilling to control the profits of German heavy industry.[1] The Enabling Act of August 1914 established the creation of war bonds which were to be the chief source of revenue for the German war effort. However, contrary to expectations, the swift victory did not materialize, and the rigidity of economic thinking together with the authorities' reluctance to tax profits as a means of financing war were cruelly exposed.

At the onset of hostilities the gold basis of German currency was in a relatively healthy position and following the advice of the Reichsbank the government decided to demonstrate faith in Germany's sound financial state. In July 1914 the gold fund of the Reichsbank stood at 1,252 million marks (with a note circulation of approximately 2,500 million). However, as a result of measures taken during the first few months of the war (or, more accurately, as a result of the failure to take bold action), this figure had more than doubled by 1917. Such a rise was due to a combination of factors that included the withdrawal of gold coins from circulation, the enacting of decrees prohibiting agio-speculation in gold sovereigns, together with special laws that forbade the export of gold.[2]

The extent to which economic and financial thinking was dictated by a belief in a short military victory can be demonstrated by Germany's refusal to count on foreign loans, and instead to finance the war out of her own resources. In this respect, the war bonds were unquestionably the most important source of revenue. The government was granted a monopoly on their issue and all other borrowers of capital were forbidden. The estimated costs of the war amounted to approximately 155 billion marks of which about 60 per cent was covered by nine issues of long-term war bonds. The rest consisted of treasury bonds and tax revenue.[3] The initial merit of using war bonds to finance the war was that propaganda campaigns could urge the public to subscribe as an act of patriotism. This proved a powerful psychological ploy, particularly for those in the home front who wished to participate in the war effort. Over $2\frac{1}{2}$ million Germans, for example, subscribed to the second war loan in 1915, the vast majority of these coming from the towns.[4] The Kaiser seized upon this support to send a well publicized telegram of congratulations to the newly appointed Imperial Secretary of Finance, Dr Karl Helfferich, who had been specifically charged with rearranging the state financial system in order to meet war expenditure.[5] In the first two years of the war subscriptions to internal loans represented a mere formality as the people were only too willing to demonstrate their readiness to support the war. However, this changed in 1916 when subscriptions to new loans began to lag behind the floating debt. Up to the fourth issue in March 1916 the amount raised was still sufficient to cover Treasury bills in circulation. But from the fifth issue to the ninth issue this became impossible. The Fifth War Loan, for example, left two billion marks of floating debt without cover. This was despite the fact that between the Third and Fourth War Loan issue a compulsory saving scheme was introduced for some three million juvenile and women workers and also that the period of subscription for the Fifth War Loan had been extended to 31 days, the longest period to date, indicating the difficulties in attracting small subscribers. Nevertheless, throughout 1916, Pan-German groups continued to point to the popularity of the war loan as a barometer of public enthusiasm for the war and the continuing willingness of ordinary people to make financial sacrifices. In fact despite frantic propaganda the percentage of small investors contributing 5,000 marks or less continued to fall for the rest of the war. At the same time there was a marked increase in the proportion of large subscribers of over 100,000 marks (consisting mainly of large saving banks, mortgage banks, state or semi-state banks). This merely represented an exchange of Treasury Bills into war loans. Thus the small subscribers' participation in the war loan sank during the second year of the war from a half of the total to a quarter with a proportional reduction in the total. At the same time the larger subscribers' contribution increased from one third to a half of the total.[6] During 1916 war loans were thus assuming more and more the character of inter-official transactions with public confidence on the wane. The margin of floating debt without cover increased with every new loan until in November 1918 an unfunded surplus debt of 51.2 billion marks had built up.

Whether this trend was a symptom of the morale of the German people from 1916 onwards is open to question. In October 1916 the Prussian War Ministry, summarizing the monthly reports it had been receiving from the Regional Commands, noted an increasing reluctance to subscribe to the new War Loan. They even noticed that in some places people hoped that the loan would fail and thus shorten the war.[7] It certainly alarmed General Ludendorff who in an order to the High Command demanded an economic declaration in order to clarify Germany's financial situation. Ludendorff was also responding to reports that soldiers on leave and in their letters home were spreading rumours about the inability of the German economy to hold out. Ludendorff argued that the situation required a massive propaganda campaign to counter prevailing views and to 'educate' both the home and the fighting fronts.[8] Special lectures at the front were put on and articles in the press published to reassure soldiers and civilians of the strength of Germany's economy and its financial system. However, the real problem was to be found in a doctrine of war finances that decided against imposing higher taxes on the propertied classes in order to pay for the war. The failure to tax was a legacy of pre-1914 policy that had ignored consumer interests and protected some at the expense of others. The decision of the authorities not to tax capital nor raise the discount rate (of the kind that was eventually introduced into Britain) led inevitably to an increase in the money supply and resulted in thirteen separate banknote issues. The full implications of such a policy only began to emerge after the war. With both the note circulation and deposit holdings increasing unchecked by consumer spending, an unprecedented crash was almost bound to follow once the war ended. Moreover the government did not even start taxing war profits until 1916. Altogether it has been estimated that only 16 per cent of the costs of Germany's war effort were covered by taxation. From the beginning of the war, a misguided nationalism dictated that the soundness of the German currency could only be demonstrated by showing that it was able to withstand the assaults of war unaided by widespread State interventionist policies. Such assumptions would not seriously be challenged for the remainder of the conflict as Germany continued to finance the war by internal loans. As a result of the methods adopted to finance the war it can be persuasively argued that Germany's post-war inflation had set in as early as August 1914.[9]

The establishment of the Raw Materials Office
The Allied blockade immediately cut off Germany's imports of raw materials and led to the establishment of the Raw Materials Office (*Kriegsrohstoffabteilung* – KRA) in August 1914, which was attached to the War Office (*Kriegsamt*) and placed under the direction of the Jewish entrepreneur

Walther Rathenau. The blockade had exposed Germany's lack of economic preparation for a long war. Although the problem of Germany's raw materials had been recognized before the war it was widely expected that in a short military exchange large supplies could eventually be seized in occupied areas. The setting up of the KRA demonstrated a remarkable organizational ability to respond to the difficulties encountered in 'total war' and the KRA continued to have a profound influence on the German economy until the end of the war.

Germany's lack of preparation for a long war and the need to control and distribute raw materials indefinitely was first highlighted by Walther Rathenau who, at the outbreak of hostilities, was head of the General Electric Company (*Allgemeine Elektrizität Gesellschaft* – AEG). On 8 August Rathenau visited Colonel Scheüch, Chief of the General War Office, and warned him that, in the event of a tight Allied blockade, Germany's stock of raw materials could last only for a limited number of months. Scheüch was sufficiently impressed with Rathenau to set up an interview for the next day at the War Office with General von Falkenhayn, the Minister of War. In the course of his interview with Falkenhayn on 9 August, Rathenau repeated the need for an immediate survey of existing stocks and persuaded the Minister to set up a central authority to coordinate such tasks within his ministry. Falkenhayn's decision to sanction the KRA there and then and moreover to appoint Rathenau as its head showed considerable boldness, not only in the speed with which it was set up, but also in delegating responsibility to a civilian and a Jew. Despite opposition from conservative elements within the ministry, the Raw Materials Office was established by ministerial decree on 13 August 1914.[10]

Falkenhayn had given Rathenau practically unlimited powers. With the help of two friends and collaborators, Wichard von Moellendorf and Professor Klingenberg of the AEG, they set about organizing a completely new concept in economic war planning by inviting other leading industrialists and financiers to participate in the KRA's administration. The precarious state of Germany's raw materials supply was revealed within a month of setting up the KRA. In an inventory compiled from some 1,000 large firms which received government contracts, the KRA discovered that existing supplies would last a year at the most. The situation called for a radical programme of rationalized industrial warfare. It was therefore decided that the procurement and distribution of all raw materials should be centralized under the control of the KRA. In order to muster the nation's raw materials by methods other than state socialism, four measures were immediately implemented. First and most important was a coercive measure whereby all raw materials (including half-finished products made from them) became 'emergency materials' (*zwangsläufig materiale*) that were to be directed according to the exclusive needs of the army. Secondly, in order to supplement German stocks a variety of raw materials would have to be procured from foreign countries, by force if necessary.[11] Thirdly, any indispensable article of war that could not be procured would have to be manufactured within Germany adopting new manufacturing techniques where the old methods were redundant. Finally, substitutes would have to replace materials difficult to obtain. (See Figure 11.)

The first problem encountered in implementing this programme was the laws governing economic life which according to Rathenau had hardly changed since the time of Frederick the Great. To this end the standing of Rathenau and the other industrialists who served on the KRA greatly facilitated the coordination of such a programme and tended to mollify many of the objections that were encountered from within the competing ministries and industry as a whole. The situation was simplified by the Bavarian, Saxon and Württemberg war ministries allowing centralization to take place under the control of the Prussian War Ministry. Nevertheless, the obscurity of the Law of Siege, which delegated so much unchecked power to uncomprehending Deputy Commanding Generals undermined many of the benefits of centralization and forced Rathenau and the KRA to act cautiously.[12]

The overriding need to reorganize economic life was achieved by two means: sequestration and distribution. The term 'sequestration' (*Beschlagnahme*) was given a new interpretation in that it did not mean that merchandise or materials could be seized by the state but rather that they had to be used for war purposes only. A blanket confiscation of raw materials was rejected on the grounds that manufacturing would come to a standstill until all goods had been reapportioned by the KRA which had neither the time nor facilities to requisition on this scale anyway. 'Sequestration', however, involved a painful transitional period particularly for industries like metallurgy, chemicals and textiles, who could no longer manufacture peace articles but were forced to adjust plant and machinery for war work. Within the KRA an Office of Sequestration (*Beschlagnahmestelle*) regulated the flow of commandeered materials and saw that these measures were obeyed. Made up of a large staff, the *Beschlagnahmestelle* sent out printed matter daily to the Deputy Commanding Generals for distribution throughout the country. The result was nothing less than the reorganization of German industry.

Equally as important as the reorganization of industry was the need to ensure that raw materials were efficiently distributed to the firms most needing them. To this end, the KRA set up the War Raw Materials Corporations

Figure 11 'There is Enough Aluminium, Copper, Brass, Nickel, Zinc in the Country. Hand it in – the Army Needs It!' Louis Oppenheim, 1917.

(*Kriegsrohstoffgeseschaften*), a system of private stock companies under government supervision charged with gathering, storing and distributing raw materials. In addition to the usual organs of stock companies, a board of governors and a supervising committee, these corporations had an independent committee of appraisement and distribution made up of government officials and representatives of commerce. Their task was to collect raw materials and to direct the flow of supply according to the needs of the firms in quantities corresponding to the orders received from the government and at prices fixed for such materials. The sharp rise in metal and textile prices towards the end of 1914 made the control of prices essential, but the Office of the Interior argued that this was unworkable. Instead, Rathenau simply entered into a series of agreements with various essential industries, fixing maximum prices for a group of goods. The first such agreement was arrived at in December 1914 with a reluctant metal industry and this set the tone for all future negotiations over price fixing.

The combination of state socialism and restricted capitalism proved to be a paradoxical situation that was not always successfully resolved although Rathenau believed (mistakenly) that it was an economic innovation destined to

Figure 12 A poster that compares favourably the combined national income of Germany to that of Britain.

become widely accepted after the war. Industry disliked the degree of state intervention in allocating raw materials and in fixing maximum prices for their goods, and local government officials resented the KRA's interference in what they believed was their domain. They particularly resented what they saw as the KRA's total disregard for their views over the question of the 'price policy'. Furthermore, it was a system that favoured the large industrialists who could afford to invest in the war corporations foregoing dividends and direct profits in the belief that they would be favourably placed in the allocation and distribution of raw materials.

On 1 April 1915, Rathenau resigned as head of the KRA and handed the whole organization over to be integrated into the Prussian War Ministry. In his letter of resignation he reported that the nation's supplies were secure, 'that a scarcity of essential materials no longer threatened the outcome of the war... the English blockade has failed'.[13] This was a widely held view at the time shared even by *Vorwärts*, who, in an editorial review of the first year of the war declared: 'Germany has stood the test so splendidly that her enemies should really give up all hope of economic defeat... Germany is supplied so abundantly with all raw materials... the war can be continued for an almost endless time'.[14] Taking up this point later, Mendelssohn-Bartholdy claimed that Rathenau's resourcefulness actually prolonged the war and led the German people to believe that winning the war was simply about the relative economic strengths of Britain and Germany (Figure 12). According to Mendelssohn-Bartholdy, 'Rathenau, when it came to politics, was an industrialist first and last'.[15] The irony was that in spite of commerce's resistance to Rathenau's reorganization of German industry to a war footing, his policies served the interests of big business and placed even more political power in the hands of the industrialists. His desire for greater scientific management in German economic affairs, with greatly increased capacity for production, led to an organizational structure that allowed industrialists like Hugenberg to use the effects of war on industry not only to increase their own economic power but also to attain specific political ends.[16] Unquestionably Rathenau exaggerated the success of the KRA when he handed it over to the War Ministry, but in recognizing the need for swift economic measures to avert a raw materials crisis, the establishment of the KRA represents a unique example of mobilization for total war whereby the government and not industry decided what was essential and what was non-essential for the successful outcome of the conflict.

The Hindenburg Programme

With the exception of the KRA which attempted to channel the supply of raw materials, the military and the industrialists had initially been reluctant to interfere in the free workings of the economy, preferring instead to support the old and trusted *laissez-faire* system. However, by the beginning of 1916 the Allied blockade and the economic superiority of the Entente had persuaded many industrialists that the total mobilization of the economy was now necessary to meet this challenge. Moreover the changing nature of the war had also placed enormous demands on the production of new war materials and more sophisticated technology. Industrialists engaged in heavy industry who would be in the forefront of this 'battle for war materials' gradually came to realize therefore that a tightly controlled economy might yield enormous profits. Such 'corporatist' ideas were also emerging within the OHL as the importance of industry in modern warfare became manifest. Colonel Bauer, for example, who was Head of Section II and who had close links with industry, was calling for greater control of the economy.[17] However, at this stage, Bauer's efforts were kept in check by Falkenhayn who was suspicious of the new breed of middle-class military technocrats. Nevertheless, the idea of an 'economic military dictator' would not go away and found resonance in the German press. Towards the end of 1915, the organ of the Roman Catholic Centre Party, the *Kölnische Volkszeitung*, called for an 'economic dictator in *military guise*' (their stress) claiming that the current feeling among the people was: 'the army will soon get the job done'.[18] Industrialists like Stinnes, Duisberg and Krupps representing the interests of heavy industry believed that if it was necessary to have greater state control of the economy they would rather do business with the army than with civilian politicians.[19]

Meanwhile at the OHL fundamental changes were taking place. Falkenhayn's failure to break through at Verdun in 1916, his deteriorating relations with Conrad von Hötzendorff, Austria–Hungary's Chief of General Staff, over Germany's refusal to provide support in the Dolomites and along the Isonzo Front, together with the successful Russian Brusilov offensive in June 1916 which caused a collapse of Austro–Hungarian forces in the East, all served to mark Falkenhayn as a general without luck. In early 1916 he had suddenly and dramatically dropped his opposition to unrestricted submarine warfare despite the obvious danger that this might bring America into the war. As the military situation seriously began to deteriorate, the Russian capture of the Bukovina was the signal for Romania's declaration of war on the Central Powers. The atmosphere of impending crisis was thickened by the initial success of the British offensive on the Somme which revealed Allied superiority in men and materials. These events only served to fuel a long-running campaign to replace Falkenhayn by Hindenburg and Ludendorff, men whose reputation in Germany had reached almost mythical proportions.[20] Falkenhayn was clearly doomed. The Kaiser, who had resolutely refused to discuss his replacement, was eventually persuaded that Falkenhayn had to go, and on 29 August 1916, Hindenburg was appointed Chief of the General Staff and Ludendorff was made his First Quartermaster General.

The appointment of Hindenburg and Ludendorff to the OHL was hugely popular with the German people. The *Büro für Sozialpolitik*, which provided the Württemberg government and its representative in Berlin with reports on economic and social issues, noted that: 'The workers have received the naming of von Hindenburg as Chief of the General Staff with great enthusiasm... Even the most radical Socialist newspapers have always expressed complete confidence in his magnificent leadership...'.[21] Under this new leadership, the Verdun offensive was abandoned and the British Somme offensive was brought to a halt in the late autumn, while in the East the second and third Brusilov offensives failed and Romania was defeated. These events only served to add new laurels to the Hindenburg–Ludendorff team. At home they abandoned the old munitions and manpower policies associated with the War Ministry and implemented the so-called Hindenburg Programme – a series of government measures designed to raise output of war materials by the forced labour of the adult population within an arbitrarily fixed period of time.

The war had taught the OHL the value of propaganda if nothing else but the Hindenburg Programme was a programme of despair which had little to do with rational economics and further increased the tendency towards a militarization of German society. The plan which has justifiably been claimed as a triumph for the joint interests of the OHL and heavy industry, and which affected every man and woman of working age, remained largely unintelligible to the man in the street. Even the name under which the plan of 1916 was implemented was calculated to mislead the population. Field Marshal von Hindenburg's name was used to obscure a programme for the adoption of a measure of forced labour simply because his was one of the few names left to conjure with in Germany. After Tannenberg, Hindenburg had been turned into a national hero. Colossal wooden statues of the Field Marshal were erected all over Germany, into which nails were hammered at the cost of one mark each in aid of the war bond drives and war charities. (See Figure 13.) Once the Hindenburg Programme had been decided, the OHL and the captains of industry embarked upon a massive propaganda campaign focusing on the authoritative figure of Hindenburg to gain wide popular support for the oppressive measures that were about to be implemented. The Field Marshal's massive head was a gift to propagandists and poster designers such as Louis Oppenheim, Bruno Paul and Hans Rudi Erdt who all contributed to perpetuating the 'Hindenburg myth'. Perhaps the most impressive design in this genre is Oppenheim's poster for the Seventh War Loan which juxtaposed the statuesque head of Hindenburg above the hand-written message: 'The man who subscribes to the War Loan is giving me the best birthday present von Hindenburg' (see Figure 14).[22]

The British offensive on the Somme in 1916 had revealed a munitions shortage in Germany comparable to that of November 1914. In 1914 the War Ministry had successfully persuaded the OHL to reject the proposals put forward by heavy industry and supported by Colonel Bauer for a radical munitions programme. Instead, the War Ministry undertook responsibility to increase the production of munitions and artillery based on a careful husbanding of Germany's resources. In 1916, however, Bauer now had the full support of Hindenburg and Ludendorff. On 23 August 1916, before they were appointed to Chief of General Staff, the *Verein Deutscher Eisenhüttenleute* had submitted a request to the government calling for the reorganization of the War Ministry and a centralized military plan to increase industrial capacity. This memorandum was handed to the Chancellor Bethmann Hollweg by the Secretary of State Dr Karl Helfferich, on 28 August before a meeting between the Chancellor and Hindenburg and Ludendorff. According to Helfferich's account of the meeting, Bethmann Hollweg was surprised to discover that Hindenburg was fully informed of the contents of the industrialists' memorandum to the government and shared their concerns.²³

Two days after Hindenburg and Ludendorff took office, the munitions programme set up by the War Ministry in 1914 was finally abandoned. On 31 August, Hindenburg, prompted by Bauer, wrote to the War Minister, General Wild von Hohenborn, demanding that the supply of munitions be doubled and that the supply of artillery be tripled by the spring of 1917. While acknowledging that the War Ministry had increased its munition programme, Hindenburg justified his demands on the basis of the enemy's superiority on the Somme and the further anticipated offensives in the coming spring. If Germany was to overcome her inferiority in manpower then still greater increases in munitions production would be necessary. According to Hindenburg this would require a structural change within German industry whereby machines would have to take the place of men who could then be released to the front and priority would be given to those branches of industry producing goods essential for the war effort.²⁴ As a result, those industries not producing essential goods might have to go under.

Although the Battle of the Somme had identified the need to increase the munitions programme, it did not justify accusations levelled by the OHL and heavy industry that the War Ministry had been negligent and inefficient, nor did it necessarily warrant the measures associated with the Hindenburg Programme. However, the material superiority of the British at the Somme was attributed to the establishment of the Ministry of Munitions and its ability to manage the British war economy and control the movement of labour (and profits) by means of the Munitions of War Act of July 1915.²⁵ Hindenburg's letter to Wild on 31 August, however, did not specify the extent to which the OHL wished to emulate the British experience. Further details of this came two weeks later on 13 September, when Hindenburg sent the Chancellor detailed proposals for what amounted to total civil conscription and for a reorganization of the War Ministry.²⁶ The OHL demanded first of all that the number of those exempted from military service should be reduced, that the military age limit be raised from 45 to 50, and legislation based on the War Production Law of 1872 be amended to allow the government to move workers away from those sectors of industry which were non-essential to the war effort. The tone of the letter of 13 September represented not only a challenge to the government and the War Ministry on questions lying outside the army's competence but it was also intended to reflect the growing sense of bitterness and impatience felt by the *Frontsoldat* with the munitions programme and the contribution of the home front. Accordingly the OHL demanded the 'maximum exploitation of all workers', compulsory work for

Figure 13 The unveiling of the colossal wooden statue of Hindenburg in the Siegeshalle in Berlin, 4 September 1915.

Figure 14 'Subscribe to War Loans. Times are Hard, But Victory is Certain.' Bruno Paul's 1917 poster of Hindenburg as the national figurehead.

childless wives who 'just cost the state money' and for women and girls who had contributed nothing, or who 'engaged in useless occupations'. With the exception of the medical schools all universities were to close, thus preventing women from gaining places and eventually taking all the good jobs away from the men and consequently neglecting their main roles as wives and mothers. All Germans in fact, including profiteers, agitators and pessimists should be subject to the 'time-honoured principle that he who does not work shall not eat'.

According to the OHL, the Hindenburg Programme was designed to solve these problems; according to Bauer it would also provide the Chief of Staff with complete control over 'all matters of war work, food and the production of war materials'.[27] Concerned about the extension of the powers of the OHL at the expense of civil government, Bethmann Hollweg passed the OHL's letter of 13 September on to his economic advisor, Karl Helfferich, who penned a reply completely rejecting the 'authoritarian measures' proposed by the OHL. Helfferich claimed that the real problem was the shortage of jobs available, not the shortage of manpower as the OHL were insisting. Extending military service to males over the age of 45 and compulsory labour for women failed to solve Germany's fundamental problems. The high wages paid by the war industries had already ensured a more than adequate supply of male and female labour. In fact the supply of women seeking jobs far exceeded the demand.[28] Helfferich produced figures which showed that for every 100 available jobs there were 80 men and 160 women seeking work. Compulsory labour service for women would, argued Helfferich, 'put the cart before the horse'. Similarly, men over the age of 45 who were capable of work were already engaged in the war economy. Taking them out of such employment and putting them into uniform would only exacerbate the situation. Furthermore, the militarization of the economy and the closing down of universities would make the transition to peacetime reconstruction all the more difficult. Rejecting the corporatist strategy implicit in the OHL proposals and fearing the effects of coercion on the workers, Helfferich concluded his memorandum by declaring: 'One can command an army, but not an economy.'

The degree of state intervention in the economy, whether it be military or civil (or both), had become a major issue among the smaller entrepreneurs for some time. As early as October 1915, the liberal *Vossische Zeitung* which was especially sensitive to financial interests and represented the views of the amalgamated employers' associations, had been attacking corporatist ideas and warning about the dire consequences of too much compulsion by the state.[29] Not surprisingly, those industrialists and entrepreneurs who were outside heavy industry felt excluded and thus viewed the implementation of the Hindenburg Programme with mixed feelings. They found support here in the shape of the War Ministry which was highly critical of Hindenburg's proposals. On 14 September Wild von Hohenborn, the War Minister, had in fact received a covering letter to the Hindenburg memorandum in which the OHL went even further and suggested the setting up of a labour office (*Arbeitsamt*) which would be responsible for seeing that all Germans worked and that no food would be allocated to those who were not working without genuine reasons. This office would also regulate wages.[30] The Ministry had opposed compulsory labour on the grounds that such measures might undermine the achievements of the German home front in adjusting to the war economy, offend workers who had made such enormous contributions to the war effort and lead to discontent and less productivity on the part of the labour force. The War Ministry also saw the Hindenburg Programme for what it was; an attempt on the part of the OHL to blame the ministry for the munitions shortage and therefore to bring it under the close control of the Supreme Command. The War Ministry responded to the Hindenburg proposals by stressing the great strides that had been achieved through *voluntary* agreements between managers and unions. Eager to show that he was responsive to the situation and anxious to protect his own position, Wild created a new Weapons and Munitions Procurement Office (WUMBA) in the early part of September.[31] WUMBA was really an amalgamation of the old Ordnance and Master's Office, the General War Department, and the Engineers' Committee placed under the unified leadership of the widely respected Major General Coupette who had previously been in charge of the Technical Institute of Artillery.

On 16 September 1916 Wild felt confident enough to convene a secret meeting with 39 of Germany's leading industrialists together with leading figures in the armed forces to discuss the economic situation.[32] Wild began by giving his support to the Hindenburg Programme and the need for industrial harmony and generally attempted to placate the industrialists without capitulating to their demands. He promised that in future more skilled workers would be exempted from military service but resolutely refused to hand the whole question of exemptions over to the procurement agencies, claiming that they were too close to industry to provide the necessary judgement. The industrialists for their part welcomed the creation of WUMBA but continued to insist that the Hindenburg Programme could not be fulfilled by spring if they had to deal with the interminable bureaucracy of the ministry. Rathenau claimed that the ministry was causing immeasurable damage simply because 'it didn't know what it wanted'. Others urged Wild to abandon 'social experiments' for the duration of the war. Replying for the ministry and WUMBA, Coupette acknowledged that there were problems but stressed that the Hindenburg Programme would guarantee greater continuity of production than had previously been the case and urged the industrialists to remember that their workers were 'human' and needed holidays. However, the captains of industry were more concerned with establishing the principle that as the new programme demanded a higher level of industrial efficiency, they should receive the vast bulk of government contracts. Some industrialists, like Rathenau, expressed regret that smaller firms would have to fold as a result, but national concerns required that labour be utilized more efficiently and the large companies could only achieve this if they were fully employed.

The meeting of 16 September and the hostility of the industrialists and the OHL directed at the War Ministry, persuaded Wild that in order to avoid direct confrontation with the Supreme Command, he would simply fail to reply to their original memorandum, hoping that with the passing of time Ludendorff and Bauer would turn their attention elsewhere.[33] The OHL, however, was not prepared to let the matter rest and was already preparing its second line of attack. For some time The League of German Industrialists had been pressing for the creation of a new agency to control labour questions. Their cause was taken up by Freiherr von Batocki, the head of the War Food Office (*Kriegsernährungsamt* – KEA), who on 20 September sent a personal letter to General Groener proposing a 'supreme war economy command' (*Oberste Kriegswirtschaftsleitung*). The idea was that all questions of labour and food be taken away from the control of the War Ministry and placed under this new office which would be headed by a General. Not surprisingly, the idea was seized upon by Ludendorff and Bauer, who in subsequent discussions with Groener expanded the original suggestion to include other agencies dealing with the war economy.[34] General Groener was the obvious candidate to head the new organization; with his exceptional organizational talents and his experience in economic matters, he had worked with Ludendorff and Bauer in the General Staff before the war and shared their dislike of the War Ministry.

On 10 October Groener was sent to Berlin to present the OHL's proposals for what was now called a 'Supreme War Office' (*Oberste Kriegsamt*) to Bethmann Hollweg. The War Office would regulate procurement, raw materials, labour and food, and WUMBA and the KRA would also be placed under its control, thus depriving the War Ministry of virtually any role in the war economy. Ironically, on the same day that Groener was persuading the Chancellor to accept these proposals, the War Ministry replied to Hindenburg's original memorandum of 13 September. Wild rejected the OHL's proposals for a Labour Office and compulsory civilian mobilization, insisting that the ministry's organizational structure had already demonstrated an ability to increase the production of war materials. Wild pointed out again the dangerous effects of such measures on civilian morale but did concede that the age of military service could be raised from 45 to 50 and that the controversial law on the state of siege might in exceptional circumstances be used to restrict the free movement of labour.[35]

Much to Groener's and the OHL's surprise, the Chancellor enthusiastically embraced the proposed War Office apparently unconcerned by the increased power it gave to the Supreme Command. The proposals as they stood, however, presented a constitutional dilemma in that if it were to be a federal office it would come under the jurisdiction of the Chancellor. Bethmann suggested that the solution lay in placing the *Kriegsamt* within the framework of the Prussian War Ministry but independent of all other sections so that in practice it would respond to the wishes of the OHL. Although the War Minister would be its official head, he would assign all responsibilities for the War Office over to a Deputy Minister.[36] Ludendorff had no alternative but to accept the implication of the Chancellor's compromise solution on condition that Wild should be replaced. Groener noted in his diary: '... the new War Minister would have to swear under oath to the new arrangement, otherwise the War Ministry's old bureaucratic spirit would continue to dominate...'.[37]

Wild had tried in vain to protect the War Ministry from the two-pronged attack of heavy industry and the OHL, but his days were clearly numbered. Furthermore he knew that as an arch opponent of Bethmann's peace moves he could not expect support from the Chancellor. He recognized this and complained bitterly of the campaign to circumvent his authority. On 28 October, Wild received a cabinet order signed by the Kaiser informing him that 'on the behest of General Field Marshal von Hindenburg' he had been replaced as War Minister.[38] His successor was General von Stein, an ultra-conservative Prussian, who immediately countersigned the order establishing the new *Kriegsamt* under the leadership of General Groener who was also made Deputy War Minister with a seat in the Bundesrat. The subordination of the War Ministry to the OHL was now complete.

The Hindenburg Programme had created an economic quasi-dictatorship under the OHL. It was designed to compensate for Germany's inferiority in manpower by creating superiority in armaments. In the name of more efficient production of war materials, this new programme represented the triumph of monopoly capitalism at the expense of the so-called peace industries. In some non-essential sectors such as glass, cotton, shoe manufacturing, and the soap industry, closures and amalgamations reduced the number of firms to below 50 per cent of pre-war figures. Documents recently recovered from the former Soviet Union and East Germany have confirmed that the Hindenburg Programme was largely, in Holger Herwig's phrase 'smoke and mirrors, an ambitious reform programme designed for public consumption'.[39] Having won a major victory at the expense of the War Ministry with the creation of the *Kriegsamt* and the dismissal of Wild, the OHL now turned its attention to securing some form of compulsory labour.

The Auxiliary Service Law and the German labour movement

For the working class the war was a mixed blessing. On the one hand it ended unemployment, brought high money wages to industries like munitions and for the first time provided thousands of jobs for women and the unskilled. However, the very rationalization required by the war which opened up these opportunities for the unskilled threatened the security and craft basis of the 'aristocracy of labour'. The increased regulation of labour was dramatized by the Patriotic Auxiliary Service Law (*vaterländischer Hilfsdienst* – PASL) of December 1916, which gave the trade unions a new degree of recognition at the expense of militarizing the labour market.[40] Although the PASL did represent certain concessions to labour it cannot be seen as some historians have suggested as a 'triumph' of labour'.[41]

The origin of the PASL can be traced back to Ludendorff's far-reaching demands for compulsory labour (including women) to be introduced along with an extension of military conscription, together with preliminary military training for youths between the ages of 15 and 17 and the closing down of the universities and factories not involved in war production. The Chancellor, Bethmann Hollweg opposed such radical demands, which amounted to a militarization of society, arguing that domestically they departed from his 'politics of the diagonal' and internationally they would provide great comfort to Germany's enemies. The OHL countered by claiming that such a law would appeal directly to the nation's patriotism by bringing home to the workforce the harsh realities of the demands now placed upon them. The OHL reasoned that this would convince the workers that their participation was vital to the war effort. The Chancellor was to discover a surprising ally in General Groener, the head of the new War Office who was to advise the OHL on labour questions.

Groener had been persuaded by the weight of Bethmann's arguments and sought a compromise between the Chancellor and the OHL. On 28 October Groener was able to present Ludendorff with his draft proposals for a 'Patriotic Auxiliary Service Law'. The main proposal was that 'every male between the ages of fifteen and sixty who is not serving in the armed forces may be required to perform Patriotic Auxiliary Service for the duration of the war'.[42] This together with another proposal that youths over the age of 15 were to be trained for military service was sufficient to persuade Ludendorff to drop his demand for the use of compulsion against female labour and to abandon the proposed extension of the Military Service Law. The following day on 29 October Groener presented his compromise proposals for an Auxiliary Service Law to Bethmann Hollweg and his ministers where it received a lukewarm response. During the meeting Groener was eventually forced to make two significant modifications. It was agreed that every male between

17 and 60 not serving in the armed forces be required to demonstrate employment in war work. Groener also agreed to drop the clause providing for preliminary military training for youths between 15 and 17. On the basis of these concessions Bethmann Hollweg ordered that a bill be drafted. However, because the government was already encountering widespread criticism from Reichstag Deputies about the extent of encroachments on civil liberties, it was decided that the bill should be promulgated by the Bundesrat under the Enabling Act of 4 August 1914.[43] Groener immediately sent off a report to the OHL and in their reply of the 30 October they supported the draft with minor amendments, but Hindenburg insisted that the Reichstag accept responsibility for the passage of the bill.[44] Furthermore the OHL, although indifferent to how the problems were to be resolved, was, nevertheless, determined that the bill be passed without wasting time on 'long discussions', convinced as they were that 'the Reichstag would not prevent the passage of the bill once they realised that the war could not be won without such a law'.[45] Bethmann and Groener on the other hand recognized that the various interest groups needed to be fully consulted in order to present a properly drafted bill that would be acceptable to the Reichstag.

The decision to mobilize the civilian population by means of a new law rather than extending the Military Service Law meant that a mechanism for the restriction of the free movement of labour would have to be found. For this reason it was imperative to reach some form of agreement between industry and labour. The rank and file of the trade union movement who were becoming increasingly disillusioned with the war were deeply suspicious of the bill.[46] The trade union leadership on the other hand welcomed the conciliatory approach of General Groener and many of the employers. Indeed Groener was able to persuade the unions to accept him as being responsible for binding arbitration and to delegate Alexander Schlicke, leader of the powerful Union of Metal Workers, to represent labour's interests in the War Office. For their part, the unions demanded concessions in return for ending the worker's right to choose his place of work freely. They insisted on establishing workers' committees, together with arbitration and mediation boards for every factory.

Although many industrialists welcomed the proposed bill as being a step in the right direction, representatives of heavy industry like Hugo Stinnes and anti-unionist politicians like Helfferich opposed the bill as a 'dangerous social experiment' that would place too much power in the hands of the labour movement.[47] Groener was able to persuade them that it was possible to make concessions to the unions without compromising the position of either the industrialists or the army. The industrialists for their part were forced ultimately to accept Groener's argument that compulsion might lead to an irreconcilable conflict between employers and workers. On 4 November, discussions were held between the War Office and the Ministry of the Interior with representatives of employers and labour. Three days later Helfferich and Groener called a meeting of the party leaders to impress upon them the need to reconcile their differences and to avoid a prolonged and divisive public debate that could be seized upon by Germany's enemies. It was agreed that all controversial clauses should be sorted out in the Budget Committee and then the bill should be passed in one plenary meeting of the Reichstag. The following day it was the turn of trade unionists to meet Helfferich and Groener. During the meeting of 8 November the differences between the two men sharpened. Helfferich was clearly reluctant to make concessions to the unions, whereas Groener was eager to meet union demands, stating as he did the following day to Bundesrat delegates that 'the war could not be won against opposition from the workers'.[48] Finally a modified version which included provision for arbitration committees, was sent, with the Kaiser's approval, to the Bundesrat on 14 November 1916.

Having demanded that the bill should become law as soon as possible, the OHL were concerned that the longer the passage of the bill was held up, the more modifications would be made. Furthermore, the military wanted an unequivocal statement from the German people that they were determined to fight for victory by passing the PASL before the announcement of Bethmann Hollweg's peace offer. Matters were brought to a head on 16 November when Bethmann received a challenging telegram from Hindenburg that was also released to the press, stating that unless Hindenburg received the support of the homeland, 'he would refuse responsibility for the continuation of the war'.[49] In spite of the Chancellor's protest that the complexity and controversial nature of the bill warranted detailed discussions, the OHL were supported by the Kaiser who demanded that the bill be passed within the next few days. Finally, after a number of amendments, the bill received the consent of the Bundesrat on 21 November and was sent to the Budget Committee of the Reichstag for discussion on 23 November.

On 2 December the Reichstag passed the Patriotic Auxiliary Service Law by 235 votes against 19, but only after the Budget Committee had transformed the original short bill into a more detailed piece of legislation. Much to the displeasure of the OHL, the preliminary discussion within the Reichstag showed quite clearly that Bethmann's fears were well founded. Reichstag Deputies, while recognizing the need for some form of labour law, objected to what they considered to be an ill-conceived and hastily drafted bill, that made little effort to meet the demands of the trade unions and failed to provide a voice for the Reichstag in the administration of the bill. The Budget Committee began to discuss the bill on 23 November. After long and sometimes acrimonious debates, the general discussion was completed on 25 November. The following day was taken up by heated discussions between Helfferich and Groener and the party leaders. On the basis of these deliberations a new draft containing certain concessions to the unions and the SPD was presented to the Budget Committee on the morning of 27 November. The draft included provision for workers' committees and arbitration courts. At one stage, Helfferich was on the point of resigning when an SPD motion to establish workers' committees and conciliation courts in the railways and agriculture was narrowly defeated. November 27 and 28 were spent by the committee in deliberating the new draft. The first reading of the bill in full session of the Reichstag took place on 29 November where political divisions resurfaced once again. The Minority Socialist Party saw the bill as an attempt to coerce the labour movement, whereas the Conservatives sought to extend the liability to Auxiliary Service for women and youths. On 30 November the second reading of the bill lasted for 12 hours when the Social Democratic Party finally accepted the bill. At the end of the third reading on 2 December only the Minority Socialists opposed it and eight Social Democrats broke ranks and abstained. The PASL was finally promulgated by the Kaiser on 5 December after being approved by the Bundesrat.[50]

The PASL provided for compulsory labour service for all men between the ages of 17 and 60 who were obliged to work for firms engaged in war production. The definition of auxiliary service was so vague that in practice it would apply almost exclusively to the working class, who unlike the upper and middle classes, were rarely able to convince the authorities that their present activities were essential to the war effort. Furthermore, anyone refusing work that had been assigned to him could be imprisoned for up to one year, or be fined up to 10,000 marks – or both. The law also ended the worker's right to choose his place of work freely; such a change would now have to be approved by a factory arbitration committee, which also assumed responsibility for mediating in internal disputes. These committees were made up of a military chairman and equal numbers of employer and employee representatives, appointed at the suggestion of both parties. Only adult males were admitted as members of these committees on the grounds that the PASL only applied to men. Both management and labour could appeal to these committees not only over the application of the PASL but also about disputes concerning wages and conditions. Similarly, under Paragraph XI, workers' committees were to be established in any company engaged in war production employing more than 50 people. The duty of the committees, according to Paragraph XII, was to 'promote a good understanding among the workers and between the workers and their employer.'[51] Other benefits included support for invalids, rent and price controls, subsidies for medical bills, the ending of outstanding trials of trade unionists, the non-drafting of union leaders and the ending of restrictions on recruitment amongst rural labourers and state workers for both unions and the SPD.

The political significance of the PASL was that for the first time trade unions were recognized as representatives of the workers and that employers were forced to negotiate with them as legitimate partners. The position of the unions within the Second Reich had been strengthened by their participation in the drafting of the new law and subsequently the war economy as a whole. The PASL also gave unions a foot in large, heavy industry plants for the first time. As a result, they could now confidently expect their membership to rise. However, the PASL imposed severe restrictions on the workers' freedom of movement and bound the unions even more closely to the war effort. Both the unions and the majority Social Democrats who voted in the legislation would eventually pay a high price for short term gains that began increasingly to be seen, particularly by the revolutionary left, as a piece of repressive legislation against the working class. *Vorwärts* defended the collaboration of the Social Democratic group in the Reichstag by maintaining that the bill would have become law in any event, but the extensive changes negotiated had provided considerable benefits to workers.[52] Eager to gain recognition as equal partners and flattered by the attention shown them, union leaders issued a short manifesto on 8 December calling on workers to support 'whole-heartedly' the bill, claiming that it represented an important step towards 'war socialism' and heralded the new role that organized labour would play in the 'rebirth of Germany after the war'.[53] A few days later some 500 union delegates, representing four million workers, met in Berlin and issued another resolution declaring that workers and employers would work as a team to 'prevent the destruction of Germany by her enemies'. The statement ended by demanding stronger measures to be taken against profiteering but called upon the government to 'give far-reaching encouragement to the legitimate demands of workmen and employees in the matter of better conditions of labour, higher wages, and guarantees for the maintenance of free association (*Koalitionsrecht*)'.[54]

The eagerness of the trade unions to cooperate with the military authorities was not simply an example of pragmatic trade unionism supporting the Fatherland in its hour of need, it was further proof of the extent to which the working class had been integrated 'negatively' into Wilhelmine society. Of course working-class radicalism existed before 1914 and in specific areas was actually growing before the war; the miners, metal workers and the building workers were traditionally hostile to an autocratic Wilhelmine State that had become more repressive in 1912.[55] In Germany there had been a sustained improvement in the real earnings of labour since the mid-1870s until the outbreak of war in 1914.[56] The implementation of various welfare schemes, together with relative job security after the economic boom of 1896 and the fact that workers were spending less time at their place of work, served to reduce work dissatisfaction and encourage a belief that capitalism could fulfil the 'bourgeois' aspirations of the working class. However, this embourgeoisement or 'negative' integration that had been a feature of some areas of organized labour began to break down in the face of 'total war' and splits between union executives and the rank-and-file became more clearly defined as the war dragged on. The sustained rise in working-class living standards was followed in 1913 by a pre-war period of real-wage stagnation caused mainly by inflation. If 100 is taken as the index for the cost of living in 1900, it stood at 134 on the outbreak of war, then rose dramatically to 168 in 1915, 221 in 1916, 329 in 1917 and 407 in 1918. This inflation more than outstripped rising wages. Therefore the situation of rank-and-file union members was deteriorating rapidly. Even the relatively high daily real wages of skilled workers in the war industries dropped by 21.6 per cent between 1914 and September 1916, while real wages of workers in civilian industries had decreased 42.1 per cent during the same period.[57] In the face of deteriorating economic and social conditions the membership became increasingly restive. The problem confronting the unions was not simply inflation. In Wilhelmine Germany, employers had formed themselves into powerful organizations effectively undermining union strike action by use of the lock-out.[58] For many unions, strikes became increasingly costly and ineffective, further undermining their position with their own rank-and-file membership. While it may well be true that the labour movement had not been as integrated into the German body politic as has often been imagined, nevertheless, a combination of inflation, powerful employers' organizations and reactionary aristocratic and military elites had resulted in a cautious and largely acquiescent union leadership by the outbreak of the war.

To some extent these factors explain why trade union executives participated in the drafting of the PASL and generally welcomed its introduction in late 1916. The new law not only recognized the unions as equal partners with employers in factory decision-making, it also gave them the opportunity to recruit in new areas, and by restricting the mobility of labour it made the unions' task that much easier to control their own membership. The unions were not slow to make use of their new powers. In particular, the elections of workers' committees allowed them to enter the large industrial conglomerates which had previously been closed to them. As expected trade union membership also began to increase from 950,000 at the end of 1916 to just under 1.3 million by the end of 1917, rising again to 1.5 million in September 1918. The increase in membership brought a radical change in the social composition, which for the first time included unskilled young and women workers. By 1918 nearly half of all German men between the ages of 15 and 60 had been conscripted. The reduction in the industrial male labour force was compensated in particular by the increase in the female labour force (the growth of juvenile labour was less important in this respect). Just before the outbreak of war the proportion of women in enterprises employing ten or more people was almost 22 per cent; in 1918 it had risen to 34 per cent.[59] By the end of the war it was not unusual for the large armaments factories to be employing more women than men under highly dangerous conditions. (See Figure 15.)

The PASL had the effect of encouraging a redistribution of the workforce away from the 'peace' industries producing primarily for civilian needs and favoured the war industries producing for military requirements. In the final year of the war the numbers working in war industries had risen by 44 per cent since 1914. In order to meet the production quotas the OHL released 1.2 million workers from the army in September 1916 and a further 1.9 million in July 1917.[60] However, the tremendous boost that this law gave to the armaments programme in particular only served to exacerbate the shortage of skilled labour elsewhere in equally important war industries such as metal processing and mining. The unexpected result of this was that armaments firms, faced with a shortage of qualified workers in an expanding sector, began to compete with each other by offering higher wages. In drafting the Bill the Reichstag had failed to secure adequate control of war profits and as a consequence this led to an uncontrolled rise in wages in sectors like munitions. Under the conditions laid out in Paragraph IX of the Bill, more and more workers in this sector were able to change jobs by convincing arbitration committees that they were being offered 'a suitable improvement of working condition'. It took some time before the military constructed effective countermeasures to curb this rise in staff turnover.

In the meantime the armaments industry, by successfully preventing restrictions on its profits, used this windfall, along with higher wages, to accelerate the process of concentration in a deliberate strategy against smaller and less efficient firms. The trend towards further monopolization forced small and medium sized firms to go out of business, leaving many workers feeling 'betrayed' and increasingly fearful of social relegation. One of the unforeseen ramifications of this process was that it undermined longstanding political loyalties and engendered a sense of disorientation and disillusionment with the political system that continued well after the war had ended. Referring to the reforms that the OHL had instigated in 1916, Michael Geyer has written of an 'explosive fusion' of the nation's manpower and material reserves, and a 'symbiotic relationship' between the military and industry in which machines replaced men as the primary agents of state-organized violence.[61]

The PASL was intended by the OHL and many industrialists from heavy industry to coerce the workers to accept some form of compulsory labour service. The military believed that such legislation would also show Germany's enemies that Bethmann Hollweg's 'peace offer' had not undermined the resolve of the nation to fight on for eventual victory. The Chancellor on the other hand, together with the likes of Groener, the union leaders and the Reichstag majority, had hoped that the law would paper over many of the cracks that were appearing between capital and labour. However, the OHL, prompted by the industrialists, became increasingly unhappy with the amended law, arguing that it did not go far enough, and began to press for changes. Heavy industry in particular complained that the law had been so drastically amended to accommodate the unions that it now created more problems than it solved.[62] Indeed, for those groups hostile to the bill, it soon became a scapegoat for all Germany's economic problems. Even the food riots and the 'turnip winter' of 1916/17 were attributed to the shortcomings of the PASL. Ludendorff referred to the law as 'neither fish nor fowl' and complained that it was not 'merely insufficient, but positively harmful in operation'. Ludendorff felt that the unchecked rise in wages was causing bitterness among the troops and undermining the morale of the army. Although claiming to recognize the delicacy of 'labour questions', he argued for a strong war policy, instead of a 'weak and submissive domestic policy'.[63]

It is against a background of growing criticism of the law that the Association of German Employer Organisations met on 28 February 1917 to discuss the situation. In a series of proposals to Groener and the War Office they outlined their concern that the original bill had been emasculated in the Reichstag and asked Groener to modify Paragraph IX to prevent workers from changing jobs and particularly moving to firms offering higher wages.[64] Groener attempted to play down these fears and reaffirmed his policy of conciliation between the unions and the industrialists by stressing the need to emphasize the *moral* imperative of the PASL rather than its compulsion.[65] Prompted by the industrialists from heavy industry, the OHL urged Groener to take decisive action, pointing out that the targets of the Hindenburg Programme were not being met and demanding a cut in wages in some sectors, a cheapening of raw materials and food, and improvements in transport facilities. The PASL, it was claimed had been responsible for an uncontrolled spiralling of wages and for workers resorting to strike action in order to press their demands for political reforms. Two recurring accusations were that the arbitration committees set up by the new law were too easily influenced

Figure 15 (a) A recruitment poster urging: 'German Women – Work in the Home Army!' The female munition worker produces the 'potato masher' grenade for the soldier.
(b) A photograph of female munition workers making shells.

Figure 15 (c) The Krupps armaments works in Essen.

by worker's representatives and allowed workers to change jobs for higher wages; and secondly that the workers' councils, which had been intended to be merely a token gesture to the unions were being used as a platform for revolutionary agitation. While there is some evidence that, for example, in the Leuna works the workers' council became the focus for the anti-war strike in August 1917, such accusations show how little the OHL understood the nature of industrial unrest.

The introduction of the PASL failed to unite the workforce behind the total war effort in the way that Bethmann and Groener had hoped and soured industrial relations – but not for the reasons that the OHL suggested. The

PASL was strongly resented by highly paid skilled workers such as the metalworkers who had previously benefited by moving from one firm to another in search of higher wages. By agreeing to more rigid factory controls and restrictions on labour mobility, union executives in the highly skilled sectors were laying themselves open to rank-and-file discontent. In the case of the powerful German Metal Workers Union (*Metallarbeiterverband*) the struggle between the union executive and the rank-and-file became more clearly defined as a result of the PASL. These oppositional elements made their voice felt at the union conference of 1917 and in the great Leipzig strike of that year, when metalworkers demanded 'the immediate repeal of the disgraceful compulsory labour laws'.[66] Such elements began to identify themselves with the Independent Socialists (USPD) who had spoken out against the new bill as a curtailment of workers' freedom. Together, this alignment organized the massive strike wave of January 1918, electing what they described as a 'soviet' to represent them in order to establish direct democracy in the factories. Such groups with their notions of industrial democracy would later play an important role in the November revolution (see Chapter 8). By opposing the PASL from the beginning the USPD benefited from the divisions within the workforce which had been created by the demands of total war and exacerbated by the new auxiliary labour law: between a 'labour aristocracy' that feared loss of status and wages and those who had been unable to profit from the changing economic situation, many of whom felt economically endangered by the restructuring process and, as a result, politically disoriented.

The OHL and the representatives of heavy industry now turned against Bethmann Hollweg, Groener and the War Office for the shortcomings of the bill, which, they contended, was delivering the country into the hands of an irresponsible and unpatriotic working class. They now demanded that wherever possible the army commanders should use the Law on the State of Siege to end strikes and silence what one industrialist referred to as 'systematic agitators'.[67] In a letter to the Chancellor on 9 March Ludendorff added his voice to the chorus of dissent by suggesting that more use could be made of the Law of Siege to deal with 'conscienceless agitators' who were 'seducing' the workers. In Ludendorff's view, workers needed to be 'enlightened' about their obligation to the Fatherland and this should not be left to 'wicked elements'.[68] Ludendorff proposed the institution of the Auxiliary Service Cross to raise the esteem in which war work and auxiliary service was held. He wrote later that his position as First Quartermaster General had provided him with a unique insight into the state of public opinion and had convinced him of its importance in winning the war. Although he would be one of the first to receive the new decoration (and claimed that he wore it proudly for the rest of the war), the introduction of this new decoration in the wake of the 'turnip winter' of 1916/17 met with little propaganda success, because workers justifiably responded by claiming that they could not eat it![69]

Some army commanders were only too happy to use the Law of Siege to intervene in labour disputes, often forbidding all strikes or actions that might encourage strikes. Worried about the consequences of such repressive measures after the horrors of the 'turnip winter' and the bitter struggle to pass the PASL, the civilian government reminded the OHL that the strikes should not be divorced from the serious food situation. This was the nearest statement to an acknowledgement that the home front had plenty to agitate about.[70] Bethmann Hollweg pointed out to the OHL that any plans to abrogate the auxiliary labour law or to use coercive measures would only weaken the authority of 'well meaning union leaders'. Instead the Chancellor urged 'certain employers in heavy industry' to make sacrifices to strengthen the position of the 'patriotic and sensible elements' of the workforce.[71] Such pleas fell on deaf ears. The OHL was convinced that the country was 'going to the dogs' and had already decided to use the shortcomings of the home front as a stick with which to beat the Chancellor and secure his dismissal.

In their blinkered manner the OHL continued to see more repression as the panacea for Germany's problems. Their critical perception of the work force as morally decadent, unpatriotic and politically corrupt shows how little they understood the motives behind the demands for greater political emancipation. Having little to show for the great sacrifices that the population had already endured, the OHL continued to underestimate the cumulative effects on morale of sustained food shortages combined with the widespread disappointment felt at the Entente's rejection of the Chancellor's peace offer. For those who had survived the shadow of famine with their hopes constantly frustrated, the success of the Bolsheviks in Russia in February 1917 provided new encouragement. Indeed the Russian slogan 'peace, bread and democracy' accurately summed up their own aims and acted as a poignant reminder of what might be achieved in Germany.

THE SHADOW OF FAMINE

The Allied Blockade cut off approximately one-third of Germany's importation of foodstuffs and as a result led to two thirds of the population depending almost exclusively on German agriculture and livestock. Furthermore, the mobilization of 1914 included many agricultural labourers and peasant farmers which together made up over four million peasant holdings in Germany. Such a situation made it extremely difficult for the authorities to make substantial increases in food production. Consumption, it was decided, had to be regulated by means of rationing, substitute foodstuffs and price ceilings on certain foods.

As 1914 drew to an end with no prospect of a military victory by Christmas, the government was forced somewhat belatedly to make provision to feed the population in the event of a long drawn-out conflict. One of the main instruments of government food policy for the rest of the war was set out towards the end of 1914 and constituted a price-ceiling policy, initially for selected foods. Almost immediately, however, the government was confronted with a dilemma they would never resolve successfully. On the one hand they wished to keep certain food prices high in order to reduce consumption and on the other hand they wanted to convince the population that food prices were being kept in check and that scarce foods in particular were being distributed fairly. By raising prices and reducing consumption existing food supplies could be stretched further but lower prices were seen as a necessary measure to prevent social unrest.[72] Lulled by the record harvest of 1913 and optimistic reports on the food situation, the public were consuming more by the end of 1914 than before the war.[73] At the same time food prices continued to increase. In Munich, for example, a fifty-pound sack of potatoes, which had been sold at three marks, suddenly rocketed to nine after the announcement of war.[74] The official explanation for this was that the increased demand of the military for foodstuffs, together with the reduction in food supply from abroad, had resulted in a genuine food scarcity. Accusing the producers of profiteering, Social Democrats waved aside such explanations demanding price ceilings and warning of possible social unrest unless the government intervened.

The man given responsibility for feeding the nation at war was Clemens von Delbrück, the Secretary of the Interior and Vice Chancellor. Delbrück's lack of urgency suggests a temperament ill-equipped to respond to the exigencies of war. Eventually, however, Delbrück's inertia was moved by the pressing need to agree on a priority between high prices or low prices. Both Reich and individual states were already opting for low prices on foods that were rising sharply. One of the consequences of this was a rise in the price of foods that were not included on the selected list. Secondly, it rapidly exhausted the reserves of low-priced food.

The situation began to alarm representatives of heavy industry who urged Delbrück to buy up food reserves in order to curtail consumption and guarantee reserves throughout 1915. Interestingly enough, the plan was bitterly opposed by the League of German Farmers who claimed with some justification that such a move would leave them open to further charges of profiteering. Nevertheless, it became clear that food and price-controls would have to be extended beyond imposing selective price ceilings. Consequently from November 1914 the government began to intervene in the production and distribution of food. War Boards (*Kriegsgesellschaften*) for different kinds of food were set up in an attempt to restrict such food to rationed consumption. The first to be established on 17 November was the War Grain Board to be followed by flour, oats, butter, eggs, potatoes, fish, etc. On the 23 November Delbrück announced a maximum price on potatoes for table use.[75] Such measures invariably led to a further increase in the consumption of and prices for products not yet controlled. This in turn led to further rationing and price ceilings until by 1916, the distribution and prices of almost all food products (including some substitute foods like acorns) were controlled by the state.

By the end of 1914, Delbrück was sufficiently alarmed by warnings given by Social Democratic leaders that the *Burgfrieden* was seriously threatened by uncontrolled price rises, to act. On 25 January 1915 and again on 6 February, the Bundesrat passed legislation (signed by Delbrück) which placed grain and flour production under government control.[76] Farmers were now required to declare their stores; wheat, rye and bread were forbidden for fodder, and failure to comply with these regulations was punishable by imprisonment for one year or a fine of 10,000 marks. Once the grain had been bought up and maximum prices imposed, an Imperial Distribution Office (consisting of 16 delegates from the Bundesrat) was established which together with the War Grain Board was given responsibility for distributing grain. Almost immediately bread rationing was introduced in some cities including Berlin, and the government began issuing posters proclaiming 'ten food commandments' which urged the public to be 'economical with bread' and always to think of 'our soldiers in the field ... who would be delighted to have the bread which you waste'. The virtues of 'war bread' (identified by the letter K), composed of rye and potato flour, were particularly extolled. The Prussian Minister of Agriculture, von Schorlemer, confidently stated in a newspaper article that the food of the German people was 'absolutely assured'.[77] However, by July 1915, bread rationing was extended throughout the Reich and bread cards were issued on Monday mornings which identified the allowances of each person in grams per week.

Ensuing food shortages in the following months confirmed the growing public feeling that farmers were deliberately producing non-controlled goods or selling in the rapidly expanding black market. The farmers for their part resented the price ceilings set by the government and opposed any extension to the 'compulsory economy' (*Zwangswirtschaft*). Agrarian leaders claimed that it was one thing to control grain which could be stored but it was far more difficult to control perishable goods. Farmers had already been forced to slaughter pigs on a massive scale for fear of a potato shortage and argued against further cuts to the fodder supply. Nevertheless, the government was coming under increasing pressure from urban consumer groups who wanted the compulsory economy extended to all food products and prices kept as low as possible.[78] On 15 October 1915, the General Committee of the Trade Unions and the Executive Committee of the SPD petitioned the Chancellor warning him of the dangers of food profiteering. The statement challenged the need to raise food prices in order to control consumption. Citing figures taken from the Co-operative Society of Berlin and Environs, they produced a table showing the rises (in percentages) in food prices since the outbreak of war: lard had increased by 176, onions by 270, beans by 172, potatoes by 133, oats by 172, wheat flour by 44 and sugar by 21. In a veiled attack on Delbrück the representatives of labour criticized the 'hesitating procedure of official agencies' and warned of the dangers of mounting dissatisfaction unless the government took decisive action against 'profiteers and unscrupulous speculation'.[79]

Delbrück responded immediately by establishing a new authority, the Imperial Office for Potato Supplies (*Reichstelle für Kartoffelversorgung*), with the power to ban potatoes for fodder and transfer potato supplies to wherever they were most needed. This was followed by the Imperial Price Examination Agency with local branches in all cities with over 10,000 inhabitants. Nevertheless, it was obvious from the German press that the country was feeling the pinch at home to a greater degree than ever before. Not only had the high prices of milk, butter and meat caused widespread alarm, but the measures taken by the government were still regarded as inadequate. The socialist newspaper *Vorwärts* referred to a report drawn up by the Chemical Research Institution of Leipzig for the year 1914 which claimed that the impossible had become a reality and that pig fat was now dearer than butter:

> that with the prevailing scarcity of fat, fats and oils of inferior quality, which under ordinary circumstances would never have been employed, were used to eke out requirements, is proved by the many complaints, which came in from the purchasing public, and not without ground.

Vorwärts concluded: 'We are confronted with an imperious necessity. Without fat, the generator of energy and warmth, man cannot subsist, least of all the men engaged in severe labour...'.[80] A few days later on 22 October, *Vorwärts* renewed its criticism of the government by ridiculing legislation that had just been introduced to outlaw profit-mongering and the new Price Examination Agency. 'The first is a pistol which looks very formidable, but which has the disadvantage of not going off; the second is a bureaucratic make believe'. *Vorwärts* called for urgent action, but not just to maintain the 'good war mood in the population'. Adequate food provision and the fight against profit-mongering should 'be an end in itself, not the means to an end'.[81]

Criticism of the government's food policy was not confined to the socialist press. The *Leipziger Neuste Nachrichten*, a staunchly nationalist paper, carried a leading article entitled 'Meatless Days', which called on the Bundesrat to improve the provision of food. The paper was critical (as indeed, was the press in general) of the fact that the Bundesrat had decreed days without meat.[82] Such legislation, argued the press, was entirely superfluous as meatless days had existed for a long time. The *Leipziger Neuste Nachrichten* suggested that such measures failed to address the real problem of food provision which was not only governed by the natural regulating force of supply and demand but also by the 'artificial retention of wares and arbitrary profit-making'. According to the paper, compulsory fast-days would accomplish little; 'there is no magic in them to spirit cheap meat into the poor man's pot.'[83] *Vorwärts* claimed that there *was* sufficient food if only the government would distribute it fairly. Accusing the government of 'half-heartedness', it rallied against profit-mongers and demanded that unless 'reasonable' maximum prices were fixed for all foodstuffs then the working class and even sections of the middle class faced the approach of winter with 'anxiety and consternation'.[84] The *Kölnischer Volkszeitung*, the organ of the Catholic Centre Party, dismissed as absurd the idea that Germany might be starved into submission. Pointing to the recent 'splendid harvest', the paper argued for the appointment of an individual with dictatorial powers to oversee the distribution of food supplies which, it suggested, was as important as 'any strategical plan of campaign or as any victory in the field'. The paper warned, however, that failure to resolve the food question could lead to a feud between producers, suppliers and consumers which, in turn, might result in 'class divisions'.[85]

The belief that producers were withholding supplies in the hope of higher prices was widespread. The Conservative papers came to the defence of the much-maligned landowners, emphasizing the difficulties and increased expenses which made it difficult for them to supply the market at cheaper prices. The *Berliner Tageblatt* retorted by publishing an explosive article by Dr Wendorff-Toitz, a Reichstag Deputy who owned estates in Pomerania. Discounting the argument that production costs had risen uniformly, Wendorff cited wage expenditure as an example of production costs actually falling. Where Russian prisoners of war were employed, wage costs diminished considerably. Even where conditions were less favourable, the rise in the price of agricultural produce had more than compensated for the increased costs of production. Referring to his own estates, Dr Wendorff reported; 'my receipts for 1914–1915 were 18 per cent higher than the average of the three preceding years'. The *Berliner Tageblatt* concluded that the government must take drastic measures for providing the population with food at 'tolerable prices' without seriously endangering German agriculture, and with 'the approval of all discerning citizens'.[86]

The allegations caused a furore and on 23 November 1915, the *Deutsche Tageszeitung* attacked the 'radical' *Berliner Tageblatt* for printing such material. It filled three columns with letters of protest, attacking Dr Wendorff personally and representing conditions on his estate in an unfavourable light.[87] Other Conservative newspapers took up the case claiming that Wendorff's estate was an exceptional one, and could not be taken as typical. The *Berliner Tageblatt* responded by stating that no amount of explanations would make townspeople understand why it was that when the potato harvest had been exceptionally abundant, no potatoes for the time being were to be had, even at higher prices;

> and it remains a simple fact that the representatives of the land-owning class have fought tooth and nail against the proposal that the State should take possession of the available food supplies, which measure would be a necessary complement to the fixing of maximum prices.[88]

The debate over food prices and food provision revealed deep-rooted feelings about hoarding and profiteering and the enmity that threatened to polarize town and country. A meeting held at the Reich Chancellery on 17 November agreed that urgent measures were necessary in order to mobilize support for the government's food policy. The task fell to the Ministry of the Interior. Having first informed the Ministry of Agriculture, the Ministry of the Interior launched on 25 November a campaign of 'public enlightenment' designed to control press coverage of the food question and provide the public with more 'official' information. To this end, a 'News Agency for Food Questions' (*Nachrichtendienst für Ernährungsfragen*) was established swiftly to refute misrepresentation and disseminate a steady stream of 'official' communiqués which the press would be expected to publish. These statements were intended to diffuse class tensions, strengthen faith in the Reich, and provide the 'simple man in the street' with clear and concise expositions of the government's food policy. Copies were also made available free of charge to regional authorities for local distribution.[89] In a further attempt to muzzle press coverage of food issues, the Supreme Censorship Office (*Oberzensurstelle*) issued a series of guidelines to the press on how the food question should be handled. The concern of the *Oberzensurstelle* was that continued press speculation over this sensitive issue would not only undermine morale at home but also strengthen the will of Germany's enemies. The guidelines stressed that rising food prices were a natural consequence of war that had to be borne by *all* classes and that such hardship was not confined to Germany. The *Oberzensurstelle* insisted that the press had

> the patriotic duty to make the people understand that they must willingly contend with a bearable rise in the cost of living... and that economic difficulties at home were nothing compared to the sacrifices made by our brave troops in defending the peace and safety of the homeland.[90]

Posters and postcards were disseminated to show that compared with England, France and Russia, the consumption of staple food such as bread, potatoes and sugar remained higher in Germany (See Figure 16).

The government's attempts to convince the population that the nation's food supply was secure and being distributed fairly, was further hampered – certainly in the latter part of 1915 – by growing dissatisfaction that less privileged Germans were having to sacrifice more than the rich. Sensing the resentment, Princess Blücher, a resident at Berlin's exclusive Esplanade hotel, recorded in her diary:

> How must a mother feel whose only son is in daily danger, when going into some hotel like 'Esplanade,' she sees people feasting in splendour, smartly dressed, talking and laughing and in every way living in the lap of luxury? Will she feel anything but hatred for these thoughtless, indifferent creatures? Will she not say: 'Is this what we are sacrificing everything for? Is this the great country, the culture that is to redeem the world?'[91]

It was during the autumn of 1915 that the first food riots occurred in the working-class districts of Berlin. James Gerard, the American Ambassador, noted that as food became scarce the card system was applied to meat, potatoes, milk, sugar, butter and soap. Only green vegetables and fruit remained exempt, together with poultry and game. Such exemptions usually meant that the rich continued to live well. Furthermore, a flourishing illicit trade supplied the wealthy with food at the expense of the poor. The manager of one of the largest hotels in Berlin was imprisoned for forcing the servants to give him their allowance of butter, which he in turn sold to rich guests of the hotel.[92] Nevertheless, despite dwindling food supplies and higher prices, the military situation continued to be favourable, accounting for the fact that only 141 strikes were recorded in Germany during the whole of 1915, with fewer than 13,000 participants.[93]

The food situation began to deteriorate even further in 1916 resulting in serious disturbances in a number of cities and towns. The German population was surviving on a meagre diet of dark bread (made without white flour), slices of sausage without fat, individual rations of three pounds of potatoes per week, and turnips. The mobilization of agricultural labourers into the

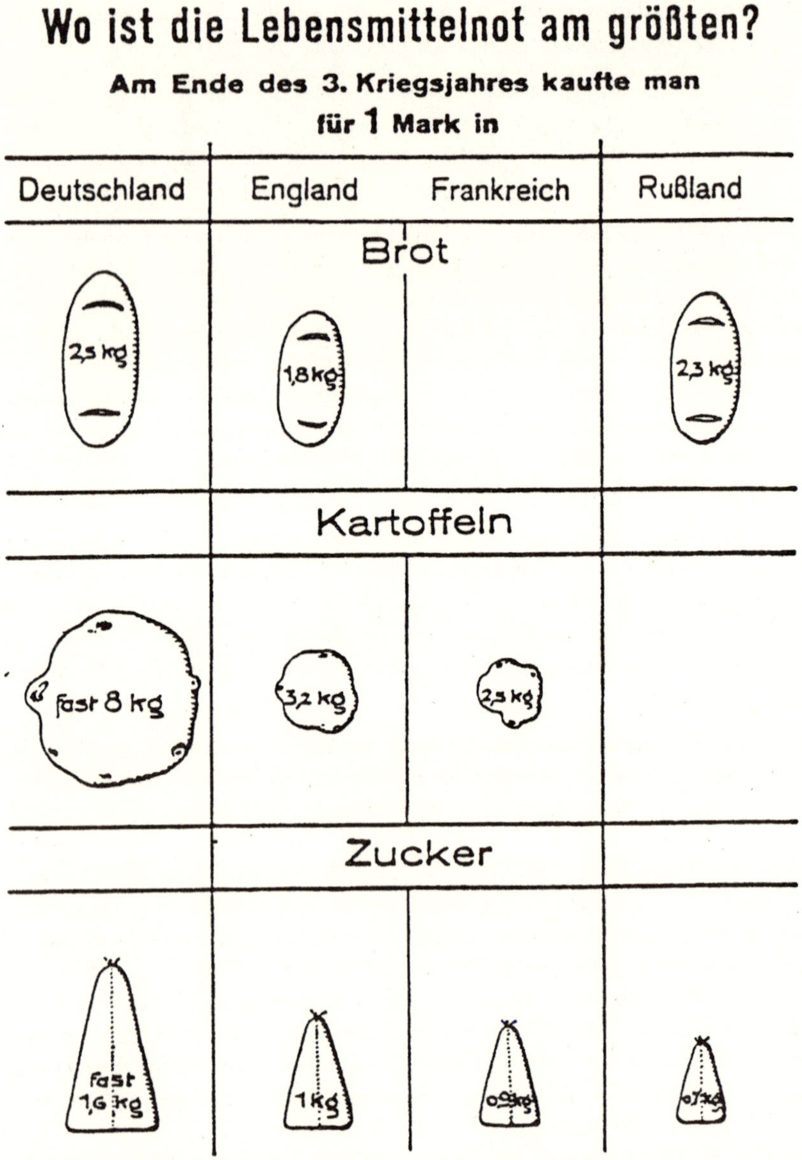

Wo ist die Lebensmittelnot am größten?

Am Ende des 3. Kriegsjahres kaufte man für 1 Mark in

Deutschland	England	Frankreich	Rußland
Brot			
2,5 kg	1,8 kg		2,3 kg
Kartoffeln			
fast 8 kg	3,2 kg	2,5 kg	
Zucker			
fast 1,6 kg	1 kg	0,9 kg	0,1 kg

Figure 16 A poster and postcard; 'Where is Food Need Greatest?' The chart shows what the populations in Germany, England, France and Russia could buy at the end of the third year of war for 1 mark. Using the examples of bread, potatoes and sugar, the chart reveals that Germans could purchase considerably more of all three.

armed forces at the start of the war made it particularly difficult to increase production. Furthermore, food imports from neutral countries began to decline, as Holland, Denmark and Switzerland feared for their own supplies. In January the Reichstag persuaded the government to set up an Advisory Food Council (*Ernährungsbeirat*). This move did little to appease public opinion, as the Council, made up of Reichstag Deputies, operated in an advisory capacity only. The press continued to voice criticism and some papers called for a military solution ('a food dictator') to the food question. A recurring criticism levelled during this period was that individual states failed to place the interests of the nation before their regional concerns. In a vitriolic article published in February, the *Vossische Zeitung* referred to the 'selfish exclusiveness of the South German states'.[94] The reluctance of primarily agricultural states, such as Bavaria, to serve the interests of urban consumers, clearly irritated Berlin, but could not obscure the fact that the government's food strategy had collapsed.

One of the results of the growing food shortages was endless queuing, often without the guarantee of food at the end of it. People were forced to waste precious time standing in line in the hope of obtaining meagre food rations. As the queues lengthened, women were starting to wait outside food shops in the middle of the night. Reports from all over the Reich suggested that people were becoming restless and local disturbances and protest meetings took place in numerous German towns. The Bavarian Ministry of War stated that morale was deteriorating rapidly and that the food question was assuming a political dimension as protesters began to call for 'bread and peace'. In Essen, it was reported that discontented and hungry Krupp's workers had gone on the rampage, breaking the windows of the mayor's residence.[95] In March angry crowds in Bonn waiting outside stores for lard began a riot when favoured customers driving up in their carriages were served first. Police had to draw swords in order to restore order, but not before the mob had smashed windows in the police station. Similar scenes were recorded in Cologne where the mayor was forced to open the food market twice in one night. In May, Princess Blücher returned to the Hotel Esplanade to find it besieged by an angry crowd that had looted the bread supplies in the belief that guests were living in a 'superabundance of luxuries', whereas, according to Blücher, they were receiving the same allowance as all other citizens, namely 1,900 grams of bread a week, including 400 grams of flour. Blücher also recorded that a peculiar form of 'Ersatz' illness was striking down the population, caused by a mixture of chemicals in the diet and the adulteration of food as a result of the widespread consumption of substitute foods.[96]

It was not only the mood of the public at home that was changing. Reports were drawing attention to the alarming frequency with which soldiers on leave or in their letters home complained of unequal treatment, insufficient food and military losses. The Bavarian Ministry of War claimed that the spreading of grievances and rumours was poisoning the mood of communities and doing immeasurable damage to morale at home. It called on officers to set an example by ensuring that their own behaviour was beyond reproach and that they were not demonstrably living a life of luxury. The Bavarian War Ministry concluded that stricter censorship was not the answer; rather officers would have tirelessly to instil into the ranks the imperative need to observe army discipline and instructions.[97] In March the Prussian War Ministry took up this theme and recommended that a concerted propaganda campaign of 'spiritual enlightenment' be directed at both the home and fighting front. The campaign was to be waged by means of leaflets, posters, the press and the use of individual figures of authority (clergy, teachers, officers, etc.) in an attempt to persuade the country that stoicism and sacrifice would eventually lead to victory. It was a strategy that, according to the War Ministry, had the full support of the Deputy Commanding Generals, who were clearly concerned at the inertia of the civil authorities (see Chapter 6).[98]

However, no amount of patriotic slogans could compensate for the scarcity of food – and in particular, meat. One of the effects of placing a maximum fixed price on beef was that it virtually disappeared from the shops. The belief gained ground that this was because producers were not prepared to sell the meat at the fixed price. One reader complained to the *Berliner Lokal-Anzeiger*;

> Wherever the would-be purchaser turned to buy beef it was always the same old cry: 'Beef sold out!' or, 'We have no beef today!'. I asked today in thirty shops: everywhere I was told that there was no beef. But veal, for which no maximum price is fixed, was offered everywhere at unheard of prices![99]

In April, the respected Berlin correspondent of the *Frankfurter Zeitung* reported that some half million meat supply cards had been recently distributed among wives of soldiers and workmen allowing them to purchase up to 2 lb of pork per week, according to the size of their families. The demand for meat was such that many butchers were having to close their shops. Meat proved so scarce that the Ministry of Agriculture recommended young crows as a 'suitably pleasant alternative'. The *Berliner Tageblatt* repeated the accusation heard in many cities that while townspeople suffered, the problem was 'non-existent' in the countryside. Medical experts suggested that colonies of children should be transported to country districts for the summer months.[100] Many farmers were indeed hoarding food and in some cases refusing to slaughter meat. The urban centres were particularly affected by the government's impotence and the resulting food shortages. It was not uncommon for soup kitchens to appear in the poorer city sectors. Industry, which had become disillusioned with the government, engaged increasingly in 'self-help', a euphemism for buying food for workers on the black market.

In the Reichstag, Clemens von Delbrück was repeatedly criticized for his failure to coordinate food administration. It came as no surprise therefore, when, on 7 May, Delbrück resigned, ostensibly on grounds of health. For his bungling incompetence he was awarded the Order of the Black Eagle. Finally, the government was persuaded to act. On 22 May 1916, the Bundesrat authorized the Chancellor to establish a War Food Office (*Kriegsernährungsamt* – KEA). The Bundesrat vested all control of the food supply in the Chancellor, who in turn passed his powers to the President of the KEA. The man appointed was the Conservative Adolf Tortilowicz von Batocki-Friebe, High President of East Prussia. In theory, the President had sweeping powers to dispose of food as he saw fit; this included the regulation of sale and consumption and if necessary expropriation. Under the Bundesrat decree, violations were punishable by an imprisonment of one year and by a maximum fine of 10,000 marks. In a transparent attempt to secure national consensus, an Executive Committee was set up to include all vested interests, both political and economic. Individuals as diverse as August Müller, right-wing trade unionist and SPD member and Adam Stegerwald, leader of the Christian trade unions, were persuaded to serve. The establishment of the KEA was initially welcomed in the press who saw it as a means of strengthening the hand of central government in its dealings with recalcitrant federal authorities and an obvious move to streamline the multiplicity of agencies concerned with food administration. However, in practice, the army remained independent of the KEA and Batocki would continue to rely on the various state ministries for the enforcement of his directives. Moreover, the Reichstag Advisory Council on Food Supply continued to function alongside the KEA.

The new 'Food Dictator', as he was called, immediately appealed to the press for their support, 'even when things come down to the bedrock'.[101] Indeed, in his first official speech to the Reichstag Budget Committee, Batocki boldly requested more funds in order that the KEA could carry out it grandiose plans.[102] Funding was not really its problem. More fundamental was the failure to define clearly its role. The KEA proved anything but a centralized, dictatorial agency, and was doomed to be a disappointment. General Wilhelm Groener, who had been instrumental in setting up the KEA and who remained a member of its Executive Committee summarized the problem thus:

> The difficulty lies in the many-sidedness of our administrative apparatus. To me, as an officer, the relationships seem like a labyrinth which is so confused that one cannot find one's way. But we cannot get away from

this administrative apparatus, cannot set up something new in its place, above all not a military organization. There has been much talk of a military food dictatorship, but the way things stand, I do not know what a military apparatus is supposed to create. Speed is necessary. It would be another matter if this had been prepared in the mobilization plans before the war.[103]

From the outset the KEA suffered from the lack of a precisely defined role. Groener had conceived it as a centralized agency that would bring about closer collaboration between civil and military authorities. Groener believed that the Deputy Commanding Generals should serve the KEA's needs and provide military efficiency in the supply of food. However, the military possessed neither the will nor the ability to serve the new organization and provide for a more effective programme of distribution. Moreover the War Ministry remained deeply suspicious of Groener's motives, and continued to view the KEA as an organization set up to weaken their own position. The KEA was further hampered by Batocki's lack of political acumen; the public had demanded a 'food dictator' but Batocki lacked the necessary ruthlessness to impose his will. Groener's hope that it would eliminate government procrastination and bureaucracy was never realized.[104]

The KEA did, however, identify the acute need to feed the urban industrial population and accordingly initiated a system of special food premiums for so-called 'heavy-task' labourers (*Schwerarbeiter*) in the heavy industries. This moderately successful policy sprang from the pragmatic consideration that the urban masses were vital to the war effort and needed to be fed – even in the face of growing hostility from producer groups – in order to sustain war production. Such a realization was not unique to Germany; in the context of 'total' war, all the protagonists recognized the political and military importance of a healthy civilian workforce. The decision, however, to maintain production and price controls by means of a centralized agency such as the KEA inevitably incurred hostility from the right. From its inception, agrarian interest groups such as Junker conservatives continued to call for the abolition of the compulsory food policy and claimed that the KEA represented a dangerous concession to the left who they believed were exploiting the food issue for political ends. The right viewed the KEA as a symbol of unwarranted state intervention, a portent of new orientations towards socialism.

Looking at events in Germany in 1916 there is little evidence to support this claim, although this would change after the 'turnip winter' of 1916–17. Generally speaking the food riots should be separated from strikes taking place during this period; they rarely had a political tendency and most food demonstrations were confined to economic demands such as increased food rations, reduction in maximum prices, etc. It was still rare for a food demonstration to turn into a strike movement. Nevertheless, food demonstrations and riots did occur in many towns. Reporting to the Prussian War Ministry in May 1916, the Deputy Commanding Generals noted that the public mood 'had taken a turn for the worse' as a result of the food shortages. The monthly report from the 10th Army Corps in Brunswick referred to the shortage of fats and potatoes but continued to highlight the authorities' failure to distribute food supplies fairly. Dismissing figures that suggested that undernourishment was widespread the report concluded that the announcement of a military victory would swiftly offset war weariness. Other reports were less dismissive. In the same month a state of siege was announced in Leipzig during three days of demonstrations that left shops looted and trams damaged.[105] In Württemberg the Ministry of the Interior was so concerned that it issued a decree supporting church and school officials in their efforts to counteract 'unfavourable' influences.[106] In July the 2nd Army Corps in Munich stated that in Königsberg, twenty eight offices had been set up to receive complaints about food shortages. They acknowledged that the available food was insufficient to feed the working population. The report suggested that there had been a dramatic reversal in fortune between the towns and the countryside and identified the rural population as being the worst hit as in many cases agricultural peasants were too weak to work. The explanation, according to the report (from a staunchly agrarian region), was that the poor potato harvest had affected the producers more as the potato was their staple diet and they did not have access to food substitutes as did those in the towns. Moreover farmers could no longer spare potatoes to feed their pigs and were now dispensing with them rather than allocating precious resources to fattening livestock with the likely consequence of a pig shortage in the future. The 2nd Army Corps also recorded that flour reserves which had been placed in storage had become unfit for human consumption with the result that bread rationing could not be lifted.[107]

Not surprisingly the Prussian War Ministry became increasingly anxious about the impact that food shortages was having on the mood of the population. In June representatives of the Deputy Commanding Generals had been called to the War Ministry to discuss how the situation could be improved. The Deputy Commanders agreed that public complaints about food were an important safety valve, but should not be allowed to get out of hand. Lieutenant General von Rogowski of the 10th Army Corps pointed out that long frustrating queuing outside empty shops created a volatile situation and also led to women being absent from their work for long periods. Rogowski outlined a two-pronged approach adopted in Brunswick; on the one hand the army was holding regular meetings with the press in order to improve relations and communications, on the other they were providing food for the towns where the shortage was felt most. This theme was taken up by Major von Braunbehrens of the 18th Army Corps who outlined the provision that had been made to provide soup kitchens and community meals. However, he warned that the situation was reaching breaking point. On the other hand, Captain Nehrkorn pointed out that in the area of the 9th Army Corps the situation was less depressing. He singled out the far-sighted planning and understanding of the political economy shown by many of the administrations in the Hanseatic towns. In Hamburg, for example communal soup kitchens were able to feed 160,000 – 180,000 civilians *of all classes* (his stress). In Württemberg the military leaders outlined their proposals for an all-out propaganda campaign designed to counter the negative effects of the food shortages and high prices.[108]

In spite of the austerities and food shortages most of the reports on civilian morale confirmed that Germans retained an undiminished faith in their military leaders. Interestingly enough, the reports rarely mention the standing of the Kaiser, still widely perceived to be above politics. The newsreels and press continued to record enthusiastic crowds wherever he went.[109] Generally the home front directed their anger at civilian authorities and continued to view the military as less corrupt and more efficient administrators. Impatience with the government was further exacerbated by the failure of the potato harvest and the poor quality of potatoes that remained. The hunger and malnourishment that followed were made all the worse by the continued belief that that there was enough to eat were it not for private hoarding. In the public's mind, government officials were invariably implicated in profit-mongering. Discussions that took place in August 1916 between the Admiralty and the Reich Chancellery acknowledged that the public attributed the food shortages and high prices to collusion between government officials and food producers. Once again a solution was sought through a concerted propaganda campaign designed to defend the food policy and persuade the population to 'hold out'.[110] Reporting to the Prussian War Ministry in September 1916 on the state of morale for August, the 7th Army Corps stated their concern that the worsening food situation would lead to exhaustion, renewed stoppages of work and dangerous civil unrest. A few days later, in early September, Major Deutelmoser outlined a wide-ranging propaganda exercise under eight main headings that was to be coordinated by the War Press Office:

1. What do our enemies' want?
2. Who is prolonging the war?
3. How are we shortening the war?
4. Can we win?

5. The cruelties of our enemies.
6. Lies of the enemy press.
7. Enemy losses.
8. War provision.[111]

The campaign was waged with the specific intention of diverting attention from domestic hardships by stimulating hatred of the enemy, particularly Britain and the British blockade. Posters were a cheap and effective means of disseminating such propaganda. A typical hate-poster showed a picture of a John Bull figure under which appeared the caption, 'This man is responsible for your hunger!' Another poster showed an ugly, snarling British military figure (curiously in Scottish uniform!) astride an equally vicious bull-dog with the caption:

> 'When, still compelled to fight and bleed,
> When, suffering deprivation everywhere
> You go without the coal and warmth you need,
> With ration-cards and darkness for your share,
> With peace-time work no longer to be done,
> Someone guilty there must be –
> England, the arch-enemy!
> Stand then united, Stay strong!
> For Germany's sure victory will thus be won.' (See Figure 17.)

But the severity of the country's food crisis undermined the government's attempt to distract attention away from the question of food supplies. 'We can hardly complain of starvation,' wrote Princess Blücher in May, 'but the whole population is being under-fed, which of course, in the long run, means a deterioration of physical and mental forces in all classes'.[112] However, the failures of the rationing system deepened inequalities in Germany. The poor, for example, were hit hardest by the terrible potato shortage which was caused by the failure of the harvest in 1916; it amounted to only 23 million tons, less than half that of 1915. Germans had consumed potatoes more than any other food. Before 1914 a fifth of Germany's cultivated land was devoted to potato production. The failure of the 1916 potato crop together with poor storage conditions which resulted in widespread spoilage, forced Germans to look reluctantly to the turnip as a potato substitute, and this would remain their staple diet for the rest of the war. Moreover as supplies of potatoes dwindled and the effects of the Allied blockade began to bite even harder, this triggered a devastating chain reaction. With meat and potatoes in short supply, the people turned to bread as a nutritional substitute. The government had already decreed that the *Kriegsbrot* (war bread) should consist of 20 per cent

Figure 17 An anti-British poster 'He is the Guilty'.

potato flour. The failure of the potato yield in 1916 meant that this figure could no longer be met and as a result bread gradually consisted of a combination of rye flour, wheat flour, and a range of substitutes. Not surprisingly the bread proved difficult to digest, although it was claimed that the Kaiser and Kaiserein had enthusiastically adopted the *Kriegsbrot*. Eventually the rye flour was replaced with turnips and the bread ration which had been set at 225 grams in 1915 fell to 160 grams in 1917.[113] (See Figure 18.)

An example of how the politics of rationing effected the population and led to inequalities can be seen from the way in which grain supplies were allocated. The government had devised a rationing policy that divided the population of 60 million into two broad groups; rural food producers who

Figure 18 A Berlin ration card allowing for 2 kilograms of bread.

accounted for 14 million and the remaining 46 million, 31 million of whom were urban dwellers, who were categorized as consumers. Seven million were drafted into military service as the war progressed. Omitted from this equation was the 1.33 million prisoners of war and internees most of whom worked on the land. They would be fed meagrely either by contractors or they would depend on food parcels. The deplorable state of Germany's food production was further exacerbated by the reduction of the grain harvest to 12 million tons from a pre-war figure of 21 million tons. The government allocated 30 per cent of the reduced grain harvest to the 7 million in the armed forces. The 14 million rural food suppliers received 12 per cent and the urban dwellers, amounting to 67 per cent of the total population, were only allocated 33 per cent. The 'heavy-task' workers received a further 6 per cent and the remaining amount was distributed for potato substitutes, seed and industrial alcohol, plus 9 per cent to army reserves.[114] Germans did not even have the meagre consolation of being able to drown their sorrows in beer, for according to one estimate, 95 per cent of the grain normally used for brewing beer was diverted to other sources. *Kriegsbier* rarely contained as much as 4 per cent alcohol.[115] In October 1917 Princess Blücher wrote that since coffee and tea had entirely run out, all varieties of berries and leaves were being steeped in hot water and used as a surrogate. Coffee, in fact, went through several stages of substitution and ended up consisting of carrots and turnips, while tea (for all but the very rich) became a euphemism for anything that could be scavenged.[116]

Figure 19 Poster of a nationwide campaign encouraging adults and children to collect acorns, beechnuts, dried fruit peel, etc., and deliver them to designated collection points.

The wartime blockade affected more than simply potatoes and grain supplies. Germany's pre-war dependency on food imports led eventually to a catastrophic shortage of concentrated fodder (*Kraftfutter*), which in turn had wide-ranging implications for the food chain. Prior to the outbreak of hostilities Germany had been importing fodder at an annual rate of five million (metric) tons. The effects of the Allied blockade gradually suffocated German imports of this source. The government responded with a nationwide campaign encouraging adults and children to collect acorns, beechnuts, dried fruit peel etc and deliver them to designated collection points (see Figure 19). In 1917 the German High Command conceded that 'all attempts to produce fodder substitutes... of cattle feed concentrates, have been unsuccessful'.[117] The result was a diminution of the nation's reserves of milk, meat and fats as the lack of fodder precipitated its own chain reaction. By the end of 1917, for example, the amount of milk available had been reduced by half just at the time when additional supplies were required to combat the influenza outbreak and malnutrition. James Gerard, the American Ambassador, reported that no one over the age of six years of age could get milk without a doctor's certificate.[118] Only expectant mothers, infants and the elderly could expect to receive milk certificates, however, such certificates could guarantee neither quantity or quality.

Milk cows were not the only animals dependent on fodder. German livestock had also been nurtured on imported fodder. As we have seen, meat cards and 'meatless days' (later extended to 'meatless weeks') were introduced and restrictions were imposed on slaughtering. However, due to the precipitous effects of the appalling 'turnip winter' livestock was slaughtered simply in order to preserve turnips and potatoes formerly considered suitable only for fodder. Much of the livestock that was slaughtered proved too emaciated to provide meat. By the final year of the war, pig stocks had been reduced by 77 per cent and cattle by 32 per cent. The weekly per capita consumption of meats, which had been 1,050 grams before the war, shrunk to a mere 135 grams by the end of hostilities.[119] An American art student in Dresden in May 1917 reported eating elephant meat; 'The restaurant was packed as long as the elephant lasted'.[120] By 1918 food scarcity was such that even Berlin's rare and admired kangaroos were slaughtered for meat.[121] Many took to killing birds and rodents. The Munich folksinger, Josef Benno Sailer, testified to the severity of the hunger in song:

> Squirrels, weasels, martens
> We did kill, and dog and cat,
> Fox and mole and jay and crow:
> Safe weren't even mice and rats.[122]

The German economist Jürgen Kuczynski has compiled the details in Table 1 from the ration cards kept by the German government. Although these figure over-estimate consumption and fail to distinguish between the original food and substitutes, they, nevertheless, reveal that, with the possible exception of potatoes, the Allied blockade drastically reduced the consumption of all foodstuffs.

The more food was rationed and price ceilings imposed, the more food drained away from the regulated market and found its way on to the black market which was already flourishing. Contemporary observers estimated that:

> from one-eighth to one-seventh of flour, meal and vegetable distribution, a quarter to a third of milk, butter and cheese and from one-third to a half of meat, eggs and fruit were distributed through the black market at insane prices that reached up to ten times pre-war price levels.[123]

Table 1 *Food rations as a percentage of peacetime consumption, 1916–18*[124]

Commodity	July 1916–June 1917	July 1917–June 1918	July 1918–December 1918
Meat	31	20	12
Fish	51	–	5
Eggs	18	13	13
Lard	14	11	7
Butter	22	21	28
Cheese	3	4	15
Rice	4	–	–
Cereals	14	1	7
Potatoes	71	94	94
Vegetable fats	39	41	17
Milling products	53	47	48

As the rural population drifted to the towns to sell their wares on the black market so a new phenomenon emerged that would travel in the opposite direction and become the embodiment of the illegal consumer economy. It was not uncommon for working-class families to compensate for their lack of wealth by relying on relations living in the countryside to supply them with food. However, this new group, known as the urban 'hamster' or 'squirrel', consisted of individuals and/or families who would travel in groups to scour the countryside in search of food. The weekends proved particularly popular and additional 'hamster trains' (*Hamsterzüge*) would be run to accommodate the rush. The Bavarian poet Oskar Maria Graf, who was then living in Munich, described this exodus:

> There were regular processions of pilgrims to the villages. Once in the countryside, in what amounted to mass civil disobedience of the rationing laws, these 'hamsters' bartered or bought food from the farmers, or if they could not buy or barter, simply stole it.[125]

The quiescence of the German home front was, not surprisingly, sorely tested as a result of increasing material hardship. In February 1916 a number of food riots were reported in Berlin involving women and youths. By the summer of 1916 most of the Reich's major cities were experiencing similar disturbances. In some instances the food riots acted as a trigger for subsequent strike action. One of the features of civil discontent was the prominent role of women and youths in protest (see Chapter 6). In 1916, male youth crimes were 50 per cent higher than 1914 figures. By 1917 the juvenile criminal rate would rise by 25 per cent reaching a peak in 1918. Most of these were petty crimes such a theft and robbery. Adults tended to put this rise down to a lack of parental discipline and talked of adolescent 'waywardness' (*Verwahrlosung*). As early as February 1915 the military authorities provided voluntary military preparation for 16 year olds in the hope that such training would imbue greater civic responsibility.[126] In the absence of fathers fighting at the front and mothers working in munitions factories, the wayward behaviour of youth signified a generation conflict and the collapse of the family structure. For male adolescents, the war had also brought about significant opportunities to earn high wages and the opportunities to spend such earnings on 'pleasure' activities. Most authorities responded by banning juveniles from visiting public houses, coffee houses or confectionary establishments (*Konditoreien*) after 8 p.m. or allowing youth to purchase alcohol for home consumption. In Bremen, for example, juveniles were also banned from cinemas, music halls, and even vocal and declamatory recitals which 'are devoid of higher scientific or artistic interest'.[127]

Wartime criminal statistics reveal not only an overall increase in criminality, but significantly the extent to which women regarded circumventing the official system of food distribution as a legitimate means of survival. Prior to the outbreak of hostilities approximately 33,000 women had been convicted of offences against property, by 1917 this figure had doubled to nearly 66,000. The number of first time offenders also increased as women resorted to crime in order to feed their families. The majority of women convicted of offences against property had either stolen food from shops or in the countryside or had been caught forging food ration cards.[128]

The 'turnip winter' had a profound effect on the home front and its attitude to the war. Ernst Gläser noted how scavenging and the struggle for survival had changed attitudes:

> And it was a hard winter right to the end. The war now got past the various fronts and pressed home upon the people. Hunger destroyed our solidarity; the children stole each other's rations.... Soon the women who stood in pallid queues before the shops spoke more about their children's hunger than about the death of their husbands. The war had shifted its emphasis. A new front was created. It was held by the women, against an *entente* of field gendarmes and controllers. Every smuggled pound of butter, every sack of potatoes successfully spirited in by night was celebrated in their homes with the same enthusiasm as the victories of the armies two years before....
>
> Soon a looted ham thrilled us more than the fall of Bucharest. And a bushel of potatoes seemed much more important than the capture of a whole English army in Mesopotamia.[129]

Table 2 *Average daily meat consumption in grams per head, by groups*[130]

Year	Army personnel	Self-suppliers	Consumers
1914	285	60	145
1915	132	60	135
1916	160	75	65
1917	145	80	48
1918	127	90	28

The failures of the rationing system deepened social inequalities in Germany. Not only were the poor excluded from purchasing food on the black market through lack of income, they were further penalized by the government's rationing policy which resulted in grossly unequal food consumption as Table 2 reveals.

One of the consequences of hoarding and blackmarketeering and illegal subsistence strategies in general was that the government reduced even further official rations, which were already significantly below the minimum level of subsistence. For the working class the precipitous decline in food consumption literally spelled death. The health of the population had been in a state of decline before the terrible winter of 1916–17, but the physical effects of malnutrition now became apparent for all to see. The American newspaper correspondent, George Schreiner, witnessed the consequence of the government's rationing policy:

> Once I set out for the purpose of finding in these foodlines a face that did not show the ravages of hunger. That was in Berlin. Four long lines were inspected with the closest scrutiny. But among the 300 applicants for food there was not one that had had enough to eat for weeks. In the case of the younger women and children the skin was drawn hard to the bones and bloodless. Eyes had fallen deeper into the sockets. From the lips all colour was gone, and the tufts of hair which fell over parchmented foreheads seemed dull and famished – a sign that the nervous vigour of the body was departing with the physical strength.[131]

The first to suffer were working-class children and the elderly. The health of the aged, many of whom were on fixed incomes, deteriorated from a combination of inadequate rations and indigestible ersatz substitutes. A confidential inquiry started in 1917 by the Reich Health Office into conditions of health in the federal states, received a chilling reply from one asylum for aged people that read simply: 'Inmates have all died'. The death rate among the old was

Table 3 *Index of child mortality (1913 =100)*[134]

Sex	Age	1917	1918
Male	5–10	156.3	189.2
	10–15	154.3	215.0
Female	5–10	143.8	207.3
	10–15	152.9	239.0

increasing at such an alarming rate that an insurance executive referred to a 'manslaughter of the aged'.[132] Infant mortality, on the other hand was high in the years leading up to the war; out of every hundred children born in Germany in 1913, fifteen died in the first year of life, but compared with other age groups, there were relatively small changes in the figures for infant mortality. This is partly explained by the dramatic fall in the birth rate. The total numbers of German children born annually fell from 1,838,750 in 1913 to 926,813 in 1914.[133] Mortality, however, increased prodigiously among children. By 1918, child mortality was almost double its pre-war level and was still rising (Table 3).

Although many mothers had sacrificed their own health in an attempt to correct the nutritional deficiencies of their children, the state of health of Germany's children became quite desperate as famine cast its shadow over helpless families. As early as 1916 the Reich Health Office had suggested that more children between the ages of 5 and 15 were dying than in any other single age group. Not only were female children more affected by food shortages by the end of the war than boys, but there is evidence to suggest that women also suffered more than men (who would normally expect to qualify for special rations in the armed forces). Figures for the final months of 1918 reveal that deaths among females in all age groups were 25 per cent higher than the combined monthly deaths recorded in peacetime for both sexes. Mortality amongst young mothers was strikingly high as many bore the brunt of feeding families on restricted rations. The health of the 5 million additional women mobilized into the workforce not surprisingly deteriorated as they attempted to balance domestic duties with the physically demanding war work on inadequate supplies of food. For every 100 women who died in the age groups 15 to 25 in 1913, 290 women died in 1918. The corresponding figure for young males before the age of call-up was 215.[135]

It is not the concern of this study to enter into the debate about the exact numbers that died as a result of starvation induced by the Allied blockade.[136] Suffice to say that although death by starvation did occur during the war, malnutrition more often lowered resistance to diseases and infections such as tuberculosis, dysentery, influenza and rickets which have a strong nutritional basis, and which ultimately were the causes of death. Undernourishment, however, remained a major contributory factor because an adequate diet would have more frequently prevented such infections and diseases in the first place.

The *Kohlrübenwinter* (turnip winter) and resulting malnutrition was having a catastrophic effect on German life and it affected all classes including Reichstag Deputies. Hans Peter Hannsen writing in his diary on 30 March 1917, noted:

> Today I happened to sit between Dr (Wilhelm) Struve and (Philipp) Scheidemann in the restaurant. The latter said that at nine-thirty last evening he had gone out with a knapsack on his back to get some potatoes, since his family had no food in the house. He had gone from place to place and had not reached home with his fifteen pounds of potatoes until two in the morning. 'Who would have thought that such a thing could ever happen,' Scheidemann burst out 'that I, who am buried in work, should be forced to spend my time begging for a few pounds of potatoes along with women and children!'
>
> According to Dr Struve, (Adolf) Groeber stated in the Committee on Employment that he was so faint as a result of the poor food in Berlin that he had become a pessimist.[137]

The peasants also became frustrated. The tensions between the interests of the community and the interests of powerful agrarian circles remained unresolved as did indeed differences between the smaller farmers and the more influential estate owners that dominated the *Bund der Landwirte*.[138] Town dwellers continued to blame all farmers for the nation's misery and although some complaints were justified, too often farmers were singled out as easy scapegoats for the government's incompetence. Indeed, by the end of the war, many farmers themselves no longer had sufficient food. Agricultural landowners had to contend with a war economy in which the state intervened and applied restrictions to agriculture more rigorously than to industry – often without reference to prevailing conditions. As the war dragged on, farmers endured acute shortages of labour (due to above average conscription in rural areas) and materials, sequestration of their horses, lack of fertilizers and over-cultivation of the land. The increasingly elaborate machinery of wartime controls regulated prices and delivery quotas and the plethora of bureaucratic directives set production targets and forbade farmers from slaughtering their own livestock. The holders of medium and small farms complained that they were no longer masters of their own holdings and resented what they believed to be the preference given to townspeople. As a result, large quantities of food were diverted to the black market. Requisitioning and the use of force were particularly resented in the rural areas. In 1917, troops were brought in to search farmsteads for hidden food stores. Ernst Gläser, who spent his summers working in the countryside, recounts that the old farmers secretly buried sackfuls of smoked sausage in the fields, and killed pigs in the woods. The police and inspectors who were posted outside threshing machines to check quantities and who 'confiscated all the harvest' were hated by the farmers 'as much as they had hated the French in 1914; even more, for they weren't able to shoot them... The word "enemy" now meant the gendarmes'.[139]

Thus the experience of war served to draw the large agrarian-dominated *Bund der Landwirte* and the smaller agricultural landowners closer together, although this should not be overstated. Their shared anxieties in the face of bureaucratic interventionism and their mutual dislike of town dwellers were not, in themselves, sufficient to offset pre-war differences and mutual distrust. Some of the smaller farmers who were particularly badly hit called for an early end to the war and a negotiated peace whereas the larger estate owners closed ranks with heavy industry to campaign for 'peace through victory' and annexations. Both groups feared organized labour and perceived interventionism as a further sign of insidious 'state socialism'. However, this rapprochement between urban and rural capitalism had limited objectives and did not bring about the permanent union of *Eisen und Roggen* ('iron and rye') that had been advocated by Bismarck. Urban and rural entrepreneurs were primarily concerned to re-establish a free market economy and to halt the 'new orientation' of constitutional reforms that had been promised at the outset of hostilities and which now appeared linked to a negotiated peace settlement.[140] However, the large agricultural estates were invariably in the hands of the reactionary Prussian Junkers, who remained the upholders of the Prussian monarchical and agrarian traditions and vehemently opposed to the democratization of the Prussian voting system or the extension of Reichstag powers.

On 3 July 1917, Friedrich Ebert made a speech in the Reichstag that summed up the growing sense of confusion and helplessness:

> The statements made by ministers compel us to direct our attention to our domestic troubles. *The food situation is unbearable.* The promises of the Government have brought us only disappointment. The bread ration was reduced this spring. The potato supply has been insufficient. During the past month labourers had to live on dry bread and little meat. Undernourishment is spreading. Conditions making for health are impaired. When we face this situation, we have to say: Our strength is almost spent![141]

Ebert called for clarification of the government's peace programme and the need to fulfil promises of a new orientation. He compared Germany's lack of political progress with reforms that were being introduced in England and Hungary. Internal unity, he warned, could only be maintained in the face of continuing hardships if the government responded to the widespread desire for democratic electoral reforms. The government, however, was not listening. While it recognized the seriousness of the food situation it had rejected thoughts of increasing provision and decided instead that increased censorship was the solution. In November 1916, for example, the Supreme Censorship Office issued five instructions to the press on how the food situation was to be treated:

1. In view of the high (food) price levels, the press are to avoid 'sensational' presentations so as not to weaken the *Burgfrieden*.
2. They must avoid general and spiteful attacks on the commercial class.
3. Reports of civil unrest due to rising food prices are to be avoided.
4. They must avoid reporting mass meetings and disturbances in front of shops and food distribution points.
5. Food shortages should not be the subject of jokes or comic leaflets.[142]

These negative measures in the face of widespread malnutrition and in some cases, starvation, revealed an alarming flight from reality on the part of the authorities. Meanwhile the food shortages persisted. In September 1917, the Deputy Commanding General in Nuremberg reported that the population had 'lost all faith in the promises made by the authorities in the administration of food'. According to General Ludendorff, waning morale at home was intimately connected with the food situation:

> the human body did not receive the necessary nourishment... for the maintenance of physical and mental vigour. In wide quarters a certain decay of bodily and mental powers of resistance was noticeable, resulting in an unmanly and hysterical state of mind which under the spell of enemy propaganda encouraged the pacifist leanings of many Germans.[143]

The bitter *Kohlrübenwinter* of 1916–17 did have a profound impact on attitudes towards the war and unquestionably weakened the morale of the home front but Ludendorff's observations made with the benefit of hindsight coldly ignored the prevailing situation and served merely to restate the *Dolchstoss* ('stab-in-the-back') myth perpetrated by the far right in Weimar Germany.[144]

UNRESTRICTED SUBMARINE WARFARE

Recognizing the importance of social stability and the imperative need to lift morale, the government made a far-reaching decision to launch unrestricted submarine warfare in a desperate attempt to counter the blockade and as an antidote to war weariness. On 19 January 1917, the Kaiser signed a decree authorizing the military campaign which was to start on 1 February and was to be prosecuted with the 'utmost energy'. On 31 January, Chancellor Bethmann Hollweg, who had opposed submarine warfare, reported to the Finance Committee that although it had been indefensible to begin submarine warfare, it would now be indefensible *not* to pursue such a strategy. Bethmann argued that the situation had changed and Germany now had more submarines and secondly the Allies had suffered a poor harvest which placed them in a vulnerable position; 'We cannot starve England, but we can place Italy and France in such an intolerable situation that they will compel England to conclude peace, while at the same time she will face rapidly increasing losses'.[145] The Chancellor, clearly uneasy with his *volte face*, was, nevertheless, supported enthusiastically by Secretary of State Helfferich who presented the Finance Committee with a scenario that bore little resemblance to reality. Ignoring Germany's precarious position and the plight of millions of undernourished Germans, Helfferich contemptuously dismissed the threat posed by America should she be dragged into the war, and as far as England was concerned: 'by the autumn the Island Kingdom will sprawl like a fish in the reeds and beg for peace!' While this delighted the Junkers, it could not disguise the desperate gamble that had been undertaken. At the same meeting of the Finance Committee, the Minister of the Marine, Admiral Eduard von Cappelle, stated that eight new and larger U-boats would be in service each month and the navy would *guarantee* (my italics) to sink 600,000 tons per month and destroy one half of England's merchant tonnage in six months. However, the decision taken in January was the most fateful since the adoption of the Schlieffen Plan. If unrestricted submarine warfare should fail to bring Britain to her knees within the allotted six month period, then it was almost inevitable that the United States would go to war with Germany.

For a brief period the question of food supplies was overshadowed by an unrelenting propaganda campaign designed to rationalize unrestrictive submarine warfare and reassure a weary home front. U-boat calendars, posters and postcards proliferated, providing wildly different estimates of enemy tonnage sunk, but all suggesting that unrestricted submarine warfare would break the blockade and bring Britain to its knees. The most famous poster in this genre was Hans Erdt's *'U-Boote Heraus!'* (U-Boats Out!) with its dominant 'U' creating a strong single motif. The submarine war was also employed to persuade the nation to contribute to war loans with slogans such as 'Help the U-Boats defeat England' (see Figure 20(a,b,c)) and 'Victory Is not Won with Words and Thoughts Alone', Juxtaposed against a U-boat engaged in a naval battle.

Official propaganda justified unrestricted submarine warfare in terms of the blockade and the worsening food situation. However, Germany had embarked upon a military campaign fraught with risks and undermined by major errors of judgement on the part of both politicians and naval leaders. Moreover the propaganda that accompanied the launching of all-out submarine warfare had created a false sense of certainty in ultimate victory. Not only did it risk drawing the United States into the war but failure to secure victory would further undermine morale at home. The German authorities had also underestimated the extent to which Allied losses would be offset by new naval construction. In the first Reichstag debate since the announcement of all-out submarine warfare, Dr Eduard David, the spokesman for the Social Democrats, questioned the figures provided by von Capelle:

> The Minister of the Marine believes that, by sinking 600,000 tons monthly, we can destroy one half of England's merchant tonnage in six months. But he overlooks the fact that we must count on 150,000 tons of new ships being built each month, and that German tonnage in the neutral countries may be seized and so give a similar increase.[146]

David's estimates proved a considerable understatement. Whereas German submarines sank an average of 550,000 tons of shipping in the last 11 months of 1917, the average decreased to 323,000 tons during the 10 months of war in 1918. Allied construction exceeded 12 million tons by the end of the war offsetting the damage caused by the U-boats.[147] Moreover the decrease in U-boat successes was also due to the toll that Allied mines were taking on German submarines. By the time the OHL launched its major offensive in March 1918 one general noted sadly that the U-boat war had turned into 'a wild goose chase'.[148]

Germany's greatest error was in underestimating American military capability. Addressing the Reichstag, Admiral von Capelle expressed a view widely shared in military circles:

> As far as the financial and economic situation is concerned, I have always laid great stress on the importance of America's entrance into the war. But from a military point of view, her entrance means nothing. I repeat: *from a military point of view America is as nothing*. I am convinced that almost no Americans will volunteer for war service . . . [149]

Figure 20 Four examples of unrestricted submarine warfare.
(a) 'Subscribe to War Loans and Help in the U-Boat War Against England'.
(b) 'U-Boats are Out!' Hans Rudi Erdt's famous poster.

Figure 20 continued
(c) An agitational cartoon from the right-wing satirical magazine, *Kladderadatsch*, of the unrestricted submarine warfare against England launched in February 1917.

The consequence of the United States entry into the conflict proved a disaster for Germany and only added to the hardships of its civilians. The US contribution would tilt the military balance in favour of the Allies and enforce the blockade with catastrophic implications for the food situation in Germany. In July 1917 President Wilson signed a general embargo on arms and foodstuffs reaching the Central Powers and generally improved the scope and efficiency of the blockade. The German government's disdain of America's fighting capacity was matched only by its contempt for the suffering of its own people. The Kaiser, or accurately, the military, had unleashed unrestricted submarine warfare in an attempt to restrict food imports reaching

Figure 20 continued
(d) U-Boat calendar claiming that unrestricted submarine warfare will eventually force Britain to seek a peace settlement.

Great Britain. U-Boat calendars hailed German successes and official propaganda claimed that ensuing food shortages and starvation would force Britain to seek an early peace settlement. (See Figure 20d.) Unrestricted submarine warfare proved futile, it failed to break the blockade and underestimated the vigour with which the Allies would retaliate. The government's failure to fulfil its promises together with worsening food shortages led to civil disobedience and to demands for reforms. The shadow cast by hunger and malnutrition acted as a catalyst for political parties, trade unions and interest groups to demand an end to famine and a negotiated peace. What is surprising is not that the fabric of German society began to disintegrate after the 'turnip winter', but that it had held together for so long in the face of intense pressures and deprivation. The inequality of hunger that was built into the system by the government's own policies led not only to an increase in tension between urban and agrarian communities, but also to a polarization of contented and discontented sections of the community. The vast mass of families of soldiers at the front had been reduced to scavengers by the winter of

1916–17. In contrast, a minority prospered as a result of the exigencies of war and became more assertive. As we shall see in following chapters, the failure to bring the war to an end in the light of the worsening food crisis led to open dissatisfaction with the government and the Kaiser from both the 'contented' and 'discontented' – although for different reasons. The stirrings of discontent and opposition could no longer be ignored. The government and the OHL responded by inaugurating a counter propaganda campaign of 'patriotic instruction' (*Vaterländische Unterricht*) designed to foster a belief in ultimate victory. However, there remained a minority of pacifists who were convinced that the war should never have been started.

5
Dissenting Voices
Pacifism, Feminist Ferment, and the Women's Movement

'Everyone has a part to play'
                                    Franz von Wandel, March 1916

The general causes of dissent and protest can be listed as follows: the impact of economic misery and the perceived disparity between the sacrifices made by the upper class and the rest of society; war weariness and a longing for peace; frustrated expectations for political and social reform; the impact of the Russian Revolution that transformed general grievances into social criticism and eventually political action. These motivational forces, which range from social criticism to political protest, increasingly pushed the hopes of 1914 for total victory ever more into the background and weakened national solidarity. By the end of 1916 growing discontent and war weariness merged with social criticism and eventually constituted a major precondition of the German Revolution. However, fundamental challenges to the German Empire only took place towards the end of the war after considerable and prolonged economic sacrifices.

Before analysing the events in Germany that followed February 1917, I want first, briefly, to look at the various forms of social protest which, while not immediately posing a revolutionary challenge to the *status quo*, were considered by Reich authorities to undermine national solidarity and the 'spirit of 1914'. These protests invariably came from what might loosely be termed the 'left of centre', and the manner in which the authorities responded largely accounts for the deteriorating relationship between official policy and public opinion for the rest of the war.

The outbreak of war and the *Burgfrieden* succeeded in the short term in pulling together disparate groups and interests in pursuit of total war and victory. As we have seen, by appealing to the nation as opposed to sectional class interests, the Kaiser integrated the SPD and the labour movement into the war effort (see Chapter 6). Nevertheless, as the promised swift victory failed to materialize, strains reappeared as the *Burgfrieden* began to fragment, at first over the government's war aims and its annexationist policy. The rapidly deteriorating supply of food to the home front only exacerbated tensions. The spectacular failure of the Reich authorities to resolve the food shortages came to be regarded as an injustice and not simply a consequence of total war. The first expressions of dissatisfaction and protest in the working class followed – culminating, in the summer of 1916, in the food riots experienced by most German cities. The war served also to raise expectations on the part of sections of the community, such as the Women's Suffrage League, which increasingly felt that participation and sacrifices made in the name of the war effort justified social and political reforms. Individuals and groups that had enthusiastically 'signed-up' to the *Burgfrieden*, in the belief that reforms would be forthcoming and inequalities dismantled, became increasingly frustrated and critical at the authorities' failure to fulfil its promises.

PACIFISM AND THE PEACE MOVEMENT

By 1916, little social progress had been made, and disillusionment and dissent set in. The outbreak of war also released anti-war sentiments which refused to subside. The pacifist movement was largely propelled by women. In fact, war split the women's movement. The majority of its members remained loyal to the Fatherland and to the government's war aims, but hoped that their emancipatory claims would be recognized. Accordingly, the women's suffrage organizations continued to press for 'votes for women' even as they undertook war work. (Deep-seated stereotypical images of women as the 'weaker sex' were so firmly entrenched in German culture that there was no question that women should be conscripted into the armed forces.) However, other women turned to radical politics, while a minority of feminists repudiated nationalism and remained wedded to the peace movement. The feminist–pacifist group saw the war as a peculiarly masculine phenomenon and continued to press for changes in the educational system and a move away from the Prussian militarist tradition.

Although the SPD and the trade unions endorsed the war efforts, sections of the working class and leftist Social Democrats were more divided on the issue. These groups objected to war on class and anti-militarist grounds. But these objections were also tinged with pacifism. Mary Nolan, for example, has shown that while some Social Democratic functionaries had demonstrated 'frenzied enthusiasm' for the war, in Düsseldorf massive anti-war demonstrations took place on 29 July 1914 after Austria and Serbia had declared war. Some 15,000 to 20,000 workers packed twelve giant Social Democratic rallies and later marched and sang through the streets. The *Volkszeitung* proclaimed that the workers had protested against a war that 'would bring unending misery and new burdens to the workers of all lands' and 'had warned those who desire war not to play with fire or they could get burned.'[1] Nonetheless, the protests that took place in Düsseldorf and other cities achieved little. As we have seen in Chapter 1, socialist and trade union leaders were reluctant to resist the call to arms in the face of the anti-socialist laws and fears of massive repression.

While radicals were disarmed and temporarily silenced by the SPD's failure to implement an anti-war strategy, it was left to pacifist organizations to continue to resist what James Shand has referred to as the 'chauvinistic power-psychosis' of Wilhelmine Germany and to rally support for international understanding and world peace.[2] Prominent among these organizations were the German Peace Society, the National Women's Committee for a Lasting Peace and the New Fatherland League.[3]

The German Peace Society (*Deutsche Friedensgesellschaft*) was founded in 1892 by Alfred Fried and Bertha von Suttner, both of whom were Austrians (the Austrian Peace Society had been formed the year before), and it constituted the major focus of German pacifism prior to 1914. The society had been established by 'bourgeois pacifists' who were neither radicals rejecting the nation-state nor religious non-conformists. Its basic middle-class, liberal stance was that the European powers must coexist together in peace and harmony. In 1898, the magazine *Die Friedenswarte* (Peace Watchtower), which was sometimes printed in Switzerland and which is still published sporadically to this day, was published for the first time. The German Peace Society, which eventually produced its own journal, *Völker-Friede*, boasted a number of distinguished members, notably its co-founders, Fried and Suttner (both of whom would receive the Nobel Peace Prize; Suttner in 1905 and Fried in 1911); Walther Schücking, a law professor (who would later form part of the German Peace Delegation at Versailles in 1919); and Ludwig Quidde, a scholar and politician. Yet the Society remained a fringe organization, largely academic by nature and devoid of any radical or socialist pretensions. At its height it never managed to attract more than 10,000 members, although it had established a network of local branches throughout the country. Occasionally it had been attacked by militarist and Pan-German groups for being 'defeatist', but generally the authorities and the population at large remained indifferent to its activities.

This situation changed once hostilities commenced in 1914. The German government's attitude to the peace movement was no different from that of other governments embroiled in the conflict; it looked on dissenters of all kinds as a threat to national solidarity in times of 'total war'. In Germany, however, because all matters affecting public order and national security passed from civilian control into military hands, it could hardly be expected that military officials would sympathize with the peace movement. Moreover, under the Prussian Law on the State of Siege and the Bavarian

State-of-War Law, the military were armed with powers to intervene in areas such as press censorship, the holding of meetings and the banning of organizations deemed to pose a threat to national security.

Interestingly enough, the military authorities did not immediately ban meetings or indeed the publications of the German Peace Society. Its journal, *Völker-Friede* continued to be published monthly, subject to the general terms of censorship that were imposed on all publications. Occasionally it appeared with a blank column and it was to avoid this form of censorship that Alfred Fried decided, at the end of 1914, to move to neutral Switzerland.[4] During the first months of the conflict the Peace Society generally adopted a low profile and refrained from criticizing Germany's role in the events leading up to war. It even distributed a pamphlet on the duty of all German civilians:

'Now that the question of war and peace is no longer an issue and our nation is threatened from all sides in a life-and-death struggle, every German must fulfil his duty to the Fatherland regardless of whether or not he believes in peace....'[5]

While it remained concerned not to isolate its members from the rest of society, the Peace Society generally stuck to its pacifist principles and hoped that the fighting would end quickly.[6] For its part, the military authorities continued to monitor the activities of the Peace Society and its leaders but were conscious that if they over-reacted they ran the risk of turning a fringe group into national martyrs.

As we shall see later in this chapter, the German women's movement as a whole became more nationalistic during the First World War (although not necessarily more right wing). Indeed, the growth of nationalist sentiment in the country at large had developed alongside the campaigns of the Navy League some four years before the outbreak of hostilities. However, a small and beleaguered faction of radical feminists continued to resist this growing nationalism in order to uphold their pacifist ideals. Anita Augspurg and Lida Gustava Heymann, the leaders of the Women's Suffrage League (*Frauenstimmrechtsbund*), had for a number of years advocated international reconciliation and campaigned against the insidious militarism in German society. These women helped to form the International Woman Suffrage Alliance, established in Berlin in 1904. Augspurg became its first Vice-President, and Käthe Schirmacher its first Assistant Secretary. Other feminists such as Minna Cauer, Anna Lindemann, Else Lüders, Frieda Radel and Lida Gustava Heymann played a prominent role in the Alliance. However, in 1909, tensions among its members over the competing claims of work for female emancipation and campaigns for peace surfaced when Augspurg and Heymann suddenly resigned, claiming that the International Alliance had allowed itself to be 'carried along in the wake of the warlike character of male politics, and was governed by the petty fear that a stand for pacifism might damage the prospects for female suffrage'.[7] (In fact when war did break out, Augspurg and Heymann believed that it was even more imperative that women should get the vote, and so be in a position to advance peace and other causes dear to them.) To contemporary European and American suffragists, who had looked upon the German suffrage movement and its leaders as inspiring and dynamic, this indictment of Alliance activities by two leading members represented a major blow.

Augspurg and Heymann were articulating a dilemma that would cause a great deal of initial confusion for pacifist and feminist groups when war was declared in 1914. For example, Helene Stöcker of the League for the Protection of Mothers (*Bund für Mutterschutz*) shared pacifist beliefs, in love and understanding yet as a radical feminist she was unable to overcome the influence of the social Darwinist right within her organization and prevent it from supporting the war effort. Nevertheless, Stöcker continued to denounce the war and militarism as destructive forms of male supremacy and urged women, the givers of life, to work for peace.[8] Individuals such as Frida Perlen and Mathilde Plank, the Suffrage League's leaders in Stuttgart, had petitioned the Kaiser requesting him to halt the war. Others like Lida Gustava Heymann, had visited the Bavarian War Ministry and called on the minister to telegraph the Tsar to end the conflict. Such women were invariably received with courtesy but ignored as misguided fanatics. The issue of war and peace polarized many in the peace and suffrage movements. Not surprisingly, a large number of resignations from the Women's Suffrage League followed. Frieda Radel, the leader of the relatively powerful Hamburg Branch, caused uproar when she resigned in September 1914 to support the war effort.

The Women's Suffrage League had approximately 2,000 members when the conflict began and many branches were only subsequently preserved through the social work they undertook – not because of their pacifist stance. Writing after the war Lida Gustava Heymann claimed that had it not been for its work in sending supplies to prisoners of war and contacting the relatives of internees, etc., the league would have been decimated.[9] Even so, a minority of radical pacifists repudiated nationalism and refused to support the war by continuing to undertake charitable work. At the other extreme, some branches of the league distanced themselves from the peace movement entirely. In 1916 in Nuremberg, for example, the city authorities inspected the membership list of the Suffrage League and reported to the War Ministry that its members had no contacts with the peace movement and that there was 'no cause for any action to be taken'.[10]

However, by the beginning of 1915, the peace movement in general began to mobilize against a protracted European war. One example of a more activist approach was the founding in Berlin of the *Bund Neues Vaterland* (New Fatherland League) in the autumn of 1914. The league represented a cross-section of society (including men and women like Ludwig Quidde and Helene Stöcker), from traditional pacifists to liberal and socialist politicians, and its founding programme talked obliquely of breaking 'radically from the existing system' – although it never specified how it would achieve this break.[11] The defining moment for both the feminists and the pacifist movements in Germany was the conference held at The Hague in April 1915.

The Hague Congress was attended by 224 English women, 49 American women led by the president of the Congress, Jane Addams, 1,700 women from Holland and numerous representatives from all over the world. Anita Augspurg led a German delegation that was restricted to only four by a hostile Foreign Office. The women at The Hague agreed not to discuss the question of responsibility but instead called for a swift end to the war and a peace of understanding without annexations. They also drew up a number of resolutions on the peace settlement that included the respect for the rights of national minorities, the compulsory arbitration of international disputes, democratic control of foreign policies, equal political rights for women, universal disarmament and freedom of the seas. Out of the Congress emerged the Central Organization for a Durable Peace, an international peace association committed to the Hague principles.[12]

Reaction in Germany to the Congress was mixed. The authorities tried to prevent some women from going, while the Federation of German Women's Associations (*Bund Deutscher Frauenvereine* – BDF) condemned it as 'incompatible with the patriotic and national duty of all German women' and banned Augspurg and Heymann from the Federation. Attempts by pacifists to arrange a second congress foundered. At a national level, Augspurg and her delegates returned to Germany and immediately set up the German Women's Committee for a Lasting Peace (*Deutscher Frauenausschuss für einen dauenden Frieden*) which attempted to apply the Hague principles to the internal war-aims controversy. The organization, which was never large, drew most of its support from the Suffrage League and remained active until the end of the war. It consisted of small groups of women who formed themselves into discussion groups at a local level. It had no constitution and possessed no official membership lists. It survived on donations instead of subscriptions. Its strongest areas of support appear to have been in Hamburg and Munich. The amorphous shape and nature of the organization made it extremely difficult for the authorities to dissolve it. The Committee (for a Lasting Peace) sent thousands of anti-war letters through the post to potential supporters. The authorities responded by placing all members' correspondence under surveillance. The Committee also distributed emotional propaganda leaflets. The following is one of the more colourful and was published in *Die Frauenbewegung*:

> Millions of women's hearts blaze up in wild grief.... Cannot the earth reeking with human blood, the flayed bodies and souls of millions of your husbands, betrothed, sons, the horrors that oppress your own sex... cannot all this inspire you to burning protest?.... The wheel of time is running with blood: you must seek to grasp it...[13]

The Committee's vehemence was echoed elsewhere. Pacifists as a whole employed sharply socialist, indeed, revolutionary tones in many of their leaflets and posters. In April 1915 an anonymous leaflet was distributed in Munich and aimed specifically 'at the women of the working people':

> Much has been made of a great brother and sisterhood between the high and the low, of a citizens' truce (*Burgfrieden*) between the rich and the poor. Now, the citizens' truce can be seen in the way the entrepreneur keeps your wages down, the way the speculators and dealers raise prices, the landlord tries to throw you on the streets. The state treats you in a niggardly fashion – bourgeois welfare care cooks you beggars soups and urges you to ration... 'Who endangers the well-being of the Fatherland?' The Fatherland is endangered by all those that become wealthy out of the needs of the masses and become masters through the oppression of others. *The working people of all countries are a brotherhood.* Only the united will of the people can put an end to the murder. *Socialism alone offers the future freedom for humanity!* Down with capitalism!... Down with war![14]

Although the fiercely agitational stance of the example above may be an exception rather than the rule, there was an intellectual overlap between pacifist and socialist objections to the war. Rosa Luxemburg, for example, spent almost the entire war behind bars for her beliefs. In Stuttgart, Clara Zetkin, editor of *Die Gleichheit* (equality) and Luise Zietz who had been one of the few members of the SPD leadership to oppose the *Burgfrieden*, together with the Spartacus League under the leadership of Luxemburg and Liebknecht, had campaigned under the banner 'Down with the war!'. However, it is important to make a distinction between the pacifists and the radical socialists like Zetkin and Zietz who placed more emphasis on the political transformation of society rather than on gender or pacifist issues. It is a distinction that the imperial authorities wilfully failed to recognize. By the autumn of 1915 the tolerance of the Prussian and Bavarian War Ministries and their Deputy General Commanders was exhausted, and they, in turn, responded by waging an unrelenting campaign that continued until 1918 against the various pacifist organizations and their leaders.

The military censors were concerned first of all that 'defeatist' literature should not be published in Germany. Their concern came to a head in the summer of 1915 when *Bund Neues Vaterland* published its provocative rejoinder to the annexationist petitions of the Six Economic Organizations (see Chapter 3). But the German Peace Society also ran into difficulties. In Munich where Dr Ludwig Quidde resided, the meetings of the Society were attended by no more than 35 to 55 people, half of them 'ladies'. The Peace Society opposed any policy of annexation, and continued to press for a peace that would allow peoples to live together. In July 1915, Quidde set out the official *Bund* position in a pamphlet entitled 'Shall We Annex?' which was distributed to sympathetic politicians and officials. The Berlin police raided the Alliance headquarters and seized remaining leaflets by order of the military. Quidde then prepared a lengthier pamphlet on 'Real Guarantees for a Lasting Peace' and 32,000 copies were printed privately in Munich but swiftly confiscated by the Bavarian military before no more than a few hundred copies had been distributed. In the same month, the Independent Religious Society of Hamburg was refused permission to hold meetings because it had circulated a pamphlet entitled 'War, the Fatherland, and Human Worth'. In June, *Vorwärts* opposed the annexationist plans of the King of Bavaria and quoted approvingly the Archbishop of Cologne's prayers for peace. In August, the press were prevented from mentioning the criminal procedures instituted against pacifists in Stuttgart for distributing a manifesto advocating peace.[15] These incidents persuaded the War Ministries in Berlin and Munich to orchestrate a campaign against the peace movement. Accordingly, in November 1915 two detailed reports were sent to their respective Deputy General Commanders, describing the activities of the various pacifist groups with recommendations for dealing with them.

The Prussian report conceded from the outset that the peace movement (referred to as 'a world brotherhood peace movement made up of a vanishing world bourgeoisie') was unlikely to penetrate sections of the population or influence public opinion. Pacifists were dismissed as 'hazy idealists' seeking international fame. Nevertheless, a failure on the part of the authorities to condemn pacifism and clamp down on its leaders would be construed as a sign of weakness by enemy and neutral countries. It was also vital that soldiers at the front should be kept immune from the blandishments of pacifist propaganda. (See Figure 21.)

The Prussian War Ministry was convinced that the activity of these tiny pacifist organizations 'borders on treason, since it is calculated to strengthen the enemy's will to resist at the cost of weakening our own firm, unwavering

Figure 21 A *Simplicissimus* cartoon attacking German pacifists: 'Once again they tried to bury the hatchet of war in the barrel of ink. Unfortunately it was too big on this occasion.' 23 November 1915.

determination to carry on the war.' However, caution was urged and legal redress under article 89 of the Penal Law Code was to be avoided as successful prosecutions 'would draw unwanted attention to the peace movement from home and abroad.' Moreover the emergency powers vested in the Deputy General Commanders under the Law on the State of Siege were sufficient to stifle the peace movement. Controlling meetings, forbidding pacifist representatives from travelling abroad together, and intensifying mail surveillance were recommended as adequate measures. The report ended unambiguously: 'The publication and spreading of pacifist articles and leaflets must not be tolerated. We must prevent them being sent abroad and to the front. Written material of this kind, including private letters which express the desire for international pacifist aims are to be confiscated.'[16]

The Bavarian War Ministry was particularly concerned that the women's movement was being infiltrated by pacifist ideas. Indeed a third of its report was devoted to the role of women in the peace movement. The ministry claimed that the war demanded 'a *Burgfriede* between the sexes' and a 'cessation of all feminist activity . . . as a prerequisite of public security'. The suffrage organizations were singled out, in particular the Suffrage League in Munich, by far the most radical centre of pacifism within the League. The Bavarian

War Ministry claimed that the 'patriotically-minded' part of the women's movement could easily lose supporters to left-wing internationalist groups of feminists, 'over whose activities it has no control.'[17]

For the most part the authorities acted on these guidelines and concentrated on preventative measures and on truncating the means of communications while at the same time condemning pacifist organizations as 'defeatist' and their members as misguided zealots. But whereas in Britain the authorities could generally rely upon the public (and particularly the working class) to shame individuals and disrupt peace meetings, in Germany the authorities had to take a more interventionist role. The explanation for this can be traced to the nature of the war aims debate in Germany (see Chapter 3). On the one hand the government was claiming a justified war of self-defence, yet on the other, it was implementing an annexationist military policy. The arguments of the peace movement exposed these contradictions and thus threatened the precarious 'political truce' that had been put in place at the beginning of the war. The authorities wrongly identified pacifism with weakness. It was a familiar line of reasoning that hardly changed during the course of the war. The government was committed to final victory that could not be compromised by delusions of a just, negotiated, peace. The 'will to hold-out' (*Wille zum Durchhalten*) was therefore fundamental to the war effort and could not be seen to weaken. If the authorities allowed pacifist agitation to continue unchecked, a misleading picture would emerge (so it was argued) of a lack of confidence and of internal division. Therefore stringent measures were taken against the peace movement and its leaders.

These measures were implemented immediately they were proposed in November 1915. The Berlin branch of the Peace Society was forbidden to hold public meetings and even private ones of its members. Under an emergency decree of 31 July 1914, the Berlin military authorities stipulated that all public meetings required a permit from the police authorities at least 48 hours before a meeting was to take place. This draconian proclamation (which was not always enforced) allowed the police to ban speeches or meetings whenever they liked.[18] The society's monthly journal, *Der Völker-Friede*, was also banned in November and the impact of harrassment was shown in the same month, when its annual general meeting in Leipzig was attended by only 13 branches. Undaunted, the outspoken president of the society, Ludwig Quidde, stated that as the Pan-German associations were clamouring for annexations, the Peace Society could not remain silent. The meeting passed a general resolution condemning all annexations 'inside Europe' and demanded a peace settlement that guaranteed the 'national interests of the German people'. In Munich, the Bavarian War Ministry forbade communication between members, ordered Quidde to cease agitating for the pacifist cause, and finally forced him (even though he was a member of the Bavarian Landtag) to hand over the Society's membership lists – with the result that its branches and members fell by almost 50 per cent.[19]

These harsh restrictions were not limited to the German Peace Society, but to all pacifist organizations. *Bund Neues Vaterland*, for example had its branch offices regularly searched and its leaders harrassed. It was forbidden to distribute its publications to both members and non-members – nor was it allowed to inform them of this persecution. In February 1916 *Bund Neues Vaterland* was virtually paralysed when it was forbidden to promote its aims for the duration of the war. As a result, little is heard of the Bund until the autumn of 1918 when it suddenly reappeared and engaged in the wider debate about the future of Germany.

On 23 November 1915 Lida Gustava Heymann was banned from making public speeches and by April 1916 the Suffrage League in Munich was closed down. Heymann, Anita Augspur and Margarete Selenka (a member of the *Bund für Mutterschutz*) were forbidden to propagandize the pacifist cause or to correspond with and visit other countries. Members of the National Women's Committee for a Lasting Peace were also banned from holding meetings in public and *Die Frauenbewegung* could no longer be printed in Germany. The Committee responded by changing tactics and sending thousands of anti-war letters through the post, whereupon all members' correspondence was placed under surveillance. The authorities were particularly concerned that the anti-war propaganda might influence women teachers, who were seen as a mainstay of the generally conservative women's movement. For example, in March 1916, the Prussian War Ministry wrote to the Ministry of the Interior expressing concern that teachers in schools were for 'pedagogic reasons', attempting to counteract hatred between nations 'by concentrating on future reconciliation'.[20] The National Women's Committee had, for some time, campaigned against the excessive militarism in schools which finally illicited a reproach from the educational authorities in Bavaria warning schoolmistresses not to meddle with pacifism. Maria Zehetmaier, a school teacher in Munich who tried to publish an article in the *Berliner Lokalanzeiger* in October 1916, was removed from her job by the Ministry for Culture specifically for spreading 'pacifist literature'.[21] Radical pacifists like Frau Dr Hoesch-Ernst printed their speeches in Switzerland before having them distributed in Bavaria. In a typical document entitled 'Patriotismus und Patriotitis' (implying that patriotism was an 'illness'), Hoesch-Ernst demanded the setting-up of secret printing works on the Russian model and increasing the tempo of women's agitation to match the riots taking place in Berlin. This last demand was rejected by her followers on the grounds that 'the South German population is not so inclined to resort to violence'.[22]

In December 1915, Lida Gustava Heymann was stopped from crossing the border into Holland, even though her passport and documents were in order. She complained directly to the Deputy Commanding General about her treatment in dismissively imperious terms: 'As an educated woman it goes against the grain for me to get into arguments with uneducated official in wartime'.[23] In January 1916, the police authorities in Munich discovered and confiscated feminist–pacifist leaflets that were being distributed in the poorest areas of the city:

> From women to women! We no longer want to watch our husbands and sons being slaughtered! We no longer wish to put up with the fathers of our children having to soil their hands with the blood of their brothers in the human race! We demand peace! Peace for everyone![24]

The police also hauled in a poster campaign that urged women (and girls) to 'Wake up! Do not weep at home! We want peace!'. Seized posters, pamphlets and leaflets were sent to the Bavarian War Ministry together with a synopsis of the material. Lida Gustava Heymann was clearly suspected by the police of being behind these campaigns and eventually in February 1917 Heymann was officially expelled from Bavaria. According to her memoirs, Heymann continued successfully to conceal both her illegal activities and her whereabouts from the authorities. These censorship measures, which were extended to the rest of Germany, were not lifted until October 1918. As late as November 1918, the Hamburg police still refused to allow Heymann to address a public meeting.[25]

In the course of 1916 the military authorities succeeded in silencing the peace movement by a combination of imprisonment, censorship and surveillance. In Berlin several women were put on trial and fined because they had circulated a message from the Archbishop of Canterbury which condemned war in general and called for peace.[26] In a detailed report on the state of morale in the army and in the home front, the Bavarian War Ministry singled out pacifist groups as a cause for concern, particularly the 'lively' propaganda emanating from the International Women's Committee for a Lasting Peace in Amsterdam (referred to as 'subversive, stateless, agitators with no conscience'). Berlin, Hamburg, Breslau, Munich and Stuttgart were identified as the main strongholds of pacifist agitation for 'peace at any price'. The report noted that peace propaganda was no longer confined to small groups of misguided idealists; rather the cry for 'bread and peace' could now be heard in larger gatherings 'in which mainly women took part'. Citing Munich as a centre 'where pacificism seems to have taken hold', women 'of moderate opinion' were, according to the report, targeted by activists for special attention. The combination of peace demonstrations and food riots represented a volatile mixture and posed a real threat to the *Burgfrieden*. The Bavarian War Ministry was especially concerned at the manner in which disturbances were exaggerated in the foreign press. One report emanating from Lyons Radio Telegram suggested that in Berlin serious disturbances had recently taken place in which 200 demonstrators had been killed or wounded by marauding troops. Not only did exaggerated rumours undermine morale at home but they also provided succour to the enemy. For these reasons the Bavarian War Ministry confirmed that the military authorities should maintain their uncompromising suppression of the organized pacifist movement.[27]

Despite the generally successful government crackdown on pacifism, activists like Ludwig Quidde, Walther Schücking, Anita Augspurg and Lida Gustava Heymann continued their illegal activities. They held meetings and issued pamphlets notwithstanding the censorship. In spite of the surveillance, pacifists circulated their literature secretly, sending them under cover to addresses where there was less danger of detection. Quidde, for example, is said to have deceived the censor and distributed 14,000 copies of his pamphlet 'Real Guarantees for a Lasting Peace' by dispatching it as 'privately printed'. Quidde's method was to only send banned literature (by post) to those that had ordered it. In other words, he was preaching to the converted – or at least, the sympathetic.[28] Quidde continued to argue, counter to the government's official stance, that tolerance shown to pacifists would be seen abroad as a sign of strength, not weakness. It would also allow the government to distance itself from the aggressive policy of the annexationists. However, the peace movement, which was never more than a fringe phenomenon, could not flourish in an underground form and tended to fade from the scene.

Annexationists, on the other hand, were not considered to represent a threat to public order and continued their activities unencumbered by censorship or threat of arrest. On 1 August 1916, the National Committees for a Victorious and Honourable Peace openly breached censorship restrictions on the discussion of war aims and held meetings in numerous German cities in which speakers openly espoused support for a *Siegfrieden* ('peace through victory').[29] In the summer of 1916 prominent pacifists, such as Quidde, Eduard Bernstein, Helen Stöcker and Gustav Landauer, formed the *Zentralstelle Völkerrechts* (Central Office for Peoples' Justice). It set out a half-hearted manifesto opposed to peace with annexations and called for international disarmament. Its membership remained small but it did petition the Reichstag. In contrast with its attitude to the Peace Society, the military allowed the *Zentralstelle* to continue its activities, which remained modest and ineffectual.

With the exception of the *Zentralstelle*, the authorities continued to view all pacifist activity during the war with extreme suspicion. Surveillance and censorship applied also to film production. In 1915, for example, the distinguished film director Richard Oswald produced *Das Eiserne Kreuz* (The Iron Cross). The film features two families, one German, one Belgian, who had been friends before the war. The sons had been drafted into the respective armies and were forced to confront each other. The film concludes with the question: 'Where will all this suffering end?' The military authorities seized the film on release and all copies were destroyed. Quite clearly, the pacifist tendencies in the film, which were deemed detrimental to the public interest, precipitated such action.[30]

As late as 1 January 1918 the High Command (OHL) were still insisting that the military commanders be as vigilant as ever in preventing pacifist literature from being sold in book shops or circulated for propaganda purposes. The military commanders were reminded by the Minister of War, General von Stein, of the guidelines laid down in 1915 and the imperative need to counter propaganda proposing 'peace at any price'. According to Stein, it was the 'ultimate duty' of all commanders to impose the most 'ruthless and rigorous measures' against pacifists agitators.[31] In July 1918 the OHL once again drew the Deputy General Commander's attention to the 'mischievous' activities of the German Peace Society. Together with the Central Office for Peoples' Justice, it had been planning a series of campaign meetings to promote a 'compromise' peace on the basis of the Reichstag's Peace Resolution of 19 July 1917 (more will be said about this in the next chapter). The military commanders were instructed to prevent all such meetings taking place.[32]

Despite the guidelines laid down by the War Ministries and the OHL the Deputy General Commanders were not consistent in the way they approached the peace movement and individual organizations. By and large they reacted by taking a sledgehammer to crack a nut. The measures generally stopped short of arrest and imprisonment as they were determined not to set up pacifist leaders as martyrs. Nevertheless, it was gross over-reaction that typified the ignorance and lack of understanding of the military authorities concerning civilian affairs. James Shand has argued that because of the latitude left to the commanders, the peace movement confronted not a solid wall of governmental determination but rather 'a shifting line of fluctuating impulses'.[33] Prussia and Bavaria imposed a rigid regime of suppression and prohibition, whereas in Württemberg, a more tolerant attitude prevailed. Even when Bethmann Hollweg partially lifted the ban on the discussion of Germany's war aims towards the end of 1916, the peace movement was still largely precluded from taking part in the truncated debate. The authorities took the line that the insignificant pacifist organizations would damage morale in Germany and provide comfort to the enemy. State officials increasingly failed to differentiate between legitimate pacifist concern and revolutionary agitation – or outright defeatism.[34] Until the formation of the Prince Max von Baden's cabinet in October 1918, when pacifists reappeared (for a brief time) to claim the moral highground for post-war reconstruction, the peace movement remained muzzled and emasculated – a symbol of repression in total war. By the time pacifists were allowed to resurface, events in Russia had shifted the political agenda away from war aims to a Marxist challenge to democracy and oligarchy. In an ironic twist, as restrictions and censorship were lifted, the beleaguered military authorities came to look on the pacifists as a moderating influence against revolutionary socialism.

FEMINIST FERMENT AND THE WOMENS MOVEMENT

The first point to be made is that the bourgeois women's movement did not represent a radical challenge to the *status quo*.[35] By and large the women's movement became even more nationalistic as the war progressed. When discussing the women's movement and the question of female suffrage it is necessary to make a distinction between the moderate and politically nonpartisan main umbrella organization, the Federation of German Women's Associations (*Bund Deutscher Frauenvereine*, hereafter BDF), that claimed authority to represent the women's movement, and individual suffrage organizations that acted as lobbyists for the cause of 'votes for women'. Whereas the suffrage organizations looked to participation and service to secure their goal of female emancipation in the short term, the BDF believed that support for the war effort would guarantee concessions – including, it was hoped, the granting of female suffrage – when the war was over. At the other end of the political spectrum, radical feminist socialists such as Clara Zetkin and Luise Zeitz, who had opposed the *Burgfrieden*, advocated a more assertive and egalitarian role for women but, more importantly, were deeply embroiled in the factional and ideological conflicts within the German Social Democratic movement. Political activists, like Zetkin and Zeitz, generally adopted the position that women's liberation and socialism went hand-in-hand and therefore women were better served fighting alongside men in the class struggle.

On the eve of war there were three rival female suffrage societies: the Suffrage Union (*Frauenstimmrecht*) and two breakaway factions – the German Alliance for Women's Suffrage (*Deutsche Vereinigung für Frauenstimmrecht*) and the German Women's Suffrage League (*Deutscher Frauenstimmrechtsbund*) led by Augspurg, Heymann and Cauer. Since the foundation of the Suffrage Union, the feminist movement had polarized on the issue of the Union's famous Section 3, which had committed it to fighting for 'universal, equal, direct and secret active and passive suffrage' for both sexes.³⁶ Feminists who were uneasy with the Unions's commitment to universal suffrage founded the The Alliance in 1911 and campaigned for women's suffrage on the same terms as men had the vote – or would have in the future. In December 1912 a number of leading radicals within the Union executive committee, including Anita Augspurg, its founder-President, resigned and formed the Suffrage League on a rigid adherence to universal suffrage and the moral reform concepts that had motivated the suffrage movement some 10 years earlier.³⁷ Augspurg and Heymann's involvement with the peace movement, once war was declared, not only led to the defection of many of their former supporters but also persuaded the Union and the Alliance to join forces in March 1916, finally discarding Section 3 and campaigning for limited suffrage. For the remaining part of the war the internal battles within the women's suffrage movement were largely acted out at a local level.

The question of votes for women had never been straightforward, particularly in a political system as complex as Wilhelmine Germany's. The suffrage movement, which had begun with such high expectations at the turn of the century, was in disarray on the eve of the First World War. Despite a decade of pressure the suffragists had little to show by way of concrete reforms.³⁸ Richard Evans has referred to 'tactical paralysis and internal dissension' as the two chief characteristics of the female suffrage movement in Germany in the last years of peace.³⁹ Direct agitation for the vote by suffragists had been largely rejected in the years leading up to the outbreak of war in favour of the indirect route of participatory engagement within local government and the main political parties. Nevertheless, the granting of female suffrage was not an entirely fanciful notion – and many Germans genuinely believed that the war would act as a catalyst for radical political change. For example, Eduard David, the SPD Deputy, had told Helene Stöcker on 30 August 1914 that the war would bring about universal suffrage in Prussia at the very least.⁴⁰

However, the assertion made by some historians that the introduction of women's suffrage in Germany can be understood as a reward for female participation in the war has now been largely rejected.⁴¹ Typical of the non-critical and slightly patronizing approach that underpinned writing on feminist issues for so long is the following, written by a British historian in the early 1970s:

> war was creating in Germany a feminine revolution at least as spectacular as that in Britain or France. The old domestic picture of the *Hausfrau* placidly passing the time gossiping with friends to the accompaniment of clicking knitting-needles was no longer typical. She knitted still when she had time, though now for strict reasons of economy rather than womanly

habit.... But many other changes were occurring. With their husbands at the front, and spending their days at work, women were becoming more self-reliant, less apt to look on the peacetime breadwinner with the former awe. They were having to cope with the problems of daily living– food queues, scarcities and high prices – and making decisions in a way that they had never done before. All this was breeding the beginnings of a sense of independence. And though there was no organized campaign for women's suffrage in Germany, the National Council of Women of Germany, with its 600,000 members, was showing signs of interest in the women's vote.[42]

There was a rise in the number of women employed in wartime industry and the nature of women's work did eventually change during the war. But the axiomatic conclusion that because of their participation in the war, women found recognition and reward by being granted equal political rights can no longer be sustained. Recent research draws attention to the absence of any significant wartime debate on suffrage, and to the reluctance of the imperial authorities to introduce women's suffrage in the last days of the Second Reich.[43]

As far as the women's movement (i.e., organized womanhood) was concerned it was dominated by the BDF. In 1912 the BDF boasted that it represented 'half a million German women'.[44] Women's social-welfare organizations formed the backbone of the movement and by 1914 many of its stated objectives had been achieved; notably the opening of German universities to women and the admission of women to targeted professions such as secondary-school teaching and medicine. Under the leadership of its chairwoman, Gertrude Bäumer, the BDF's attitude to female suffrage was ambivalent, to say the least. (Radical feminists claimed that it was openly hostile.) Although the BDF was non-partisan, it included groups that spanned the political spectrum. On the left were radical groups affiliated to the *Verband Fortschrittlicher Frauenvereine* (League of Progressive Women's Associations) which advocated women's suffrage. Bäumer argued that the inclusion of suffrage groups within the BDF proved that the women's movement supported political equality for women. On the other hand, the BDF accommodated within its ranks the right-wing German-Evangelical Women's League (*Deutsch-Evangelischer Frauenbund* – DEF), which had continued to oppose the advance of radical feminism since it was founded in 1899 under Pastor Weber, the leader of the Morality Associations. The DEF rejected the unrestricted franchise for women and, instead, pressed for 'responsible cooperation' with men in the sphere of public affairs. By joining the BDF, it hoped to infuse the umbrella organization with its uniquely religious outlook which encouraged a 'religious-ethical renewal' while at the same time advocating access for women to higher education and expanded occupational training.[45] Furthermore, affiliated to the BDF were a number of temperance societies, some of whom were not interested in the emancipation of women, and others, such as the Ladies Aid (*Frauenhilfe*), who were vehemently opposed to it. Under Bäumer's leadership and her desperate attempts to retain the support of the evangelicals, the BDF consciously abandoned social and political radicalism.

The shift towards conservatism had, in fact, begun well before 1914. In 1907, the BDF had refused to join the call from international women's organizations (including the International Council of Women) and demonstrate for 'world peace', arguing that it did not wish Germany to disarm. The BDF had always been staunchly nationalistic, indeed, it was one of the strongest supporters of the Tirpitz naval expansion programme and of German foreign policy in general. Since she had taken over the presidency of the BDF in 1910, Bäumer had steered the association towards conservative policies and along nationalistic lines. Despite the fact that the BDF was never a truly homogeneous organization, being made up of numerous affiliated groups with sectional interests, the government, nevertheless, found it convenient to consult its leadership on the grounds that it was the 'mouthpiece of German womanhood'. By the outbreak of war, not only had the BDF successfully integrated into the mainstream of the political system but, moreover, it was becoming increasingly conservative. The SPD's women's magazine *Die Gleichheit* noted as early as 1910, 'bourgeois feminism is on the march towards the right'.[46] The BDF continued to march in this direction for the duration of the war at the expense of any social critique of the prevailing political structure. The war would accelerate this process as the BDF's member associations cooperated even more formally with the authorities.

Thus when war came the BDF was one of the government's strongest supporters. It abandoned all question of challenging the Wilhelrmine political system, preferring, instead, to encourage women to adopt conventional and stereotypical roles. The role assigned to women in Germany in the first year of the war emphasizes the stereotyping that took place in all belligerent states. Women were initially seen as 'comforters' – the bedrock of the home front. In her appeal on 2 August 1914, Queen Marie Therese of Bavaria summed up the social paradigm of the role expected of women in total war:

> Of you, who are not granted the privilege of defending the dignity of the Fatherland with blood and life, I ask most fervently that you contribute with all your strength to easing the suffering of every brave man wounded by the enemy bullet or thrown ailing to the ground by the hardships

of war. Like my daughters Hildegard, Helmtrude and Gundelinde, put yourselves...at the service of the Red Cross..., As in 1870–71, Bavaria's women and virgins will fulfill their patriotic duty, this I know, for such service of women is pleasing to God.[47]

Even before mobilization had been introduced, on 31 July 1914, the BDF leadership had concluded its own *Burgfrieden* by calling on all affiliated associations to form the National Women's Service (*Nationaler Frauendienst*). Supported by the Prussian Ministry of the Interior, the National Women's Service was very much the brainchild of Gertrud Bäumer and was intended to assist over-stretched and under-resourced municipal authorities by taking responsibility for looking after 'war families', food provision, and job placement for women. They also functioned as counselling centres in matters of welfare. To this end, the BDF had urged all women's associations to contact the Patriotic Women's Associations (*Vaterländische Frauendienst*), which was a support organization of the Red Cross providing war welfare.[48] When in January 1917, the National Central Women's Service of Germany (*Deutsche Zentrale des Nationalen Frauendienstes*) was formed, there were sixty local organizations dispensing war welfare that ranged from setting up soup kitchens to improvised hospitals for the homeless and wounded.

Writing in the *Jahrbuch der Frauenbewegung* for 1916, Gertrud Bäumer outlined what she believed this new formal relationship with the state would achieve – and what the benefits for women were:

> Women have been recruited to help run various departments of government, such as the Military Office, the Food and Clothing departments etc. To some extent, this constitutes the achievement of the demands of liberalism with reference to the position of our women in government. Women are to come into contact with the State and with legislation; civic consciousness of women is to be awakened, trained and educated.... Women.... will still bring their talents and interests to bear in the interests of the Fatherland even in times of peace; that is the desire of many women, that has been said from the women's point of view. Now it is also being said from the point of view of the State itself.[49]

The idea of a vocational 'Women's Year of Service' had been proposed before the war as a means of educating young women in the techniques of social work and the German virtues of obedience and duty. BDF leaders such as Bäumer believed that service to the community in times of war provided an opportunity to prove to the state the value of the services that women offered. The modified scheme of the National Women's Service not only formalized the new relationship of the women's movement to the state but was seen by Bäumer (and others) as a prerequisite for the extension of women's rights and eventually concessions when the war was over. This school of feminism dominated BDF strategy and was grounded in gender difference, as opposed to equal-rights feminism. Bäumer argued that because women and men were inherently different, a just society required a reappraisal of maternal and patriarchal responsibilities that allowed women to assume an increased public role.

Writing after the war, Gertrud Bäumer referred to the 'liberating' aspect that resulted from this partnership with the state in which, for the first time, women were given responsibilities. Bäumer described in almost mystical terms the manner in which this experience of 'service to the Fatherland' transcended the 'individualistic' gains that women had traditionally sought through suffrage:

> A different order than the militaristic, technical one of the nineteenth century prevailed and we felt an enormous feeling of liberation. An order not of achievement and reward, risk and profit, effort and advantage, but of life and death, blood and strength, effort as such, absolute, in every case. This is what we experienced then: being lifted into a totally different order, one that opposed the individualistic principle of achievement. It was, in a special form, the decisive *antithesis* of the industrial-capitalist way of life. Public feeling was completely transformed, taken off the hinges of rational connections and transported up to the world of values such as: homeland, soil, family, camaraderie. New destinies awoke new feelings, or ancient ones that were frozen and faded.[50]

James Gerard, the American Ambassador, commented favourably on the work undertaken by the National Women's Service:

> But perhaps the most noteworthy was the National Frauendienst, or Service for Women, organized the first day of the war. The relief given by the State to the wives and children of soldiers was distributed from stations in Berlin, and in the neighbourhood of each of these stations the Frauendienst established an office where women were always in attendance, ready to give help and advice to the soldiers' wives. There were card indexes of all the people within the district and of their needs. At the time I left Germany I believe that there were upwards of 7,000 women engaged in Berlin in social service, in instructing the women in the new art of cooking without milk, eggs, or fat, and seeing to it that the children had their fair share of milk. It is due to the efforts of these social workers that the rate of infant mortality in Berlin decreased during the war.[51]

It was precisely this type of charitable work that radical pacifist women objected to on the grounds that it was supporting and perpetuating the war.

Dissenting Voices 161

In contrast to the BDF who believed that war had made the task of gaining votes for women a secondary issue and had therefore put aside its demands for political and social emancipation for the duration of the conflict, the Suffrage League continued to press for an extension of the franchise on the grounds that as women had been denied participation in the political process they could not be held responsible for the disaster brought about by this 'men's war'. Lida Gustava Heymann wrote that it is for this reason that 'the political emancipation of women requires a fundamental change in the nature of the State.'[52] The Bavarian War Ministry, which called for a cessation of all feminist activity during the war, argued that such demands were a means of achieving not the equality of women, 'but their superiority'.[53] The OHL even suggested closing down universities for fear that they would be filled with women who would take away the good jobs from the men and neglect their traditional roles as mothers and wives. Hindenburg, in particular, pressed for 'drastic measures' to be taken against 'female agitation' for equality.[54]

In their determination to crush feminist ferment, the military authorities occasionally made howling errors of judgement. An example was brought to the attention of Major Deutelmoser, Head of the War Press Office in Berlin. The influential *Büro für Sozialpolitik* expressed 'astonishment' that in Stuttgart the Deputy Commanding Generals had banned a conference of the Women's Social Democratic Union on 15 March 1916. The *Büro* suggested that the commanders had confused the branch with the more radical wing associated with Clara Zetkin, the editor of *Die Gleichheit*. The theme of the conference was 'Women's War Work' and the speaker, according to the report, 'was not Frau Zetkin but Frau Anna Bios'. The *Büro* pointed out indignantly:

> Frau Blos is not only liked and well regarded in moderate party circles and by the trade unions, but she has won friendly respect in the Stuttgart region for her honourable work in war aid. She has been nominated for honours and she has also belonged for many years to the Protestant Schools' Council. Moreover, Frau Blos was not making inflammatory statements – simply enlisting the support of the Social Democratic women's groups to participate in the war effort.

The *Büro* warned Deutelmoser to expect the far left to make political capital out of the 'unfortunate' incident.[55]

In spite of the worsening food situation and the economic deprivations suffered by the home front, the military authorities continued to stress the importance of the population's will to 'hold out'. Pacifist or suffrage groups who pressed for changes to the system were labelled as *'Reichsfeinde'* and their claims dismissed as 'defeatist'. In such an openly hostile atmosphere, the question of women's suffrage could not be discussed in public without accusations of 'unpatriotic behaviour' being levelled by the authorities at feminists who insisted on pressing their cause. The issue of female labour raised by the OHL was a highly sensitive one for feminists and non-feminists alike.[56] General Groener in the War Office had appointed Marie-Elisabeth Lüders, a younger member of the BDF leadership, and her colleague Agnes von Harnack as consultants in charge of female labour. Their task was to mobilize women into all areas of the workforce with the greatest possible speed. Lüders referred to this as 'the mobilization of women by women'.[57] The organizational plan submitted by the women in November 1916, after consultation with various women's representatives, identified the close connection between labour procurement and labour welfare. Lüders's report drew a distinction between willingness to work and an ability to work. Major obstacles to successful mobilization into the war economy were women's work and obligations within the family. Groener was sufficiently persuaded by these arguments to oppose the extension of obligatory auxiliary service to women, preferring instead to tailor social policy to the needs of women and families.[58]

In this context, the bourgeois women's movement was extremely reluctant to be seen making political capital of the new opportunities for employment that had opened up as a result of male mobilization. In a lecture for the Association of Women's Interests in January 1916, Elisabeth Altmann-Gottheiner summarized their position:

> That this was not so, is undoubtedly the greatest proof of the patriotic attitude and the deep feeling of responsibility on the part of the organized German women's movement. Every German woman who consciously considers these things is aware that she is, during the war, just the substitute for the man who held her position earlier, and she must step down as soon as he returns home and reclaims his position. In wartime, a truce [*Burgfrieden*] prevails between the sexes, and German women emphatically reject the desire to extract a possible 'war profit' from the war.[59]

The increase in female employment was, in fact, relatively small. The reality of the German war economy was that the conscription of male labour led to high unemployment among women particularly unskilled female labour. As far as the 'war profit' was concerned, the structural changes brought about by the war, as women took over skilled jobs, had no lasting effect beyond it. The migration of female labour out of domestic service and agriculture into areas of work previously designated 'men only' had already begun before 1914. The war accelerated this shift and the trend continued after 1918. However, many of the gains that were made during the war were quickly dissipated by the process of demobilization in 1918 and 1919, when soldiers returned from the front to reclaim their old white collar and industrial jobs.[60]

Thus, 'responsible', middle-class women, were not expected to profit from the wartime situation, despite their achievements in the war and the positive role many wished to play in post-war reconstruction. Although the women's movement renounced 'cheap triumphalism' in economic affairs, it maintained its patriotic support for the government's war aims. The women's movement rarely deviated from its staunchly pro-government position. Typical were propaganda posters such as Oswald Polte's 'For the Fatherland', showing a determined 'mother-figure' offering her jewels and gold for the war effort; and perhaps, most famous of all, the female munitions worker placing a grenade in the hand of a soldier beneath the words: 'German Women Work in the Home Army!' (see Figures 15(a) and 22).[61] To celebrate the contribution made by women to the war economy a 'Hymn to the German Women' was composed and circulated to all municipal, church and women's organizations. It openly glorified the role of women in the war effort. The first stanza reads as follows:

> Work, which up to now man
> did with strong hands,
> is now done by women,
> and so we want to praise them.
> Let it loudly sound in all areas
> the high song of the German Women;
> Hail to our Women!
> Hail to our German Women![62]

In early 1917, after President Wilson issued his Peace Note, the BDG rejected it out of hand – as it later repudiated the Armistice Terms (see Chapter 7). Hindenburg was so moved by the BDF's display of solidarity that he sent a telegram of thanks to Gertrud Bäumer: 'We German men bow down our heads before the German women in reverence'.[63]

In spite of the BDF's unwavering support, the government refused to grant political equality to women. By 1917, however, the longevity of the conflict, combined with the economic hardships, began to revive calls for political change. In his 'Easter Message', Kaiser Wilhelm promised the people that he would make political concessions and extend the franchise. The Kaiser's message seemed to bode well for the women's movement and meetings were held throughout the country on the question of female suffrage. Petitions were handed in to the Reichstag calling for votes for women. Although these petitions were discussed in the constitutional committee of the Reichstag in June 1917, the majority of the political parties declared their opposition: the

Figure 22 'Collect Combed-Out Women's Hair! Our Industry Needs it for Drive Belts.' This campaign in Magdeburg was organized by the German Red Cross and the poster designer, Jupp Wiertz, employed a crucifix-like image for the campaign – presumably to symbolize the sacrifice that was being made by women.

Conservatives and the Catholic Centre on principle, the National Liberals on the grounds that the time was not yet right. Only the socialists supported the women. It is revealing therefore that official opinion had changed little on the subject of female suffrage since the pre-war days.[64] Despite the sacrifices that women had made and in the light of their unquestioned contribution to the war effort, the political parties refused to support even modest reforms. Nevertheless, the stance of the BDF in calling for women's suffrage because of their achievements in the war eventually persuaded the German-Evangelical

Women's League to disaffiliate. It had always opposed women's suffrage and, from the BDF's point of view, retaining the Evangelicals was unlikely to change the traditional hostility of the majority of the parties to feminist emancipation.

The exigencies of war would not, in themselves, usher in political reform of the system and provide votes for women – although women's leaders affiliated to the BDF were bestowed semi-official status. It would take the wholesale dismantling of the Wilhelmine system to achieve the feminist goal of political equality. In November 1918, a parliamentary republic was proclaimed in Germany. The Weimar Republic, which was born out of turmoil and defeat, granted all women over the age of 21 the vote.[65]

Throughout the war, official propaganda disseminated carefully constructed positive images of the 'patriotic woman' – images which depicted women comforting families of soldiers at the front; working in soup kitchens for the homeless; or supplying ammunition for the armed forces. (See Figures 15(b) and 36.) These images, however, were in stark contrast to another side of women at war; namely, starving mothers in the vanguard of the food riots in the urban conurbations, pacifists calling for a negotiated peace without annexations and radical feminists demanding universal suffrage. In February 1917, for example, women and children took to the street in Altona and Hamburg demanding 'Food and Peace'. Such demonstrations, which were widespread, led to serious riots.[66] The actions of such women did not always spring from new politicized notions of 'class war'. Often they were undertaken reluctantly as acts of desperation in the struggle for survival. In the industrial conurbations of Upper Silesia women demonstrated against food shortages and when their demands were not met they looted food shops and distributed the food amongst themselves.[67] Such actions transcended class and political affiliations, yet in the longer term may have politicized women in bringing them to the realization that the government could be held accountable for their difficulties. However, with the exception of Rosa Luxemburg among the Spartacists, who came from a Russo-Polish tradition, few women could claim to hold prominent political positions. These 'alternative images' of feminist ferment, which were heavily censored, symbolized the failure of the Wilhelmine system to come to terms with the exigencies of total war and the government's continuing reluctance to recognize the legitimacy of public opinion that did not pose a revolutionary threat, but equally, did not correspond to a militaristic view of German society in total war.

For most of the war the authorities were able to dismiss the suffrage cause by focusing their own propaganda on the mass participation of women's associations in the National Women's Service. Official propaganda could point, furthermore, to the areas where women had been brought into the decision-making process alongside men; through the BDF, welfare provision, and the work placement boards in the War Office. However, the failure to include women in the political concessions following the Kaiser's 'Easter Message' undermined both the position and strategy of the BDF. Promises of female emancipation in the future were no longer a substitute for concrete reforms.

Dissenting voices within the feminist movement embraced suffrage and pacifism. As we have seen, the two often overlapped. The peace movement, which was largely dominated by women, was effectively muzzled through state censorship and surveillance. If all else failed, pacifists could be labelled as 'enemies of the Empire' (*Reichsfeinde*) and ostracized. An analysis of 'dissenting voices' and organized protest within war-ravaged Germany suggests an intriguing gender difference that warrants further research. Women tended to be more humane and sensitive to the nature of the conflict and were thus were more critical of the war and the way it was being conducted. Not having to face death in combat was one factor. Another was that as the men departed for the fighting front, the home front became increasingly 'feminized' as women remained behind. Not only did women assume an important role in the war economy, they continued to suffer privations – and not simply material hardship – specific to a largely female homefront. That is not to say that women were weaker, more prone to capitulation – or unable to 'hold-out' for victory; simply that an organized minority expressed their critical stance towards the war at an earlier stage and generally remained immune to the blandishments of imperial propaganda.[68] It is also fair to say that the military and civil authorities found it more difficult to deal with both organized and spontaneous women's protests and feminist ferment than with masculine dissent. Women, unlike men, could not be threatened with being moved to the front, although if they transgressed certain sexual codes with prisoners of war, they were severely dealt with. In some districts, 'war wives' had their Family Aid allowance withdrawn, although in most cases this was for their alleged refusal to work.[69] To impose punitive measures, whether it be for the purposes of labour mobilization, sexual promiscuity, or to truncate feminist ferment, risked undermining soldiers' morale at the front, which, in turn, might antagonize the Social Democrats and the trade unions and destroy the *Burgfrieden*.[70]

However, the disintegration of the *Burgfrieden* was exposed by the demands of another group who could not be denied so easily. The continuing disquite within the far left of the SPD over the question of war aims posed a much more serious threat to national solidarity. By the end of 1916, the question of war aims had flared up again and this time the OHL and the Chancellor would be forced to respond. Moreover, the outbreak of the Russian Revolution in February 1917 provided a new political and ideological impetus to leftist Social Democrats. By the end of the year the German Social Democratic movement would polarize and finally split and the government's policies would be in disarray as the country at large began to question the moral legitimacy of its own state.

6
War Aims Again

'A colossal rift divides our people'

MB Report, October 1917

In December 1916, the Reich made a first attempt to begin peace negotiations but these were turned down by the Allies. The Germans reacted to this refusal by becoming determined to win victory at all costs and resolved at home to guard against any democratic 'softness'. The Chancellor, Bethmann Hollweg, was dismissed. His successor, Michaelis, was completely under the influence of the OHL. Hindenburg and Ludendorff now enjoyed not only military leadership but also *de facto* political control.

In 1917 the 'Inter Group Committee' was formed by the SPD, the Centre and the Progressive People's Party. Its aim was: the establishment of a parliamentary monarchy and a negotiated peace without victors or losers. The programme formed the basis of the Reichstag's peace resolution in July 1917. For a section of the SPD representatives the ideas of the 'Inter Group' did not go far enough. As committed internationalists they refused to agree to further war credits and broke away from the SPD to form the 'Independent Social Democratic Party' (USPD). The USPD formally joined the 'International Group' which, under the leadership of Karl Liebknecht and Rosa Luxemburg, had been actively opposed to the war policies of the Reichstag majority since 1915 under the banner of 'Down with the war!' As the 'Spartacus League' the 'International Group' formed the germ cell of the future German Communist Party (KPD).

The military and political tensions of 1917 caused Wilhelm II to think about a possible reform of the three class voting system in Prussia. However, the leadership of the Reich, under the influence of the OHL, only agreed to any real political concessions after the military situation had become hopeless: the October reforms of 1918 introduced by the Chancellor, Prince Max von Baden, represented the first real step towards a parliamentary system of government – too late, as was already apparent.

PUBLIC OPINION AND PROPAGANDA, 1916

By the end of 1916, strikes and riots were not uncommon in Germany, but they were almost always fuelled by economic grievances.[1] Openly anti-war activities remained confined to small and isolated minorities in the pacifist and radical socialist camps. The history of the pacifist and feminist movement point not to ideologically trained revolutionaries intent on overthrowing the Second Empire, but to fairly spontaneous protests at inequalities within the Wilhelmine system and demands for piecemeal changes.

However, during the course of 1916, subtle, yet discernible shifts took place. German electoral reform became an integral part of the discussion of the objectives of war – which continued to dominate the political landscape. The Russian Revolution of February 1917 not only revived hopes for peace, but it also intensified demands for political reform. For the first time, the mood of dissatisfaction contained an explicitly domestic dimension and occasionally manifested itself in open calls for revolution. The ensuing debate culminated in an historic split within the Social Democratic movement and the resignation of the Chancellor, Bethmann Hollweg.

1916 was marked by the two great battles of Verdun and the Somme. Although they had been launched by the German military with the intention of bringing France to its knees, Germany paid a fearsome price with estimated casualties exceeding 330,000. The battles imposed enormous strains on the German home front to supply the necessary armaments for the armed forces and provide hospital care for the sick and wounded. Moreover, the Allied blockade, as we have seen in Chapter 4, was beginning to affect the supply of food, resulting in the 'turnip winter', war-weariness and resentment.

To outside observers, the nation's morale appeared unaffected. Edward Bullitt, the American newspaper correspondent, wrote that in spite of war-weariness, the Germans remained 'amazingly solid': They have a habit, as have no other people, of obeying.'[2] However, many of the reports percolating back from the Regional Army Commands to the OHL and the War Ministries in Berlin and Munich painted an alarming picture of dissatisfaction and social criticism. In its summaries of the monthly reports, the War Ministries occasionally put a brave gloss on the information by suggesting that faith in victory remained unshaken. But increasingly the reports made for depressing reading as the food situation clearly undermined public confidence in the nation's leadership. In February 1916, the Bavarian War Ministry conceded that low morale at home 'might force us to conclude a premature peace treaty'. The War Ministry listed pacifist activity, malicious letters from wives to soldiers at the front complaining of hardship and misery, careless talk in the press and the repression of the 'Liebknecht group' as evidence that might be construed by Germany's enemies that it was 'on the brink of moral and economic collapse'. The report called for a major propaganda campaign to counter these erroneous impressions by 'deeds and facts':

> Immediate action should be taken to convince the people that the war is not about the Fatherland's possessions, but about their own homes and affairs and that victory is for the taking providing the population is prepared to make enough sacrifices. If, on the other hand, the German people now have doubts about final victory, then the great sacrifices made up to now will have been in vain. All for the lack of resolve and the desire for a swift, inglorious peace'.[3]

The campaign should also convince the home front 'how petty their little cares and burdens are compared to the brave soldiers risking their lives at the front.... it must be made the holy duty of all those at home to keep their domestic worries and complaints to themselves and not to dishearten their loved-ones in the field of battle'.[4] Deputy General Commands would enlist the support of 'patriotic' groups such as the Church, teachers ('who are the advisers of the people through good and bad times') and affiliated sections within the Federation of German Women's Association. The techniques of persuasion were to include film, theatre, posters, public lectures and confidential talks in small, closed, circles. 'War Wives! Help Your Men to Victory', a recently published pamphlet, was cited as an example of cleverly crafted propaganda that could be emulated.[5] The purpose of the report (which was unsigned) was to persuade the Bavarian Minister of State to support a concerted counter-propaganda campaign designed to 'mobilise the spiritual and morale resources of the nation'.[6]

Ironically, on the same day that the Bavarian War Ministry criticized the resolve of the home front, it claimed in a separate decree that soldiers on leave and in their letters from the front were responsible, as a result of *their* complaints 'about real or imagined injustices for poisoning the mood of whole localities'.[7] The civil and military authorities could not agree whether it was the civilians who were demoralizing the soldiers or whether soldiers were inciting civilians and then returning to the front wearier of the war than before. The Bavarian War Ministry concluded that the outcome was the same: exaggerated, frivolous or malicious reports, whether from the fighting or home front were doubly harmful in that they undermined national solidarity and strengthened the morale of Germany's enemies.[8]

In March 1916, the Prussian War Ministry reported to the Minister of the Interior with its suggestions for improving morale. The report, which was signed on behalf of von Wandel, came to similar conclusions to that of its counterpart in Munich. It bracketed the peace movement (particularly female pacifists) together with the activities of minority radical groups within the Social Democratic movements as areas of particular concern. In Prussia, the War Ministry sensed a change in the mood of the people that needed to be addressed. It was especially concerned for German youth – 'the bearers of our future military might' – as they no longer 'identified with traditional values of obedience and service to army'. Special attention must be given, it argued, to 're-educating' youth along 'healthy principles'. The author of the report, von Wandel, also pointed out that the population should be made aware of the positive measures the government was taking to combat inflation and rising prices. To this end, domestic grievances should be set against the Allies' desire to annihilate Germany: 'Each individual should have imprinted on his conscience that this war is a matter of life and death for Germany and that everyone has a part to play'.[9]

In May, it was the turn of the Württemberg Ministry of the Interior to support a campaign using the Church and schools to counter the growing discontent among the population. The intention was to promote confidence in final victory and to raise morale in the countryside, which was particularly low due to the worsening food situation.[10] The following month on 6 June, the Prussian War Ministry called together representatives of the Deputy Commanding Generals to discuss the mood of the home front.[11] The meeting began with an optimistic summary from Colonel von Wrisberg of the War Ministry. Wrisberg conceded discontent and accepted that morale could be improved, but warned against over-reacting, suggesting that complaints about the food situation, for example, acted as an important 'safety valve'. Next to speak was Lieutenant General von Rogowski of the 10th Army Corps who claimed that public opinion was largely shaped by the popular press. In order to engender greater trust, his officers (in Brunswick) held meetings with the press every four weeks – as a better informed press, he suggested, were more likely to work with the military in the national interest. The first note of dissension was struck by Major General von Magirus of the Württemberg War Ministry who warned that unless action was taken, the *Burgfrieden* could not be sustained through another winter. The time had come, Magirus suggested, to establish a central propaganda organization.[12] There was support for Magirus, however, the meeting was sidetracked by numerous local demands and ended inconclusively. The issue of a central propaganda organization was resurrected on 24 June when leading representatives of all the political and military authorities met with the League of German Scholars and Artists (*Bund deutscher Gelehrter und Künstler (Kultur-Bund)*.[13]

The high-powered meeting was opened by Walter Rathenau of the *Kultur-Bund*[14] who set out three objectives: to establish a *neutral* (his stress) office under official control, to appoint a director, and to construct an organizational network to facilitate 'patriotic enlightenment' at both national and local levels.[15] In a detailed and thoughtful outline, Rathenau was, in effect, offering the 'good-offices' of the *Kulter-Bund* to front the proposed new operation. Major Nicolai of Section IIIb agreed that there was a need to coordinate the activities of the two fronts and in particular to convey to the home front the unflinching spirit of the German army. Referring to the effects of enemy propaganda as 'biting into the soul of the German people', Nicolai welcomed the support of the *Kultur-Bund* and assured them of his cooperation. After a lengthy discussion the meeting decided to petition the Chancellor with a somewhat contradictory recommendation to set up an independent propaganda office, indirectly controlled, but supported by government and not private funding. It was further agreed that the *Kultur-Bund* would become involved and that to facilitate this, the monthly reports from the Deputy Military Commands would be made available to its representatives. (The outcome of these discussions forms the basis of the final chapter.)

However, by the end of the year plans to establish a quasi-independent propaganda organization and to appoint a director had failed to materialize. It was proving difficult to come up with the name for a director and also to agree where this new power constellation should reside. A major obstacle proved to be the power struggle that was taking place between Hindenburg and Ludendorff, recently appointed to the High Command, and Chancellor Bethmann Hollweg. As we saw in Chapter 2, the establishment of the War Press Office (*Kreigspresseamt* – KPA) had allowed the OHL considerable control over all matters to do with censorship. Ludendorff in particular was determined to make greater use of the KPA for his own political ends. One of the first measures that the new High Command took was to dismiss Deutelmoser, the Head of the KPA, whom they considered to be too sympathetic to the Chancellor's political policy of a 'new orientation'. Deutelmoser was transferred to the Foreign Office and replaced by the more compliant Major Stotten. Hindenburg and Ludendorff were now free to use the KPA to manipulate censorship against the left-wing press and to intensify their attacks on Bethmann Hollweg. However, the whole question of censorship was unpopular with the German press and with the political parties left of the Conservatives. The OHL was determined to control the press, yet was anxious not to be closely associated with unpopular decisions. In a typically Machiavellian move, Ludendorff suggested that the press should be controlled by a central agency working under the direct control of the Chancellor. ('A firm directing hand in Press matters would materially facilitate our general policy'.)[16] Acting on the advice of Deutelmoser, Bethmann rejected the suggestion as both men recognized the transparency of Ludendorff's suggestion. The Chancellor (and not the OHL) would be blamed for restrictive censorship while an increasingly interventionist Supreme Command would continue to maintain ultimate control by insisting that 'purely military' questions were involved.[17] The Chancellor, moreover, had no wish to be caught in the cross-fire between the Supreme Command and the Reichstag as to how propaganda should be disseminated. Fortunately for the Chancellor the Bavarian War Ministry also appeared to be unpicking Ludendorff's proposals. In a critical note on the proposed measures, the Head of the Press Department, von Sonnenburg, opposed further centralization and feared antagonism 'to all things Prussian'. While he hoped that the transfer of Deutelmoser to the Foreign Office might improve relations with the press, he questioned whether the War Press Office was the most appropriate conduit between the OHL and public opinion. Too often, in the view of the Bavarian War Ministry, the KPA wanted to 'shape the press from a purely military standpoint'. In a none too subtle criticism of the OHL and Berlin, Sonnenburg concluded dismissively that in Bavaria they had achieved a relationship of trust and in fact were encountering few problems with the press.[18]

The analyses of the mood of the people contained in these official reports provide a revealing insight into official attitudes. On the one hand they reflect the authorities' concern constantly to gauge public moods and acquire information about public opinion and they also reveal the indifference to the suffering that was being reported. A vast network of informers from all walks of life were employed by the Counter-Intelligence Department (*Abwehrabteilung*) of the Deputy General Staff to collect information. To assure themselves of continued popular support was an unwavering concern of the government and of the OHL in particular.

In explaining the mood of dissatisfaction among the people, genuine domestic hardships and grievances were accorded little significance. The home front was described variously as 'defeatist', 'weak-willed' and 'fainthearted'.[19] By October, *Monatsberichten* from all over the country were confirming that the vast majority of the people were war weary. Nevertheless, 'holding-out' (*Durchhalten*) remained synonymous with government policy and its exhortation invariably formed part of the summary attached to the Commanding General's reports. Little serious thought was given to the causes of growing discontent and low morale or the fact that the population was exhausted after three years of fighting and deprivation. Increasing effort was expended, instead, on 'enlightenment' campaigns intended to bolster morale and counter growing perceptions on the part of the working class that food shortages and general deprivation were injustices and not a war-related misfortune. Propaganda campaigns were launched to counter popular feelings of social injustice, as notions of 'them' and 'us', which prevailed prior to the 'spirit of 1914', reappeared. The poor felt that the rich were not subjected to the same restrictions as they were, and that the manufacturers and traders were making huge profits out of the war. 'The feeling of hatred daily grew stronger for the factory owners, the rich shopkeepers, and business-men who dealt in army supplies of all kinds, and for officers of the army and navy.'[20] A letter to a German prisoner of war intercepted by the British reveals the sense of despair felt by many working-class Germans:

> We are having an infernal time here with regard to food. I feel like smashing the shop windows. Nothing can be had for love or money. There is food enough for us all, but the wretches will not part with it. They feed themselves fat, fill their purses, and leave us to eat dirt..... there is nothing that we can hope for. The luckiest are the men who are killed and dead. The others, the wounded and the mutilated, are patched up only to be sent back to the front to be martyred again... There is precious little food for human beings; meat, bacon, sausage, and all fats are short. We are vegetarians, we are salad-soldiers and as limp as rags. They can't take us for long marches any more, else they would have to come and collect us in hay carts.[21]

Exaggerated rumours that the rich did not share in the general deprivation caused enormous resentment and did untold damage to morale. In May, Princess Blücher returned to her hotel in Berlin to discover it to be in a state of siege: '... being surrounded by a cordon of police and a rather threatening looking mob, who it seemed, had already stolen the bread supplies for the hotel, evidently supposing that we were living in a superabundance of luxuries.' Reports from Bavaria claimed that the public believed, given the high war profits of manufacturers, that the war was being prolonged for 'the interest of big capital'.[22] In August 1916 it was reported that 'the war against the English is phoney, because in his heart the Emperor sides with the English. He doesn't want to destroy his relations with the English as his money is invested in the Bank of England!'.[23] In dealing with the question of food shortages, the Chief of the Press Office in the Admiralty suggested that official propaganda should distinguish between middle-class intellectuals who were more 'intelligent and politically minded' and the masses whose low morale was almost entirely driven by 'difficulties in obtaining food'.[24] A poster campaign entitled 'Where is food need the greatest?' favourably compared the provision of basic foodstuffs such as bread, potatoes and sugar in Germany to that in the Entente nations.[25] (See Figure 16.) The Chancellor, in a condescending speech in the Reichstag on 5 April, spoke of the great moral reserve that had allowed the German people to maintain a substantially improved standard of living during the last decade. The following day Haase pointed out that large sections of the labour and middle class did not share in the rising standard of living:

> How could the masses restrict themselves more? Food prices are as a rule beyond their means.... The well-to-do and the rich are now subject to some restrictions and annoyances – and we freely admit this. However, anyone having money is still in a position to buy sufficient food and sweets. The poor and the less well-off suffer deprivation again and again.... The differences between the various classes become more apparent than ever.[26]

Linked to the worsening economic and food situations was the growing perception that the misery of war was meaningless. The authorities decided therefore to replace the negative imperative of 'we must hold-out' by a more positive version 'we must win'. The War Press Office coordinated a massive leaflet campaign to convince the home front that a lost war would mean that the present generation of Germans had thrown away the achievements of innumerable preceding generations.[27] The working class and the political parties to the left of the Conservatives were repeatedly reminded that victory would be achieved if they remained true to the 'spirit of 1914'. For nationalists, viewing the growing embitterment in domestic politics and the failure of the military push at Verdun, the *Burgfrieden* had now assumed the myth of salvation. Huge advertising campaigns were undertaken to persuade the population to 'hold out' and 'help us win' by subscribing to war bonds, which were viewed by the authorities, and the OHL in particular, as a plebiscite for continuing 'total war'.[28] In October 1916 in its summary of the monthly reports, the Prussian War Ministry noted a marked reluctance to subscribe to the new Fifth War Loan. Even more worrying was its conclusion that ordinary citizens saw this as a means to shorten the war. Some sections of the community even expressed the hope that the loan would fail.[29] In February 1917, the Prussian War Ministry received reports from its Deputy Commanding Generals that soldiers ('in large numbers') were writing to their wives warning them against subscribing to war loans as this would prolong the conflict.[30] In the midst of the 'enlightenment' campaigns, the German people employed gallows humour. A garrison leader in Kaufbeuren recounted the following joke circulating in Bavaria on German versus Austrian morale: 'What is the difference between the morale in Germany and in Austria? The answer is that with us, its optimistic but serious whereas in Austria its pessimistic, but merry!'[31]

The growing embitterment and the lukewarm response to the Fifth War Loan only served to convince the military that the politicians and the civilian population lacked the necessary resolve. Writing after the war, Ludendorff encapsulated the arrogant mentality of the military technocrat:

> The Reichstag, and with it the whole of the people, had to share responsibility ... I hoped that the government would be prepared to adopt the great principle of universal service, and to bring the people to consider what further powers and resources they could devote to their country. It required an unselfish understanding on the part of the people to shake themselves free from the self-seeking of domestic politics, to devote themselves wholly to the war, and to translate into action the proposals of G.H.Q.'.[32]

Such arrogance underpinned the perception doggedly held by OHL and the War Office. The 'self-seeking of domestic politics' referred to by Ludendorff was a retrospective criticism of the Chancellor, the 'defeatist' stance of many pacifists and feminists, coupled with increasing opposition from left-wing socialists opposed to the course of the war. We witness here the roots and antecedents of the 'stab-in-the-back' legend. The military solution was 'more of the same' – only with greater fortitude. Gradually, however, the divisions within the SPD, and calls for a negotiated peace and internal reforms, which gave rise to these concerns, placed the question of war aims back on the political agenda. This time the OHL was unable to stifle debate – although it would do its best to shape the framework of the discussion.

THE DIVISIONS OF THE LEFT

As discontent increased and the mood within the country became more pessimistic, old conflicts within the SPD, which had temporarily been papered over by the *Burgfrieden*, resurfaced over the question of war aims and attitudes towards the war. The Social Democratic Party, since its formation in 1875 out of two pre-existing parties with different traditions, had long experienced tension between its reformist and revolutionary wings. Moreover, the SPD leadership had failed to develop a common strategy to deal with the possibility of war. It is too simplistic to suggest that the party's attitude towards the war destroyed the Social Democrats. Deep ideological differences already existed before the 'spirit of 1914' appeared to bring it together behind the façade of a defensive war to protect the Fatherland. The longing for peace and the question of war aims had a profound effect on the Social Democratic movement (and the German labour movement), and eventually led to a tragic split in its ranks in 1917.

In the course of 1916, Karl Liebknecht became the embodiment of conscientious resistance to the war. Just as pacifist objections to the war were often couched in socialist rhetoric, so it was that radical socialist criticism of the government's war aims was sometimes tinged with pacifist sentiments. At a meeting of the parliamentary party held at the beginning of the year, Liebknecht, who had voted for war credits on 4 August, declared that the 'real sin' of the majority was not voting for war credits, but the preservation of the *Burgfrieden* which undermined 'the most elementary principles of Social Democracy'. Liebknecht demanded that attitudes to war be conducted in future along socialist principles.[33] This attack from a maverick voice of the radical wing of the party struck at the heart of the dilemma that had confronted the Social Democratic movement since its historic compromise to support the *Burgfrieden* in August 1914. In a recent book, Wolfgang Kruse has persuasively argued that the Social Democrats' vote for war credits in 1914 was not simply an act of blind patriotism. Rather it was a tactical decision on the part of the majority SPD parliamentary group who rationalized that in return for supporting the Kaiser, they could expect to receive a degree of civil equality and would finally cast aside the ignominy of being labelled *'vaterländischen Gesellen'*. From being the enemy within, the Party was now being offered the unparalleled opportunity to become part of a broad patriotic front. Kruse demonstrates that on 4 August most SPD Deputies did not believe that Germany was fighting a defensive war. They were fully aware that Germany's aims were aggressive and had come about as a result of the machinations of the Austro-Hungarians, supported by the German government. Moreover, most of the SPD leaders recognized the anti-war mood among their followers. Kruse cites the anti-war rallies in the last week of July as evidence that the working class were not 'war enthusiastic'. Although some within the Social Democratic movement did genuinely undergo a patriotic 'August experience', the principal motivation for the main body of the SPD leadership was to be part of a future integrated nation. Indeed, Kruse argues, integration became a goal in itself. But not all the party shared this vision. For a minority on the extreme left this political realignment was at the cost of repudiating its socialist political tradition. It was this division within SPD ranks that led to its eventual split and decades of recrimination.[34]

In 1914 the German working class was divided by occupation, tradition, region and religion. Similarly the SPD movement which claimed to represent the working class, was equally divided into a number of ideological camps. These ranged from the far left, which later became the *Spartakusbund*, to the nationalist right. The wings were buttressed by a main body motivated by what Geoff Eley has referred to as 'hard-headed but class conscious pragmatism . . . infused with nationalism'.[35] In 1916 it is possible to identify at least four different groups on the left of the party; moderates such as Haase and Bernstein, whose opposition sprang from pacifist rather than revolutionary sympathies; individuals such as Ledebour and Hoffmann who supported the Zimmerwald movement,[36] and the Spartacists and the left radicals of Bremen and other north German towns.

Karl Liebknecht and Rosa Luxemburg, both of whom had taken part in the Russian revolutionary movement of 1905, were the figureheads, together with Franz Mehring and Clara Zetkin, of the radical opposition known as the 'extreme left wing'. The most important ideological difference between the 'left wing' and the 'extreme left wing' was that the former believed in reformist programmes in collaboration with the proletariat and bourgeoisie while the 'Liebknecht group' called for an end to the imperialist war and for a revolutionary class struggle to overthrow capitalism and its institutions. The decision of August 1914 had marginalized the extreme left and it would take time before disquiet and opposition manifested themselves.

By the beginning of 1915 Liebknecht and Luxemburg had denounced the war and called for 'peace, not annexations'. Rosa Luxemburg had been imprisoned for having publicly encouraged civil disobedience (to the law), even before the outbreak of hostilities. In her *Junius Pamphlet*, which was printed in Switzerland in 1915, and distributed secretly in Germany, Luxemburg attacked the SPD for its 'treacherous action' in supporting a capitalist war for imperialistic expansion.[37] Although party discipline persuaded the extreme left to abide by the caucus decision to support the *Burgfrieden*, Liebknecht broke ranks on 2 December 1914 and voted against war credits. Liebknecht justified his action in a speech before the Main Committee of the Reichstag:

> This war, which the people did not want, did not blaze up for the welfare of the German or any other people. It is an imperialistic war, a war for the capitalist monopoly of world markets and the political control of worthwhile settlements for industry and capital.[38]

By the third vote on the war credits on 20 March 1915, Liebknecht was joined by Otto Rühle, with another 30 Deputies abstaining. Wolfgang Heine accused Liebknecht and his supporters of hoping for a military defeat as a precondition for social revolution within Germany. On 5 March 1915 a group of leading left-wingers formed the Group International, establishing the first organizational opposition and its own mouthpiece, *Die Internationale*. In Berlin, 5,000 copies were sold within a few days. Rosa Luxemburg contributed an article calling for the resumption of the class struggle on the basis of the SPD's pre-war programme: 'There is only one alternative: either Bethmann Hollweg or Liebknecht, either Imperialism or Socialism'.[39] The authorities quickly confiscated all remaining copies and imposed a strict preventative censorship on any further publication. In May Liebknecht denounced the war and called for reconstruction on an international front claiming that the real enemy was German imperialism: 'The German people must fight imperialism, fight in a political struggle, in cooperation with the proletariat of the other countries who must in turn oppose their own imperialists... stop this genocide!'[40] In Düsseldorf revolutionary workers to the left of Group International, formed the General Workers' Union with strong syndicalist tendencies. Meanwhile, rightist Deputies (such as Eduard David) and trade union leaders were seizing the opportunity to 'cleanse' the party of Marxist elements. The moderate centre finally responded in June and Bernstein, Haase and Kautsky issued their manifesto 'The Demand of the Hour' which, in turn, galvanized the leadership to disavow officially a war of annexations.[41]

In December 1915, when the vote on the fifth war credits was taken the number of opponents rose to 38 with 20 more SPD Deputies abstaining. At the same time, links were established in neutral Switzerland, with women's and youth organizations meeting in Zimmerwald (September 1915) and Kienthal (April 1916). Nevertheless, leftist radicals were still reluctant to break with the party and continued to work with leaders of centrist opposition, such as Ledebour and Hoffmann, who led the German delegation at Zimmerwald. Writing in *Vorwärts* in January 1916, Rühle declared that while he felt unable to promote a party split, he recognized that a genuine socialist struggle would only be possible when it happened.[42] Ironically the split was precipitated from the right when, on 12 January 1916, Liebknecht was expelled from the Reichstag faction by 60 to 25 votes, whereupon Rühle resigned in solidarity. In March Haase made his historic speech on socialism and Germany's war aims in which he attacked those whose war aim was the 'conquest of world power and who for this purpose pursued the most extravagant plans for conquest'. Haase's speech was in many way a defining moment for the SPD. His speech caused furious protests from his own ranks and particular from right-wing Social Democrats. In the opinion of Hans Peter Hanssen, Haase's speech had the effect of splitting 'the mighty German Social Democratic Party'. The extraordinary events in the chamber were recorded by Hanssen as follows:

> Today, when I entered the Reichstag, Haase was sitting in his place with material for a speech before him.[Gustav] Hoch was standing in front of him, gesticulating violently. A number of passionately excited Deputies soon gathered around Haase's desk. It was clear enough that he wished to speak and that his party associates wished to prevent him, because of the probable result.

The meeting opened. A few interpellations were answered. Then Haase took the floor. At once there was commotion in the chamber. Keil was unmanageable. He completely lost control of himself; he darted like an arrow towards Haase, threatened him with clenched fists and shouted: 'Treachery! Treachery!' A shower of abusive words followed, accompanied by applause and shouts of 'Bravo!' from the civil parties. Foremost in these ranks was [Julius] Kopsch, who as an Independent is theoretically a 'Philosemite.' Now he shouted: 'Again a Jew! A Jew! What do the Jews want here? Bravo Keil!'

Heine and David also lost their self-control and, shouting venomously, yelled themselves hoarse. Ledebour and [Friedrich A.K.] Geyer waved their arms, threatened with their fists, and were onthe point of starting a fight. The whole chamber was in wild uproar.... When Haase came down from the speaker's stand, the mighty German Social Democratic party was split.[43]

The division within the SPD was not a staightforward issue of the right wing versus the Left. Eduard Bernstein, who belonged to the party's right wing, went over to Haase and shook his hand – as indeed did Kautsky. Others such as Paul Lensch, who before the war were on the left of centre, now joined the right wing of the majority socialists. Haase was condemned by the parliamentary majority for 'a breach of discipline and of faith'. Nevertheless, 15 Deputies expressed their solidarity with Haase and formed the Social Democratic Working Group (SAG), with Haase and Ledebour as joint chairmen and Dittmann as the secretary. Eighteen Deputies voted against the government's emergency budget and were promptly expelled from the SPD parliamentary party by a vote of 58 to 33. In the meantime, the Group International reconstituted themselves under the name Spartacus from the pseudonym attached to the *Spartakusbriefe* – which were open letters, largely written by Liebknecht and Luxemburg, to the German people. The split in the parliamentary party inevitably led to a wider split in the Social Democratic movement. Following a hastily arranged conference in September the executive decided to move against the left and in October took control (unconstitutionally) of *Vorwärts*. Opposition groups convened a conference in January 1917 and when they were expelled from the party, they formed a separate Independent Social Democratic Party (USPD) which was launched at Gotha in April.[44] The Spartacus League was allowed to join the new party although extremists insisted on maintaining their independence and freedom of action. By 'joining' the USPD as a tactical marriage of convenience, the Spartacists opened up new divisions and created new ideological conflicts.

Not until December 1918 did these radical splinter groups unite to form the German Communist Party (KPD).[45] Since its formation in 1875, the Social Democratic Party had continually experienced tension between its reformist and revolutionary wings; in seeking to respond to the exigencies of war, the Social Democrats found it impossible to contain such tensions within its own ranks. The split in 1917 produced a new configuration of the left which would form the basis of the Weimar Republic in 1919.

WAR AIMS AGAIN

Following the parliamentary party's disavowal of a war of annexations, the Reich authorities monitored activities within the SPD even more closely than before. In August 1915 the Prussian War Ministry issued a series of instructions to Deputy Commanding Generals on how they were to deal with the Social Democratic movement in general and the propaganda distributed by leftist factions within the SPD. On 18 August the War Ministry set out its general position that the SPD was committed to the *Burgfrieden* and a successful prosecution of the war but radical groups 'clustered around Liebknecht' were intent on promoting war weariness and political divisions by resurrecting 'tendentious discussions about war aims'. It was therefore important to act with 'restraint' and not to create martyrs or give the impression that the party itself was under attack. Political agitators and strike leaders were to be arrested and either tried for treason or sent into the army. Workers on strike were to be ordered to return to work and threatened with punishment if they refused. ('Only serious and provable offences, such as treason, should be pursued ruthlessly'.)[46] On 27 August, the War Ministry expressed concern that radical socialist propaganda, by means of leaflets and political pamphlets, was being freely circulated among soldiers at the front. Military commanders were referred to an earlier decree of 26 June and instructed to confiscate all agitational material likely to weaken military solidarity and the pursuit of victory.[47] In June 1917, following the historic split in the SPD's ranks the Supreme Command reminded Deputy Commands of the decree of 26 June 1915 and the imperative need to remain vigilant to USPD literature, which, it claimed, was intent on both polarizing the Social Democratic movement and undermining the *Burgfrieden* by persuading the proletariat that peace can be concluded speedily 'in the spirit of the Internationale'. Paradoxical attitudes towards the USPD continued nevertheless. For example the USPD's manifesto was banned and confiscated by the police yet the party's flagship, the

Leipziger Volkszeitung, continued to be published – albeit under the watchful eye of the censor.[48]

Radical socialists that had split with the majority SPD were quick to make political capital of the growing bitterness and unrest as a result of food shortages. Leaflets blaming the capitalists and the government for the plight of the people continued to be distributed despite the censorship regulations and penalties for capture:

> HUNGER!
> What was bound to come has come! Hunger!! In Leipzig, in Germany, in Essen, and in many other places there are riots started by hungry masses of people.
>
> Herr Bethmann Hollweg says England is the cause of the hunger in Berlin, and other officials repeat this. The German Government should have known it would come to this. War against Russia, France, and England had to lead to the blockade of Germany....
>
> Why has the government done nothing? Because the government, the capitalists, the Junkers do not feel the pangs of hunger of the masses....
>
> The workers can either continue in silent obedience and go to a sorrowful end, or they can rise up, do away with the Government and the ruling classes, and force peace....
>
> Arise, you men and women!
> Down with the war!
> Hail to the International Solidarity of the Proletariat![49]

The government's strategy of restraint was severely tested in May 1916 when Karl Liebknecht was seized while attempting to address a May Day rally at the Potsdamer Platz in Berlin. Organizers had called for an anti-war demonstration for 'Bread! Freedom! Peace!'. The thousands that assembled were matched by the size of the police contingent which attempted to disperse the crowd. Liebknecht was heard to cry, 'Down with the war! Down with the Government!', before he was arrested. The demonstrators continued to chant 'Down with the war! Long live the International!' while the police confiscated over a thousand leaflets calling for class war. At the end of June, Liebknecht was tried for treason, having been stripped of his Reichstag immunity, and sentenced to two and half years' penal servitude. On appeal (by the prosecution) his sentence was increased by a higher military court to four years and one month. In court, Liebknecht remained defiant: 'I stand here to accuse not to defend myself. Not political truce, but war is my slogan. Down with the war! Down with the government!'[50]

The trial and conviction of Liebknecht precipitated the first political strikes of the war and demonstrated the strength of popular anti-war feelings. In

June, 55,000 Berlin workers in approximately 40 armaments factories came out on strike. Organized by a small group of radical shop stewards against the arrest and trial of Liebknecht, the strike was led through the streets of Berlin by skilled workers chanting 'Long live Liebknecht – Long live Peace!'. Small demonstrations in support of Liebknecht occurred in other cities including Hamburg, Essen and Stuttgart, where they were hurriedly suppressed by the police. Calls from supporters of Liebknecht for a 'general strike' never materialized, except in Berlin and Brunswick (both strongholds of the extreme left) where workers used Liebknecht's situation to protest about wider issues such as food shortages, censorship and civil liberties. The Spartacists also made political capital out of Liebknecht's imprisonment. The Spartacus letter of 5 November was addressed to Liebknecht who was now portrayed in its propaganda as a martyr to the cause of revolution:

> No you have not fallen! You are gone from us... but you remain at your post as a fighter and leader for our holy cause and each day that you spend in prison is a thorn for the German working-class, and each clanging of your chains is a trumpet-call to us all: To the fight! To the fight for your and our liberation![51]

Rosa Luxemburg wrote to a friend that the Reichstag's refusal to uphold Liebknecht's immunity marked 'the political suicide of parliamentarianism'.[52]

Liebknecht's determination to fight against the war on socialist principles raised, once again, the spectre of Germany's war aims. It is worth mentioning that Liebknecht was arrested demonstrating against the war. Anti-war demonstrations took place on May Day in all the major German cities. Radical leaders were arrested and their leaflets were confiscated. Under the decree of 26 June 1915 many were conscripted forcibly into the army for causing riots. In Stuttgart and other cities, socialist youth organizations were closed down for participating in the peace demonstrations. Heavy-handed, coercive measures failed, manifestly, to stifle debate on Germany's war objectives. As we have seen in Chapter 2, press censorship, although as efficient as the French and British censorships, was not severe enough to prevent numerous indiscretions by German socialist and even bourgeois press. According to Lutz in his study of the Fall of the German Empire:

> More suppressed pamphlets circulated secretly throughout the Empire during the war than in any other belligerent power. The censorship failed to close this channel of communication with an iron hand, and the inevitable result was that revolutionary propaganda of the enemy thus entered Germany.[53]

Lutz exaggerates the case but there is an element of truth in this. It explains how such an acrimonious debate on war aims was conducted in public and continued for much of 1916–17. That is not to suggest that freedom of opinion prevailed. The censorship apparatus that I outlined in Chapter 2 remained in place. The ensuing discussion was shaped very much within the contours of the guidelines laid down by the various regulatory bodies, notably the War Press Office and the Supreme Censorship Office. Nevertheless, socialists in particular would transgress these guidelines in the Reichstag and in the press just as some pacifists were able to circumvent letter censorship and surveillance. Socialist speeches, critical of the war, given from the floor of the House, were published in full and often in pamphlet form, as parliamentary debates were not subject to the official censorship.[54]

On 24 May 1916 a full-scale debate on censorship took place in the Reichstag. The SPD tabled resolutions intended to safeguard the freedom of the press and civil liberties against encroachments from the military. The minority socialists also submitted a resolution calling for the abolition of the Law on the State of Siege. Wilhelm Dittmann delivered a vigorous attack on the government on behalf of the Social Democratic Labour Association.[55] The call to review the role of censorship in wartime Germany was taken up by *Vorwärts* at the beginning of 1917:

> The time has come to withdraw a forgotten sentinel who has remained in place ever since the beginning of the war. We still have the censorship. But we probably have it only because nobody has bothered himself to think about the reason for it.

In a passionate editorial, *Vorwärts* argued that the *Burgfrieden* should no longer prevent healthy political debate citing the 'unrestricted public debate about war aims' as an example of the necessity for public discussion.[56]

The question of war aims refused to disappear. Not only had it served to split the SPD but it could justifiably be claimed that the divisions within the Social Democrats mirrored the polarization in the country at large. Ironically, given that it breached the principles of the *Burgfrieden*, the war aims discussion was first made public by annexationists in the middle of 1916 and thereafter conducted practically unrestricted in public. It reached a first climax with the peace resolution in July 1917 and the founding of the Fatherland Party in September of the same year (see Chapter 7).

The Supreme Censorship Office had forbidden the press to discuss the SPD's reservations to an annexationist war and their principles on the question of war aims as early as August 1915.[57] By the middle of 1916, the question of Germany's war aims had become inexorably linked to political reforms of the Wilhemine system. The monthly reports from the Regional

Army Commands also reveal a decisive shift in the mood of the population, and make for depressing reading for the authorities. In June 1916, the 10th Army Corps referred to the public mood as taking a 'turn for the worse'. In Brunswick-Lüneburg it was reported that radical elements within the SPD were exploiting war weariness and food shortages to attack the 'propertied classes'. Describing public morale as 'low' it suggested that only a military success could lift the mood of the population.[58]

Hanssen's diary entry for 2 June recorded the wild enthusiasm in the Reichstag over the naval battle at Jutland: 'The Navy reported that it ended with a brilliant victory for the Germans.... England had suffered heavy losses'.[59] The following month, however, the 2nd Army Corps in Munich reported that the desire for peace was getting stronger and that this was undermining the government's negotiating position. It lamented the public's failure to grasp Germany's strong military position and her military capabilities – particularly submarines. It is highly unlikely, given the extensive propaganda campaign, that the public would have remained unaware of the high hopes of the military and right-wing groups for submarine warfare.[60] In August the Deputy Commander in the Marks noted with concern the rise of political extremism among industrial workers. The metal workers in particular were deserting traditional allegiance to the main body of the SPD and the trade union movement and gravitating to the Sparticus League – referred to as 'rabble-rousers' and 'terrorists'.[61] The report talked of a 'politicised' labour-force refusing in some cases to work overtime unless it was guaranteed more food. By means of its own intelligence network, the OHL had thwarted widespread civil disturbances planned for 1 August by drafting workers' leaders into the army. According to the report, such precipitative action on the part of the OHL had successfully focused the minds of the workers back to the war effort. In Essen, the 7th Army Corps reported on the 'tense mood' of the workforce. In an SPD-trade union conference held in Düsseldorf in July a speaker claimed in front of invited representatives from the Deputy Commanding Generals and civilian authorities that: 'all trust in government is gone'. In the same month, the 10th Army Corps assessed that food shortages and agitational propaganda spread by radical socialist groups had weakened workers' morale. Leaders were arrested and the *Bremer Bürgerzeitung* – the mainspring of socialist agitation in the area – was subjected to stringent pre-censorship. An editor of the *Bremer Arbeiterzeitung* was discovered to be eligible for army service! Such action, according to the report, tends to 'nip unrest in the bud'.[62] In early September, the 7th Army Corps cited 'extensive strikes' in the Düsseldorf area linked to the food situation and whipped up by the radical wing of the Social Democratic movement. The seriousness of these reports finally persuaded the Supreme Censorship Office (*Oberzensurstellen* – OZS) in November to construct five ground rules to be observed by the press. These rules were to be enforced by all the regional censorship offices, and included:

1. To guarantee the *Burgfrieden*, no sensationalist stories of high food prices.
2. Press to avoid general or spiteful attacks on commercial classes.
3. No reports of civil unrest due to rising price of food.
4. No reports of mass meetings held in front of stores or distribution points.
5. Shortage of food forbidden to be made the object of jokes or comic leaflets.[63]

As the OZS attempted to put a brave face on mounting political and social unrest, it also tried to prevent a wider discussion of war aims and political reforms. Conservative power-elites insisted on linking the *Burgfrieden* to war aims which they saw as a means of ensuring political and social harmony. The 'spirit of 1914' created a number of convenient myths: that Germans were 'enthusiastic' for the war; that it had led to the birth of a new 'national community' (*Volksgemeinschaft*) at the expense of class struggle and that it would lead to salvation and victory. Its unifying force had, in fact, been based on fundamentally different interpretations. To the Social Democrats it represented an undertaking on the part of the ruling elites to reform the worst excesses of the Second Reich in return for working-class support against the Allies. For Conservatives, the *Burgfrieden* was a blank cheque from the labour movement to allow them to conduct the war without the need to change the distribution of power at home. It was therefore imperative that the *Burgfrieden* remain unchallenged to continue as an effective agent of social and political control. The proclamation of war aims based on annexations and an expansionist programme was therefore openly divisive and destructive of an ambiguous political truce that had been tied to the vocabulary of a defensive war. In the latter half of 1916 the German people were split into two camps: those who promoted a *Siegfrieden* ('peace through victory') based on annexations and those who advocated a *Verhandlungsfrieden* (a negotiated peace) on the basis of the territorial *status quo ante*. Interestingly enough, the division was not always along traditional class lines. By no means all workers were opposed to an expansionist foreign-policy programme. Equally, some commercial interests (particularly from the banking sector) supported anti-annexationist policies. The *Volksbund für Freiheit und Vaterland* (People's League for Freedom and Fatherland), for example, saw itself as a moderate opposition to the Fatherland Party and Pan-German aspirations. It remained a largely ineffective counter to the flood of Pan-German propaganda.

It is not surprising that civilian and military authorities were reluctant to allow a debate on Germany's war aims. Not only could such a debate expose the ambiguity of the *Burgfrieden*, it could also highlight the internal divisions on the question of military victory and of a compromise peace. As we have seen, the OZS had forbidden the press to discuss the SPD's reservations to an annexationist war in August 1915.[64] By the middle of 1916, in spite of censorship restrictions, the question of Germany's war objectives became inexorably linked to demands for political reforms. No one was more acutely aware of the danger implicit in allowing wider discussion of war aims than Bethmann Hollweg. A beleaguered Chancellor now found his policy of 'new orientation' buttressing two irreconcilable camps. Hans Peter Hanssen noted in his diary that:

> the Chancellor is being sorely tried.... But his mouth is closed for the purposes of public utterance, although his opponents are continuing to agitate openly with irresponsible gossip.... The Chancellor was tense, tired, and nervous.... His hair has become white, his face is lined with deep furrows. He seems the personification of despair ...[65]

Criticism of the Chancellor was mounting and his opponents, notably the newly appointed third OHL, were demanding his removal. In April 1916 Bethmann Hollweg called an important debate in the Reichstag to bring together different opinions on the conduct of the war. The day before the debate, the OZS had given the press the broad contours of the Chancellor's speech with instructions on how it was to be reported.[66] In his speech the Chancellor declared: 'It is for Germany, not a piece of foreign soil, that Germany's sons bleed and die.'[67] *Vorwärts* reported that those hoping the Chancellor would offer the prospect of provisional peace negotiations were 'deeply disappointed'. Instead he appeared to accept the *status quo ante* with the promise that Germany would not oppress any nationalities.[68] The debate was dominated by a powerful speech from Stresemann for the National Liberals urging the House 'to use all means at our disposal to their full extent in order to safeguard Germany's peace and future'.[69] The ensuing discussion failed to cast new light on the government's attitude to a negotiated peace. One of its few clear statements had been made by the Chancellor in December 1915 when he informed the House that the longer the war continued the greater would be the guarantees required for Belgium. The vagueness of this, and subsequent statements, served only to fuel speculation both at home and abroad.[70] Annexationists interpreted the Chancellor's remarks to support their expansionist programme, while moderates took comfort in the view that guarantees did not necessarily mean that more territory would be annexed.

The annexationists were themselves divided. The issue of Prussian electoral reform served to confuse the discussion surrounding the objectives of the war. Thus National Liberals would join with the Progressives and the SPD on the issue of political reform but would support the Conservatives on questions of war aims and foreign policy. Broadly speaking, the Pan-Germans favoured annexations, above all in the west, linked to an extravagant colonial policy. The Conservatives, National Liberals and the minority wing of the Centre Party also supported extensions of the German frontier with France because of its economic importance, but generally favoured an Anglophobe programme. According to Ebba Dahlin, the Conservatives hated England for political reasons while the National Liberals hated England for economic reasons.[71] Anglophobes favoured annexations in the west and colonial expansion. They believed in unrestrictive submarine warfare in the pursuit of *Siegfrieden* and opposed peace proposals on the grounds that they were a proof of weakness. Numerous annexationist pamphlets were circulated in Germany. In Munich, for example, the Independent Committee for a German Peace, an organization of professional men and academics (also known as the Schäfer Committee after its chairman, Professor Schäfer), distributed 300,000 copies of its twenty-seventh annexation pamphlet. Needless to say, such literature encountered few restrictions from the censors. The German Colonial Society that included members from the Centre Party and the National Liberals as well as the Conservatives, demanded the return of colonies lost in the war and the acquisition of new ones. Other interest groups such as the Committee of Christian National Workers asserted that peace could not be permanent unless Germany's colonial aspirations were satisfied. The Pan-German Union's position was encapsulated in the phrase 'to be imperialist in the East' meaning the annexation of Poland, Lithuania, and Courland and parts of Russia for agricultural purposes.[72] There was also considerable public interest in the Lutheran pastor Naumann's suggestion for a 'Mittel-Europa' solution which involved much less displacement than the Pan-German programme. Divisions of opinion also surfaced on the question of indemnities. Pan-Germans and Conservatives pressed for large indemnities, Progressives believed that Germany alone should not pay for the cost of the war while some sections in the Social Democratic movement argued that areas currently occupied by Germany should be used as indemnity in the division of the final cost of the war.[73] In 1917 the arguments employed by Pan-German newspapers become increasingly defensive, suggesting that it was losing popular support. Their argument for indemnities became an argument of despair.

The Centre Party began 1916 supporting the Conservatives but as the year progressed the more moderate wing swung round to support the Chancellor. *Germania*, the party's moderate paper, approved of the Chancellor's declaration in the Reichstag in April while the *Kölnische Volkszeitung* remained more cautious.[74] Matthias Erzberger deplored the internal divisions being created by the question of war aims and ascribed it to the failure of Bethmann Hollweg's weak leadership. In April, following the debate in the Reichstag, Erzberger wrote in a memorandum:

> The government must seize the leadership in the public discussion of war aims. If the government fails to give a lead to public opinion private interest groups will induce the people to oppose the government and voice views calculated to prolong the war. The German people has shown throughout the war that it is eager to follow a government which knows its own mind.[75]

However, by the end of 1916 the Centre Party's *volte face* was complete and it supported the Chancellor's position on a 'negotiated peace'. The Centre Party was especially well qualified to reconcile social antagonisms because of its Christian principles and, in part, because it was expressing the views of so many diverse social and economic groups within the party. As a party reflecting moderate views it was inevitable that eventually it should be more concerned with progress towards a negotiated peace than annexations.

In July, *Vorwärts* illustrated the complexity of the issue when it referred to differences of opinion between the party executive who continued to oppose annexations and those within the SPD who were prepared to accept a strictly limited annexationist programme.[76] There were some members of the majority like Lensch and Quessel, who were naked imperialists, but they were an exception. A small group clustered around Scheidemann supported the Chancellor, interpreting 'guarantees' as meaning a rectification of the frontier, but the vast majority continued to oppose all plans for conquest. In July the executive of the SPD together with the trade unions drafted a petition to the Chancellor demanding an early end to the war.[77] The following month the SPD published its own resolutions on the war aims. In what was clearly intended to be the 'official' position of the party, the executive committee talked of 'influential German circles . . . propagating plans for conquest'. Arguing that 'chauvinistic annexationists' were more likely to prolong the war, the document called on the Chancellor to rescind the ban on the discussion of war aims and allow the 'German people to take a free and unhampered position in regards to these plans of conquest'.[78]

One factor that was rarely alluded to in official communiqués was the question of rising casualties. War losses had a profound effect on the people and made more frequent explanations of war aims necessary. Towards the end of October 1916, Major Nicolai representing the OHL, informed the War Press Office that war aims could only be discussed in a 'neutral, non-provocative manner'. The open discussion that the SPD had called for in its August resolution was strictly forbidden as this would highlight internal division and provide comfort to Germany's enemies. Instead, the press was to be reminded that this was a defensive war, forced on Germany. Supporting the annexationist position, Nicolai stated that a war of defence gave Germany the right to demand indemnities against all future reparations to nations that had been occupied. The War Press Office was instructed that should guidelines be breached then offending newspapers could expect stringent pre-censorship.[79] Major Nicolai's guidelines drew a swift response from the Imperial Navy who felt that they did not go far enough nor reflect the seriousness of the situation. On 7 November the Head of the Admiralty and the Secretary of State for the Imperial Naval Office in a joint statement suggested that to allow a discussion of any kind could only weaken the resolve of the people to fight or persuade them to call for an end to the war. Rejecting Nicolai's framework for 'limited discussion' as 'a contradiction in terms', they urged the Chancellor to take full responsibility and centralize the discussion of war aims. As a postscript they insisted that any form of 'limited discussion' must include the need for overseas bases and colonial possession.[80] Although there was some rivalry between the OHL and the Admiralty, Bethmann sensed that he was being placed in an invidious position by the Admiralty and in danger of being trapped. His reply to the navy was conciliatory but firm. The question of war aims, he suggested, would only be resolved if the Chancellor could rely on the support of all government offices. In a side-swipe at the OHL, he demanded that sensitive press releases should be authorized by his office alone. To this end a specialist section in the news department of the Foreign Office was to deal with war aims.[81] Representatives of military and civilian authorities had met on 20 November to set out directives explaining the government's war aims and boost morale during the third winter of the war. Major Nicolai explained that the Supreme Command placed great store by the maintenance of a favourable public opinion and demanded that something be done in this respect. The OHL already had in place its own directives which included the use of 'enlightenment' (*aufklärung*) instead of 'propaganda'. Nicolai outlined that the main principle of public enlightenment must be truth, 'but exaggerated objectivity was to be avoided'. Truth, according to Nicolai, would strengthen the trust of the people, and there could be no doubts over the veracity of OHL reports.[82] On 27 November, the Chancellor and the OHL agreed to lift partially the ban on the discussion of war aims. In a much heralded statement of unity, they claimed that it was in response to public opinion.[83] However, two days prior to this announcement, the OZS had issued a stern 16-point programme to regional censorship offices imposing strict guidelines on what could and could not be published. On the question of annexations, point 14 was unequivocal: 'Those who think it right to confiscate a gun from a bandit and a revolver from a robber can have no objection to our wish to annex to the German Reich areas that threaten our security'. The civil and military authorities together with the press were also provided with a 'new definition' of the *Burgfrieden* intended to shape future discussion on the question of war aims:

> The *Burgfrieden* can be expressed as the attempt to uphold the spirit of resolve and devotion to the great national aims, in avoiding anything that might endanger the unity of the German people and in never allowing the impression to be given that the strong national will for victory is wavering.[84]

In December 1916, a slender opportunity for conciliation was offered in the form of a vague peace proposal from the German Chancellor. On 12 December the German government offered to discuss peace terms. It has been suggested that Bethmann was using the possibility of unrestricted submarine warfare as a threat to lead President Wilson to act as a peace intermediary.[85] A more likely explanation is that Germany had been placed in a position of strength from which to launch its initiative after the collapse of Romania's capital, Bucharest, on 6 December.[86] In a heavy-handed peace initiative, the proposal stated simply that Germany was willing to begin negotiations in order to stop the terrible conflict which had begun for the 'defense of their existence and for the freedom of their national development'. The proposal, which also protested against Britain's 'starvation' policy, was passed on to the diplomatic representatives of the United States, Spain and Switzerland and read out in the Reichstag.[87] The object of the proposal was to be a complete surprise and not even party leaders were informed until the last moment.[88] Two days later, an embarrassed Wilson sent a note to the belligerent powers for a statement of peace terms. He had in mind a peace without victors or vanquished.[89] The German government replied on 28 December that it favoured a 'direct exchange of views' and repeated its proposal of 12 December that delegates representing the belligerent powers should meet on neutral territory. The Entente was deeply suspicious of German motives. Briand informed the French people that the vagueness of the German peace move was a thinly disguised trap, not for peace but for continuing the war. Lloyd George famously remarked that he did not wish to 'buy a pig in a poke'. In a joint statement the Allies repeated the charge that the Central Powers, by violating neutral Belgium, were alone responsible for the war.[90] As Christmas 1916 approached the possibilities of a negotiated peace appeared to have been dashed. Street lights and Christmas decorations were dimmed to conserve electricity. The Mayor of Berlin compared the current hardships with those endured in 1813 and concluded his New Year message with the forlorn hope that 'May the bells of peace sound out in the New Year'. James Gerard, the American Ambassador, observed a 'melancholy' Berlin and recorded a Christmas party given by his embassy for poor children in the capital: 'One little kid got up and prayed for peace, and everyone wept.'[91]

POLITICAL REFORMS, 1917

The refusal of the Entente to consider opening peace negotiations on the terms laid down by the German government strengthened the defence motif in German war aims and provided a new impetus for the resumption of unrestricted submarine warfare. On 31 January 1917, Bethmann Hollweg told the American Ambassador that he had been compelled to take up ruthless submarine war because it was evident that Wilson could do nothing to achieve a negotiated peace.[92] Gerard, for his part, believed that had the decision rested with the Chancellor and the Foreign Office instead of the military then unrestricted submarine warfare would not have been resumed.[93] Bethmann recognized that the Entente's rejection of his peace proposal and the harsh tone of its rejection had outwitted his half-hearted attempt to find a 'third way'. 'We *were* ready for a peace of understanding', he informed the Reichstag in February.[94] Following a tense, confrontational meeting with the OHL at Pless on 29 December, the Chancellor returned to Berlin convinced that Hindenburg and Ludendorff were determined to militarize the entire life of the state. Hindenburg, on the other hand, informed the Emperor that Bethmann was indecisive and that the OHL could no longer work with him. The question of unrestricted submarine warfare had become extricably bound up with Bethmann's political future. His peace move had failed and he had nothing tangible to offer. The OHL had demanded the rejection of the Entente's reply and now were insisting that if the Chancellor did not agree to the resumption of unrestricted submarine warfare he should be forced to resign. In June 1916 Bethmann had attacked the Pan-Germans and Conservatives. 'Does submarine warfare,' he asked, 'bring us closer to, or take us farther from, a victorious peace?'[95] Recognizing the popularity of Hindenburg and Ludendorff and the precariousness of his own position, he chose to capitulate in the interests of preserving the unity of the Reich.[96] Writing in exile some years later, the Kaiser criticized Bethmann's 'remoteness' from political realities and condemned his 'inadequacy' as Chancellor: 'Deep down in his heart he was a pacifist and was obsessed with the aberration of arriving at an understanding with England.'[97]

The resumption of submarine warfare in February 1917 effectively blocked immediate peace moves. Attention focused instead on political reforms. 1917 was marked by spreading industrial strikes, the deteriorating food situation, undernourishment, and resulting political and social unrest. One writer referred to the 'drama of the battlefield' being changed to the 'drama of the larder'.[98] Princess Blücher described the mood of the people in February 1917 when she wrote in her diary:

> People are beginning to think that the torments of Dante's *Inferno* are capped by the hardships of this deadly winter of 1916–17.... As for the mood of the people, the heroic attitude has entirely disappeared. Now one sees faces like masks, blue with cold and drawn by hunger, with the harrassed expression common to all those who are continually speculating as to the possibility of another meal.[99]

Food shortages continued to dominate social life in Germany and in the political realm electoral reform became an integral part of the debate on the objectives of war. Socialists and some Progressives now considered the reform of the Wilhelmine system a war aim and worked energetically to achieve its adoption. The combined failure of Bethmann's peace move and the continuing slaughter on the battlefields had a profound impact on the people. The outbreak of the Russian Revolution of February 1917 briefly revived hopes for peace and politicized sections of the work-force. In March, the Württemberg War Ministry noted that news of the role played by the industrial workers in Russia has 'persuaded German workers to believe that they can extend their influence both within the workplace and in politics. Employers often hear workers talking of emulating the Russian example'.[100] In April, the Reichstag heard of strikes and demonstrations against the government and calls for the setting up of workers' councils patterned after those in Russia.[101]

It was believed in some quarters that political reform, set against the backdrop of the Russian Revolution, might counteract the considerable effects of these events and neutralize growing radicalism of socialists and extremists within the labour movement. While war aims had polarized the nation, the political reform debate was structured very much along class lines and used to further political aims. The Conservative annexationists continued to view total victory as a means of staving off radical political changes and maintaining the *status quo*; those who supported a defensive war came to see a negotiated peace as a necessary precursor for a new political orientation. Whereas the bourgeois women's movement believed that their achievements in the war effort deserved recognition, and felt frustrated by the government's refusal to extend the franchise to women, socialists were no longer prepared to be hamstrung by the *Burgfrieden*. The government's failure to explain war aims adequately, its reluctance to introduce political reforms, and the Napoleonic ambitions of the OHL all became major issues of conflict in 1917. No longer was the mainstream Social Democratic movement prepared to support uncritically the continuation of the war – and by implication, the *Burgfrieden*.

The strains of war not only split the Social Democratic movement but it placed the SPD majority in a very difficult position. The impact of the Russian Revolution sharpened its dilemma. One of the consequences of its (continuing) compromise with the *status quo* was that the SPD leadership had adopted an increasingly nationalist stance in the interests of maintaining the *Burgfrieden*. Although it remained firmly committed to the gradualist reform of parliamentary structures, in the short term its goal was the defence of the Fatherland. This involved distancing itself both from the anti-war dissidence of its former left wing and the unofficial militancy of disaffected groups of labour. The result, as Eley has pointed out, was that in attempting to keeping working-class aspirations in check, the SPD was turning into the policeman of the working class.[102] The party executive was, nevertheless, determined not to become the government's puppet and continued to defend working class entitlements in the face of encroachments from the military and civilian authorities.[103]

The SPD never lost sight of the need to reform Wilhelmine Germany and continued to press for changes. Its position was partly enforced by the decline in rank-and-file support and the need to defend the interests of the working class in the face of the increasing militarization of civic life. In August 1916 the Regional Army Commands reported an alarming shift in workers' allegiance from the SPD to the more radical *Spartakusbunde*.[104] In fact the Spartacus League made relatively little in-roads in SPD membership – partly because their leaders were in prison or serving involuntarily in the trenches! The main beneficiary of the decline in the SPD's membership was the USPD, although conscription was an important factor.[105] Some SPD leaders, however, conceded that the appeal of the more radical USPD proved attractive to an increasingly 'politicised' working class.[106]

The Chancellor had been attempting to relieve mounting internal conflict by holding out the prospect of political reform, to be implemented after the war. As we have seen, Bethmann Hollweg recognized that war aims were intrinsically divisive and remained determined not to open the debate on Germany's war aims for fear of unveiling the ambiguity of 'the spirit of 1914'. His policy of 'a new orientation' explicitly offered, in return for the support of the SPD and the working class, an undertaking to reform the worst aspects of the Wilhelmine political and social system. A beleaguered SPD executive now recognized the need to cash in their cheque as a *quid pro quo* for keeping working-class rank-and-file demands in line. Both military and civilian leaders recognized that the war could not be won without the support of the SPD and the working class, but neither were prepared to commit themselves to reform the existing system substantially. The Chancellor had spelt this out when he warned the party: 'the leaders of the Social Democratic Party must understand that the German Reich, and particularly the Prussian state, can never permit any weakening of the firm foundations on which they built.'[107]

However, the Chancellor's strategy satisfied neither side and the relentless press campaign against the Chancellor continued, fuelled by the OHL and the radical right. The retention of the *Burgfrieden* as a bulwark to political reforms had now become inexorably associated with the nature of German political culture. For extreme nationalists, the 'spirit of 1914' had created a transcendent national unity underpinned by the idea of German superiority. They believed that the *Burgfrieden* had provided the basis for a *Volksgemeinshaft* in which Germans recognized their common ethnic identity. Its retention in the face of challenge from the left and the introduction of parliamentary democracy became therefore a matter of political salvation. Bethmann Hollweg viewed the *Burgfrieden* in a different light. The participation of the people had convinced him that reforms bent on achieving more equality were now necessary. Calls for reforms included the eminent voice of Max Weber, who argued that only a government of the people could achieve success. After the debacle of Verdun, the Chancellor agreed, and set in motion a reform of the Prussian suffrage law. The OHL, Pan-German groups and, after its inception in September 1917, the Fatherland Party, responded violently and unleashed a press campaign against the Chancellor which grew increasingly savage.

One aspect of the Bismarckian Constitution that was in urgent need of reform was the Prussian franchise with its three-class system guaranteeing a permanent Conservative hold over the Lower Chamber (*Landtag*).[108] Although reforms had been suggested shortly after the outbreak of war in 1914, little progress had been made until January 1916 when in a speech from the Throne, electoral reform was promised. The Kaiser's speech had been eagerly anticipated for weeks. The press had been led by the government to expect a political landmark.[109] The Kaiser spoke of a 'new orientation' but in oblique terms. Reform of the Prussian suffrage was mentioned only in the following passage:

> The spirit of mutual understanding and confidence will continue to work in the co-operation of the whole people in state affairs likewise in times of peace. It will pervade all our public institutions and will find active expression in our administration, our legislation, and the establishment of foundations for the representation of the people in our legislative bodies.

Socialists and liberals expressed disappointment at its ambiguous tone while Conservatives reacted violently. Wild von Hohenborn, the Prussian War Minister, was approached by a group of Landtag Deputies to arrange a secret audience with the Kaiser to express their concerns. Wild refused to circumvent the Chancellor but noted that it 'was a sign of the deep feeling against Bethmann'.[110]

However, as the mounting political, economic and military factors began to expose the fragility of the *Burgfrieden*, the Chancellor came under increasing pressure to introduce political reforms immediately, and not to wait until after the end of hostilities. He found support in the unlikely form of the distinguished conservative historian Friedrich Meinecke, who called for immediate reforms:

> Right now is the psychological moment to start a reform in our internal policy, above all a reform of the Prussian franchise, and thus to fulfil not only one of the chief desires of our working classes, but also to strengthen the bonds of understanding between them and the national state ...[111]

A new political alignment of Socialists, National Liberals, the Centre and Independents pressed for moderate reforms as a means of strengthening the home front and providing Germany with an opportunity to achieve its war aims. Bethmann, however, continued to favour changes after the war. Addressing the Prussian *Abgeordnetenhaus* (House of Representatives) in March 1917, he argued:

> the experiences of this war must and will lead to a reconstruction of our internal political life in important respects, and that in spite of all possible resistance.... For the gentlemen of the Left the cardinal point in their wishes regarding internal policy is the reform of the Prussian Government. The Government, however, has repeatedly said ... that it would not propose such a reform, which would undoubtedly lead to bitter internal disputes, and which could not be undertaken at a time when we are still confronting the external enemy ...[112]

Ironically, on the same day that Bethmann was attempting to placate his critics on the right, Hindenburg asked the Kaiser to dismiss him – which he refused to do. The 'Adlon Group', a coalition of representatives from heavy industry and the radical right led by Carl Duisberg had been conducting a vindictive propaganda campaign supported by the OHL to replace the Chancellor with stronger leadership.[113] Bethmann's pathetic appeals to Hindenburg and Ludendorff for restraint in the interest of national unity,[114] were rejected on grounds that the OHL could not intervene in 'purely political matters' and could only take action when the interests of the military command were threatened.[115] This proved to be an effective method of censoring the left-wing press and frustrating the Chancellor. Articles supporting internal reforms, a negotiated peace or attacking annexationist programmes were considered by the military as threatening the *Burgfrieden*. Pan-German demands to retain conservative privilege at the expense of parliamentary democracy encountered no such difficulties. When the OHL was accused of being politically biased, it contemptuously dismissed such criticism by stating that it was only interested in military matters:

> It is the urgent wish of the Supreme Command not to be involved in partisan controversies and not to be drawn into political quarrels, as this would seriously interfere with the conduct of the war. Articles and public lectures likely to have such an effect are prohibited.[116]

Bearing in mind the OHL's meddling in all aspects of politics and its relentless campaign to force Bethmann out of office, this was a disingenuous statement – to say the least.

By the end of March, however, the new alignment in the Reichstag was gathering momentum. The OHL had flirted with Duisberg's plan for a military dictatorship, but pulled back for fear that it would undermine their own popularity. On 29 March, Stresemann made an extraordinary speech on behalf of the National Liberals, in favour of suffrage reform:

> We no longer want the military absolutism we have submitted to for three years. Our party has changed its opinion on the date of reforms and believes they ought to be carried out immediately; the war lasts too long and demands too many sacrifices from the people.[117]

It was clear that a majority in the Reichstag now favoured suffrage reform. When the Russian Provisional Government declared in April that it favoured a peace based on self-determination, Bethmann later wrote that 'The colossal importance of the Russian Revolution was clear'.[118] Prompted by Bethmann, who was reluctant to lose the momentum that had been generated in the Reichstag, the Kaiser agreed to make a statement on suffrage reform in Prussia in his Easter message. Speaking the day after America had declared war on the German Empire the Kaiser proclaimed:

> After the victorious completion of the war.... We charge you to submit proposals... which is fundamental for the improvement of Prussia's internal structure. After the tremendous efforts of the whole people in this terrible war, there can be no place, in our opinion, for the three class franchise in Prussia.[119]

The message was couched in guarded terms, but a promise to change the Prussian franchise, albeit after the war, had nevertheless been made.[120]

The OHL was furious that it had not been consulted by Bethmann over the content of the Kaiser's Easter message. Ludendorff dismissed the content of the Kaiser's message as obsequious deference to events in Russia and even claimed that it had been directly responsible for unleashing the strikes that erupted in April.[121] Although some officers at the OHL recognized that the army could boost its popularity by supporting internal reforms, the leadership saw it as divisive, and sought to postpone all discussion of the suffrage question.[122]

The Kaiser's Easter message had failed to unify the nation or to satisfy those who were demanding constitutional change. Hopes of a separate peace with Russia were dashed and unrestricted submarine warfare had failed to bring England to its knees as promised. On the contrary, it was a major factor in America's entry into the war. A serious political crisis was brewing. In his speech of 15 May to the Reichstag, Bethmann returned to the question of war aims, refused to make a statement, but declared that 'I am in full harmony with the Supreme Army Command'.[123] This apparent unanimity between the OHL and the Chancellor incensed Hindenburg and Ludendorff who were intent on getting rid of Bethmann. By maintaining silence on the question of war aims Bethmann failed once more to satisfy his critics on both the right and the left.[124] The socialists again asked him to renounce annexations and indemnities while the conservatives demanded that he reject the socialist formula.[125] Dissatisfaction with the Chancellor, both inside and outside the Reichstag, increased. In Germany the conflict on war aims had not only split the nation but the debate was expressed in stereotypes that became catchwords for respective attitudes: 'A Scheidemann peace' versus a 'Hindenburg victory!'.

The dynamic interaction of opposing political forces came to fruition in the so called 'July crisis'. Towards the end of June, Graf Roedern, the Secretary of the Treasury, had revealed that the war credits would be exhausted by the middle of July, and that the Reichstag would have to be recalled to vote for new credits. The resumption of submarine warfare together with widespread strikes had placed an intolerable strain on an already overstretched German war economy. Roedern calculated that the cost of maintaining the war was running at three billion marks per month.[126] The debate was likely to be stormy for there was no automatic guarantee that war credits would be approved. Bethmann found himself beleaguered on both sides and, faced with irreconcilable demands, he had intended to use the debate to placate the Reichstag 'Fraktion' and promise future reforms. The OHL and heavy industry were determined to manipulate the crisis to remove the Chancellor.[127]

In early June, Hindenburg complained to the Kaiser that the Chancellor had conspicuously failed to give the OHL his full support. The Field Marshal then wrote to Bethmann on 19 June warning him against giving the impression that the war would be over by autumn. Having failed to receive a satisfactory response, Hindenburg wrote to the Emperor again:

> Our greatest anxiety... is the decline in the national spirit. It must be revived or we shall lose the war.... The question arises whether the Chancellor is capable of solving these problems – and they must be correctly solved, or we are lost![128]

The Kaiser was not, as yet, prepared to dismiss the Chancellor. The OHL was determined to force the issue and both Hindenburg and Ludendorff threatened to resign if Bethmann did not go.[129] The Chancellor's position depended solely on the goodwill of the Kaiser and this could no longer be assured.[130] During the Reichstag debate on war credits a new note of warning was struck, when, for the first time in the House, a Deputy spoke of the possibility of revolution in Germany. Addressing the Main Committee of the Reichstag the Majority Socialist Gustav Hoch claimed that: 'There is always talk of whether the revolution will come or not; we can only say that the German people are already in the midst of revolution'. Referring to the growing discontent in the country he warned:

> The feeling in Germany is such that things cannot go on as they are at present, for otherwise it will come to conflicts of the worst kind. The Government ought to take heart of Goethe's words: 'The revolution from below is always due to the sins of omission of those above'.[131]

The mounting crisis took a new turn on 6 July when Erzberger made an extraordinary speech in the Reichstag in which he maintained that the submarine campaign was hopeless and that it was quite impossible for Germany to win the war. Calculating that it would cost at least 50 billion marks and 200,000 (German) lives to continue the war, Erzberger made a passionate appeal; 'Kaiser, hear thy people!' and called for negotiations for peace to begin immediately.[132] Although the Reichstag had very little influence on the decision-making process, Erzberger's speech represented a devastating blow for both the Chancellor and the OHL.[133] It also acted as the catalyst for an inter-party agreement the following evening demanding the 'parliamentarization of Germany'. The merging of war aims and political reforms had now gathered momentum and representatives from the SPD, the Centre and the Progressives (known as the 'renunciation majority') united to draft a peace resolution.[134] When the OHL were informed of this they were determined to have it modified. Hindenburg's view was that a 'peace of renunciation' would be seen by the Entente as a sign of weakness and blamed Bethmann for lack of strong leadership. The question of internal political reform reached a climax on 11 July when the Kaiser and the Chancellor signed a decree promising that franchise reform would be completed in time for the next elections. The conflict between Bethmann and the OHL came to a head. Equal suffrage in Prussia and the possibility of parliamentary reforms posed a direct threat to the unique position of the army in German society. Loebbel and the entire Prussian Ministry of State also threatened to resign if electoral reform was introduced. Meanwhile the OHL was letting it be known that it was in favour of bringing parliamentarians into government and that it was the Chancellor who had prevented discussion taking place. Although Bethmann persuaded the Kaiser that he was able to control the Reichstag and that negotiations on war credits were continuing, he recognized that he could no longer resist the Supreme Command. The Kaiser was coming round to this view as well, having discussed possible replacements for Bethmann with Valentini on the evening of 8 July.[135] On the following day, Bethmann had to withstand a blistering attack from Stresemann in a packed Reichstag. In one of his final speeches as Chancellor, Bethmann stood up and appealed to the House:

> Let not those who desire my dismissal be blinded by personal prejudice. Our condition is far too serious for that. We all possess the same love for the Fatherland, but there is a danger that the dissension, which has been much in evidence today, will influence decisions. See to it that this does not happen. I repeat: I personally mean nothing, the Fatherland is everything ...[136]

The majority of members had already decided that Bethmann was a hindrance to peace and must go. The OHL, on the other hand, considered him an obstacle to the winning of the war. His position was untenable.

On the same day that Prussian suffrage reform was announced by Imperial Decree, the Crown Prince arrived in Berlin to support the OHL's case against Bethmann. Furious with Hindenburg and Ludendorff for their constant meddling in political affairs, a hesitant Kaiser still was not prepared to ditch his Chancellor unless written statements demanding the change were produced. The following morning, in a constitutional first, the Crown Prince asked representatives from the Reichstag their views on whether Bethmann should be dismissed. With one exception (who was Payer) all those consulted favoured replacing the Chancellor.[137] On the evening of 12 June, Hindenburg and Ludendorff dispatched their resignations to Berlin after notification had been sent to General von Lyncker in the afternoon. On receiving the

Crown Prince's report the Kaiser now decided to accept the resignation of Bethmann. A few days earlier he is reported to have said of Bethmann to Valentini: 'I am supposed to dismiss that man who stands head and shoulders above all the others.'[138] Hindenburg and Ludendorff arrived in Berlin on 13 June determined to reassure politicians that Germany must hold out since a 'peace of renunciation' would have a disastrous effect on the army. Instead they found themselves caught up in the speculation surrounding the peace resolution and tried desperately to disassociate themselves from its deliberations.[139] They were also determined to have a say in the appointment of the new Chancellor. After a number of names were suggested, Georg Michaelis emerged as a compromise candidate.[140] The hapless Michaelis appeared ill-suited for the Chancellorship. He was a colourless Prussian civil servant who had stumbled to the position of Imperial Grain Officer (see Chapter 4). He had not sought the office and his position rested solely with the generals who saw him as a compliant puppet likely to do their bidding. Honourable but harmless, he suited the OHL as an interim Chancellor.[141]

On 19 July, a week after Bethmann's resignation, the Peace Resolution was passed in the Reichstag. Gothein, the leader of the Progressives, wrote the original draft and despite objections from the OHL, it was published by Scheidemann in *Vorwärts* on the morning of 14 July. Scheidemann and Erzberger claimed disingenuously that they were unaware that further discussion of the draft had been contemplated.[142] The government was now persuaded to publish it officially. The resolution was presented by Fehrenbach of the Centre Party during the debate on war credits on 19 July. He described it as not being a peace 'offer', but a peace 'announcement'. It read as follows:

> As on 4 August, 1914, so today, on the threshold of the fourth year of the war, the German people stand upon the assurance of the speech from the throne: 'We are not impelled by the lust of conquest.' Germany took up arms in defence of its liberty and independence and to secure the inviolability of her territorial possessions. The Reichstag aims for a peace of understanding and lasting reconciliation between nations. Force acquisitions of territory and political, economic, and financial violations are incompatible with such a peace.
>
> The Reichstag rejects all plans aiming at an economic blockade and the stirring up of enmity among peoples after the war. The freedom of the seas must be assured. Only an economic peace can prepare the ground for the nations to live together in freedom.
>
> The Reichstag will energetically promote the creation of international political organizations. So long, however, as the enemy governments do

not accept such a peace, so long as they threaten Germany with conquest and violations, the German people will stand together as one man, hold out unshaken, and fight until the rights of Germany and her Allies to life and development are secured. The German nation united is unconquerable.

The Reichstag knows that in this announcement it is at one with the men who are defending the Fatherland; in their heroic struggles they are assured of the undying gratitude of the whole people.'[143]

The resolution was preceded by the new Chancellor's inaugural speech. Michaelis explained his understanding of Germany's war aims, and then undermined the original intention of the resolution by adding: 'These aims may be obtained within the scope of your resolution as *I understand it* (my italics).'[144] In effect the Chancellor had interpreted the resolution to fit the ideas of his masters at the OHL. Writing a few days later to the Crown Prince, Michaelis explained that: 'The notorious resolution was carried by 212 votes to 126 with 17 absent. Through my interpretation of it I stripped it of its most dangerous intentions. With the resolution as it stands we can make any peace we like.'[145] The peace resolution was deliberately couched in vague terms that supported international conciliation and understanding without limiting the government's freedom of manoeuvre by declaring precise war aims. There was no mention, for example, of restoring Belgium independence. The wording was such that it defended a 'peace of understanding' that might, or might not, include annexations. The vagueness of the resolution saved its sponsors from further embarrassment when, some months later, the terms of Brest-Litovsk were discussed.[146] It also eased the way for critics of the government to vote for war credits. The party leaders, moreover, had no definite programme to establish parliamentary government. The new Chancellor's tenure had begun well, but it was not to last.

Hindenburg and Ludendorff returned to GHQ triumphant; they had removed Bethmann and replaced him a with a compliant Chancellor; they had rendered the Peace Resolution meaningless and they had established their right to dictate foreign policy and intervene in internal political affairs. The Reichstag had voted for war credits and the Kaiser, once the embodiment of German authority, now was a farcical figure, his power emasculated by his generals. The third Supreme Command appeared all powerful. Following the Peace Resolution the forces of reaction came together to form a concerted opposition to a diminution of war aims and the introduction of internal reforms. Hypnotized by visions of new conquests, annexationists and Pan-Germans acting through the OHL and heavy industry refused to recognize the opportunities for a peace without annexations and indemnities. The OHL had demonstrated little understanding of the causes of popular dissatisfaction and unrest. Instead of heeding Goethe's warning, recited by Hoch to the Reichstag, that 'the revolution from below is always due to the sins of omission from above', the OHL remained convinced that only a spectacular military victory could now avert the threat of domestic revolution. In place of reform and peace, the OHL offered 'patriotic instruction' as a palliative for more suffering and a continuation of the war. Germany was to become a parade ground, and the people were expected to 'fall-in'.

7
Civilians 'Fall-in'

'Good propaganda must keep well ahead of actual political events. It must act as pacemaker to policy and mould public opinion without appearing to do so. Before political aims are translated into action, the world has to be convinced of their necessity and moral justification.'

General Ludendorff

THE RISE OF THE FATHERLAND PARTY AND PEACE THROUGH VICTORY

Having prised the political initiative away from the Chancellor and eroded the authority of the Kaiser, Hindenburg and Ludendorff were determined to consolidate their position. Martin Kitchen has referred memorably to the politics of the Supreme Command under Hindenburg and Ludendorff as a 'militarised form of bonapartism'.[1] The mass popularity of Hindenburg gave the OHL a plebiscitary dimension that Ludendorff (and Pan-Germans) was quick to exploit. The OHL embodied the Pan-German aspirations of important sections of society, notably the heavy industrialists and the agrarians. However, the form of military dictatorship that unfolded and the military solutions offered were incapable of solving Germany's problems. A huge gulf opened between the extreme annexationist programme and the possibility of achieving, by means of military conquest, imperialist aims. As the new Chancellor was soon to discover, these aims could not be abandoned without confronting the power and authority of the Supreme Command and substituting it with a new power base.

A major concern of the OHL was the decline in morale of the population. Ludendorff, in particular, recognized the importance of public opinion in an age of 'total war' and the need to shape it by means of propaganda, persuasion and coercion. He recognized also the need to preserve the *Burgfrieden* and restore a degree of harmony to a war-weary and divided country. In the view of the OHL, the weak and prevaricating Bethmann Hollweg had failed to provide strong leadership. Although it had succeeded in replacing Hollweg, the OHL remained incensed with the Reichstag's Peace Resolution which it was determined to undermine.

Jurgen Kocka has argued that the war stimulated a new type of antiparliamentary mass movement that pushed Hindenburg and Ludendorff towards a plebiscitarian military dictatorship.[2] Indeed, Ludendorff was virtual dictator of Germany during the last two years of the war. He was an intriguing character who, through considerable professional dedication, rose from Major General in 1914 to Senior Quartermaster-General in September 1916. While Hindenburg remained the popular hero of Tannenberg, his energetic and ruthless subordinate assumed the dominating role within the OHL. He shrewdly exploited the vacuum created by an indecisive and vacillating Kaiser and the frailty of the civilian leadership. Whether he set out to make himself indispensable is open to question. Politically he was more astute than the traditional Prussian type of officer. One of his earliest biographers claimed that a sense of dedication to what he believed to be the best interests of Germany, rather than naked lust for power, dictated his actions. Ultimate responsibility for his mistakes must rest with the Wilhelmine system that allowed quasi-dictatorial powers to fall into the hands of a professional soldier patently ill-equipped to deal with such responsibilities.[3]

While Ludendorff possessed the virtues and vices of the Prussian officer corps and embraced some of the conservative leanings of the late-nineteenth-century cavalry officer, he did not hanker back, unlike Hindenburg and other aristocratic officers, to the good old days of cavalry charges.[4] He was an annexationist and vehemently opposed to internal reforms. He firmly believed that Germany's claims to control Belgium were justified to protect the Ruhr; and in the East, he favoured huge annexations of Poland and the Baltic to prevent Russia from invading East Prussia. Like most of his fellow officers in the OHL, he opposed the reforms of the franchise in Prussia ('The connection between the franchise decree and the Russian Revolution was too obvious') and feared above all that an increase in parliamentary government could only be at the expense of the Prussian military tradition and its elevated position in the Reich.[5] But, in contrast to the aristocratic officers corps in the OHL, Ludendorff was a middle-class, radical technocrat – a modern-style advocate of 'total war'. He recognized the importance of industry, technology and propaganda in modern warfare and held the view that official propaganda should be employed more scientifically to uphold morale and exhort the population to fight on. For Ludendorff, morale was sufficiently important to be considered as an adjunct of military strategy. 'The German people', he wrote, 'both at home and at the front, have suffered and endured inconceivable hardships in the four long years of war. The war has undermined and disintegrated patriotic feeling and the whole national *morale.*'[6]

Ludendorff was convinced that in order to achieve more effective control over public opinion, the organizational structures for the dissemination of propaganda needed to be reshaped and better coordinated. In November 1916 the OHL had called together civilian and military representatives from the news gathering and information service for this purpose. This proved an important meeting and the forerunner of more radical schemes that were to follow. Three areas of activity were identified as being in need of coordination: at home; at the front; and in neutral countries. The meeting established the ground rules for future strategy. 'Enlightenment', not propaganda, should be carried out as unobtrusively as possible and that 'truth' (although not excessive objectivity) be the guiding principle in all public enlightenment campaigns. In order to facilitate better coordination it was agreed that they should meet at least once a month.[7] Heads of departments were asked to summarize their specific activities. Lieutenant-Colonel von Haeften outlined the work of the *Militärischen Stelle im Auswärtigen Amt* (Military Office for Foreign Affairs – MAA) and particularly its activities in neutral countries ('neutral reporters are cleverly and subtly influenced to write in our favour, but in keeping with the taste and style of their own country'). Major Warnecke spoke for the War Press Office (KPA) and set out out Four areas of responsibility: (1) the maintenance and strengthening of trust in the OHL and the military leaders, to the Kaiser and Reich; (2) strengthening of the desire to win the war and readiness to sacrifice oneself; (3) explaining the mood at home to those at the front; (4) explaining the imperative necessity of individual cooperation in the home front. Warnecke was followed by two colleagues in the KPA, Major Buchmann and First Lieutenant Garnich. Buchmann provided a short summary of the aims of the *Deutschen Kriegsnachrichten* (German War News), which appeared on Monday, Wednesday and Friday and a diatribe on avoiding political antagonism with the press. Officials were requested to recognize the sensitivity of the relationship between the military and the press before handing over news material for publication. Garnich spoke of the special responsibility he had been given for providing and distributing appropriate patriotic material to youth leaders and youth organizations.[8]

One of the consequences of this meeting was a new definition of the *Burgfrieden* agreed by civilian and military leaders. Little progress was made, however, in centralizing and coordinating propaganda activities. This remained a burning issue for Ludendorff who continued to press for a Ministry of Propaganda. The OHL was particularly concerned to counter the effects of the July Peace Resolution and to strengthen its control over the War Ministry and the Deputy Commanding Generals. To achieve these ends, Ludendorff strengthened the responsibilities of Major Nicolai who had commanded Section IIIb since the beginning of the war. Despite his interest in shaping popular opinion, Ludendorff rarely attended meetings with representatives of the opinion-forming agencies. His two 'mouthpieces' – Nicolai, and from spring of 1918, von Haeften, were allowed to exercise a degree of independence. It was not uncommon for these two men to initiate ideas that would be sanctioned by Ludendordff who would then issue directives and expect them to be implemented.[9]

Shortly after the Reichstag's Peace Resolution in July, Pope Benedict XV made a fresh initiative to secure a negotiated peace. On 30 August, 1917, a copy of a telegram handed by the British Ambassador to the Holy See on behalf of the Entente was passed to Michaelis. It asked for clarification of German intentions with regard to the future of Belgium. The telegram was accompanied by a letter from the Papal Nuncio, Pacelli, urging the Chancellor for a conciliatory reply. Despite Michealis' efforts to persuade the OHL that Belgium's economic dependence on Germany would render military occupation unnecessary, Hindenburg and Ludendorff remained completely intransigent over Belgium and refused to move from their extremist annexationist position.[10] The Chancellor waited for almost a month before refusing to provide a definitive statement on Germany's intentions regarding Belgium. The Vatican took this to mean a rejection of their peace move and effectively this snub brought the Papal peace mediation to an end. The OHL had triumphed again and Michealis' position was now untenable. Although he had been described in the press as possessing a 'clear head with iron willpower' he was in fact a meek and pliant character unable to chart a politically independent course.[11] Michaelis had leaned too heavily to the extreme annexationist position and like his predecessor, Bethmann Hollweg, had failed to steer a sufficiently independent middle course. By October the Reichstag were calling for his resignation.

The failure of the Pope's initiative was greeted with a triumphant howl of approval not only from right wing groups who were attempting to undermine any moves made by Catholic and pacifist elements, but more surprisingly, by the Protestant Church which was in favour of a continuation of the war. The attitude of the clergy to the war was summed up in a circular issued by the Bishop of Limburg on the Lahn that claimed 'paid agents of the enemy' were inciting the German people against its princes so as to undermine the national power of resistance and strength. It called on the clergy to resist such attempts 'with all determination'.[12] It was only in the latter half of 1917 that a small group of pastors in Berlin had the courage to instigate moves towards peace by collecting signatures for a peace protest. According to Princess Blücher the official attitude of the Protestant Church was governed by a traditional hostility that prevented it from following any lead headed by the Pope. The Princess recorded its war cry with disdain:

'We hope for a good German peace from God, and not a bad international one from the Pope.'[13]

While the Chancellor continued pathetically to appease the OHL and reassure the Reichstag of his honourable intentions, military pressure groups such as the Army League (*Wehrverein*) and Pan-Germans were concerned that peace mediation might raise false hopes in Germany thereby weakening the resolve of the people. The Navy League (*Flotterverein*) in particular launched a mendacious propaganda campaign promising a *Siegfrieden* through submarine warfare. On 21 August, Michaelis read out a confident statement to the Reichstag from Hindenburg: 'All fronts show that at the beginning of the fourth year of war we stand in a more favourable position than ever from a military point of view'.[14] A massive counter attack was now launched in opposition to the Peace Resolution and against all opponents of the OHL. The East Prussian civil servant, Wolfgang Kapp (who was later to lead a *putsch* against the Weimar Republic) and Grand Admiral Tirpitz, together with various right-wing pressure groups and nationalist organizations founded the *Deutsche Vaterlandspartei* (German Fatherland Party), an ultra right-wing nationalist movement. Encouraged by Hindenburg and Ludendorff and financed by the army and heavy industry, the *Deutsche Vaterlandspartei* was founded in September under the leadership of Prince John Albert of Mecklenburg and von Tirpitz (referred to by Hans-Ulrich Wehler as 'a professional failure') with Kapp as its chairman.[15]

The aims of the Fatherland Party were set out in its manifesto of 11/12 September 1917 ('the Day of Sedan').[16] Once established, it rapidly gained support and spearheaded right-wing propaganda against parliamentarianism, socialism, and the Reichstag resolutions for a negotiated peace without forced annexations. By July 1918 it claimed to have increased its membership to 1.25 million with over 2,500 branches.[17] Although it referred to itself as the Fatherland Party, it was established as a movement outside the existing party system to support and defend a strong government resolutely committed to victory. Claiming that the Reichstag no longer represented the will of the people, its manifesto argued that 'nervous and weak peace' resolutions only postponed peace. In the face of 'the all-devouring tyranny of Anglo-Americanism', its manifesto called for courage and endurance to secure a 'Hindenburg Peace'. Anything less would result in a 'starvation peace' (*Hungerfrieden*). Recalling the Iron Chancellor, Otto von Bismarck's titanic struggle against 'destructive party strife', the Fatherland Party pledged itself 'to guard and defend the German Fatherland in this gravest hour of German history from the evil of disunion and division' with the aim of 'welding together the whole energy of the Fatherland without distinction of party politics'.

In reality the *Vaterlandspartei* was a broad-based coalition of the right whose roots and antecedents can be traced to the *Sammlungspolitik* (coalition politics) of the late nineteenth century. Far from wishing to bring disparate groups and sectional interests together it was a deeply reactionary grouping, determined to maintain the *status quo* at home ('questions of internal politics must be postponed until after the war'), while waging an aggressive, agitational campaign, for a 'peace with victory' and large-scale annexations in the East and the West. It was particularly concerned to restore the prestige and authority of the Kaiser as a bulwark against a strident parliamentarianism. Much of its propaganda was consumed, therefore, with countering the 'cunning enemy's lies to encourage Germany's sons to abandon their Imperial Chief. The *Vaterlandspartei* was supported politically and financially by industrialists such as Kirdorf, Hugenberg, Roetger and Stinnes and the chemical and manufacturing industries of Borsig, Duisburg and Siemens. Thus there was no lack of funds and, moreover, while the propaganda of the left was repeatedly obstructed by censorship, surveillance and intimidation, the massive propaganda launched by the *Vaterlandspartei* was disseminated largely unhindered thanks to the support of the Supreme Command and big business.[18]

The Fatherland Party advocated also the repression of all opponents of the OHL and its quest for a *Siegfrieden*. The determination to stamp out dissent led directly to an alarming rise in anti-Semitism. Since the eighteenth century Jews had been a periodic target of vicious anti-Semitism. The economic crash of 1873 stimulated a revival of anti-Semitism which Bismarck exploited whenever it suited his political ends. The years leading up to the outbreak of war were marked by an increase in anti-Semitic literature disseminated largely by Pan-Germans groups who attacked the growing Jewish influence in German society and called for Jews to be barred from positions of importance. Such views were not uniquely German, or indeed, all pervasive, but help to substantiate the arguments put forward by some historians that stress the role of traditional elites and the continuities in social structures and ideology linking imperial Germany with the Nazi era.[19] Despite the insidious anti-Semitism that pervaded German culture, the partial assimilation of the German–Jewish population had, nevertheless, made considerable advances in the period leading up to 1914, albeit through 'negative integration'.[20] The tensions unleashed by war, however, resulted in a more virulent anti-Semitism.[21] The *Vaterlandspartei* and nationalist groups in general attempted to deflect criticism of the war and social deprivation into anti-Semitic sentiments. The search for scapegoats allegedly responsible for weakening German unity and strength focused on Social Democrats and Jews who were depicted as dangerous revolutionaries – or if they were demanding peace – as 'Jewish subversives'. In October 1916 the War Office even conducted a count of

Jews among soldiers and officers.[22] A plethora of contradictory accusations were levelled at Jews, including draft-dodging and war profiteering. Jews had traditionally been identified with capitalism and the war was frequently described in the monthly reports from the Deputy Commanding Generals as a *Geldkrieg* ('money war'). Nationalists drew the simplistic conclusion that the war was being prolonged because Jews had not yet made enough profit from it.[23] In the Reichstag, moreover, it was not uncommon for a political opponent to be labelled a 'Jew' as a term of abuse.[24] The *Vaterlandspartei* and nationalist pressure groups deliberately inflamed anti-Semitism to distract attention from genuine economic hardships and as a means of obfuscating class divisions. The President of the Pan-German League, Heinrich Class, called for a 'ruthless campaign against Jewry, against which the all too justified wrath of our good, but misled, people must be directed'.[25]

Viewed by some as a precursor to Nazism, the *Vaterlandspartei* did not last long enough for substantive comparisons to be sustained. Its manifesto concentrated on foreign affairs and proposals for territorial expansion, referred to by Volker Berghahn as 'hallucinations about empire'.[26] Little thought was given to a coherent economic programme. Nevertheless, comparisons with the NSDAP continue to be made and similarities undeniably exist. Both parties advocated dictatorship and demanded the repression of all political opponents, and both were virulently anti-Semitic and anti-Slav. Moreover the Fatherland Party included in its ranks Anton Drexler, founder of the German Workers' Party which was the forerunner of the Nazi NSDAP. For some, this connection is proof enough that a path can be traced from the Fatherland Party to the National Socialism that followed. The distinguished Conservative historian Friedrich Meinecke was convinced that such links could be made and wrote after the Second World War that 'the Pan-German League and the Fatherland Party had been true curtain-raisers for the rise of Hitler'.[27]

The first great rally of the new right wing alliance took place on 25 September 1917 in the Berlin Philharmonic Hall. The principal speaker was Admiral von Tirpitz who continued to maintain that Germany's demands on Belgium were entirely justified to protect her industrial heartland and that her military and particularly naval superiority would guarantee victory with annexations. The *Vaterlandspartei* remained ultimately propagandists for a *Siegfrieden*. Through its excessive demands, its unequivocal advocation of a 'Hindenburg Peace', its branding of everyone who disagreed with its policies as a *Staatsfeinde*, the Fatherland Party was unquestionably a divisive force and contributed to the polarization of opinion in Germany and the general decline in morale. Not surprisingly it elicited strong opposition which became increasingly vociferous. The nature of this opposition is described later in the chapter. Within a month of its foundation, Princess Blücher was moved to observe that internal disputes were 'being swallowed up in the vital conflict of the two great parties, the democrats and the *Vaterlandspartei*, which is daily increasing in vehemence'.[28]

'MUNITIONS OF THE MIND': 'PATRIOTIC INSTRUCTION' AND THE REORGANIZATION OF IMPERIAL PROPAGANDA, 1917–18

The *Vaterlandspartei* had been established in response to the 'July crisis' that led to the resignation of Bethmann Hollweg but also to a resurgent Reichstag. Its supporters were determined that Germany's war aims should continue along the lines set out by the OHL and not undermined by agitation for peace and domestic reform. With the resignation of Bethmann, the OHL believed that it was in the political ascendency now that a compliant Chancellor was prepared to implement its bidding *vis-à-vis* the Reichstag. Hindenburg had declared in August that Germany's military position had never been stronger. Nevertheless, Ludendorff had felt for some time that the OHL had been losing the battle for public opinion at home. He remained convinced that public opinion could be assuaged more easily if propaganda and censorship was centrally coordinated by the OHL. One of the major failings of Germany propaganda during the war was that an overburdened *Kriegspresseamt* (KPA) had been established with dual responsibilities to supply war news to the press and maintain the morale of the German people and the troops. Partly because it lacked a sophisticated understanding of the psychology of modern warfare it had failed to set up specialized units within its organization and, as a result, chose to concentrate on war news at the expense of morale. Moreover it was staffed by military personnel whose first priority was waging war. It appreciated too late that modern warfare required as much attention to the 'munitions of the mind' as to planning battles.[29]

In May 1917 the Prussian War Ministry held a meeting chaired by Colonel Ernst von Wrisberg and attended by representatives from all the major ministries, including Major Nicolai representing the OHL. The meeting, which lasted for two days, was ostensibly to coordinate measures to counter anti-monarchist propaganda, but inevitably it covered a broader agenda.[30] Recognizing that Allied propaganda was having a demoralizing affect on both the home front and troops, the meeting agreed to recommend a number of measures. The Reich Chancellor was to set up a central agency for the collection and coordination of propaganda and closer links were to be established with Section IIIb of the OHL (two measures that Ludendorff had urged in December 1916).[31] Not only did this strengthen Nicolai's position but it was also intended to overcome the endless conflicts that had bedevilled the military and civilian censorship bodies.[32] Funding was to be allocated for a new campaign of 'patriotic enlightenment' that would enlist 'important' individuals to write articles for the press, or give speeches to combat enemy propaganda and counter harmful rumours.[33] The churches, the schools and patriotic women's organizations were all to be used as agencies for 'enlightenment', providing meetings and lectures based on specially selected material sent by the War Press Office.[34] The meeting unanimously agreed that urgent measures were needed to restore the popularity of the Kaiser. In an attempt to engender better public appreciation of the work carried out by Wilhelm, the Kaiser, together with the Kaiserin, were to be placed in the Forefront of the counter-propaganda campaign. The press was to convey in words and pictures his 'extensive contribution to the good of the Fatherland'.[35] For his part, the Emperor would be asked to make trips to the smaller towns and villages to raise his profile in the eyes of the people. He would also be given more credit for alleviating the food shortages and greater efforts would be made to establish a closer identification with the workers, particularly in the industrial conurbations.

The authorities had been concerned for some time at the declining popularity of the Kaiser and the increase in enemy anti-monarchy propaganda flooding into Germany. On 29 April in a telegram sent to Secretary of State Zimmermann, Legation Secretary Freherr von Lersner outlined Ludendorff's concern at the Allies' attempt to drive a wedge between the German people and the Hohenzollerns.[36] Lersner reported that the military cabinet had received numerous letters from the public asking that the Kaiser abdicate and that Ludendorff had sent Nicolai to Berlin to confer with the Minister of War to counter anti-monarchist propaganda sentiments. Ludendorff favoured stringent censorship in the German press and as a result of Lersner's telegram, Deutelmoser, now installed as chief of the News Division in the Foreign Office, instructed the Censorship Office and the Post Supervision Office to classify anti-monarchy material as 'dangerous' and to pass them on to the military censor, who had instructions to suppress such material from appearing in the press.

Attempts to determine the place of Wilhelm II in German history and to analyse the importance (or otherwise) of the Kaiser invariably involves the historian in making judgements about the so-called *Sonderweg* thesis and the conditions which permitted the rise of Hitler to power. Much of this debate, however, focuses on Wilhelm II's role in the pre-1914 period.[37] The outbreak of war marked a sharp decline in the personal influence of the Kaiser. The prestige of the monarchy had declined so much that by the time Wilhelm II had reluctantly acceded to public demand for the appointment of

Hindenburg and Ludendorff, the 'Supreme Warlord' (now an empty title) had been relegated into the background. Although Wilhelm II was inquisitive and enthusiastic by nature, he lacked the staying power to ensure that his ideas were translated into policy.[38] By the middle of 1916, popular acceptance of his constitutional infallibility had perceptibly waned. Aware of this, Wilhelm was less inclined to exert Imperial rule in the face of the challenge posed by Hindenburg and Ludendorff. The importance of 'kingship mechanism', a term used by Norbert Elias to describe the desire within the governmental and administrative elite to procure the Kaiser's favour, also became less important during the course of the war. Obsequiousness and servility remained a feature of court life and undoubtedly contributed to the poor quality of government in later Imperial Germany. But these were the vestiges of a political system that was failing to respond to what Arthur Marwick has referred to as the 'test' of war.[39] Apart from periodic sabre rattling and the symbolic maintenance of hierarchical protocol, which was a characteristic of German society, Wilhelm II was very much a spent force. Nevertheless, for propaganda purposes, it was important to maintain the pretence that the Kaiser retained the support of his subjects.

Unlike Bismarck, Hindenburg and Ludendorff had no intention of disguising their power under the constitutional cloak of monarchical authority. Wilhelm was aware of the seriousness of the threat to his own position posed by the populist Third Supreme Command but his shortcomings were such that he was unable to provide the constitutional balance between weak political leadership and the strength of the OHL. By 1917 the Kaiser's reputation had slumped alarmingly; reports from the Deputy Commanding Generals refer to the open scorn in which he was now held by Germans. In Bavaria it was rumoured that he had been wounded in an assassination attempt in Austria. Bavarians, held him personally responsible for prolonging the war and cared little whether he survived or not, claiming: 'Austria wanted peace, but the Prussian Swine keeps holding it up'.[40] In the summer of 1917 Princess Blücher wrote in her diary that, 'the Kaiser is daily growing more and more the shadow of a king, and people talk openly of his abdication as a possibility very much desired'.[41] Hermann Gunsser, an Independent Deputy from Württemberg, boasted that: 'Public opinion is at a high pitch in South Germany. If the Kaiser were to enter a village in my electoral district he would scarcely come out of it alive'.[42]

The extent to which the Kaiser had been replaced in the minds of his people by the populist figures of Hindenburg and Ludendorff can be gauged by the intensive propaganda campaign that was launched for the Sixth War Loan in the spring of 1917.[43] The campaign was spearheaded by Bruno Paul's famous poster 'Times are Hard, But Victory is Certain' containing

Figure 23 'Help Us Win! Subscribe to the War Loans.' Fritz Erler's 1917 haunting poster for the Sixth War Loan.

the monumental profile of Hindenburg as the new national symbol (Figure 14). Another famous poster associated with the Sixth War Loan was Fritz Erler's 'Help Us Win! Subscribe to the War Loans', which became the most widely distributed German poster of the war. An infantryman wearing the steel helmet that was introduced in 1916 stares defiantly from the trenches. He is surrounded by barbed wire, a gas mask on his chest and two 'potato masher' grenades in his pouch, the intensity of his eyes and his defensive position in the trenches captured the siege mentality of Germany in 1917 (see Figure 23).[44] The Admiralty played an important role in the campaign. A typical advertising statement was released by its News Department on 21 March:

> The war is drawing to a decisive phase on land and sea and the words of Frederick the Great have special significance. He said, 'to wage war, money, money, and more money is needed'. Let everyone think of this and contribute to victory by subscribing to the Sixth War Loan.[45]

The public response to the flotation was surprisingly enthusiastic, although it had been launched before the 'July crisis' and the Reichstag's peace resolution, both of which had a dramatic effect on public opinion. The pro-German *Continental Times* ('Independent Cosmopolitan Paper for Americans in Europe') reported enthusiastically on the success of the Sixth War Loan under a cartoon entitled 'In the Land of the Free and the Home of the Brave':

> Some of the latest subscriptions to the Sixth War Loan are truly remarkable. They tell eloquently of the spirit of patriotism and confidence which exists through-out the country. It must be remembered that none of the frantic style of advertising which recently took place in England where the entire country was placarded with screaming posters, papers crowded with overwrought and hyper-sensational advertisements, imploring, admonishing or cajoling the people, and statesmen like Bonar Law even using threats of coercion if people did not subscribe. Here all has been done quietly. In simple words and modest form the people have been asked to subscribe from motives of patriotism. Posters have been used but in no sense have they been loud or sensational ...[46]

Despite the relative success of the Sixth War Loan, Ludendorff continued to argue that propaganda had failed to provide the German people with a sense of what they were fighting and dying for. By continuing to press for more centralized control over the means of communication, Ludendorff was swimming against the prevailing public mistrust of state authority. Civilian and military authorities were encountering widespread aversion to their 'enlightenment' campaigns immediately the public became aware that propaganda material emanated from official channels.[47] An alarming challenge to government information control had developed since the winter of 1916/17 in the form of a 'counter public' (*Gegenöffentlichkeit*) that subverted official news and information about the war with rumours, gossip, jokes, and criticisms of the war, etc. Such opportunities presented themselves wherever people gathered in groups, be it in a food queue, a cinema or an overcrowded train compartment. These channels of communication proved impossible to regulate although it had been made an obligation to notify authorities of the spreading of false information since January 1917.[48] Municipal authorities and regional commands collected this information but could do little with it, while some Deputy Commanding Generals tried (unsuccessfully) to make the spreading of false rumour a punishable offence. Official responses varied from one region to another but there was widespread agreement that false rumours (that remained unchecked) contributed to the growing antipathy to the war. Rumours also acted as the catalyst for spontaneous collective action that could ignite into a food riot or even a strike.[49]

Unperturbed by reports suggesting a widening gulf between state authority and popular feeling about the war, Ludendorff decided to press on and cultivate his, and Hindenburg's popular base, through a major propaganda programme of 'patriotic instruction' (*Vaterländische Unterricht*). A start would be made on the troops and the campaign was launched by Ludendorff on 29 July 1917.[50] On 17 July 1917, Ludendorff penned a memorandum claiming the success of the sixth war loan had been due to the organizational structure that the military had established for enlightenment purposes. This was to be the basis for a much wider campaign of 'patriotic instruction' intended to raise the morale of the troops as the vanguard for a decisive victory.[51] Outlining the importance of 'patriotic instruction', Ludendorff wrote that 'a natural longing for home and family after three years of war had sapped the fighting spirit of the troops'. The object of patriotic education was to impress upon German soldiers the realization that the 'greater the burdens on the spirit of the army, the greater is the necessity that conviction, duty and whole-hearted resolution should become the army's fighting strengths'.[52] For some time the OHL had claimed that sections of the army had been infiltrated by USPD agitational propaganda and that this had lowered morale and undermined discipline amongst the troops.[53] To counter the dual problem of enemy propaganda and political agitation of the far left, an extensive organizational apparatus was established.[54] Ludendorff remained in overall charge although Section IIIb under Nicolai was responsible for the day-to-day running of the programme. A permanent coordinating organization was established at GHQ and in each army corps district a specialist propaganda officer was appointed who would receive advice and material from the War Press Office on how best to disseminate the patriotic propaganda in the district units.[55] These 'directors of propaganda' were to be attached to the General Staff and would decide on the methods adopted according to the needs of individual units although the commanding officers would have ultimate responsibility for the patriotic education of the men under their command.[56]

Ludendorff recognized that there was a direct correlation between the spirit of the army and the morale of the public. For this reason patriotic

Civilians 'Fall-in'

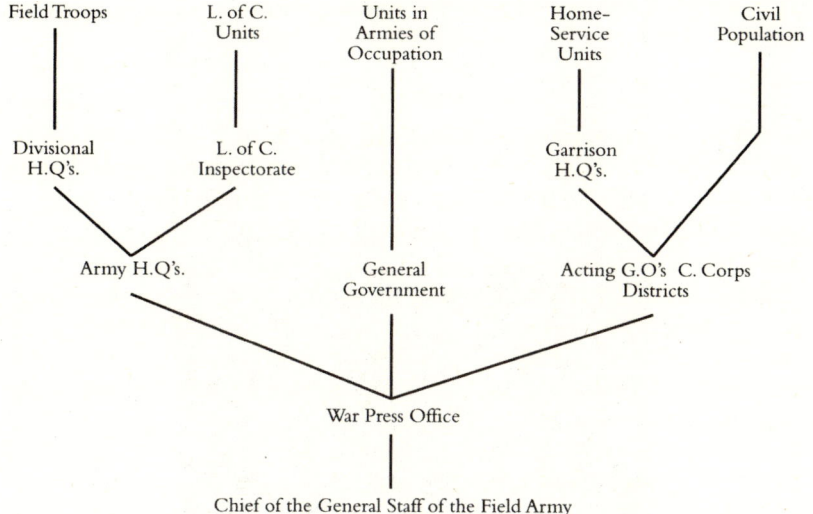

Figure 24 The Organization for 'patriotic instruction'.[57]

propaganda at home was to be brought in line with that of the army. 'Patriotic instruction' would apply equally to the home front (Figure 25). Typically, the military decided on the same organizational structure for the dissemination of *Vaterländische Unterricht* to the civilian population.

Although the principle that governed 'patriotic instruction' was that propaganda should be adapted to local requirements it was stipulated by Ludendorff that discussion should not be permitted. Instead patriotic instruction was to be confined to certain points and repeated many times.[58] Four themes were indentified:

1. *The Causes of the War.* The economic development of Germany, its importance and the consequences of a lost war, particularly from the point of view of the working class.
2. *Confidence in Final Victory.* The war was turning decisively in Germany's favour and devotion to duty and manly pride are to be encouraged.
3. *The Necessity and Importance of Leadership* (the army, the government, civil administration, industry and commerce). Hence the necessity for authority and it corollary, obedience. There must be unflinching confidence in the Emperor and the princes of the federal states, as well as the military leaders.
4. *The Enemy,* who is placing all his hopes on our economic and political collapse must be convinced that we cannot be beaten in the field.

Figure 25 'Through Work to Victory! Through Victory to Peace!' A symbolic handshake between the fighting front and the home front. Alexander Cay, 1917.

The immense importance that Ludendorff attached to the campaign can be gauged by the fact that he addended a personal statement to the order of 29 July. Public morale had fallen to a low ebb, he argued, and this had affected the army as well ('public opinion at home has in some cases actually infected the army already, as countless letters show'). Left-wing agitators and pacifists were predictably condemned for provoking discontent and what Ludendorff termed 'rampant vulgar cares' were endangering the troops and final victory. Calling on all commanding officers to take the lead against 'agitators, gamblers and weaklings' he promised that once the campaign had got off the ground, specialist army personnel ('directors of propaganda') would be infiltrated into civilian life to raise the morale of the general public.[59] 'Directors of propaganda' were appointed to each army unit and given the responsibility for organizing compulsory lectures on specific themes at least twice a week. The content of these lectures, which were to be the focus of patriotic instruction, was strictly circumscribed and had to develop out of the guiding principle that: 'the *love of the mother country* springs from the knowledge of the *worth* of the mother country.' This resulted in tortuous lists of instructions, constantly updated, of how the lectures were to be delivered. War aims and party politics were strictly forbidden; the war was to be portrayed as being forced on Germany by the unscrupulous Entente powers who were not interested in German offers of peace. A weak peace therefore meant economic disaster for Germany. The troops had to be taught the imperative need to fight on, convinced by jingoistic history lessons on past military triumphs and current U–boat successes that victory was assured. War profiteers were condemned and workers in the armaments factories who went on strike were accused of fratricide.[60] The lectures were supplemented by visiting speakers, film propaganda and mobile libraries stocked with nationalistic literature especially chosen by the *Aufklärungstelle*.[61] (See Figures 7 and 25.)

One of the first tests of the new programme was the flotation for the Seventh War Loan in the autumn of 1917. Interestingly enough having established a centralized organization for the dissemination of 'patriotic instruction', the public's response to the Seventh War Loan was lukewarm. This reflected the duration of the war, the demands of the military upon the civilian population and the unprecedented economic burdens that led to war weariness and a longing for peace. Unfortunately for the OHL reports were indicating that the public was no longer concerned with the question of war aims, rather when will the war end.[62] No amount of centralization could persuade the population to invest enthusiastically in war bonds if they believed such an act might prolong the war. As one official put it succinctly; 'The people are saying that "enthusiasm is not a herring that one can salt".'[63]

In August the War Press Office had set up a conference to review the question of public morale. The Head of the WPO, Major Stotten, informed the participants that the Entente had been extraordinarily successful with slogans. Apart from 'The Freedom of the Seas', Germany had been woefully inept at using slogans for propaganda purposes. He therefore proposed a contest and prizes for the best slogans ('words which can illuminate ideas like a flash of lightning'). The Bavarian War Ministry suggested that more use should be made of the placard, claiming that in England, 'entire houses had been covered with war loan posters'. Stotten reaffirmed the importance of the 'artistic poster' and cited Erler's poster for the Sixth War Loan as an example of successful propaganda. The WPO, however, was reluctant to embark upon blanket coverage as posters were expensive, but it would continue to target station depots, factories, worker's dining rooms, etc.[64]

Although the Seventh War Loan campaign in October proved to be a disappointment for the OHL, it used some particularly striking posters. The campaign coincided with the celebrations for the 70th birthday of Hindenburg. Louis Oppenheim designed a poster with the Field Marshal's massive head over a signed statement: 'The man who subscribes to the War Loan is giving me the best birthday present. von Hindenburg.'[65] Another war-loan poster showed a determined Teutonic knight brandishing a sword and shield but wearing an infantryman's steel helmet. F.K. Engelhard's poster, 'No! Never!' showing a grasping, claw-like pose of an enemy soldier set to engulf Germany (depicted in terms of both town and countryside) was intended to be an unequivocal reminder of what capitulation and defeat would mean. A recurring theme in 1917–18 was that in prolonging the war and rejecting an unfair peace, Germany was fighting for freedom. Lucien Bernard's poster of the mailed fist was a powerful symbol of aggression that throws down the gauntlet: 'This is the Way to Peace – the enemy wills it so! Therefore subscribe to the War Loans!'. (See Figures 26–29.) A broadsheet showed John Bull being toppled by the 13.1 billion marks that was collected in the campaign. Similarly, Gerd Paul encouraged the nation to subscribe by showing a Siegfried-like warrior beating a cowering British lion with the caption: 'The last blows are necessary for final victory. Subscribe to the War Loans'.

German propagandists were quick to employ children in the campaigns (as indeed were all the belligerent nations), often with the intention of embarrassing the adult population. Typical was a propaganda leaflet which showed a group of German schoolchildren reading a rhyme in a book: 'Everyone up 'till the last row. Is joyfully subscribing to the War Loan. The young ones show themselves today to be cleverer than many grown-ups.' A later campaign used a conversation between a teacher and pupil to illustrate the point. Under the heading 'The Subscribing Hour':

> *Teacher.* How many War Loans have you subscribed to, Else? *Else* (daughter of an innkeeper): I Miss? *All Nine!*[66]

Film was also widely used for propaganda purposes. The most popular film used to promote the Seventh War Loan featured the leading German movie star, Henny Porten, in a Messter production entitled *Hann, Hein und Henny*. The 'Henny' in the film is Porten playing herself. Hann and Hein are two U-boat sailors who have written to her for advice on how best to raise money for the war effort. Receiving them in an opulent apartment, Porten explains to the sailors with the aid of an animated dream sequence that they are not to worry as she has had a premonition that the public's generosity

Figure 26 'This is the Way to Peace – the Enemy Wills it So! Therefore Subscribe to the War Loans!' Lucian Bernhard's powerful poster for the Seventh War Loan of the mailed gauntlet.

will ensure that the government's target for the loan drive will be met. The film press reported that the film (referred to as a *'Kriegsanliehe-Filme'*) was an 'overwhelming success' with cinema audiences.[67]

As Christmas 1917 approached it became obvious that the patriotic instruction programme was having little success (Figures 31 and 32). The home front had been urged to 'think German' and avoid all foreign influences while continuing to suffer deprivations. Women were encouraged to use food substitutes, not to complain to husbands fighting at the front, and above all not to have sexual intercourse with prisoners of war.[68] At the front, troops laughed at sermons that tended to consist of nothing more than chauvinistic claptrap. As early as May 1917 it had been noted that there was a shortage of suitable teachers to provide suitably 'patriotic' lectures – especially to the

Figure 27 Another variation of the Teutonic knight – brandishing sword and shield but wearing a First World War steel helmet. Poster for the Seventh War Loan.

disoriented youth in the conurbations.[69] The exception was in the field of entertainment, and particularly film entertainment, where war-time developments were to have long-term implications for the German film industry. (Figure 33.) One of the ramifications of *Vaterländische Unterricht* was the increasing state intervention in the film industry. Throughout 1917, Ludendorff had been stressing the importance of film as a propaganda medium and calling for the industry to be centralized. As a result, a new umbrella organization financed jointly by the state and private industry was founded on 18 December 1917 and became known as *Universum-Film-Aktiengesellschaft* (Ufa).

The imperial government's involvement in the founding of Ufa was set out in a secret meeting in January 1918 attended by all the major political and military representatives.[70] They had been called together to decide how they

Figure 28 'Subscribe to War Loans. Help those who watch over your Happiness.' An archetypal German family from the Nibelungen legend.

would make use of its facilities, both during the war and in the years of peace which followed. The War Ministry was particularly concerned to keep official involvement in the new combine hidden from the public, thus reflecting its reluctance to be seen to be indulging openly in propaganda. Although the OHL was keen to see Ufa become commercially successful (hence its stated reason for not taking a larger share in the company), it nonetheless had to ensure that the state's political interests were safeguarded at every level within the new organization. Interestingly, although the founding of Ufa had been announced for some six weeks, it had still to be registered officially as a going concern and government departments had yet to decide its precise role.[71] The War Ministry, which dominated the proceedings, identified three immediate tasks, suggesting that Ufa would spearhead both domestic and foreign film propaganda and coordinate the activities of the commercial film industry.[72] Reassurances were given to the Reichsbank that Ufa would be expected to make substantial profits for all concerned. The armed forces,

Figure 29 A dramatic poster for the Seventh War Loan depicts President Wilson as a warlike dragon.

individual ministries and municipal authorities would even have to pay for the services of Ufa out of their own budgets. The only faintly dissenting voice came from the Ministry of Culture which expressed the hope that such commercial considerations would not be allowed to undermine its efforts to raise the status of film. Within this new economic and political framework, the position of film organizations like Deulig and Bufa were discussed.[73] The OHL was clearly annoyed with the lack of cooperation from Deulig. Bufa, on the other hand, was to be absorbed within the new combine and given a subordinate role.

Although the government and the OHL were determined to keep official involvement in Ufa a secret, they were clearly excited by the possibilities offered by film in promoting its campaign of 'patriotic instruction'.[74] Ufa was

Figure 30 Gerd Paul's dramatic poster for the Seventh War Loan depicting a Siegfried-like warrior beating a cowering British lion with the caption: 'The last blows are necessary for final victory. Subscribe to the War Loans'.

envisaged as the catalyst through which film production, facilities and film theatres would be improved and increased. Film production was no longer to reflect the lowest tastes of the masses. Film was now to have an educational and cultural role and would reflect sectional interests in German society – the armed forces, big business, trade unions, local authorities, the police, and even Germany's colonial achievements. The anticipation of a national film archive (one of Bufa's new responsibilities) suggests also a sophisticated awareness of the richness of film as a source of historical record.

Ufa was established too late to make a a major contribution to the war effort. After the war, the German government's involvement in Ufa was exposed in a celebrated debate in the National Assembly where it was strongly

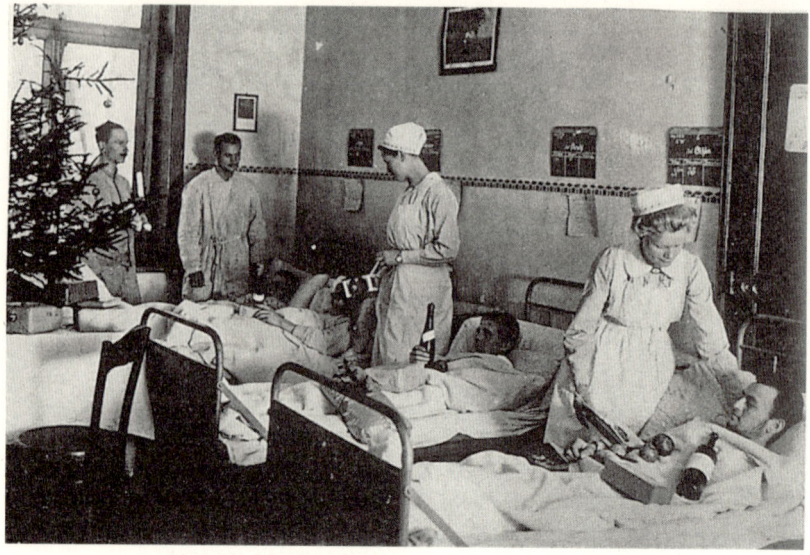

Figure 31 A German hospital ward on Christmas day.

criticized. The state was eventually forced to sell its holdings in the company. Even so, despite the turmoil in Germany in 1918, Ufa quickly asserted its independence in the field of film production. It rapidly became the largest film enterprise in Europe and four years after the war, Germany's film production was second only to that of the United States.[75]

In September 1917 Ludendorff reviewed the 'patriotic instruction' campaign, stressed again its importance to the war effort and seemed satisfied with it success. He agreed that terms such as 'patriotic propaganda' and 'propaganda officer' could be misconstrued as having political implications (*sic*) and should be substituted by 'patriotic education' and 'education officer'. He also confirmed that there was no need for the campaign to remain secret.[76] Ludendorff remained sensitive to accusations that *Vaterländische Unterricht* was politically biased in favour of right-wing annexationist propaganda. Hence his concern that party politics should be kept out of the campaign. In practice, of course, it was a politically driven, undisguised attack on the left. It conceived that the military 'solution' to increasing polarization was a *Siegfrieden* that would render democratic and socialist reforms unnecessary. Not surprisingly the patriotic instruction programme incurred widespread hostility from political opponents.

The roots and antecedents of these objections can be traced to the proliferation of Pan-German propaganda from the spring of 1917. In Württemberg,

Figure 32 Erich Gruner's wood-cut poster: 'Thanks. Offering from the Kaiser and the Nation to the Army and Navy. Christmas Gifts for 1917'. Note the symbols of the crown and the clasped hands.

Haussmann, a Progressive Deputy complained that the propaganda made neutrals hate Germany.[77] Other Deputies claimed that Pan-German campaigns for annexations irreparably damaged relations with America.[78] In October these complaints reached their climax with a socialist interpellation in the Reichstag. In the course of the debate on the new war loan, the OHL, the Fatherland Party and Pan-German groups were roundly attacked and accused of manipulating the patriotic instruction campaigns for the purpose of annexationist propaganda. Hasse (USPD) pointed out that it had been the Supreme Command and not the Reichstag that had appointed the new Chancellor – 'a confidant of Hindenburg and Ludendorff. Haase reaffirmed the socialists' manifesto for peace, namely: 'No annexations, no indemnities, self-determination and the struggle against any imperialistic government that rejects this programme or even replies to it evasively...'.[79] The new

Figure 33 A still from the final scene of *Der Knute entflohen* (*Escaping from Tyranny*).

Secretary of State, Richard von Kühlmann, was asked to make a statement on the question of Belgium independence but remained implacably evasive: 'What we shall fight for to the last drop of blood are not fantastic conquests, but the inviolability of the German Reich'. It was left to Otto Landsberg of the SPD to launch a measured, but nonetheless, devastating attack on the patriotic instruction programme. Landsberg exposed the Pan-German claim to decide what was German and what was patriotic. Citing numerous examples of unhindered Pan-German agitation and army excursions into party politics, Landsberg claimed that the whole propaganda exercise, although ostensibly to fortify the soldiers' courage, was directed at the Reichstag's Peace Resolution of 19 July which had attempted to revise drastically the expansionist war aims of Imperial Germany.[80]

Although the Reichstag approved the new war loan, the socialist majority voted for the first time with the minority against the credits as a protest against Pan-German annexationist activity.[81] The Reichstag seized the opportunity offered by the patriotic instruction campaign to flex its new found political muscle. Having sought the assistance of the parliamentarians to remove Bethmann Hollweg in July, the OHL was now faced with the wholly unanticipated event of a concerted Reichstag majority demanding that Michaelis be replaced. On 22 October, a coalition of SPD, Progressives, National-Liberals and Centre Party Deputies called for a new Chancellor who would agree to its five-point programme of political principles that included a relaxation of censorship, reform of the franchise and a conciliatory reply to the Papal peace initiative. There is a certain irony that the Reichstag should demand the removal of Michaelis at precisely the same time that the OHL was demanding discipline and obedience by exhorting the people to follow leadership figures such as the Kaiser and Hindenburg. Having bowed to the wishes of Ludendorff and the OHL, Michaelis had failed to gain the support of the Reichstag majority. The Chancellor's inept handling of the naval mutiny, the growing anti-war sentiment and the spate of political strikes, persuaded even supporters such as Kühlmann that he would have to go. On 2 August, approximately 600 sailors on the battleship *Prinzregent Luitpold* left their ship to protest at conditions on board. They were quickly joined by sailors from other ships moored in Wilhelmshaven. The *Prinzregent Luitpold* was placed under siege and the sailors were charged with mutiny and political conspiracy having been accused of consorting with the USPD and with planning to make political mischief at the forthcoming Socialist Congress in Stockholm. On 26 August, five sailors were convicted and in September two were executed and three given lengthy prison sentences. Michaelis compounded the injustice of the whole affair by Falsely accusing the USPD of plotting with one of the convicted sailors against the Kaiser. Having caused uproar in the Reichstag by his political ineptitude, Michaelis' position was no longer tenable.[82] Within six months of coming into office he was replaced by the 74-year old Count Georg von Hertling, former Prime Minister of Bavaria. Hertling was not particularly liked by either Hindenburg or Ludendorff but by appointing a conservative Catholic as Chancellor it was hoped that he might split the Centre Party and neutralize the effects of Erzberger's Peace Resolution.[83]

Ludendorff's insistence that *Vaterländische Unterricht* was effectively countering people's negative perceptions of the war was not shared by officials from within the War Press Office who reported that the programme had failed to imbue the people with a 'strong national self-consciousness'; 'Like children they must be told what they have to do'.[84] The Deputy Commanding Generals were also expressing misgivings. One report suggested that attempts to manipulate opinion were doomed as the public viewed all attempts at enlightenment as 'cheap propaganda'.[85] Moreover, the programme of patriotic instruction was being constantly tampered with. In November, at the time that Reichstag politicians were calling for the dismissal of Michaelis, Ludendorff commended a 'new syllabus' for directors of patriotic education that was intended to refine the programme and make it more meaningful to the troops and the home front.[86] A lack of suitable speakers, however, was proving a major obstacle to the successful implementation of the programme. The War Press Office had informed the War Ministries as early as May that the call-up of large numbers of teachers had created a crisis particularly for school and youth authorities.[87] In fact the problem was more profound than simply a lack of speakers, although this was important; the campaign was fundamentally ill-conceived and flawed from the outset, both psychologically and politically. As men and women were collapsing in the factories for lack of food, they were being subjected to the most banal and jingoistic claptrap. Soldiers who refused to believe that the war was almost won, were 'fortified' by horrific stories of atrocities committed against German prisoners of war.[88] Writing after the war to discredit the *Dolchstoss* myth perpetuated by right wing nationalist groups that the German army remained undefeated on the battlefield, Ludwig Lewinsohn painted a different picture of low morale among demoralized troops:

> The means of strengthening their morale, defensive war from the homeland, was decried as a lie. The *Vaterländische Unterricht*, which was conducted by young officers, was laughed at. Hate was in the troops. Hate not for the enemy who were suffering the same, but hate for those who prolonged the war'.[89]

Not only was the programme psychologically flawed but it also continued to be hindered by the OHL's insistence on retaining organizational control and its refusal to distinguish between propaganda for the troops and for the home front. Ludendorff steadfastly refused to contemplate establishing a Reichs Press Office responsible for civilian morale that would complement the War Press Office.[90] Such intransigence reflected Ludendorff's organizational fetishism and his belief that the morale of the people could be transformed by new, centralized, organizational structures. Little thought was given to the complexity of the issues involved – both personal and political. *Vaterländische Unterricht*, and the organizational restructuring that accompanied it, was the 'final solution' to complex political and economic problems from an increasingly eccentric and isolated general.[91] It was also the last desperate attempt on the part of the *status quo* to pre-empt a feared 'revolution from below'.

8
Defeat and Revolution

Soon it will be all over,
Spirits are low, strength is ebbing,
Only discipline is matchless!
                            Polybius

BREST-LITOVSK: 'VICTORY IS OURS'

As Christmas 1917 approached it became obvious that the patriotic instruction programme was having little success.[1] The mood of the German people during the fourth year of the war was influenced by a deep longing for peace and strong dissatisfaction with its own government for its failure to negotiate a peace settlement. The government, or more precisely, the OHL, responded to public indifference to the war with patriotic instruction, tough regimentation and increasing repression at home. Strikers, for example, were now regularly sent to the front. Yet despite the hardship and fatigue imposed by the exigencies of total war the fabric of German society remained intact. The political infrastructure at both national and local level continued to function; the army remained loyal, and, with the exception of the small and isolated Spartacists, there existed no revolutionary challenge to the *status quo*. The conditions that had led to revolutionary breakdown in Russia had therefore not been reached in Germany.[2]

Nevertheless, the German people were approaching the limits of their endurance. Cupboards remained bare, food queues extended even longer (encouraging ever more alarming rumours to spread) and coal was in short supply. Electricity and power proved insufficient to maintain the cities. Overcrowding became a feature of everyday life on the transport systems. On Christmas Day 1917, the *Berliner Tageblatt* reported that due to the high prices, the capital remained littered with unsold Christmas trees.[3] Shortages of food that had led to hoarding and blackmarketing drove a wedge between town and countryside and rich and poor and increased class hatred. Bavarians now firmly believed that the war was being prolonged in the interests of Prussian militarists and Junkers. Front-line soldiers came to despise the profiteers and draft-dodgers who demeaned their sacrifices. The Kaiser was a pathetic figure who no longer represented the symbol of national unity. The *Burgfrieden* which had been the focus of official propaganda since 1914, could hardly be mentioned without illiciting howls of derision. Half the population had lost interest in the outcome of the war and the other half believed that it was already lost. The Entente was also close to exhaustion; the French army had been shaken by mutiny and Europe was running out of fighting men.

Thus towards the end of 1917, the mood of political unity that had been a feature of the 'spirit of 1914' was rapidly disintegrating. One writer noted: 'In August 1914 one rejoiced with it. At that time it was in truth the representative of the people's will and the universal spirit. Since then a grey layer of increasing disenchantment has come over the entire land'.[4] While the moderate faction in the Reichstag was talking about peace without annexations, the OHL had rejected the opportunity of a negotiated peace in the belief that only a spectacular military victory could avert the threat of domestic revolution. The winter of 1917–18 was dominated by the peace negotiations between Russia and the Central Powers at Brest-Litovsk. The Bolsheviks, exploiting the failure of the Kerensky government to make peace with Germany, seized power in November 1917. Lenin saw the immediate necessity of ending the war. The German government was anxious to secure a formal peace treaty that would allow the despatch of troops to the Western Front. Considerable differences between the civilians' representatives led by Foreign Secretary Richard von Kühlmann and the military led by Ludendorff prevented, however, a speedy conclusion to a peace settlement.[5]

Negotiations between German and Russian delegates began in the small town of Brest-Litovsk on 22 December and concluded three months later on 3 March with a treaty that the Kaiser hailed as one of the 'greatest successes in world history'.[6] Under the terms of the treaty, Russia lost over one million square miles of land, and 62 million people, whose fate would be determined by Germany and Austria, were now incorporated into the Second Reich.[7]

Germans followed the negotiations with intense interest. For many war-weary citizens the peace negotiation offered new hope. 'Christmas was, of course, but a sorry season,' recorded Princess Blücher:

> although the unexpected and seemingly successful peace movement in Russia undoubtedly created a brighter atmosphere for people here than they have known since the war begun. Brest-Litovsk, mingled with the divine proclamation of 'Peace upon earth and goodwill amongst men', moved our hearts to a new throb of hope. It remains to be seen how far people are justified in believing this to be the first weak wavelet of the great peace-tide which is gradually but surely going to inundate Europe[8]

Formal peace negotiations began on 27 December with all discussion, at Lenin's insistence, made public. However, the Russian delegation headed by Trotsky broke off negotiations when the punitive nature of the German demands became known. Talks resumed in early January but the Bolsheviks refused to continue under Germany's terms ('no war, no peace') and returned to Russia. Towards the end of January the first political strikes took place in Berlin and spread throughout the Reich. The talks were reopened again in February and in March Lenin ceded to the annexationist demands of the OHL. Opinion in the Reichstag divided along predictable lines although only the Independent Socialists expressed outright opposition by voting against war credits. Stresemann and the National-Liberals argued that if the Supreme Command felt it necessary Germany should annex certain territories in order to protect its existing frontiers. Ledebour and other Social Democrats objected to the government's intervention in the domestic affairs of Russia and warned the OHL against annexing parts of Poland, insisting that the negotiations must be based on self-determination. Haase for the USPD denounced the rectification of frontiers as annexation and accused Herding, the new Chancellor, of working as an agent for the military and the annexationists.[9] In March, Haase resumed the attack by criticizing the secrecy surrounding the negotiations and declaring his party's opposition by voting against war credits. Although Lenin had insisted that the negotiations be made public, the tension in the German camp between civilian and military objectives led to severe censorship in the German press.[10] At a meeting of the Reichstag's Finance Committee held on 3 January 1918, the SPD's Eduard David complained that committee members remained in the dark about what was going on at Brest-Litovsk: 'The enemy as well as the neutral people are much better informed concerning the actual state of affairs than is the German Reichstag'. Ebert demanded that all publications of the Russian government and accompanying resolutions be laid before the House.[11] The Reichstag was not kept fully informed of the peace negotiations and failed to stop the plans of conquest. Whether it would have had the courage or desire to flex its legislative muscles and block the OHL's posturing at Brest-Litovsk is open to doubt.

When the terms were published in March, Hindenburg and Ludendorff's megalomaniacal plans for the East were exposed for all to see. The OHL had been determined to hold the Ukraine for its grain, and to control the Donets basin for its coal and the Caucasus for its oil.[12] Ludendorff and Hindenburg had revealed their hand and were determined to brook no opposition or allow politicians to whittle down their expansionist goals. During the negotiations both men had offered their resignations and when Chancellor Hertling had made a half-hearted attempt to act as a broker, he was informed in no uncertain terms that they 'bore responsibility before the German people for the conduct of the war and its end result'.[13] The two generals were interested only in a 'victor's peace' that would effectively emasculate Russia as a military force and allow, for the first time in the war, an all-out offensive in the West.[14]

The vindictive nature of the peace treaty with Russia was in sharp contrast to the lofty idealism of President Wilson's Fourteen Points that he set before a joint session of Congress on 8 January 1918. Wilson referred to the 'compelling voices of the Russian people' that lay helpless 'before the grim power of Germany', and called, among other things, for an end to secret treaties and secret diplomacy and for the establishment of a 'general association of nations' to protect the 'political independence and the territorial integrity' of 'great and small states alike'.[15] In his memoirs, the ex-Kaiser claimed that the harsh terms would have been revised had Germany emerged from the conflict as victors.[16] Brest-Litovsk turned out to be as 'annexationist' as the socialists had feared and an abandonment of the Reichstag Peace Resolution the previous July. However, when it was submitted to the Reichstag for approval on 18 March the Social Democrats abstained from voting and it was left to the USPD to speak out strongly against the treaty. Hugo Haase's rebuke that 'He who sows the wind, reaps the whirlwind' echoed the similarly prophetic comment of Karl Radek, to a German delegate: 'One day the Allies will impose a Brest-Litovsk on you.'[17]

While Pan-Germans and nationalists celebrated, others saw it as an opportunity lost to bring the war to a swift conclusion.[18] In February, Haase claimed that the strikes in January took place because peace negotiations at Brest-Litovsk were being held up by German demands for territorial gains and that the people understood that this was not a defensive war.[19] In fact the strikes that swept the Reich in January did have political motives and indeed were supported by minority socialists. But the strikers were also driven by hunger, war weariness, and disillusionment with the ambiguity of the government's war aims.

The roots and antecedents of the strikes can be traced back to December 1917 when a group of radical shop stewards demanded that the leadership of the USPD call a general strike. Shop stewards of the powerful Metal Workers' Union (*Metallarbeiterverband*) led by Richard Müller formed themselves into the Revolutionary Shop Stewards and in January met with USPD leaders to discuss strategy.[20] Haase and the majority of USPD Deputies argued that mass action might destroy the party but agreed that a manifesto be drafted ('the hour has struck') sharply critical of the government's negotiating stand at Brest-Litovsk and demanding peace without annexations.[21] On 25 January workers at the Torpedo Yard in Kiel downed tools in protest against the decision of the Navy Office to send several shop stewards to the front as punishment for participating in food demonstrations. In Berlin the strike movement started on 28 January when, according to official reports, 45,000 workers came out. Two days later the police estimated that their numbers had risen to 185,000 from 299 factories.[22] Thereafter it declined. *Vorwärts* put the figure much higher at 300,000.[23] Inevitably with strikes on this scale, there were acts of violence and some clashes with the police.

On the 28 January worker's representatives had met in the trade union house presided over by the Revolutionary Shop Stewards and Richard Müller and Paul Eckert. The strikers made seven demands of the government that included: immediate peace without annexations or indemnities in accordance with the principles established by the Russian People's Commissioners in Brest-Litovsk; participation of worker's representatives at the peace conference; better food, an end to the state of siege; the release of all political figures, and the vote in Prussia for all men and women over the age of 20.[24] As the strike began to spread, Hindenburg's warning: 'To strike is treason', was posted on streetcars, bulletin boards, in hotels, restaurants, etc. Some trade unions such as the Free Trade Union and the National Workers' and Professional Union distanced themselves from the strike movement and appealed to the patriotism of workers to remain loyal to the Fatherland.[25]

Hans Peter Hanssen decided to visit Berlin-Moabit where the first violent confrontations between workers and police had taken place to glimpse the strength of the strike movement. Expecting to encounter intense political activity, he was shocked to discover the misery brought about by the effects of hunger. Daily food consumption had fallen from 3,000 calories in peacetime to 1,400 by 1918:

> I stopped outside the market hall, where a number of women, old men, and children had gathered together. They were poor, dried up, miserably clad figures, ragged and half-naked, with wretched, and in many instances, impossible footwear.... About a hundred and fifty persons were standing in line. It seemed that goat bones were being sold: shoulder and ribs scraped of every particle of meat, sixty-five pfennigs per pound.... That picture of hunger, want, and misery is one that I shall never forget.[26]

The reaction of the military was both swift and brutal. The majority of military leaders attributed the strikes to SPD and USPD agitation and compared the meeting of the workers' representatives at trade union house to that of Workers' Councils on the 'Bolshevik model'. Although the strike committee had invited the USPD and SPD to each appoint three representatives to join them, the impetus for the strike had clearly come from the Revolutionary Shop Stewards.[27] The demands of the workers for peace and democracy were not specifically socialist although they illustrate the depth of anti-government feeling. The nature and speed of the strike action both surprised and embarrassed the SPD leadership. While it did not wish to be associated with a worker's council on the Bolshevik model – or major strikes in munitions factories – it recognized that the labour movement was moving to the left and that the party could not afford to lose its grass roots support.[28] The driving force for change was coming from rank-and-file activists who were dictating to the SPD leadership. On 30 January, an incandescent Ludendorff had instructed Hertling to arrest the strike leaders in Berlin. On 31 January, General Gustav von Kessel, the Commander-in-Chief of the Marks, pronounced a 'severe state of siege' under whose ordnances extraordinary military courts were set up and factories subjected to military law.[29] 'Law-abiding citizens' were warned not to attend public meetings and to refrain from loitering. Persons of military age who contravened the order were called up for military service.[30] On 4 February the strike collapsed and the workers returned unconditionally to work still under threat of the military code of justice. The police and the military had effectively crushed the strike without granting concessions.

On 5 February, the War Minister, von Stein, informed the Kaiser that the workers had been led astray by events in Russia and the strikes in Austria–Hungary a month earlier.[31] The following day, the Kaiser was assured that 'soviets on the Russian model' would not be tolerated, that munitions factories were now under martial law, and strike leaders were being sent to the front.[32] *Vorwärts* was banned for allegedly exaggerating the numbers participating in the strike and the USPD Deputy Wihelm Dittmann was arrested and sentenced by an extraordinary military tribunal to five years imprisonment for 'attempted treason' and 'resistance to authority'.[33] Deputy Commanding Generals also tightened their own censorship in the districts against peace demonstrations, food disturbances and the distribution of socialist leaflets. By 6 February it was estimated that 150 strike leaders had been arrested and between 3,500 and 6,000 strikers sent to the front as a result of the militarization of the factories.[34] The military authorities drew the lesson from their 'victory' that conditions in Germany could not be equated with those in Russia and that the population was 'perfectly content'. Von Kessel concluded that the discontent was due to agitation and that the 'misled' masses understood only force.[35] To counteract the effects of the January strikes the OHL began a massive anti-Bolshevik campaign during a lull in negotiations at Brest-Litovsk designed to show the horrors of life under communist rule.[36]

The January strikes had placed the SPD executive and the trade unions in a difficult position. Worried by the growing radicalism of its grass roots it wished to control popular protest and channel it in ways that would not lead to revolution. On 16 February in an open address to the strike movement, Ebert attempted to justify the SPD's position. He reiterated that his party declined all responsibility for the movement but had agreed to join only on condition that the SPD be given corresponding influence in its leadership; 'Our purpose was to bring the strike to an orderly conclusion... the more so because it had fulfilled its purpose as a demonstration'. Criticizing 'conquest politicians' for sanctioning the excessive brutality and persecution of strikers under the state of siege, Ebert called upon the government to respond positively to the workers' demands.[37] The War Ministries in Berlin and Munich were determined, however, not to make concessions but to stress, instead, the threat posed to the Fatherland.[38] Ebert's demands were taken up by Scheidemann in a magnificent speech to the Reichstag. 'It was a shameless lie', he said, 'to accuse the strikers of treason.... The strikers wished only to demonstrate for peace, liberty and bread'. Referring to Kessel's brutal suppression of the workforce as his 'only victory in this war!', Scheidemann attacked the Minister of the Interior, Wallraf, as 'an heirloom bequeathed to us by Michealis'. Comparing unfavourably his handling of the strike to the statesmanlike approach of Lloyd George (who met with striking Welsh miners), Wallraf, had, according to Scheidemann delegated all responsibility to the military. On one day alone, 136 persons were sentenced to 146 years' imprisonment, 3 persons together received 39 years' imprisonment with hard labour and children of 15 were sentenced to 6 and 9 months:

> I maintain that there are Englishmen and Frenchmen who fire on Germans only because they have to. But, on the other hand, there are Germans who dance with joy at the idea of Germans firing on Germans. Such people would like to see themselves the ornament of the nation; we, however, regard them as the scum of the German people.[39]

In reply, an unbowed Wallraf dismissed the strikes as 'small in number' and engineered by 'Bolsheviks' intent on undermining the foundations of the state. He continued to justify the government's refusal to talk with workers on strike and warned Scheidemann that he hoped that his government's stance might help prevent 'the heads of the German people from being again bewildered by such [Bolshevik] ideas...'.[40] The extent and seriousness of the disturbances raised once again the question of how long law and order could be maintained. By remorsely crushing the strike and removing many of its leaders, the military had, in the short term, saved the existing political system from collapse. Radical economic improvements and political changes demanded by the workers' had resolutely been refused. In the months that followed, strikes, both major and minor, erupted in many regions while the attention of the public continued to be dominated by food shortages at home and events at Brest-Litovsk.[41] Boosted by the dictated peace terms of Brest-Litovsk, the time seemed propitious for a decisive military breakthrough in the West.[42]

THE FINAL THROW OF THE DICE

The onslaught on the French and British armies reinforced by some 300,000 Americans began on 21 March 1918 and was code-named 'Operation Michael' in honour of the Reich's patron saint. Referred to in the right-wing press as the *Freidensturm* ('the Assault to Peace') a more appropriate aphorism might have been *Weltmacht oder Untergang* ('world power or collapse').[43] Commanding officers reported that morale was high but noted that the troops viewed the offensive as the last throw of the dice. The OHL also recognized that because American reinforcements were arriving in such large numbers this was Germany's last chance to secure a *Siegfrieden*.[44] Although the Great Offensive was christened the *Kaiserschlacht* ('Kaiser's Battle') few expected the Emperor to act as a brake on the OHL. Kurt Riezler noted that the Kaiser had abdicated his role as Supreme Warlord and that Germany was being run by the 'barely veiled military dictatorship' of Hindenburg and Ludendorff.[45] At the height of the January strikes Colonel Bauer at the OHL had even suggested that Wilhelm II be asked to resign as 'for some time he had become superfluous to the war effort'.[46] The offensive proved a costly adventure and nearly 20,000 soldiers died during the first day of the offensive, including Ludendorff's son. A British soldier present at the carnage later wrote: 'When I think of all those brave German infantry, walking calmly and with poise into our murderous machine-gun fire, now, and as then, we had nothing but admiration for them. Unqualified courage. Poor devils!'.[47]

Despite heavy losses to both sides the Germans made some territorial gains and claimed victory. In an extraordinary, almost defining moment in German history, one detects a real sense of a nation collectively holding its breath – suspending judgement – as it waited for the army to deliver the promised victory. Newspapers reported that the 'English' defences had been breached and the Kaiser informed his court over champagne that the 'battle is won, the English have been utterly defeated'. On 25 March, schools were ordered to close in celebration of a famous victory.[48] An ecstatic Wilhelm II, assured by Ludendorff that the British were beaten, boasted in front of his entourage that 'if an English delegation came to sue for peace it must kneel before the German standard for it was a question here of victory of the monarchy over democracy'.[49]

To coincide with the *Freidensturm*, Ludendorff planned one final propaganda offensive. The OHL had been given a further boost when the Treaty of Bucharest was signed on 7 May and effectively reduced Romania to a German vassal state. The victor at Bucharest, Field Marshal Mackensen famously remarked that 'This time the pen has secured what the sword has won'.[50] While Ludendorff did not believe that the pen was mightier than the sword, he still retained enormous faith in the importance of effective propaganda. The *Vaterländischen Unterricht* had proved a great disappointment but Ludendorff remained wedded to the idea of a centralized Propaganda Ministry. On 20 March Ludendorff wrote to the Chancellery suggesting that insufficient measures had been taken for a uniform control of the press and for the enlightenment of public opinion. The news that Lord Beaverbrook had been placed in overall charge of a new Ministry of Information and that responsibility for enemy propaganda had been delegated to Lord Northcliffe provided the impetus for von Haeften at the MAA to draft a paper demanding a German Ministry of Propaganda. Haeften argued that the appointment of Deutelmoser as Press Director to the Chancellor had failed and called for a Propaganda Minister ('a man with an authoritative position in public and political life') to coordinate and control the press and to keep them supplied with prompt and well selected information. The new minister would also have responsibility for organizing a comprehensive system of propaganda for maintaining morale at home and for weakening the enemy's home front. Ludendorff supported Haeften's suggestion (whom he referred to as 'an officer of unusually high intelligence and glowing patriotism') for an Imperial Ministry of Propaganda and his proposal that Secretary of State at the Colonial Office, Dr Solf, be appointed to head the new ministry.[51] There is something faintly ridiculous in Ludendorff's wounded, but insistent pleas for a Ministry of Propaganda bearing in mind that he constantly flouted his position and interferred in political matters when it suited him. One is reminded of Scheidemann's remark in April 1918 that 'the constitutional situation in which we live is after all only military absolutism, tempered by fear of a parliamentary scandal'.[52] Hertling, nevertheless, refused to grant Ludendorff's wish for an Imperial Propaganda Ministry, fearing that even more power would be concentrated in the OHL, and argued instead that the Foreign Office should retain overall responsibility for propaganda work abroad.[53]

The rift between the OHL and the civilian government widened still further when Ludendorff established the *Deutsche Kriegsnachrichten* (German Press Service) intended to disseminate military propaganda direct to the civilian population without the need to go through the domestic press. The OHL decided also to step up its recruitment of distinguished 'civilians' to raise the morale of the German people and explain the OHL's war aims. A major obstacle to the successful implementation of 'patriotic instruction' in the army had been the lack of suitable propaganda officers.[54] Having failed to persuade the Chancellor to set up an organization similar to that of Beaverbrook's in Britain, Ludendorff and the Deputy Commanding Generals recruited 'multipliers of opinion' from within the ranks of trades unions, churches, women's organizations, teachers, professors, artists, etc., to raise the morale of the civilian population.[55] Evidence of a more spirited campaign was the appearance of the *Flugblätter der deutschen Korrespondenz*, a series of pamphlets dealing with various aspects of German life written by distinguished 'specialists' with the objective to 'bring about a healthy political understanding among the people'.[56] The *Flugblätter* was a belated attempt to combat Allied and Bolshevik propaganda that had attempted to drive a wedge between the armed forces, the home front and the Emperor. The government was clearly concerned at the impact that such propaganda was having on both troops and civilians. In his address to the Reichstag in February, Minister of the Interior, Wallraf, referred to the concerted propaganda campaign that had been waged against Germany.[57] Leaflets, singlesheet newspapers, small pamphlets and books were dropped over German lines by aircraft and balloons. Most of the material sought to combine words and images in the form of cartoons, photographs or maps showing German soldiers the quickest route home! The Kaiser was depicted as the main obstacle to a peace settlement and German workers were encouraged to strike as the surest means of securing peace.[58] The Allied propaganda offensive was directed against the evils of the German government using caricatures of the Kaiser or attacks upon Prussian militarism and German imperialism. One of the most famous leaflets showed the Kaiser and his six sons in full military regalia, all unscathed by war, marching blindly by as hundreds of skeletal arms reach out to them in anguish. The caption of the drawing reads: 'One family which has not lost a single member.' [See Figure 34(a)].[59] Another leaflet depicted the Kaiser and Hindenburg, seated on a stockpile of shells, being carried on the shoulders of wounded, emaciated civilians and a soldier, treading warily across a path of skulls. Hindenburg says to the Emperor, 'Your Majesty, the people are depressed and groaning constantly,' to which the Kaiser replies, 'Why are they groaning? We feel no hardship.' (See Figure 34(b).)

The German authorities responded by encouraging soldiers and civilians to hand in all propaganda artefacts distributed by the enemy. The military took to organizing their own counter-propaganda. General von Hutier's order to his troops in the 18th Army Corps suggested that by turning in leaflets and pamphlets to their commanding officers they were hastening the hour of victory. According to Hutier, the enemy propaganda onslaught was a sign of desperation: 'Fortunately, Northcliffe (referred to as the 'most

Figure 34 Two examples of British propaganda leaflets intended to drive a wedge between the Kaiser and his people:
(a) One of the most famous leaflets showing the Kaiser and his six sons in full military regalia, all unscathed by war: 'One family which has not lost a single member'.

thorough-going rascal'), the "Minister of Destruction of the German Confidence," forgets that German soldiers are neither Negroes or Hindus, nor illiterate French, English, or Americans, incapable of seeing through such machinations'.[60] Hindenburg claimed that in May, German soldiers handed in 84,000 enemy leaflets to their officers and by July this figure had risen to 300,000.[61]

In the wake of Brest-Litovsk, the socialist press renewed its challenge to the government to resolve the questions of war aims and political reforms to the Prussian electoral system. The *Leipziger Volkszeitung*, representing the USPD, asked:

> Why did the government abandon the political, domestic, and foreign policy of the Reichstag majority? Why did it not renounce annexations in the East and in the West? Why did it not recognize the right of peoples to self-determination? Why did it negotiate with representatives of the Fatherland Party, but refuse to receive the workers?[62]

Vorwärts, on the other hand, juxtaposed the twin concepts of 'liberty' and 'conquest', critically highlighting attempts by 'Pan-German mailed-fist

Figure 34 (b) Hindenburg warns the Kaiser that the people are buckling under their burdens. The Kaiser replies: 'Why are they groaning? WE feel no hardship!'.

politicians' to isolate SPD leaders and suppress the working-class press while 'intoxicating the masses by a gospel of patriotism'.[63] In reappraising German war aims in this way, *Vorwärts* was taking up a major theme employed by Allied propaganda since the foundation of the *Vaterlandspartei;* namely, that the war was being unnecessarily prolonged to satisfy the interests of German militarists and Prussian Junkers.⁶⁴ A German soldier writing immediately after the war commented bitterly that

> the English knew and told it.... Elections scandals, the thousands of soldiers' grievances, compensation, and the food situation, the fanatical annexation idea – all were thrown to us in the midst of the battle. How could it help but have an effect on the physically drained, half-starved troops?⁶⁵

In June, a troop transport in Limberg was found to have the following inscription: 'We are fighting not for Germany's honour – We are fighting for the millionaire's.'⁶⁶

A major test of the mood of public opinion in the light of Brest-Litovsk and Operation Michael was the flotation of the Eighth War Loan in February. The public's oscillating response reflected the general sense of uncertainty during this period. In February, when the loan was launched, there had been a marked reluctance to subscribe. News of the expansionist terms dictated at Brest-Litovsk did little to assuage people's concerns that the war might be prolonged. However, by April, *Monatsberichten* were reporting that the initial success of the *Freidensturm* had been greeted with 'overwhelming jubilation and relief.⁶⁷ The ambivalent attitude of the population was encapsulated in the propaganda posters for the Eighth War Loan. Karl Sigrist's poster with the dove of peace and the German eagle captured this mood; on the one hand the desire for peace on the part of large sections of the population juxtaposed against the determined stand of the OHL and the annexationists for a military victory. (See Figure 35.) Equally, Ferdy Horrmeyer's pessimistic poster 'German Women, Work for Victory' revealed the bleakness of women munition workers in Germany after the January strikes. (See Figure 36.) Eventually seven million citizens contributed 15 billion Marks for the Eighth War Loan, which was the largest amount ever collected.⁶⁸ No doubt many individuals and companies were persuaded to subscribe by hopes of victory drummed up by a frenetic right-wing press. Despite the exaggerated claims and the jingoism of sections of the press, the mood of the home front remained sober. The triumphant end to the war with Russia and the initial success of Operation Michael could not dispel the sense of gravity.⁶⁹ The mood of the people was never euphoric – more a feeling of relief that reports of victories in France would place Germany in a stronger position to sue for peace. Moreover, ordinary citizens were unaware of the extent to which military censorship had been cruelly distorting Germany's vulnerable military position.

The spring offensive soon ground to a halt, largely as a result of the OHL's lack of a definite plan for operations and Ludendorff's uncertainty on how to

Figure 35 Karl Sigrist's poster for the Eighth War Loan with the dove of peace and the German eagle.

exploit the penetration gained in the March offensive. As German casualties mounted, an increasingly anxious Ludendorff demanded that the government send him soldiers who had been released to work in munitions factories and decided to call-up all 17-year-olds.[70] In early May, Colonel von Thaer noted in his diary that everyone understands that 'the hope for victory has been dashed'.[71] On 31 May 1918, the first American troops to fight in the conflict were pressed into action and helped to halt the German offensive in the Château-Thierry region. By 6 June an American brigade attacked German forces west of Belleau Woods, and on 18 June, Foch deployed American troops in the Allied counter-offensive. The battles in mid-July marked a decisive turning point in favour of the Allies. Prospects of a German victory faded rapidly.

In order to combat what Ludendorff had referred to as the feeling of 'profound depression' at home, the Women's Home Army (*Heimatsheer der*

Figure 36 'German Women, Work for Victory!' A 1918 recruitment poster urging women to contribute to victory by working in the munitions factories.

Frauen) was established by the OHL with the aim of raising morale and opposing 'defeatism'. Reichstag Deputy Hans Peter Hanssen experienced the activities of the Berlin group at first hand:

> Every Saturday afternoon, four or five hundred women meet at the Royal Conservatory of Music at Charlottenburg for lectures and instructions. Last Saturday they were urged to bring their servant girls with them.
> These women are given special instruction in espionage. They are to pay attention to conversation on the streets, in public halls, on streetcars, in short, everywhere. Should they run into *Flaumacherei* ('defeatism'), they are to oppose it energetically. If they hear people making improper utterances, they are to demand their identification immediately and turn them over to the state attorney. In places where music is played, they are to request repeatedly that patriotic numbers be given, especially *Heil dir im Siegerkranz* and *Deutschland, Deutschland über alles*, even to join in and to

request others to sing, too. They are to post themselves in front of food shops to prevent complaints. If they hear criticisms, they are to shame the parties concerned...[72]

The presence of the Women's Home Army did not, however, act a major deterrent. Complaints continued as physical and material conditions deteriorated. By the summer of 1918, Reich officials had virtually ceased attempting to control the black market accepting that it now regulated the supply and price of foodstuffs. *Vorwärts* complained sadly that 'everyone is a black marketeer'.[73] It was not uncommon for war contractors, like the Rhine Metal Works in Düsseldorf, to trade routinely in the black market in order to supplement the rations of their workers. Local authorities in Düsseldorf, and elsewhere, were aware of the practice but 'simply closed their eyes to it'. In Stuttgart, meat consumption fell to one third below prewar level and below that which would be consumed during the Great Depression of 1929.[74] Philip Scheidemann summed up conditions in Berlin as follows:

> We don't have any more meat, we can't deliver potatoes because every day we are lacking 4000 freight cars; fats are simply not available. The need is so great that it is a riddle when one asks how people in the north and east of Berlin are able to even live.[75]

Under such conditions exhortations on the joys of acorns and fruit of the hawthorn as ersatz coffee were hardly likely to raise morale. Moreover, inflation was now beginning to bite. Germans had never seen so much paper money. Silver had been withdrawn from circulation in 1917 and gold was in short supply with the result that paper money was rapidly becoming worthless. By the end of 1918, note circulation in Germany had increased by 1,141 per cent over late 1913. Profiteering as a result of illicit trading and hoarding were endemic and for many, a way of life. Many middle-class professionals such as civil servants, teachers, bank clerks, etc., who had enthusiastically supported the war, were now descending into poverty while others were surviving only by exhausting their savings. Industrial workers from the 'lower classes' had, on the other hand, done well financially. The Deputy Commanding Generals issued frequent warnings about the growing bitterness of middle-class professionals, and particularly state employees on fixed incomes, who felt increasingly alienated from the state. A report from Königsberg in the spring of 1918 drew attention to higher grade civil servants:

> that the *Mittelstand* is becoming increasingly squeezed between newly-formed capital on the one hand and the growing might of the working class on the other.... Several professions, whose members devote themselves to public and cultural tasks, watch with concern how the provision

of the simplest means of subsistence makes such heavy demands on all their resources that they are forced down to a lower social level.

One senior manager in Posen complained that he had become 'nothing more than a proletarian'.[76] For many lower-middle-class groups who sank into a *déclassé* position with concomitant loss of status, the war proved a traumatic experience; probably more profound, given the importance of social position in Wilhelmine society, than for the working class. The *Monatsberichten* feared that the loss of traditional socio-economic advantages would shift political allegiances to the left. The evidence, however, suggests disorientation and disillusionment rather than a drift to revolutionary politics.[77] With the notable exception of sections of the upper classes, who were widely suspected of evading the burdens of war, the lack of food, undernourishment and mounting resentment against profiteering had helped to disillusion *all* sections of society and unite them in demanding an end to war. In May 1918 Princess Blücher commented on the worsening food situation:

> Food is growing scarcer from day to day and we have been reduced to killing and eating our kangaroos. They have been kept here as a great curiosity and rarity for years past. Yesterday my husband received a letter from one of the provision-dealers in Breslau, saying he would give any price my husband liked to mention if he would sell him a kangaroo.[78]

The Berlin police warned that the public was no longer prepared to suffer another winter of war and was demanding 'peace at any price'.[79] (See Figure 37.)

As German forces reached the Marne, demands for a negotiated peace appeared to be boosted when the Foreign Secretary von Kühlmann informed the Reichstag on 24 June of his belief that the war could no longer be ended by 'purely military decisions alone.'[80] In fact it was Chancellor Hertling who had been due to speak to Parliament but two days beforehand he asked Kühlmann to take his place, citing exhaustion. Kühlmann's unremarkable attempt to temper OHL's expansionist ambitions with political pragmatism badly misfired and the speech caused a storm of protest from the right. Graf Westarp accused Kühlmann of defeatism and suggested that diplomatic negotiations could only begin once Germany had achieved a military victory. Stresemann talked of the 'shattering effect' of the speech.[81] Next morning, at a hastily arranged press conference, the OHL distanced itself from the Secretary of State whose attempt later that day to return to the Reichstag to clarify his speech served only to cloud the issue.[82] Approbation that followed from the left and in particular *Vorwärts'* headline 'No End to War By Military Means' marked the end of Kühlmann's political career.[83] Hellferich

Figure 37 An extraordinarily simple but powerful poster advertising a 'Day of sacrifice' (1917).

commented that Kühlmann had dared to work for peace over the heads of the OHL and what followed was 'a struggle over his political corpse'.[84] Hindenburg and Ludendorff were determined not to have a protracted struggle and by 8 July, Kühlmann was removed from office.

The removal of Kühlmann was to be Hindenburg and Ludendorff's last major political victory. Reports from the front confirmed the concerns of the more perceptive officers at the OHL that the war was already beginning to turn against Germany. As hopes of military victory finally faded, attention turned to domestic affairs and once again to electoral reform in Prussia. On 30 April the Prussian *Abgeordnetenhaus* (Lower Chamber) decisively rejected the proposal to replace the three-tiered system with equal suffrage. Despite Chancellor Hertling's intervention that reforms will come eventually 'either without disturbances or after serious internal conflicts', the vote reflected wider political divisions, with only the socialists voting in favour.[85] The stubborn oligarchy dominated by the alliance of Junkers and big business continued to ignore the writing on the wall, claiming that if equal suffrage was granted, the socialists would have a crushing majority.[86] Resistance to change could also be found within the ranks of the polarized middle class concerned at the rising ambitions of the workers and anxious about their status once the war was over. Max Bauer writing to the Crown Prince succinctly expressed the deep anxiety of the German bourgeoisie: 'Democratisation would lead to Bolshevism...'.[87] The labour movement saw the failure to grant equal suffrage as a rebuff for its constructive participation in the war effort. Philipp Scheidemann viewed it as a 'slap in the face of the German labouring class' and called for a great offensive against Prussian reaction: 'The struggle is being waged about equal suffrage without safeguards, and it will not end until victory is ours'.[88] In Berlin, Hans Peter Hanssen noted that 'a mysteriously heavy and oppressive atmosphere was hovering' and concluded that 'morale was below zero'.[89] (See Figures 38 and 39.)

With Allied forces being reinforced by increasing numbers of American troops, discipline was finally fragmenting within the German army. One of the problems later identified to the *Untersuchungsausschusses* (Parliamentary Committee of Investigation) by General von Kuhl was that many of the young recruits had been dragged unwillingly from safe, well-paid work in munitions factories. As a result many deserted or went sick.[90] By mid-July, Foch's great tank-led offensive stormed the Siegfried Line causing thousands of exhausted veterans to desert. Transport trains returning the wounded back to base hospitals were often seized by rebellious troops.[91] Concerned at the impact that Allied agitational propaganda was having on troop discipline, Colonel von Haeften penned a memorandum on necessary countermeasures to raise morale. Referring to the 'thrust of the sword being the best

Figure 38 Ludwig Hohlwein's moving 1918 poster 'Ludendorff Fund for Disabled Veterans'.

propaganda' Haeften claimed that newspaper reports of recent German victories had allowed German propaganda to regain lost ground, both at home and abroad. He identified three immediate needs; money, statesmanlike speeches and a Propaganda Ministry. The latter was imperative and, according to Haeften, 'it just has to be done'.[92]

On 1 August the Kaiser, in his Annual Proclamation, attempted to reassure the population that the 'worst is behind us'. Blaming the enemy for prolonging the war, he claimed that the Allies were intent on destroying Germany and for that reason alone 'we have to fight on until the enemy recognizes our right to survive'.[93] Against the backdrop of desertions and a breakdown of order and discipline at home,[94] Hertling finally relented and on 29 August agreed to establish the Central Office for Propaganda under the direction of the Secretary of State of the Foreign Office.[95] Hertling's plan was to coordinate and intensify official propaganda by dividing responsibility into a political division under the control of his Press Chief, Deutelmoser while placing Haeften in charge of the military side with instructions that the two directors secure 'perfect co-operation'. Although Haeften would have access to the Chancellor's press briefings, this division of labour was never likely

Figure 39 'Heroes Back From the Front! Your Country Greets You!' The small child, the symbol of Munich, welcomes returning soldiers back from the front as heroes (Walter Ditz).

to prove successful – partly because of personality clashes between the two directors – but also due to the strained relations between the OHL and the Chancellor. Deutelmoser continued to act as Hertling's Press Chief while Haeften had replaced Nicolai as the OHL's expert on propaganda.[96] Although Ludendorff had been granted his wish with the establishment of a centralized propaganda agency, he remained deeply dissatisfied with Hertling's compromise, referring to it as 'an unhappy appendage, devoid of real authority'.[97]

By this time, however, Ludendorff had more urgent matters on his mind. He had been suffering from severe depression for some days and simply refused to accept defeat, believing that he could still break the Entente's resistance by an act of will. In July, half a million German soldiers had been struck in their trenches with a virulent influenza virus and thousands more were suffering in hospitals. When informed of the debilitating effect that this was having, Ludendorff is claimed to have responded that they would need to get on with it 'as he knew of no influenza'.[98] The OHL was becoming seriously divided as disenchantment grew among the officers with Ludendorff's physical and mental state.[99] As Ludendorff's personality changed he appeared to be suffering a nervous breakdown, demanding more draconian sentences for disobedience or desertion and blaming each setback on his operational chiefs or on the limitless supply of American manpower.[100] Refusing to acknowledge his own indecision he continued to live in the fantasy world of an annexationist peace. By 8 August, Allied forces had pushed through German lines at Amiens forcing dispirited and weary German troops to pull back to the Hindenburg Line.

By September, hopes of a military breakthrough had turned to despair. The 2nd Army Corps reported solemnly that the mood of the people is 'poor' (*schlecht*).[101] Undeterred the Pan-Germans continued to insist that a *Siegfrieden* was possible. In August, the *Büro für Sozialpolitik* had warned of the grave dangers of arousing exaggerated hopes of victory.[102] In order to booster the population's resolve in a period considered critical by the OHL, Hindenburg was called to 'speak' to the nation. Photographs of the hero of Tannenberg in various martial poses accompanied the hand bills and posters distributed throughout the country that contained Hindenburg's address. Drawing on historical parallels with Germany's powerlessness during the Thirty Years' War, the Field Marshal called on the 'German Army and the German Home' to remain united and not to listen to (or read) enemy propaganda.[103] Hindenburg offered platitudes but not the reassurance that victory was in sight. The Deputy Commanding Generals recorded that his address failed to lift morale or indeed alter the widespread belief that America's involvement in the theatre of war meant inevitable defeat.[104] The conservative press instinctively heaped extravagant praise on the Field Marshal and called on the people once again to 'stand firm'.[105] More significant, although hardly reported in the press, was a deputation to the Chancellor from the trade unions declaring that the food supply, the increased price of clothes, electoral reforms, censorship, and the state of siege were the immediate concerns of the people. Calling on the government to promote a peace of understanding the unions also requested an 'open' discussion of the Pan-German plans for annexations.[106]

On 4 September Hertling appeared before the Constitutional Committee of the *Herrenhaus* and declared with exemplary frankness that he supported equal suffrage, not because he believed in it, but because it had been promised by the Kaiser. Exhibiting his usual lack of political wisdom, Herding appealed also to the 'noble and the exalted' not to put the monarchy to a too exacting test.[107] In October he resigned rather than preside over the parliamentarization of the government. Princess Blücher referred to his going: 'Hertling the good old polished man of learning as he is, has accepted the situation, and has made his exit with the quiet courtly bow of the last representative of the *ancien régime*, and a new era has set in'.[108] He died four months later, heartbroken at Germany's defeat.

In the last months of the war, the government relied increasingly on censorship to prevent the worsening military situation from becoming known. Newspapers continued to talk optimistically about final victory even after the successful American offensive in early October. However, no amount of censorship could disguise the fact that Germany was losing the war. Rumours circulating in the 'counter-public' (*Gegenöffentlichkeit*) provided stark relief to official propaganda and served only to increase the distrust of authority. In a sense, government had come full circle since the introduction of the State of Siege in 1914, when extensive use of censorship had helped frame Germany's spurious war aims. In September, one of the main organs of the government and the chief exponent of the views of the Foreign Office, the *Kölnische Zeitung*, denounced the War Press Office as the main instrument by which the German people had been deceived into expecting victory. It claimed that it had taken Germans four years to realize that they had been hoodwinked – not just over the military situation – but the economy and the food situation was much worse than had been reported.[109] By October, with the notable exception of small groups of Pan-Germans who continued to demonstrate against a peace settlement, it was clear to even the most patriotic citizens that the war was lost. The Supreme Command reluctantly had also arrived at this conclusion and on 3 October it surprised the political leadership by demanding an immediate armistice. The OHL's plans had been worked out at a meeting held at the Hotel Britannique(!) in Spa on 29 September.[110]

Ludendorff and Hindenburg agreed that power should be handed over to a civilian administration in order that as many people as possible should shoulder the opprobrium for the way the war was to be ended. In accepting plans for a 'revolution from above', the OHL was already propagating the myth of a 'stab-in-the-back': the betrayal of a valiant and undefeated German army by pacifists, 'slackers', Jews and Bolsheviks from within.

At the press conference on 4 October newspaper chiefs were briefed on the military situation. Having been fed misleading information for so long, the truth came as a considerable shock and some editors feared public reaction to the shattering news. There was also a veiled hint that Ludendorff was about to resign. Led by Georg Bernhard, the editor of *Vossische Zeitung*, the press representatives pointed out the incompatibility of a war that was being won with the hasty pursuit of peace. Accusing the government of cynically manipulating the press, the editors demanded to know the truth and called for clarity. Amidst acrimony and recriminations the press conference was brought to an end by a military spokesman who suggested that 'this group has completely lost its nerve'.[111]

The appointment of the liberal aristocrat Prince Max of Baden to replace Count Hertling signified more than simply a change of Chancellor; it symbolized a belated recognition of the need for political reforms. On 5 October at a special session of the Reichstag, Prince Max outlined the policies of his new government and towards the end of his speech stunned the assembly with the announcement that he had asked President Wilson to broker a peace settlement based on his Fourteen Points. Significantly the appeal for an armistice had been signed by the new Chancellor and his cabinet. The instrumental role of the OHL was concealed from the public. A few days later a Reichstag Deputy observed that 'people seemed almost happy and contented that peace is in sight'. The only fear was that it might slip away at the last minute.[112]

Groups of Pan-Germans on hearing that the government was about to abandon the gains in the West demonstrated against a peace settlement and demanded that the opinions of other generals be sought. Walther Rathenau, head of German General Electric (AEG) attempted to mobilize support for a *levée en masse*, a rising of the people in the best tradition of the French Revolution.[113] A nervous Prince Max consulted Ludendorff and was relieved to discover that OHL recognized the absurdity of the scheme and, moreover, had no wish to turn the proud Imperial Army into a *Volkssturm* (civilian militia).[114]

On 8 October, Wilson replied to Prince Max's proposal by informing the Chancellor that an armistice would not be possible while German troops occupied foreign territory. On 16 October, Wilson's second note was much

Figure 40 The Kaiser's visit to Kiel, October 1918.

firmer and demanded an end to the 'illegal and inhuman practices' of submarine warfare and for changes in the government asserting that negotiations would not continue with 'the power which has hitherto controlled the German nation'.[115] The note was dismissed as 'frivolous insolence' by the Kaiser, who recognized the vulnerability of his own position.[116] (See Figure 40). Ludendorff was equally dismissive claiming that to halt submarine warfare amounted to 'capitulation'. An obdurate Ludendorff refused to abandon submarine warfare unless there was a guarantee that Germany would not have to sign a 'dishonourable peace'.[117] Wilson's third note on 23 October, was unequivocal and stunned the Germans. It removed any remaining illusions of an armistice based on the Fourteen Points. Wilson refused to negotiate with the 'King of Prussia' and to the 'monarchical autocrats of Germany', he offered only 'surrender'.[118] In what amounted to an open challenge to Prince Max's peace initiative, Hindenburg issued an order to all army commanders that the conditions laid down by Wilson were unacceptable to the German army and that the war would have to continue. Gathering his officers around him, Hindenburg drew his sword and proclaimed: 'Long Live His Majesty, our King, Emperor, and Warlord!'[119]

Secure in the knowledge that his cabinet supported his negotiating position, Prince Max drafted a letter to the Kaiser offering his resignation unless Ludendorff was dismissed. On 26 October the Kaiser met with

Figure 41 Mutiny of the Fleet in Wilhelmshaven, November 1918.

Hindenburg and Ludendorff in a stormy session and accepted Ludendorff's offer of resignation. When he learned that Hindenburg had agreed to remain in office, Ludendorff accused him of treachery.[120] Two weeks later Ludendorff fled in disguise to Sweden to write his memoirs, thus bringing to an end the 'silent' military dictatorship that had dominated German political and military affairs since his appointment to the OHL in 1916. The liberal and socialist press hailed his departure as a victory for democracy and the general feeling was that he had contributed to his own fall by his excessive ambition and arrogance.[121] Prince Max had been spared a confrontation with the OHL and wrote to Wilson on 28 October that Germany would comply with the demands for democratization. The following day sailors, who had been ordered to fight one final suicide battle refused, and mutinied in Wilhelmshaven and Kiel. (See Figure 41.) As revolt spread from the docks to the streets, Wilson informed the Germans on 5 November that, 'Marshal Foch has been authorized... to receive properly accredited representatives of the German government and to communicate to them the terms of an armistice'.[122]

A few days earlier Hans Peter Hanssen observed a demonstration by Pan-Germans outside the Reichstag at Bismarck's statue:

> They were passionately urging that peace negotiations be broken off and that the struggle be continued to the end. Patriotic songs were sung between speeches; *Deutschland, Deutschland, Die Wacht am Rhein, Heil Dir*

Figure 42 Demonstrations in Berlin, 9 November 1918.

im Siegerkranz. A noncommissioned officer jumped up on the pedestal and protested against the continuation of the war. The people became enraged.[123]

Such demonstrations were rare and represented the last vestiges of a decaying order and its dream of an annexationist victory. In early October the District Commands declared that the 'patriotic spirit had died' and that respect for authority and the laws of the land 'had virtually collapsed'.[124] On 30 October the Commander of the 14th Army Corps reported that the masses no longer cared about the consequences of a peace settlement, they simply wanted peace 'at any price'.[125] (See Figure 42.) In the popular mind, however, the Kaiser had become the major obstacle to peace. After Wilson's third note, the Kaiser had steadfastly refused all suggestions that he should abdicate ('a successor of Frederick the Great does not abdicate') and even swore his six sons by way of a handshake that they would not succeed him.[126] Had he abdicated in October in favour of one of his sons the monarchy might have been saved. Instead Wilhelm harboured some fantastic notion that he might return to Berlin at the head of his army to restore order and re-establish his authority. On 9 November General Groener, who had replaced Ludendorff, disabused him of this notion. Earlier in the day, Groener had taken soundings from his most senior army commanders and later informed the Kaiser (who

Figure 43 Front page of the SPD newspaper, *Vorwärts*, 9 November 1918, announcing the abdication of the Kaiser. The brief statement is signed by the Chancellor Prince Max von Baden who has ordered the armed forces not to use their weapons: 'No shots will be fired!'.

had stationed himself at Spa) that he could no longer count on the support of the troops and that if the army was to remain intact, the Emperor would have to go.[127] Within hours Wilhelm II crossed into Holland and exile, thus ending over 500 years of Hohenzollern rule in Germany. 'We are not shedding any tears after him', wrote *Simplicissimus*, 'for he has not left us any to shed.' (See Figure 43.)

While a delegation headed by Erzberger was sent to Compiègne to receive the armistice terms from the Allies; Philip P. Scheidemann proclaimed the birth of a German Republic from the balcony of the Reichstag.[128] Prince Max's last-ditch effort to salvage what he could from the enveloping chaos and disorder was doomed to failure. Although his hastily assembled cabinet consisted of moderate Social Democrats it was tainted by association with Wilhelmine Germany. The Deputing Commanding Generals had been reporting since September of a breakdown in trust between the state and its citizens. When the truth of Germany's military situation became known in October the collective psychological shock of defeat was soon replaced by a sense of betrayal that the government had been peddling lies for four years and that the peoples' suffering and sacrifices had been in vain.[129] Official propaganda now came to be associated with lies and falsehood and served only to widen the distance between the population and the state. When Karl Liebknecht, the implacable opponent of the war and imperial oligarchy, was released from prison on 21 October a huge crowd of jubilant workers greeted his arrival at the Anhalter station in Berlin.[130] The change in mood was recorded by Kurt Riezler, who wrote in his diary: 'The end of all hubris'.[131] The old order had been discredited and the people were looking for change (although not necessarily on a Bolshevik model). Princess Blücher compared the collapse of the *Kaiserreich* to a sinking ship:

> It is a pitiful sight to watch the death-throes of a great nation. It reminds me of a great ship slowly sinking before one's eyes, and being swallowed up by storm-driven waves. I feel intensely for Germany and her brave long-suffering people, who have made such terrific sacrifices and gone through so much woe, only to see their idols shattered and to realize that their sufferings have all been caused by the blundering mistakes and overweening ambition of a class of 'supermen'.[132]

Conclusion: 'The Sins of Omission'

'We were hypnotized by the enemy propaganda as a rabbit is by a snake.'
                                                                    Ludendorff

'Enslavement for a hundred years to come. The end of the universe for all time.
The end of all hubris.'
                                                    Kurt Riezler, 1 October 1918

By the end of November 1918 not only had the war come to an end but so to had the social revolution. A revolutionary tide sparked off by a sailors' mutiny in Wilhelmshaven and Kiel at the end of October led to the setting up of 'sailors', soldiers' and workers' councils' who wrested control from local authorities. However, a Soviet-style Bolshevik revolution failed to engage the deepest sympathies of the German masses. Instead, a historic pact was agreed between Groener representing the army and Ebert of the moderate Social Democrats, to maintain law and order and suppress the revolutionary groups. After four years of suffering and deprivation Germans had little energy left for radical politics. They had signalled their desire for change but continuities with imperial Germany in the form of military, judicial and economic elites remained, reflecting the limited nature of the 'revolution'. Even after the war had ended in humiliating defeat and the blockade remained, the vast mass of the people continued to give support to those who had been closely associated with Wilhelmine Germany.

Not surprisingly, the population was not disposed in 1918 to analyse the populist appeal of the Supreme Command which had been largely responsible for the war and the Armistice terms. Hindenburg and Ludendorff never claimed 'supermen' status but were widely fêted as heroes and saviours when appointed to the OHL in 1916. Once in power, Ludendorff in particular used the means of communications to legitimize an anti-parliamentary and plebiscitory military dictatorship that propagated a militarist, nationalist, and expansionist vision of Germany. Hidden beneath the collective psyche of the masses was an uncomfortable yearning for strong leadership. In the absence of a benevolent Emperor unable (or unwilling) to uphold his constitutional position, the OHL exploited a weak parliamentary system for its own ends. Under the 'silent dictatorship' of Hindenburg and Ludendorff, free speech had been curtailed, troublesome factories were 'militarized' and agitators were either incarcerated or sent to the front. The official (German) position in the last months of the war was that the people were content, the discontent that erupted in the January strikes was due to agitation and that any concessions would only increase the avarice of the 'unenlightened masses'.[1] Firm leadership and stern measures would put them straight. In the aftermath of the failed revolution Princess Blücher observed that in the absence of the exiled Kaiser, Germans still looked for some mythical Siegfried-like figure to provide leadership:

> I believe myself that the German people in reality need something for their imagination – a figure-head that represents in some way the phantastic, the unusual, the ideal. There is no poetry in the figure of a short stout President, with a bald head, a top-hat, and a black coat. All the old fairy tales begin in the same way: 'Es war einmal ein König!' and the Olympic figure with the clanking sword, the golden crown and the purple mantle will be sadly failing in the history of the future.[2]

Blücher's prophetic observation was to be tragically realized when Hitler came to power in 1933. However, the proclamation of the Republic and the understandable desire to return as quickly as possible to some sort of normality after the deprivation and suffering imposed by war postponed any serious reappraisal of the support given by the German masses for anti-parliamentary groups. In 1945 such profound questions, reinforced by unconditional surrender and the crimes of the Nazi regime, were to force Germans to come to terms with their past. However, that came at the end of the Second World War; at the beginning of the Great War, Germans would rejoice in the invocation of the 'spirit of 1914'.

Like Britain, Germany on the eve of World War I was beset by numerous internal tensions. When war was declared antipodal forces resolved to work for victory by means of a *Burgfrieden*. This proved a fruitful theme in German propaganda. The belief that the war was foisted upon Germany as a result of enemy encirclement persuaded all sections of the community to put aside their differences. However, the *Burgfrieden* depended on victory – and a swift war. As the conflict dragged on tensions resurfaced. The imperial authorities failure to respond to the genuine grievances and demands for reform stretched the *Burgfrieden* beyond bearable limits and, by the end of 1917, it had lost its credibility as a unifying theme. In the final period of the war, the issues that galvanized the people were shortages of food, inequalities in the war burden and the refusal to grant certain groups political and civil rights.

There were a number of myths surrounding the notion of the *Burgfrieden*. First of all there was the belief that the 'spirit of 1914' heralded a new community that would transcend political differences and bring class struggle to an end. There was also the myth of salvation; that provided the people remained united and true to the spirit of the *Burgfrieden* then victory was ultimately assured.[3] Wilhelmine political society was deeply divided and the *Burgfrieden* was intended to turn socialists, conservatives, liberals, the *Mittlestand*, workers and artisans, into 'Germans'. The Kaiser had laid the foundation for such a grandiose vision when he had declared in 1914 that 'I recognize no parties, but only Germans'. For radical nationalists, foremost the OHL, the *Burgfrieden* was a means of persuading 'Germans' to share their militarist, annexationist vision. Social Democrats on the other hand were less jingoistic (although not entirely averse to nationalist rhetoric) and viewed the *Burgfrieden* as an inclusive mechanism for transforming Germany, peacefully, into a more equal society based on socialist principles of civil rights and social welfare. Thus the *Burgfrieden* legitimized fundamentally different political visions.

Inevitably, as the war continued without signs of victory, these visions began to sharpen around antipodal camps. War aims and internal political reform polarized German society. The interaction of propaganda and public opinion manifested itself most strongly around these two issues which continued to divide the population. Nevertheless, the 'spirit of 1914' remained a powerful unifying symbol and even in July 1917 could still be used to remove Bethmann Hollweg on the grounds that his (policy of) 'new orientation' threatened the *Burgfrieden*.

The failure, however, to reform the Prussian suffrage law suggested that the *Burgfrieden* was increasingly employed by conservative and military elites as an empty slogan to maintain the *status quo*. The *Burgfrieden* became for the government and the OHL a synonym for morale and was frequently invoked to inspire citizens to hold out and remain united. While some intelligentsia talked about the 'spirit of 1914' transforming Germany from a *society* into a *community*, many radical nationalists took this a stage further, claiming that the *Burgfrieden* was evidence that German society had transmogrified into the *völkisch* vision of a *Volksgemeinschaft* (people's community) whereby Germans recognized their common ethnic identity. The vast propaganda campaign of 'Patriotic Instruction' (*Vaterländische Unterricht*) was the final desperate attempt to persuade Germans of their inherent racial superiority and the need to follow strong leadership that only military dictatorship, not parliamentarianism, could provide. Defeat challenged the notion of a racially superior people. The *Dolchstosslegende* helped to explain this away and to provide a basis for right-wing nationalist groups in the Weimar Republic to take up where the Fatherland Party had left off. The stab-in-the-back legend blamed internal disunity caused by 'Jews and Bolsheviks' for undermining the *Volksgemeinschaft*. The nationalist fervour of 1914, the spirit of a united nation ready and eager for a justifiable war, remained a potent force for the German Right throughout the inter-war period and appeared to have come to fruition in the 'fighting community' of 1933.

Unlike 1945 when Germany was forced to accept unconditional surrender, the armistice had brought the war to an end in a manner that encouraged powerful right-wing groups to fabricate a wholly distorted history of an undefeated German army returning to the homeland in good fighting order. For the Kaiser and the OHL responsibility for military defeat, particularly after the spring offensive in 1918, was placed firmly on the home front. Max Bauer wrote: 'We shall win the war when the home front stops attacking us from behind'.[4] The stab-in-the-back legend was already being rehearsed to justify defeat and humiliation. Ludendorff concluded that the collapse in morale was due to agitational Bolshevik and Spartacist propaganda encouraged by the Allies; 'While our will to conquer remained unshaken we had every prospect of victory and, what was just as important, need not bow to the last drop of blood. Many Germans were no longer prepared to die for their country'.[5] In Ludendorff's famous phrase the home front had been hypnotized by the enemy propaganda 'as a rabbit is by a snake'.[6] It was a view shared by the Kaiser. In his memoirs written in exile in the 1920s, Wilhelm II claimed:

> For thirty years the army was my pride. For it I lived, upon it I laboured, and now, after four and a half brilliant years of war with unprecedented victories, it was forced to collapse by the stab-in-the-back from the dagger of the revolutionist, at the very moment when peace was within reach!.[7]

These extraordinary rationalizations for defeat by discredited and culpable leaders reflected the bankruptcy of the *Kaiserreich* and the extent to which the military elites had retreated into mythology. Germany's military strategy in 1914 (revolving around the Schlieffen Plan) had been a reckless gamble that had failed. However, the unenviable responsibility for negotiating peace fell to civilians, not soldiers.

In Germany, the *Kaiserreich* was replaced by a democratic republic in which leaders of the left played a prominent role. Despite the perpetuation of the *Dolchstosslegende* it was not the home front that stabbed the army in the back. Francis Carsten has argued that it was the army that carried its mood of despair back to the home front.[8] In the light of my analysis of the interaction between politics, propaganda and public opinion, a more likely explanation is that both fronts had endured enough suffering and, despite all the propaganda, had simply lost the will to continue a war that they no longer believed could be won. The government no longer retained the whole-hearted support of its people. The deterioration in morale unfolded over a considerable period of time. Indeed, until the last months of the war both fronts remarkably continued to 'hold out'. This may have been due to propaganda, or more likely, a combination of propaganda and a traditional sense of German patriotism.

After the war the *Dolchstosslegende* took root on the far right which continued to perpetuate the myth that the Second Reich had been undermined by a combination of enemy propaganda and failure on the part of the government to use propaganda as effectively as the enemy. In *Mein Kampf*, Hitler devoted two chapters to the study and practice of propaganda. Hitler maintained that in Britain propaganda was regarded 'as a weapon of the first order, while in our country it was the last resort of unemployed politicians and a haven for slackers'.[9]

Hitler's thoughts on propaganda were largely a reflection of the prevailing nationalist claims that Allied propaganda was responsible for the collapse of the German Empire in 1918. What I have attempted to demonstrate is that these accusations were unjustified. In fact the Second Reich was aware of the need to employ propaganda and established an impressive organizational apparatus for the dissemination of official propaganda.[10] Reich officials lacked, however, a sophisticated appreciation of the relationship between the dissemination of propaganda and its reception by different publics. The German government recognized that morale was important in 'total war' but relied on the traditional obedience of a largely subservient public to accept authority from above. German public opinion, which was comparatively sophisticated and literate, was not a static force and the population was not prepared to receive official propaganda uncritically. While the government's declared wish to 'place a finger on the pulse of the people' resulted in a national network of monitoring stations designed to provide feedback about public opinion (ranging from the monthly reports of the Deputy Commanding Generals to paid informers on the transport system), it manifestly failed to respond to what the population was saying.[11] Partly this was because the reports were viewed from a military and not a civilian perspective. The support of impeccably conservative groups was held up to justify official policy whereas complaints or open dissent were seen as a challenge to hierarchical authority and dismissed as 'defeatism'. The shifting attitude of the population to increasing economic hardship was viewed in sanguine terms by the military as a lack of resolve. The OHL launched crude polemics against 'unpatriotic' Social Democrats and constructed a grotesque caricature of the ordinary German worker as a 'shirker' unfit to be mentioned in the same breath as soldiers at the front sacrificing their lives. The need to look for scapegoats for impending defeat was a feature of the OHL in the last months of war. Parliamentary democracy was to be discredited for seeking an armistice with the enemy. Although this scenario did not square with reality it provided the necessary subterfuge to allow the army to resist reform and straddle the Weimar Republic virtually unscathed. To speak of collapse in physical and mental terms did not square with right-wing racist notions of German superiority. It was more convenient to perpetuate the myth that the army and Emperor were stabbed in the back by enemy propaganda and *Staatsfeinde*, such as pacifists, Jews and Bolsheviks, who had undermined solidarity.

While imperial propaganda during the First World War was more sophisticated than critics from the far right were prepared to concede, nonetheless it was hampered by a number of problems. As a result of the militarization of society, its propaganda was closely tied to military success. German war aims rationalizing incursions through neutral Belgium were predicated on the grounds that a short, defensive war, to break enemy encirclement, justified violations of international law. Having been the aggressor in Belgium, Germany was forced on to the defensive, a stance which it never entirely shook off for the rest of the propaganda war. When the terms of Brest-Litovsk became known the annexationist ambitions of the OHL were revealed for all to see. Having failed to anticipate that the Allied blockade would result in such severe food shortages, the imperial government did not prepare the morale of the people for a long war.

Secondly, the imposition of a State of Siege in 1914 handed over to the military control of the means of communications and responsibility for shaping public opinion. The War Press Office and Section IIIb of the OHL were more concerned with the management of news and the morale of soldiers. Their scant regard for the home front reflected their overriding fear that the civilian population would affect adversely the morale of the troops.

Finally, although diverse sections of society signed up to a *Burgfrieden* in 1914 (albeit with varying degrees of enthusiasm), not all groups were prepared indefinitely to participate in the war effort and suffer deprivations without significant political and economic reforms. No amount of 'patriotic instruction' could obfuscate the imperial authorities failure to grant such demands and negotiate a just peace. The question of war aims and a long, drawn-out, conflict are therefore crucial to an understanding of the relationship between imperial propaganda and public opinion. The government never successfully overcame the contradictions inherent in a military strategy that could not be spelled out in its propaganda. The OHL had reopened the debate on war aims towards the end of 1916 confidently expecting to present an unchallenged campaign for conquest and annexations that would unite the nation and destroy Bethmann Hollweg's policy of a 'new orientation'.

It had failed to grasp the nature of a *Burgfrieden* that had sanctioned a short, defensive war. Moreover while the OHL controlled the means of communications and much of the responsibility for censorship, it was never able to exert full control over the press or to establish an effective Ministry of Propaganda. The OHL underestimated public opinion and political dissent in the Reichstag. It is ironic that in late November 1918 and with Ludendorff in self-imposed exile, Matthias Erzberger, a civilian politician, assumed control of all propaganda activities at home and abroad.[12]

The final campaign of 'Patriotic Instruction' launched by Ludendorff in the summer of 1917 came too late to regain the public's trust. By appealing to national unity and patriotic notions of sacrifice and courage – at a time of mounting casualties and food shortages – the OHL had played out its hand. The 'spirit of 1914' had been allowed to disintegrate. The blame for this lies squarely with the OHL, the Kaiser and weak political leadership. The new type of military leader, symbolized by Ludendorff, recognized the importance of propaganda but refused to accept that public opinion could assert itself. Propaganda for Ludendorff and, by extension the OHL, was a means of manipulating public opinion. The OHL's contempt for the masses and parliamentary democracy can be traced back to the pre-war years. Such Germans viewed the outbreak of war as an opportunity for rolling back social democracy and retaining their privileged position in a rigidly hierarchical society. The symbol of reaction was Wilhelm II who had initially presented himself as the *Volkskaiser* ('People's Kaiser'). The exigencies of war would relegate Wilhelm II to a secondary and discredited figure. In 1914 the Kaiser had been the figurehead for German *Weltpolitik* and imperialist ambitions, a symbol of authority and continuity. By the end of the war he was widely perceived within Germany to be an intransigent barrier to peace.

The *Burgfrieden* offered a unique opportunity to incorporate piecemeal change into the Wilhelmine Reich. Its stubborn oligarchy failed, however, to appreciate that the 'spirit of 1914' was a 'platform' upon which to build trust and cooperation. The OHL took it for granted, ignored genuine political and economic grievances and continued to exclude the Reichstag from decision making. Propaganda that focused on unifying themes and on the enemy struck a resonant chord with the people, but such heightened nationalism could not be sustained indefinitely. Subordinate individuals and groups who questioned annexationist war aims and demanded a negotiated peace, were dubbed 'enemies of the Empire' (*Staatsfeinde*). By 1917, the OHL's decision to ignore the chance of achieving peace, but more importantly its failure to respond to demands for reform, resulted in a breakdown in trust between the people and state authority. Hitler's account of the German débâcle in 1918 and the failure of German counter-propaganda throughout the war became the 'official' truth in the inter-war years and was subsequently repeated by the younger generation of National Socialists and by right-wing activists in general. According to this view, 'in the Wilhelmine age the German intelligentsia had lived in complete ignorance about the nature of propaganda'.[13] The failure of imperial Germany to survive the test of war can be found not in inept propaganda, but in the imperial government's blind contempt for the suffering of its own people and their aspirations. Viewed from this perspective the sins of omission came unquestionably from above – not from below.

Notes

PREFACE TO THE NEW EDITION

1 A notable exception is Christopher Clark's magnificently nuanced study of the war's origins. Clark argues that every belligerent had its strategic and ideological reasons for going to war in 1914. Each sleepwalked into it. C. Clark, *The Sleepwalkers: How European Went to War in 1914* (London, 2012).

INTRODUCTION

1 In 1998, to coincide with the eightieth anniversary of the end of the Great War a number of works were published. See in particular: J. Keegan, *The First World War* (London, 1998); N. Ferguson, *The Pity of War* (London, 1998); M. Brown, *The Imperial War Museum Book of 1918* (London, 1998); H. Strachan (ed.), *The Oxford Illustrated History of the First World War* (Oxford, 1998).
2 East German scholarship is represented by the dense, three-volume survey edited by Fritz Klein, *Deutschland im Ersten Weltkrieg*, 3 vols (East Berlin, 1968–9). L.V. Moyer's, *Victory Must Be Ours: Germany in the Great War, 1914–18* (New York, 1995) is a competent, 'popular' account that embraces the home front but is much more comfortable when discussing military history. Holger Herwig has recently produced an excellent comparative analysis of Germany and Austria–Hungary, *The First World War. Germany and Austria–Hungary 1914–1918* (London, 1997). Herwig's history of the war is intended to provide a corrective to the military, Anglo-centric edifice erected by Liddell Hart. In this context, compare the revisionist goals of Hugh Cecil and Peter H. Liddle, (eds), *Facing Armageddon: The First World War Experienced* (London, 1996). Richard Bessel's *Germany After the First World War* (Oxford, 1993), despite its title, covers some aspects of the social history of the home front during the war. More recently, Roger Chickering has produced a short student textbook of the military, political and socioeconomic effects of the Great War. See Chickering, *Imperial Germany and the Great War, 1914–1918* (Cambridge, 1998).
3 A. Hitler, *Mein Kampf* (London, 1939), p 169. For a brief analysis of Hitler's view of the failure of imperial war propaganda see, Welch, *Hitler* (London, 1998), pp 26–30.
4 For the Schlieffen Plan and German military planning see the brilliant analysis by A. Bucholz, *Moltke, Schlieffen, and Prussian War Planning* (New York and

Oxford, 1991). Somewhat dated but still of interest is G. Ritter, *The Schlieffen Plan. A Critique of a Myth* (New York, 1958). For analyses of the 'illusion' of a short mobile campaign that underpinned German military at the outbreak of war, see L.L. Farrar, *The Short-War Illusion: German Policy, Strategy and Domestic Affairs, August–December 1914* (Santa Barbara, CA, 1974) and Stig Förster's excellent article, 'Der deutsche Generalstab und die Illusion des kurzen Krieges 1871–1914: Metakritik eines Mythos', *Militärgeschichtliche Mitteilungen*, 54 (1995), pp 61–95. For a brief analysis of the Schlieffen Plan in the context of the origins of World War I see, D. Welch, *Modern European History 1871–2000. A Documentary Reader* (London, 1999), pp 70–4.

5 E.H. Carr, *The Twenty Years' Crisis, 1919–39* (New York, 1964), p 132.

1 DAYS OF DECISION: GERMANY ON THE EVE OF WAR

1 For background information to the Second Reich including numerous statistical materials see V. Berghahn, *Imperial Germany, 1871–1914: Economy, Society, Culture, and Politics* (Oxford, 1994). See also Wolfgang Mommsen's substantial work on Wilhelmine Germany, *Bürgerstolz und Weltmachtstreben: Deutschland unter Wilhelm II 1890 bis 1918* (Berlin, 1995). General histories of the period can also be found in H. Holborn, *A History of Modern Germany*, vol 3, *1840–1945* (London, 1969); H. Böhme (ed.): *The Foundation of the German Empire, Selected Documents* (Oxford, 1971); G. Mann, *The History of Germany since 1789* (London, 1974). A brief, stimulating account can also be found in K. Epstein, *Matthias Erzberger and the Dilemma of German Democracy* (Princeton, 1959), pp 19–37.

2 For the early history of German labour and the Social Democrats see the following: G. Roth, *The Social Democrats in Imperial Germany. A Study in Working Class Isolation and National Integration* (Totowa, 1963); C.E. Schorske, *German Social Democracy 1905–17. The Development of the Great Schism* (Cambridge, Mass., 1955); R.P. Morgan, *The German Social Democrats and the First International 1864–1872* (Cambridge, 1962); R.W. Reichard, *Crippled from Birth, German Social Democracy 1844–1870* (Iowa, 1969); F. Balser, *Sozial-Demokratie 1848/9–1863* (Stuttgart, 1965); D. Groh, *Negative Integration und revolutionärer Attentismus. Die deutsche Sozialdemokratie, 1909–1914* (Berlin, 1973); H. Wachenheim, *Die deutsche Arbeiterbewegung 1844 bis 1914* (Cologne and Opladen, 1967); G. Ritter, *Die Arbeiterbewegung im Wilhelminischen Reich* (Berlin, 1963).

3 Unlike other states which later introduced democratic franchises, Prussia retained its undemocratic parliament until 1917. Indeed the *Herrenhaus* (the upper chamber of the Prussian *Landtag*) managed to oppose these reforms until as late as the summer of 1918.

4 The traditionally held view of the role of the army in imperial Germany can be found in the following: M. Kitchen, *A Military History of Germany* (Bloomington, 1975); M. Messerschmidt, 'Die Armee in Staat und Gesellschaft' in M. Stürmer (ed.), *Das kaiserliche Deutschland* (Düsseldorf, 1970), pp 89–118; and W. Deist, 'Die Armee in Staat und Gesellschaft, 1890–1914', in Stürmer (ed.) *Das kaiserliche Deutschland*, pp 312–29. For an interesting 'revisionist' interpretation

see, D.E. Showalter, 'Army and Society in Imperial Germany: The Pains of Modernization', *Journal of Contemporary History*, 18 (1983), pp 583–618.
5 G.D. Feldman, *Army, Industry and Labour in Germany 1914–18* (Princeton, 1966), p 12. This work is still a *tour de force* despite its age.
6 Quoted in M. Balfour, *The Kaiser and his Times* (London, 1975), p 159.
7 An excellent analysis can be found in G. Eley, *Reshaping the German Right. Radical Nationalism and Political Change after Bismarck* (New Haven, CT 1980). For specific works see: M.S. Wertheimer, *The Pan-German League 1890–1914* (New York, 1924), and more recently R. Chickering, *We Men Who Feel Most German. A Cultural Study of the Pan-German League 1886–1914* (London, 1984); H.J. Puhle, *Agrarische Interessenpolitik und prüßicher Konservatismus im wilhelminischen Reich* (Hanover, 1966); A. Kruck, *Geschichte des Alldeutschen Verbandes 1890–1939* (Wiesbaden, 1954); H.-U. Wehler (ed.), *Der Primat der Innenpolitik* (Berlin, 1976); H. Herwig *'Luxury' Fleet. The Imperial German Navy 1888–1918* (London, 1980); H. Schottelius and W. Deist (eds), *Marine und Marinepolitik im kaiserlichen Deutschland 1871–1914* (Düsseldorf, 1972); W. Deist, *Flottenpolitik und Flottenpropaganda. Das Nachrichtenbureau des Reichsmarineamtes 1897–1914* (Stuttgart, 1976). See also M. Shevin Coetzee, 'The Mobilization of the Right? The *Deutsche Wehrverein* and Political Activism in Württemburg, 1912–14', *European History Quarterly*, 15, 4 (October 1985), pp 431–52.
8 F. Fischer, *Krieg der Illusionen. Die deutsche Politik von 1911–1914* (Düsseldorf, 1969), p 366 (tr. as *War of Illusions*, London, 1975).
9 Fischer, *Krieg*, p 231; see also his, *Juli 1914: War sind nicht hineingeschlittert. Das Staatsgeheimnis um die Riezler-Tagebücher* (Reinbeck, 1983); J. Röhl (ed.), 'An der Schwelle zum Weltkrieg: Eine Dokumentation über den "Kriegsrat" vom 8 Dezember 1912', *Militägeschichtliche Mitteilungen*, 1 (1977); J. Röhl, 'Die Generalprobe. Zur Geschichte und Bedeutung des "Kriegsrates" vom 8 Dezember 1912' in D. Stegmann, B.J. Wendt, P.C. Witt (eds), *Industrielle Gesellschaft und politisches System* (Bonn, 1978). For a discussion of the wider domestic issues influencing foreign policy see W.J. Mommsen, 'Domestic Factors in German Foreign Policy before 1914' in J. Sheehan (ed.), *Imperial Germany* (New York and London, 1976).
10 H.-U. Wehler, *The German Empire 1871–1918* (Leamington Spa, 1985), p 194.
11 Critics of Fischer include A. Hillgruber, *Deutschlands Rolle in der Vorgeschichte der beiden Weltkriege* (Düsseldorf, 1970); L.C.F. Turner, *Origins of the First World War* (London, 1970); for an appraisal of Gerhard Ritter's criticisms of the 'Fischer school' see K. Epstein, 'Gerhard Ritter and the First World War', *JCH*, I, 3, (1966), pp 193–210; see also K.H. Jarausch, *The Enigmatic Chancellor: Bethmann Hollweg and the Hubris of Imperial Germany* (London, New Haven, 1973); the diaries of Bethmann Hollweg's close adviser, Kurt Riezler, have also been used to discredit Fischer's views: see K. Riezler, *Tagebücher, Aufsätze, Dokumente*, intr. and ed. by K.D. Erdmann (Göttingen, 1972); W.C. Thompson, *In the Eye of the Storm: K. Riezler and the Crisis of Modern Germany* (Iowa City, 1980). Cf. D.E. Kaiser, 'Germany and the Origins of the First World War', *Journal of Modern History*, 55 (1983), pp 442–74; see also James Joll's thoughtful and balanced analysis, *The Origins of the First World War* (London, 1984). The 'Fischer controversy' is

analysed in J.A. Moses, *The Politics of Illusion: The Fischer Controversy in German Historiograpy* (New York, 1975). Cf. the more recent analysis of research since the initial 'Fischer controversy' by B. Thoss, 'Der Erste Weltkrieg als Ereignis und Erlebnis: Paradigmenwechsel in der westdeustchen Weltkriegsforschung seit der Fischer-Kontroverse' in W. Michalka (ed.), *Der Erste Weltkrieg: Wirkung, Wahrnehmung, Analyse* (Munich and Zurich, 1994), pp 1012–43. For two excellent surveys of the wider literature on the Second Reich see, R. Chickering (ed.), *Imperial Germany: A Historiographical Companion* (Westport, 1996) and J. Retallack, *Germany in the Age of Kaiser Wilhelm II* (New York, 1996).

12 Riezler, *Tagebücher*, p 180, entry for 30 July 1911, quoted in W.J. Mommsen, 'The Topos of Inevitable War in Germany in the Decade Before 1914' in V. Berghahn and M. Kitchen (eds), *Germany in the Age of Total War* (London, 1981), pp 23–45. The military clearly felt during this period that they could persuade the nation to take up arms. Cf. Ludendorff's famous memorandum of December 1912, quoted in W. Kloster, *Der deutsche Generalstab und der Präventivkriegs-Gedanke* (Stuttgart, 1923), p 48.

13 K. Wernecke, *Der Wille zur Weltgeltung. Aussenpolitik und Öffentlichkeit im Kaiserreich am Vorabend des Ersten Weltkrieges* (Düsseldorf, 1970), pp 248–9. Similar conclusions can be found in V. Berghahn, *Germany and the Approach of War in 1914* (London, 1973), and J. Röhl, *1914: Delusion or Design?* (London, 1973).

14 Mommsen, *Topos*, p 24. See also J. Joll, *1914, The Unspoken Assumptions* (London, 1968), pp 22–5. Niall Ferguson, on the other hand, has recently argued that Germany's leaders acted out of a 'sense of weakness' in 1914: Germany believed it had lost, or was losing the arms race, 'which persuaded its leaders to gamble on war before they fell too far behind'. N. Ferguson, *The Pity of War* (London, 1998).

15 Fischer, *Krieg*, p 53; see also A.J. Mayer, 'Domestic Causes of the First World War' in L. Krieger and F. Stern (eds), *The Responsibility of Power: Historical Essays in Honour of Hajo Holborn* (New York, 1967), pp 286–300.

16 For an interesting interpretation of the *Burgfrieden* see J. Kocka, *Facing Total War. German Society 1914–18* (Leamington Spa, 1984), pp 42–3. All references will be to the revised English edition. For the original German edition see *Klassengesellschaft im Krieg: Deutsche Sozialgeschichte 1914–18* (Göttingen, 1973).

17 *Vorwärts*, 27 July 1914.

18 E. Dahlin, *French and German Public Opinion on Declared War Aims 1914–18* (Stanford, 1933), p 18; an evocative if somewhat superficial account of life in Germany in the days leading up to war can be found in J. Williams, *The Home Fronts: Britain, France and Germany 1914–18* (London, 1972), pp 5–9.

19 Quoted in Williams, *The Home Fronts*, p 8.

20 *Vorwärts*, 1 August 1914. Also quoted in R. Lutz (ed.), *The Fall of the German Empire, 1914–1918*, 2 vols. (Stanford, 1932), pp 18–19.

21 J.W. Gerard, *My Four Years in Germany* (London, 1917), p 89.

22 The document setting out the contingency plans in case of war was signed by von Falkenhayn. Letter from the Prussian War Ministry dated 25 July 1914, can be found in W. Deist, *Militär und Innenpolitik*, 2 vols, I (Düsseldorf, 1970),

pp 188–92. Of the extensive literature on the Law of the State of Siege, still unexcelled is H. Boldt, *Rechtsstaat und Ausnahmezustand* (Berlin, 1967); see also M. Kitchen, *The Silent Dictatorship* (London, 1976), pp 50–3; and Feldman, *Army, Industry and Labor*, pp 31–2.

23 The two areas that proved particularly sensitive were the implementation of censorship and the law of preventive custody. I shall be discussing both of these in the following chapters.

24 Gerard, *My Four Years*, p 89. The writer Carl Zuckmayer later recorded his own recollection of the scenes in Berlin: 'I have experienced such a physical and moral condition of luminosity and euphoria two or three times since, but never with that sharpness and intensity.' Quoted in Eric Leed, *No Man's Land: Combat and Identity in World War I* (New York, 1979), p 39. Cf. M.C.C. Adams, *The Great Adventure. Male Desire and the Coming of World War I* (Bloomington and Indianapolis, 1990).

25 C. Geyer, *Die revolutionäre Illusion* (Stuttgart, 1976), p 43; see also F.L. Carsten, *War Against War* (London, 1982), p 16. Quotation taken from R. Chickering, *Karl Lamprecht: A German Academic Life* (Atlantic Heights, 1993), p 433.

26 A. Hitler, *Mein Kampf* (tr. R. Mannheim with introduction by D.C. Watt, London, 1973), p 145. For a brief analysis of the photograph of Hitler in the Odeon Platz and popular attitudes in Germany to the announcement of war see, D. Welch, *Modern European History, 1871–2000. A Documentary Reader* (London, 1999), pp 12–14.

27 H.P. Hanssen, *Diary of a Dying Empire*, intr. by R. Lutz, ed. by R. Lutz, M. Schofield and O.O. Winther, (Bloomington, 1955), entry for 2 August 1914, p 14. See Volker Ulrich's analysis of working-class responses to the outbreak of war, 'Everyday Life and the German Working Class, 1914–1918' in R. Fletcher (ed.), *Bernstein to Brandt. A Short History of German Social Democracy* (London, 1987), pp 55–64. Ulrich claims that there was little evidence of enthusiasm for the war, rather bewilderment and resignation. See also below, n. 44. For similarly 'anxious' responses in Darmstadt see, M. Stöcker, 'Augusterlebnis 1914', in *Das Augusterlebnis 1914 in Darmstadt: Legend und Wirklichkeit* (Darmstadt, 1994): for Düsseldorf see, E. Tobin, 'War and the Working Class: The Case of Düsseldorf 1914–1918', *Central European History*, 18 (1985), pp 257–99 and M. Nolan, *Social Democracy and Society: Working-Class Radicalism in Düsseldorf, 1890–1920* (Cambridge, 1981).

28 Princess E. Blücher, *An English Wife in Berlin: A Private Memoir* (London, 1920), entry for 6 September 1914, p 24.

29 Cf. the Kaiser's address to the people (*'An Deutsche Volk'*) a year later on 1 August 1915. While the Kaiser's address restates German justifications for the war and German virtues, the tone of the message is far more sober, calling for sacrifices in the name of the Fatherland. The address can be found in Hauptstaatsarchiv Stuttgart (hereafter HSS), *E 741, BG 170 (Vaterländische Hilfsdienste)*.

30 These expressions of support were invariably given wide coverage in the press, cf. the following cross-section: *Nationaler und Berufsverbände, New Prüssische Zeitung*, 1 August 1914; Vaterländische Frauen Verein, *Norddeutsche Allgemeine*

Zeitung, 2 August 1914; Verband der deutschen Juden, *Schwäbischer Merkur*, 4 August 1914; Berlin Hochschulen, *Deutsche Zeitung*, 7 August 1914; Berliner Verband Evangelische Arbeiterverein, *Norddeutsche Allgemeine Zeitung*, 14 August 1914.

31 The Exceptional Laws restricted the rights of certain classes of German citizens. For example, the law of 4 May 1874 regulated the Roman Catholic clergy in Germany; the law of 21 October 1878 outlawed the Socialist Party; the Jesuit Law of 4 July 1872 severely curtailed the activities of members of the Order of the Society of Jesus. For further discussion of this law see, Ch 2.

32 Feldman, *Army, Industry and Labor*, p 27.

33 *Stenographische Protokolle der Verhandlungen des Reichstags*, 4 August 1914, p 2; see also Hanssen, *Diary*, p 26.

34 *Verhandlungen des Reichstags*, 4 August 1914, pp 8–9; also Lutz, *The Fall of the German Empire*, I, pp 15–16.

35 For a survey of German wartime poetry see P. Bridgewater, *German Poets of the First World War* (London, 1985). For a comparative account see J. Silkin (ed.), *Poetry in World War One* (London, 1983).

36 F. Wedekind, *Prosa: Erzählungen, Aufsätze, Selbstzeugnisse, Briefe* (Berlin and Weimar, 1969), p 259; also quoted in R.E. Sackett, *Popular Entertainment, Class, and Politics in Munich, 1900–1923* (Cambridge, Mass., 1982), p 70.

37 Quoted in G.B. Bruntz, *Allied Propaganda and the Collapse of the German Empire in 1918* (Stanford, 1938), p 169.

38 For a more detailed analysis of the attitudes of SPD leaders in 1914 see Ch 6, 'The Divisions of the Left'.

39 Jürgen Kocka argues that by creating a 'fog of unreality', the *Burgfrieden* actually laid the foundations for the 'stab-in-the-back' legend. Kocka, *Facing Total War*, pp 43–4.

40 See Chapter 7 and my discussion of Pan German war aims and the Fatherland Party. For a collection of essays on the *völkisch* movement during this period see, U. Puschner, W. Schmitz and J.H. Ulbricht (eds), *Handbuch zur 'Völkischen Bewegung' 1871–1918* (Munich et al., 1996).

41 Letter by Max König to the *Vossische Zeitung*, 5 May 1916, quoted in A.J. Ryder, *The German Revolution* (Cambridge, 1967), pp 44–5.

42 The socialist paper, the *Leipziger Volkszeitung*, noted this and commented somewhat sardonically, 'all the enemies of Tsarism join in the chorus against the bloody tyranny of the Tsar... Liebknecht has free speech against Tsarism... It was not always so. For many years the German Conservatives were friends of the knout and the Cossacks's sword.' *Leipziger Volkszeitung*, 31 July 1914, quoted in Dahlin, *French and German Public Opinion*, pp 20–1.

43 *Deutscher Reichsanzeiger*, 6 August 1914, quoted in Lutz, *The Fall of the German Empire*, I, p 21.

44 Jeffrey Verhey controversially claims that most Germans did not experience 'war enthusiasm'. During the August days, enthusiasm concentrated in the larger cities and whereas few Germans resisted the draft or publicly opposed the war, Verhey maintains that the middle classes embraced the war while the lower classes

accepted it. I would support this thesis. Where I do part company with Verhey is when he talks about 'war enthusiasm' whereas I believe that the 'enthusiasm' in August was not for war, rather a patriotic solidarity against encirclement and perceived enemies. I am most grateful to Jeffrey Verhey for providing me with a synopsis of his PhD dissertation, '"The Spirit of 1914": The Myth of Enthusiasm and the Rhetoric of Unity in World War I Germany' (University of California, Berkeley, 1991). See also J. Verhey, 'Krieg und geistige Mobilmachung: Die Kriegspropaganda', in W. Kruse (ed.), *Eine Welt von Feinden: Der grosse Krieg 1914–1918* (Frankfurt am Main, 1997) pp 176–82. See also, W. Kruse, 'Die Kriegsbegeisterung im Deutschen Reich zu Beginn des Ersten Weltkrieges: Einstehungszusammenhänge, Grenzen und ideologische Strukturen', in M. van der Linden and G. Mergner (eds), *Kriegsbegeisterung und mentale Kriegsvorbereitung: Interdisziplinäre Studien* (Berlin, 1991), pp 73–87. Baumgarten estimates that the solidarity to go to war generated by the events in August 1914 lasted for 18 months. O. Baumgarten et al., *Geistige u. Sittliche Wirkungen des Krieges in Deutschland* (Stuttgart, 1927), pp 43–45. Interestingly enough the first anti-war leaflet campaign of any significance appeared in Munich in December 1915 (see Ch 5, 'Pacifism and the Peace Movement'). Recent interpretations of the 'spirit of 1914' in different localities can be found in M. Stöcker, *Das Augusterlebnis 1914 in Darmstadt* (Darmstadt, 1994); B. Ziemann, *Front und Heimat. Ländliche Kriegsfahrungen im südlichen Bayern 1914–1923* (Essen, 1997); C. Geinitz and U. Hinz, 'Das Augusterlebnis in Südbaden' in G. Hirschfeld et al. (eds), *Kriegsfahrungen. Studien zur Sozial- und Mentalitätgeschichte des Ersten Weltkriegs* (Essen, 1997). For an interesting comparative account see T. Rathel, *Das 'Wunder' der inneren Einheit. Studien zur deutschen und französischen Öffentlichkeit bei Beginn der Ersten Weltkriegs* (Bonn, 1996).

45 Zentrales Staatsarchiv Potsdam (hereafter ZSAP), *Reichskanzlie, Allgemeines, 2398/8*, Bericht des Berliner Polizeipräsidenten, 4/5 September 1914. These reports have now been compiled by I. Materna and H.-J. Schreckenbach (eds), *Dokumerte aus geheimen Archiver. 4: Berichte des Berliner Polizeipräsidenten zur Stimmung und Lage der Bevölkerung in Berlin 1914–1918* (Weimar, 1987). See also, U. Daniel, *The War from Within. German Working-Class Women in the First World War* (Oxford, 1997), p 20 (German edn, *Arbeiterfrauen in Kriegsgesellschaft. Beruf, Familie und Politik im Ersten Weltkrieg* (Göttingen, 1989)). All references to the English translated edition.

46 Riezler, *Tagebücher*, entry for 14 August 1914.

2 THE MOBILIZATION OF THE MASSES

1 These reforms will be discussed in more detail in Ch 4. I have leaned heavily on Feldman's excellent, *Army, Industry and Labor in Germany*.

2 Further information about Erzberger's role can be found in K. Epstein, *Matthias Erzberger and the Dilemma of German Democracy* (Princeton, 1959), pp 103–5. See also Erzberger's brief account in 'Die Mobilmachung' in *Der Deutsche Krieg*, vol 5 (Stuttgart, 1914).

3 The effectiveness of the Nauen station was constantly undermined by Marconi operators in Britain who were able to monitor its messages. The revelation of the decoded Zimmermann telegram, for example, which revealed Germany's clumsy attempts to establish a German-Mexican alliance against the United States, played a considerable part in inducing the US Congress to accept the idea of war with Germany.

4 Much of this information comes from a fascinating intelligence report of German propaganda up to 1917, unearthed by the British War Office in 1939 and sent to the Foreign Office for possible comparison with Nazi propaganda. Public Records Office (PRO), INF 1/715, 11 May 1939. I am grateful to Philip Taylor for drawing my attention to this source.

5 Different aspects of German propaganda directed at American public opinion can be found in the following: H.C. Peterson, *Propaganda for War: The Campaign against American Neutrality, 1914–17* (Oklahoma, 1939); A.R. Buchanan, 'European Propaganda and American Public Opinion, 1914–17', unpublished PhD thesis (Stanford University, 1935). See also the series of pamphlets issued by the Committee on Public Information (Washington), including: 'Conquest and Kultur of the Germans in Their Own Words', W. Notestein and E. Stoll (eds), No. 5, January 1918; and 'German Plots and Intrigues', E.E. Sperry (ed.), No. 10, July 1918.

6 Very little work has been published on this subject. In 1916 the German Foreign Ministry conducted a report into its own propaganda in neutral countries and appeared quite satisfied with its performance. Foreign Office Library, GFM/HO 58169–58172, dated 1916. At the time of writing these photostat German Foreign Ministry documents were in the process of being returned to the PRO. Certainly during 1915 the British War Ministry was complaining bitterly to the Foreign Office about the failure of British propaganda to match Germany's success in neutral countries, Cf. PRO/FO 371/ Vol. 2579/188244, War Office to Foreign Office December 1915. Comprehensive documentation of German propaganda abroad can be found in Bundesarchiv Militärarchiv Freiburg (hereafter MAF), *RM5* (Admiralstab der Marine), Bd I, *3769–3782, 3809–11*.

7 Quoted in H.Y. Fyfe, *Northcliffe, An Intimate Biography* (London, 1930), p 205.

8 Ibid, p 174ff.

9 Cf. Letter from the Acting General Command of the 8th Army Corps to the Ministry of Interior, re: How to deal with Social Democrats, 19 August 1914: Deist, *Militär und Innenpolitik* 2 vols. (Düsseldorf, 1970), vol. 1, pp 194–6. While the military did not expect immediate problems with 'clever' SPD Deputies the letter made it clear that should Social Democrats transgress the *Burgfrieden* then 'severe measures' would be taken against them. For a general discussion of the notion that the Great War was pre-eminently a propaganda of war aims, see H. Lasswell, *Propaganda Techniques in the World War* (New York, 1927).

10 The full text of the law of 27 July 1914 is reproduced in full in W. Deist, *Militär und Innenpolitik*, vol 1, pp 188–92.

11 J. Schellenberg, 'Die Herausbildung der Militärdiktatur in den ersten Jahren des Krieges' in *Politik in Krieg 1914–18* (Berlin, 1964), p 33. For a perceptive analysis

of Falkenhayn see H. Afflerbach, *Falkenhayn, Politisches Denken und Handeln im Kaiserreich* (Munich, 1994).

12 A succinct summary of the organization of the High Command can be found in Martin Kitchen's greatly underrated book, *The Silent Dictatorship* (London, 1976), pp 45–63.

13 Proclamation from Chief of General Staff to War Ministries and the Deputy Commanding Generals re: Safeguarding the *Burgfrieden*, 13 August 1914; Deist, *Militär und Innenpolitik*, vol 1, pp 193–4.

14 Wolff's main global rival was Reuters whose chief executive at the time was Baron Herbert Reuters. Baron Herbert had spent his whole life in England and regarded Reuters as safely 'British'. Nevertheless, he bore a German name after its founder, Julius Reuter. Once the arrangement between WTB and the German government became known in Britain, questions were asked about whether Reuters had also been subverted by German influence. In fact, according to Donald Read, in his official history of the Reuters organization, Reuters placed its reputation as well as its network at the service of the British government. 'At Reuters', wrote one Department of Information (DOI) official revealingly on 11 July 1917, 'the work done is that of an independent news agency of an objective character, with propaganda secretly infused... it is essential that independence should be preserved'. D. Read, *The Power of News. The History of Reuters* (Oxford, 1992, 2nd edition, 1998), pp 127–8. The German government remained convinced that Reuters was a propaganda agency for the British and depicted the organization in its propaganda as 'the Lying Toad' (*'Die Lügenkröte'*) seated on telegraph wires spewing out its propaganda. (See Figure 4.)

For a somewhat protracted narrative on the organization of the German press during wartime see K. Koszyk, *Deutsche Presspolitik im Ersten Weltkrieg* (Düsseldorf, 1968). For a brief and rather superficial comparative analysis see A.G. Marquis, 'Word as Weapons: Propaganda in Britain and Germany during the First World War', *Journal of Contemporary History*, 13 (1978), pp 467–98.

15 A concise account of the role of the press in the nineteenth century Germany can be found in M. Eksteins, *The Limits of Reason. The German Democratic Press and the Collapse of Weimar Democracy* (Oxford, 1975), pp 13–27. For a more detailed analysis see K. Koszyk, *Deutsche Presse im 19. Jahrhundert* (Berlin, 1966). Koszyk memorably referred to the press of the Wilhelmine era as a 'mirror of its epoch'. Ibid, p 264. See also, H.D. Fischer (ed.), *Deutsche Zeitungen des 17. bis 20. Jahrhundert* (Munich, 1972) and H.D. Fischer, *Handbuch der politischen Press in Deutschland 1480–1980. Synopse rechtlicher, struktureller und wirtschaflicher Grundlagen der Tendenzpublizistik im Kommunikationsfeld* (Düsseldorf, 1981).

16 Eksteins, *The Limits of Reason*, p 13; Koszyk, *Deutsche Presse*, pp 307f.

17 Koszyk, *Deutsche Presse*, pp 267ff.

18 See A. Hall, *Scandal, Sensation and Social Democracy. The SPD Press and Wilhelmine Germany, 1890–1914* (Cambridge, 1977). *Vorwärts* daily circulation increased from 56,000 in 1902 to 165,000 in 1912. This increase reflected the growth of the SPD. See, V. Schulze, *'Vorwärts'*, in H.D. Fischer (ed.), *Deutsche Zetungen*, pp 331–42.

19 From a censored article by Arthur Bernstein of the *Berliner Morgenpost;* see Eksteins, *The Limits of Reason*, p 29. Circulation figures for the press can be found in O. Groth, *Die Zeitung* (4 vols, Mannheim, Berlin, Leipzig, 1928–30), I, pp 251–3.
20 The full text of the Chancellor's proclamation is printed in Koszyk, *Deutsche Presspolitik*, pp 22–3. For a detailed discussion of press censorship during the war see H.D. Fischer (ed.), *Pressekonzentration und Zensurpraxis im Ersten Weltkrieg* (Berlin, 1973). See also, W. Deist, 'Zensur und Propaganda in Deutschland während des Ersten Weltkreiges,' in Deist, *Militär, Staat und Gesellschaft: Studien zur preussisch-deutschen Militärgeschichte* (Munich, 1991), pp 153–64.
21 MAF, *RM5, Bd. 1, 2413,* Instructions from military authorities to the press, 1.8.1914. The original 26 prohibitions slapped on the press by Bethmann Hollweg were now added to by the military.
22 W. Nicolai, *Nachrichtendienst, Presse und Volksstimmung im Weltkrieg* (Berlin, 1920), p 53. See also Nicolai, *The German Secret Service* (London, 1924). Nicolai is an illusive figure, although he was probably the most important single individual associated with the dissemination of German propaganda. The surviving papers show that he was not a great innovator but a conscientious and devoted administrator. Cf. Ludendorff's comments, *My War Memories, 1914–18* (2 vols, London, 1919), I, p 17. Wherever possible I have used the English translation of Ludendorff's memoirs penned in exile. However, when the English edition fails to provide a sufficiently precise translation or an exact 'flavour' of Ludendorff's thoughts I have cited the German edition; *Meine Kriegserinnerungen 1914–1918* (Berlin, 1919).
23 MAF, *RM3 (Akten des Reichsmarineamtes),* Bd. 4, *10294*, 10.8.1914.
24 *Vorwärts*, 1 August 1914.
25 Lutz, *Fall of the German Empire,* I, p 169.
26 *Vorwärts*, 9 August 1914; also Lutz, *Fall of the German Empire,* pp 169–70.
27 Hanssen, *Diary of a Dying Empire,* p 51, in conversation with Rudolf Hilferding (one time editor-in-chief of *Vorwärts*).
28 *Vorwärts*, 2 September 1914; Lutz, *Fall of the German Empire,* p 20.
29 Hanssen, *Diary of a Dying Empire,* p 64.
30 Quoted in Lutz, *Fall of the German Empire,* II, p 12.
31 This episode can be found in Hanssen, *Diary of a Dying Empire,* pp 83–4.
32 Order of the Deputy General Command of VIII Army Corps to the civil and military authorities, 28.11.1914, Deist, *Militär und Innenpolitik,* I, pp 83–5. It had been decided on 1 September that the police authorities should not exercise such powers. See letter from Bavarian War Ministry to military commanders in Deist, p 71.
33 MAF, RM3, Bd. 4, *10294,* telegram from Secretary of State von Jagow to the Foreign Office, 28 August 1914.
34 Telegram from the Imperial Chancellor to the Foreign Office regarding the guiding principles for the handling of censorship over the question of war aims, quoted in Deist, p 40.

35 MAF, RM3, Bd. 4, *10294*, Deputy General Staff to Bavarian War Ministry, 1 September 1914. A former German journalist catalogued six different censorship and 15 other bureaus through which a single news item might theoretically travel. See, K. Mühsam, *Wie Wir Belogen Wurden* (Berlin, 1920), p 130.
36 MAF, *RM3*, Bd. 4, *10294*, Deputy General Staff to Imperial Naval Office re: setting up a Supreme Censorship Office, 3 October 1914.
37 The meeting setting up the Supreme Censorship Office took place on 3 December 1914. For a discussion of its development see Nicolai, *Nachrichtendienst*, p 73ff.
38 The events leading up to this incident are described in Hanssen, *Diary of a Dying Empire*, pp 79–80.
39 MAF, RM3, Bd. 4, *10294*, Prussian War Ministry to Military Commanders, 9 November 1914.
40 MAF, RM3, Bd. 4, *10294*, minutes of press conference held in the Reichstag, 3 November 1914.
41 The Secretary of State (Staats Sekretär) was the head of an administrative department in the imperial government. He was appointed by and responsible to the Chancellor.
42 *Verhandlung des Reichstags*, 3 December 1914, p 20; see also Hanssen, *Diary of a Dying Empire*, pp 86–8. The Reichstag renewed their attack on the Exceptional Laws on 10 March 1915, but again with little success.
43 Deputy General Staff to Military Commanders, 10 December 1914, quoted in Deist, pp 87–8.
44 MAF, RM3, Bd. 4, *10294*, Prussian Minister of Interior to Oberpräsident, 9 February 1915.
45 MAF, RM3, Bd. 4, *10305*, Supreme Censorship Office to censorship office of Acting General Command of XVII Army Corps, 12 March 1915.
46 MAF, RM3, Bd. 4, *10305*, Chief of Acting General Staff to Military Commanders, 26 March 1915.
47 MAF, RM3, Bd. 4, *10296*, Cabinet Order of Wilhelm II to Prussian War Ministry, 4 August 1915.
48 MAF, RM3, Bd. 4, *10317*, Acting General Staff's plans for the organization of the War Press Office, September 1915.
49 This remained a constant source of complaint. As early as February 1915 the German Publisher's Association unsuccessfully asked the General Staff to distribute war communiqués directly rather than through the WTB, Koszyk, *Deutsche Presspolitik*, p 29. For a detailed outlined of the new format of the *Deutsche Kriegsnachrichten* see, MAF, RM5, Bd. 2, 3722, 8 September 1916.
50 See Note 48. The document contains a separate section dealing with the responsibilities of the Supreme Censorship Office. See also folder on press censorship for the period 15 September 1914 to 25 December 1915, Militärarchiv, Stuttgart (hereafter MAS), *M77/1 (Stellvertretendes Generalkommando XIII)*, Bü 60.
51 MAF, RM3, Bd. 4, *10317*, War Press Office to representatives of the press, 6 November 1915. For an analysis of the War Press Office see, M. Creutz, *Die*

Pressepolitik der kaiserlichen Regierung während des Ersten Weltkriegs (Frankfurt am Main, 1996).

52. This argument is central to Koszyk's work, *Deutsche Presspolitik;* cf. also Eksteins, *The Limits of Reason*, pp 28–9; Marquis, 'Words as Weapons', p 476.

53. For different estimates see the following works: F. Zglinicki, *Der Weg des Films* (Frankfurt, 1956); O. Kalbus, *Vom Werden deutscher Filmkunst*, vol 1 (2 vols, Altona, 1935); C. Moreck, *Sittengeschichte des Kino* (Dresden, 1926); J. Toeplitz, *Geschichte des Films*, vol 1, 1895–928 (Munich, 1975); H. Knietzsch, *Film, gestern und heute: Gedanken und Daten zu sieben Jahrzehnten Geschichte der Filmkunst*, 3rd edn (Leipzig, 1972).

54. For a perceptive analysis of leisure, especially among younger and single workers in Düsseldorf and Bochum, see, L. Abrams, *Workers' Culture in Imperial Germany. Leisure and Recreation in Rhineland and Westphalia* (London, 1992). The wider relationship between war and culture is outside the scope of this work. German historiography has paid relatively little attention to the role of intellectuals in the Great War. From the work that has been carried out it is clear that poetry was the preferred form of cultural expression in Germany at the outbreak of war. The Berlin critic, Julius Bab, estimated that in August 1914 50,000 poems were written daily and Thomas Mann talked about a nation revealing it poetic soul. However, by mid-1915 literary journals were closing down their poetry sections due to the abysmal standards of writing. It would appear that the war did not greatly enhance cultural standards and this applied to fiction and drama as well. For an interesting, albeit depressing, collection of essays devoted to the arts see, W.J. Mommsen (ed.) *'Schriften des Historischen Kollegs, Kolloquiem 34'* (Munich, 1996). See also, Mommsen's, 'German Artists, Writers and Intellectuals and the Meaning of War, 1914–1918,' in J. Horne (ed.), *State, Society and Mobilization in Europe during the First World War* (Cambridge, 1997), pp 21–38. On the war's cultural significance see, M. Ecksteins, *Rites of Spring: The Great War and the Birth of the Modern Age* (Boston, 1989); S.D. Denham, *Visions of War: Ideologies and Images of War in German Literature before and after the Great War* (Berne, 1992); and M.P.A. Travers, *German Novels on the First World War and the Ideological Implications, 1918–1933* (Stuttgart, 1982).

55. This is not intended to be a comprehensive account of the relationship between the cinema and the state in nineteenth-century Germany. I have leaned heavily on Gary D. Stark's excellent 'Cinema, Society, and the State: Policing the Film Industry in Imperial Germany', in G.D. Stark and B.K. Lackner (eds), *Essays on Culture and Society in Modern Germany* (Texas A & M University Press, 1982), pp 123–66. More recently, Stark, 'All Quiet on the Home Front: Popular Entertainments, Censorship and Civilian Morale in Germany, 1914–1918,' in F. Coetzee and M. Shevin-Coetzee (eds), *Authority, Identity and the Social History of the Great War* (Providence and Oxford, 1995), pp 57–80. See also, D. Welch, 'Cinema and Society in Imperial Germany 1905–1918', *German History*, vol 8, no. 1, February 1990, pp 28–45.

56. E. Altenloh, *Zur Soziologie des Kinos* (Jena, 1914), p 55. The survey showed that the most devoted cinema-goers were workers and artisans.

57 Altenloh, *Zur Soziologie*, pp 55–6; Stark, 'Cinema, Society, and the State', p 125.
58 J. Kocka, *Facing Total War, German Society 1914–18* (Leamington Spa, 1984), p 13, n.8. Cf. German edition, *Klassengesellschaft im Krieg: Deutsche Soziolgeschichte 1914–18* (Göttingen, 1973), p 152. All future references will be to the English edition.
59 V. Schulze, 'Frühe kommunale Kinos und die Kinoreformbewegung in Deutschland bis zum Ende des ersten Weltkrieges', *Publizistik 22* (January–March 1977), pp 6–71; Stark, 'Cinema, Society, and the State', pp 131–3. In 1906 the average film had been 150–300 metres long; in 1910, 400–700 m; 1910–14, 700–1,000 m; 1915–18, 1,000–2,000 m. Figures taken from W. von Bredow and R. Zurek (eds), *Film und Gesellschaft in Deutschland. Dokumente und Materialen* (Hamburg, 1972), p 18.
60 See R. Schenda, *Volke ohne Buch: Studien zur Soziolgeschichte des populären Lesestoffes 1770–1910* (Frankfurt, 1970); R.A. Fullerton, 'Towards a Commercial Popular Culture in Germany: The Development of Pamphlet Fiction, 1871–1914', *Journal of Social History*, vol. 12, (1979), pp 489–511.
61 Stark, 'Cinema, Society, and the State', p 133; see also V. McHale and E. Johnson, 'Urbanization, Industrialization, and Crime in Imperial Germany', *Social Science History*, vol 1, (1976), pp 45–78 and vol. 2, (1977), pp 210–47.
62 Films had to be submitted at least three days before they were due to be exhibited. Staatsarchiv Potsdam (hereafter StA.P), Rep. 30 Berlin C, Th. 123, Berlin police decree 5 May 1906.
63 Hauptstaatsarchiv Stuttgart (hereafter HSS), E 151c/II, No. 270b, Bavarian Interior Ministry decree 27 January 1912. (This folder was in the process of being reclassified with a new file number).
64 Stark, 'Cinema, Society, and the State', p 139.
65 Brunswick had followed the Prussian example in 1911. Both the Brunswick and Württemberg laws are summarized in K. Zimmereimer, *Die Filmzensur* (Breslau, 1934), pp 72–4. After the outbreak of war, Munich imposed the most restrictive censorship by refusing to differentiate between adults and children when issuing distribution certificates. If a film was 'forbidden for children' it was also deemed unsuitable for adults. A curious decision that remained in force even when, during the war, children under the age of seventeen were refused admission to cinemas in Bavaria! For the most complete list of censorship decisions in Germany before and during the war see, H. Birett, *Verzeichnis in Deutschland gelaufner Filme, Entscheidungen der Filmzensur 1911–1920* (Berlin, Hamburg, Stuttgart Munich, 1980).
66 *Verhandlung des Reichstags*, 25 February 1914; Zimmereimer, *Filmzensur*, p 49; Stark, 'Cinema, Society, and the State', p 153.
67 Altenloh, *Soziologie des Kinos*, pp 42–3.
68 Figures for cinema audiences can be found in H. v. Boehmer and H. Reitz, *Der Film in Wirtschaft und Recht* (Berlin, 1933), p 5. Cf. also O. Kalbus, *Vom Werden*, I, p 17. The Navy League were the exception in that they had been exploiting the possibilities offered by film before 1914. See W. Deist, *Flottenpolitik und*

Flottenpropaganda. Das Nachrichtenbureau des Reichsmarineamtes 1897–1914 (Stuttgart, 1976).

69 StA.P, Rep. 30 Berlin C, Th. 134, Berlin police memorandum, 11 August 1914.
70 StA.P, Rep. 30 Berlin C, Th. 134, Kessel to Police-Präsidium, Theatre-Censor, 20 October 1914.
71 StA.P, Rep. 30 Berlin C, Th. 134, undated newspaper clipping quoting Dr. Günther in the *Berliner Morgenpost*.
72 StA.P, Rep. 30 Berlin C, Th. 134, Berlin Police report to Minister of Interior, 27 September 1914.
73 See note 71.
74 StA.P, Rep. 30 Berlin C, Th. 134, Prussian War Minister to Local Military Commanders, 15 December 1914.
75 Zglinicki, *Weg des Films*, p 388.
76 StA.P, Rep. 30 Berlin C, Th. 134, *Merkblatt für Kinematographentheater*, 13 January 1915.
77 See M. Hardie and A. Sabin, *War Posters issued by Belligerent and neutral nations 1914–19* (London, 1920); M. Rickards, *Posters of the First World War* (London, 1969); J. Darracott and B. Loftus, *First World War Posters* (HMSO/IWM, 1972); J. Darracott, *The First World War in Posters* (New York, 1974); P. Paret, B. Irwin Lewis, P. Paret, *Persuasive Images. Posters of War and Revolution* (Princeton, NJ, 1992).
78 IWM, Weekly Report on German and Austrian Papers, Foreign Office, 15 May 1915–1 January 1916, quoting *Kölnische Zeitung*, 18 May 1915. For a more detailed account see Chapter 3, pp 58–64.
79 StA.P, Rep. 30 Berlin C, Th. 134, copy of Reichstag sitting, No. 103, of 2 March 1915.
80 Quoted in Zglinicki, *Weg des Films*, p 367.
81 *Verhandlung des Reichstags*, 20 May 1916, p 1157.
82 StA.P, Rep. 30 Berlin E, Th. 135,8 March 1915.
83 StA.P, Rep. 30 Berlin E, Th. 135, singing was forbidden on 18 May 1915 and instructions to close cinemas at 11 p.m. was issued on 10 May 1915. At the very end of 1916 all cinemas and theatres and other places of entertainment were ordered to close at 10 p.m. (issued on 31 December 1916). Two months later, cinema owners had to leave an interval of $1^1/_2$ hours between two showings (issued on 21 February 1917).
84 *Bremer Bürger-Zeitung*, 11 May 1916. The article (which is partly taken from the *Schwäbischer Merkur* of 3 May) also printed a table of the breakdown of convictions for the age group 12 to 18 years of age. The Bremen assembly subsequently banned the sale of alcohol to juveniles for home consumption on risk of a 150M fine or even imprisonment.
85 Cf Berlin police instructions for 11, 13 July 1916 and 23 July December 1916, StA.P, Rep. 30 Berlin E, Th. 135.
86 *Verhandlung des Reichstags*, 30 May 1916, p 1309.
87 Ibid, p 1296.

88 Works on the subject include: K. Demeter, 'Die Entwicklung des deutschen Films zu einem Fakto der Weltpolitik und Weltwirtschaft', *Archiv für Politik und Geschichte*, No. 5, (1925); G. Bub, *Der deutsche Film im Weltkrieg und sein publizistischer Einsatz* (Berlin, 1938); F. Terveen, 'Die Anfänge der deutschen Film-Kriegsberichterstattung in den Jahren 1914–16', *Wehrwissenschaftliche Rundschau*, No. 6, (1956); H. Barkhausen, *Filmpropaganda für Deutschland im Ersten und Zweiten Weltkrieg* (Hildesheim, 1982).
89 See K.W. Wippermann, *Die Entwicklung der Wochenschau in Deutschland: 'Eiko'-Woche Nr. 36/1915*, (Göttingen, 1970) and Wippermann, *Die Entwicklung der Wochenschau in Deutschlands: Besuch Kaiser Karls I von österreich im deutschen Grossen Hauptquartier 1917* (Göttingen, 1970).
90 O. Messter, *Mein Weg mit dem Film* (Berlin, 1936), p 99.
91 Traub maintains that there were as many as 96 applicants for these licences, but this is probably an exaggeration. H. Traub, *Die Ufa. Ein Beitrag zur Entwicklungsgeschichte des deutschen Filmschaffens* (Berlin, 1943), p 131.
92 Cf. Wippermann, *Die Entwicklung... 'Eiko'-Woche*, p 12.
93 *Kinematograph*, No. 407, quoted in Terveen, 'Die Anfänge der deutschen Film', p 324.
94 The full contents of this newsreel can be found in Traub, *25 Jahre Wochenschau der Ufa* (Berlin, 1943), p 13; and Terveen, 'Die Anfänge der deutschen Film', p 324n13.
95 A summary of this newsreel can also be found in Wippermann, *Die Entwicklung... 'Eiko'-Woche*, pp 14–15.
96 *Kinematograph*, No. 414, 2 December 1914.
97 A copy of this newsreel can be viewed at the Imperial War Museum, which holds Messter-Woche No. 43–8. The Imperial War Museum also hold a rare example of an early 'careless talk' film that would become such a feature of British and German propaganda in World War II. The film, which is undated (but probably 1917), is entitled *'Bei Allen Gesprächen'* warns German soldiers against the fatal consequences of accidentally letting the enemy discover secret information. Orders for an attack are passed down from GHQ to officers in the field. Trench mortars and gas cylinders are prepared and reinforcements arrive. The British are unaware of the forthcoming offensive until a soldier picks up a casual remark by a German over the field telephone. This gives the British time to prepare their own defences and when the Germans begin their offensive and advance across no-man's land (red-tinted film) they are repulsed. While the German command wonders how the enemy gained advance warning of the attack, the soldier responsible for its failure lies wounded and has time to realize the consequences of his indiscretion before being killed by a well-aimed enemy shell. IWM, GWY, 0778.
98 For an interesting personal account of the difficulties encountered by the newsreel cameramen see F. Seldte, *Through a Lens Darkly* (London, 1933). See also Martin Kopp's account in *Kinematograph*, No. 437, 12 May 1915.

99 Zglinicki, *Der Weg des Films*, p 390. Ludendorff received these views from Professor Dr v. Schjerning of the General Staff, who suggested somewhat sardonically that such newsreels were a valuable 'medicament'.
100 *The Cinema*, 6 May 1915. Cf. 'Germany's Official Cinema Bureau', *Bioscope*, vol XXVI, No. 437, 18 February 1915. Both the War Office and the Foreign Office were clearly conscious of the need to counter German film propaganda which they acknowledged had gained an important lead. Cf. PRO, *FO/371/2579, 188244*, December 1915.
101 PRO, *FO/371/2538, 89982*, Rice to Grey, 24 June 1915.
102 The name 'Sascha' derived from the nickname of Graf Alexander (Sascha) Kolowrat-Krakowsky, the Austrian film pioneer.
103 Messter, *Mein Weg mit dem Film*, pp 132–3.
104 Zglinicki, *Der Weg des Films*, p 392.
105 For the background to the establishment of Deulig, see MAF, RM3, Bd. 4, 9901. Plan for the establishment of Deutsche Lichtbild Gesellschaft (Deulig), 3 August 1916. The plan for the establishment of Deulig had therefore been set out for three months before it was announced officially in November 1916. Cf. also Barkhausen, *Filmpropaganda*, pp 78–80, 88–9.
106 HSS, E151c/II, No 287, 12 January 1917. Later confirmation can be found in MAF, RM3/r 9901, 30 January 1918.
107 The first paragraph of its statute described it as a 'military institution'. Traub, *Die Ufa*, p 137. For how the War Ministry wished other departments to view Bufa and its policy of 'film enlightenment' see, memoranda of 27 February 1916 and 22 March 1916; MAF, RM3, Bd. 4, 9901. Cf. also the pamphlet written by Dr Wagner and produced by the War Press Office, *Das Bild- und Film-Amt und Aufgaben* (Berlin, 1917). It can be found in MAS, *M I/3, (Vaterlandische Hilfsdienst und Kriegspropaganda) 499*. This was based on a lecture given by Dr Wagner to a conference on 'Enlightenment' on 7 August 1917.
108 BHStA, Kr, MKr, 2334, Meeting with War Press Office with Enlightenment Directors, 6–9 August 1917; see also Daniel, *The War From Within*, p 256.
109 Cited in Ay, *Enstehung*, p 65.
110 See D. Welch, 'A Medium for the Masses: Ufa and Imperial German film propaganda during the First World War', *Historical Journal of Film, Radio and Television*, vol. 6, No. 1, (1986), pp 85–91.
111 Writing after the war on 'Vodka, the Church and the Cinema', Trotsky argued that the cinema was the most powerful means of collective education for the working class: 'it amuses, educates, strikes the imagination by images, and liberates you from the need of crossing the Church door. The cinema is a great competitor not only of the public-house, but of the Church. Here is an instrument which we must secure at all costs!'. L. Trotsky, *The Problems of Life* (London, 1924), pp 34–43.
112 Zglinicki, *Der Weg des Films*, p 328.
113 Boehmer & Reitz, *Der Film in Wirtschaft und Recht* (Berlin, 1933), p 5; Kalbus, *Vom Werden deutscher Filmkunst*, vol 1, p 17.

114 Traub, *Die Ufa*, p 19; Boehmer & Reitz, *Der Film in Wirtschaft*, p 6.
115 The full text of Ludendorff's celebrated letter can be found in Traub, *Die Ufa*, pp 138–9; Zglinicki, *Der Weg des Films*, pp 394–5; Barkhausen, *Filmpropaganda*, pp 259–61. The role of film propaganda during the final two years of the war will be discussed in Chapter 7.

3 WAR AIMS

1 This discussion of German war aims owes much to Wolfgang Mommsen's excellent summary in 'The Debate on German War Aims' *Journal of Contemporary History*, (1966), 47–72. Holger Herwig argues that Germany did not go to war in a bid for world power, but to secure her borders of 1871. Herwig, *The First World War*. For my own views on German *Weltpolitik* including Bethmann Hollweg's September Programme see, Welch, *Modern European History 1871–2000*, pp 6–14, 66–76.
2 F. Fischer, *Griff nach der Weltmacht, Die Kriegszielpolitik des Kaiserlichen Deutschland* (Düsseldorf, 1961), p 841 (transl. as *Germany's Aims in the First World War*, London, 1967). Fischer's thesis was immediately supported by I. Geiss, *Der Polnische Grenzstreifen 1914–18* (Lübeck & Hamburg, 1960); and W. Basler, *Deutschlands Annexionspolitik in Polen und im Baltikum 1914–18* (East Berlin, 1962). See also Roger Chickering's concise summary of the current state of play in the major historiographical debates in his Introduction to, R. Chickering (ed.), *Imperial Germany. A Historiographical Companion* (London, 1996).
3 J.W. Gerard, *My Four Years in Germany* (London, New York, 1917), p 222. Gerard also noted:

> Everyone is familiar with Lissauer's 'Hymn of Hate'. It is not extraordinary that one man in a country at war should produce a composition of this kind; but it is extraordinary, as showing the state of mind of the whole country, that the Emperor should have given him the high Order of the Red Eagle of the Second Class as a reward for having composed this extraordinary document.

4 *Kölnische Zeitung*, 7 August 1914; also cited in W. Mommsen, *Bürgerstolz und Weltmachtstreben: Deutschland unter Wilhelm II bis 1918* (Berlin, 1995), p 563. For the postcard of Grey see also, T. and V. Holt, *Till the Boys Come Home. The Picture Postcards of the First World War* (London, 1977), p 13. For the expunging of foreign words see, Gerard, *My Four Years*, p 299. For a detailed analysis of anti-English agitation in Germany see, M.P. Stibbe, 'Vampire of the Continent. German Anglophobia during the First World War, 1914–1918' (unpublished D.Phil. dissertation, University of Sussex, 1997).
5 Hanssen, *Diary of a Dying Empire*, p 23.
6 Cited in Daniel, *The War From Within*, p 34n11.
7 H. von Gerlach, *Die grosse Zeit der Lüge* (Charlottenburg, 1926), 48.

8   Quoted in J. Gloag, *Word Warfare* (London, 1939), p 117. In September 1916 the wife of an American newspaperman was attacked in the street and two secretaries assaulted because they were speaking English: cited in Gerard, *Kaiserism*, pp 116, 121.

9   Cf for example *Simplicissimus*, 2 November 1914; and *Simplicissimus*, 22 December 1914. An excellent sample of the use made of German propaganda pamphlets for patriotic purposes can be found in Hauptstaatsarchiv, Stuttgart, (hereafter, MAS), *J 150 (Flugschriftensammlung)* Nos 211, 212.

10 *Norddeutsche Allgemeine Zeitung*, 29 September 1914, quoted in J.M. Read, *Atrocity Propaganda 1914–1919* (Yale University Press, 1941 & New York, 1972), p 20 (references to 1972 edn).

11 *Münchner Neueste Nachrichten*, 28 May 1915. See also *Greueltaten russischer Truppen gegen deutsche Zivilpersonen and deutsche Kriegsgefangene* (Berlin, 1915). Interestingly enough, German claims that the French placed prisoners in front of their lines to protect their troops, was also levelled against the Germans by the British. Cf *The War Illustrated*'s account of how German troops used captured Belgian miners as a human shield in order to enter Charleroi: 'This may be Teutonic cunning, but who can imagine the Allies adopting such barbarous methods?'. *The War Illustrated*, 12 September 1914, p 85.

12 Bernhard Duhr (ed.), *Lügengeist im Volkerkrieg* (Munich, 1914). Memorandum reported in *Norddeutsche Allgemeine Zeitung*, 3 September 1914, quoted in Dahlin, *French and German Public Opinion*, p 40.

13 The manifesto claimed that: 'In the East... the blood of our women and children drenches the earth and in the West the dum-dum bullets tear apart the breasts of our warriors. Those who ally themselves with Russians and Serbs, and incite Mongols and Negroes on to fight the white race, have the least right to call themselves defenders of civilization': cited in C. Roetter, *Psychological Warfare* (London, 1974), p 46. A more detailed analysis of the manifesto and its significance can be found in J. Ungern-Sternberg von Pürkel and W. von Ungern-Sternberg, *Der Aufruf und die Kulturwelt: Das Manifest der 93 und die Anfänge der Kriegspropaganda im Ersten Weltkrieg* (Stuttgart, 1996). For an interesting account of how the Russians were depicted in the German press leading up to 1914 see, T. Paddock, 'Still Stuck at Sevastopol: The Depiction of Russia during the Russo-Japanese War and the Beginning of the First World War in the German Press', *German History*, vol 16, No 3, (1998) pp 358–76.

14 Known as the Bryce Report, its full title was the Report of the Committee on Alleged German Outrages. The Committee's findings, published only five days after the sinking of the Lusitania, proved particularly damaging and generated a wave of anti-German feeling in America and other neutral countries. Post-war commissions, however, failed to substantiate the allegations made in the Bryce Report. See, Read, *Atrocity Propaganda*, pp 201–8; T. Wilson, 'Lord Bryce's Investigation into Alleged German atrocities in Belgium, 1914–15', *Journal of Contemporary History*, 14, (1979) pp 369–81.

15 For German accounts of British atrocities during the Boer War see, *Frankfurter Zeitung*, 16 September 1915; Walther Unus, *England als Henker Frankreich* (Berlin, 1915). British misrule in Egypt can be found in *Norddeutsche Allgemeine Zeitung*, 21 April; 8, 23 June 1916. In 1916 after the Irish rebellion the German press aimed their propaganda chiefly at America. Cf. *Norddeutsche Allgemeine Zeitung*, 29 April 1916; *Frankfurter Zeitung*, 29 April 1916; particularly illuminating is the *Vossische Zeitung*, 29 April 1916. It starts by presenting a lurid picture of the suffering of the English colonies (especially India) under British rule and ends with a detailed description of the 'reign of terror' in Ireland, where 'what the knout cannot achieve is affected by famine'. The last sentence asked: 'Will this cry of Ireland at last open President Wilson's eyes to where lies right and where lies wrong, where is truth and where is falsehood?'.

16 *Norddeutsche Allgemeine Zeitung*, 27, 31, January 1915, quoted in Read, *Atrocity Propaganda*, p 123. In the last two years of the war, German propaganda continued to denounce the Allies for maltreating prisoners and for using coloured troops. The first, they claimed was an atrocity in itself; the other led to atrocities. For a detailed analysis of German counter-propaganda aimed mainly at neutral countries see Read, Ch 5.

17 *Frankfurter Zeitung*, 9 October 1915. The report is taken from 'Weekly Report on German and Austrian Papers', Foreign Office, 15 May 1915–1 January 1916, vol October 10–17, p 3.

18 German accusation of atrocity were flatly denied by the British who claimed that the shooting of the submarine crew was a justifiable act of war. The German Foreign Office eventually released a volume containing all the notes from Berlin and London; *Auswärtiges Amt, Der Baralong-Fall* (Berlin, 1916).

19 *Deutsche Tageszeitung*, 16 January 1916. Graf Ernst Reventlow was the editor of this paper and both were staunch supporters of Pan-Germanism. It was claimed that von Tirpitz gave him a title from which time on 'E.R'., as he was known, spent his time planning annexations. Reventlow became the leading exponent of German navalism and played a leading part in embarrassing the Chancellor over the submarine question.

20 Telegram from von Jagow to Foreign Office, 28 August 1914, quoted in Deist, *Militär und Innenpolitik*, I, p 69.

21 Legation Secretary Riezler to Foreign Office: censorship and the handling of question of war aims, 19 October 1914. Quoted in Deist, *Militär und Innenpolitik*, I, pp 78–9.

22 Cf the introduction to H. Lasswell, *Propaganda Technique in the World War* (New York, 1970 edition), pp xix–xxvi.

23 R. Luxemburg, *Gesammelte Werke*, vol 4, (Berlin, GDR, 1979), pp 51–2.

24 An interesting brief discussion of these issues can be found in Dahlin, *French and German Public Opinion*, pp 34–8.

25 Fischer, of course, claimed that Bethmann Hollweg deliberately led Germany into the war and thereafter worked tirelessly for the aggrandisement of German power. Fischer, *Griff nach der Weltmacht*, p 230ff. This view was countered

by Ritter in his introduction to *Staatskunst und Kriegshandwerk. Das problem des 'Militarismus' in Deutschland*, vol 3, Ch 6, *Die Tragödie der Staatskunst. Bethmann Hollweg also kriegskanzler (1914–17)* (Munich, 1964); by examining the diaries of Bethmann's assistant and confidant, Kurt Riezler, Andreas Hillgruber stressed the theory of the risks of war that may have guided the Chancellor in July 1914. A. Hillgruber, 'Riezlers Theorie des kalkulierten Risikos und Bethmann Hollwegs politische Konzeption in der Julikrise 1914', *Historische Zeitschrift*, vol 202, Heft I, 1966; for more in-depth analyses cf. Karl Heinz Janssen, *Der Kanzler und der General* (Berlin, 1967) and Fritz Stern's sympathetic essay, 'Bethmann Hollweg and the War: The Bounds of Responsibility' in Stern, *The Failure of Illiberalism* (London, 1972).

26 Th. von Bethmann Hollweg, *Betrachtrungen zum Weltkriege*, vol 1, p 98. 2 vols (Berlin, 1919, 1922). See also, Friedrich Thimme (ed.), *Bethmann Hollwegs Kriegsreden* (Stuttgart & Berlin, 1919).
27 Kitchen, *The Silent Dictatorship*, p 26.
28 Cf. his telegram to the Foreign Office regarding censorship and the handling of war aims, 22 October 1914. Quoted in Deist, *Militär und Innenpolitik*, I, p 80.
29 *Verhandlungen des Reichstags*, 2 December 1914. Bethmann's emphasis on the defensive nature of Germany's war aims was fully supported during the debate by Johannes Kaempf, the President of the Reichstag.
30 Feldman, *Army, Industry, and Labour*, p 137.
31 *Vorwärts*, 25 February 1915.
32 *Vorwärts*, 14 March 1915.
33 *Vorwärts*, 29 March 1915.
34 *Munchener Neueste Nachrichten*, 21 April 1915.
35 The six Economic Associations consisted of: the Agrarian League (*Bund der Landwirte*), the German Peasants League (*der Deutsche Bauernbund*), the Christian German Peasants Union (*der Vorort der Christlichen Bauernvereine*), the Central Union of German Industrialists (*der Zentralverbande deutscher Industrieller*), the League of Industrialists (*der Bund deutscher Industrieller*), and the League of Middle Class Citizens (*der Reichsdeutsche Mittelstandsverband*). The petition, which was presented to the Chancellor on 20 May 1915, is quoted in full in Lutz, *Fall of the German Empire*, II, pp 312–20.
36 *An die Kulturwelt!; To the Civilised World* (Berlin, 1915).
37 *Verhandlungen des Reichstags*, 28 and 29 May 1915. A summary of these debates can be found in IWM. 'Weekly Report on German and Austrian Papers', Foreign Office 15 May 1915–1 January 1916.
38 The interpellation of Liebknecht made the *Kölnische Zeitung* (the mouthpiece of the Foreign Office) particularly angry. On the following day they wrote: 'One would almost feel tempted to supply an Achilles to this national Thersites!'. *Kölnische Zeitung*, 30 May 1915.
39 The declaration is quoted in Lutz, *Fall of the German Empire*, II, pp 329–30.
40 The figures are quoted in *Vossische Zeitung*, 26 June 1915, which published the circular.

41 *Leipziger Volkszeitung*, 19 June 1915.
42 K.P. Schulze, *Proletarier-Klassenkämpfer-Staatsbürger* (Munich, 1963), pp 118–19. Haase signed the manifesto not in his official capacity as Party Chairman, but as a private individual. For the British interpretation of these events see, IWM, 'Weekly Report on German and Austrian Papers', Foreign Office, 22–30 June, 'Opinion in Germany', pp 1–3.
43 This is the famous article: 'Zur Klarstellung', *Vorwärts*, 22 June 1915. In some editions it was published a day earlier.
44 *Vorwärts*, 26 June 1915.
45 MAF, RM3, Bd. 4, 10295, Telegram from the Oberzensurstelle of 26 June 1915. On the same day the *Norddeutsche Allgemeine Zeitung* (the semi-official organ of the government) printed an official statement on the suppression of *Vorwärts*.
46 *Kölnische Zeitung*, 1 July 1915.
47 *Kölnische Zeitung*, 27 June 1915.
48 *Berliner Tageblatt*, 25 June 1915. In the fourth group it mentioned, among others, Heine, Lensch, Schippel and Kloth.
49 *Die Hilfe*, 1 July 1915.
50 Cf. the call made for Haase's resignation by the Social Democrat, Dr Lensch, quoted in *Vossische Zeitung*, 28 June 1915.
51 *Vorwärts*, 2 July 1915.
52 'To the German People', *Norddeutsche Allgemeine Zeitung*, 1 August 1915, printed in full in Wolff Telegraph Bureau, in HSS, E741, BG. 170, 1 August 1915; Lutz, *Fall of the German Empire*, II, pp 327–8.
53 *Verhandlungen des Reichstags*, 19 August 1915. Bethmann is quoted as saying that the aim of German policy in Poland was 'to create an autonomous Poland which must remain militarily and politically completely in German hands': cited in Kitchen, *The Silent Dictatorship*, p 43, n. 50.
54 Hamburg-Polizibehörde, *Zensur-anordnungen*, No. 6214, 7 September 1915, p 177. See also Lutz, *The Fall of the German Empire*, I, where it is listed as Documents XIIf & XIIg, pp 185–6.
55 *Verhandlungen des Reichstags*, 20 August 1915. The following day the *Oberzensurstelle* imposed restrictions on what the SPD could publish regarding their guiding principles on war aims! The authorities insisted that all references to the 'reconstruction of Belgium' be struck out. It also recommended that discussion of the party's guiding principles in the press be forbidden. MAF, RM3, Bd. 4, 10296, Supreme Censorship Office on Question of SPD's Guiding Principles on War Aims, 21 August 1915.
56 *Vorwärts*, 24 August 1915.
57 *Verhandlungen des Reichstags*, 27 August 1915. After this debate the House adjourned until 30 November.
58 *Frankfurter Zeitung*, 29 August 1915.
59 *Kölnische Zeitung*, 25 August 1915, quoted in IWM, 'Weekly Report on German and Austrian Papers', 22–28 August, p 1.

60 *Deutsche Tageszeitung*, 28 September 1915, quoted in Lutz, *The Fall of the German Empire*, pp 333–4.
61 Quoted in *Vorwärts*, 17 October 1915.
62 MAF, RM3 Bd. 4, 10312, Press conference held by General Staff in the Reichstag over the question of releasing details about war aims through the Censor, 3 September 1915.
63 *Vorwärts*, 3 October 1915.
64 *Vossische Zeitung*, 14 November 1915.
65 *Vorwärts*, 21 November 1915.
66 *Verhandlungen des Reichstags*, 9 December 1915. On the question of 'guarantees' the Chancellor concluded his speech rather ominously by declaring that he did not know what guarantees the government would require for Belgium, but that the longer the war continued the greater would be the guarantees necessary.
67 By the end of March 1915, the Berlin police reports were indicating that 'war-weariness' was already setting in and in July it was reported that a deep-seated longing for peace was being expressed 'particularly by working class women'. See *Bericht des Berliner Polizeipräsidenten*, 34, 2398/2, Bl. 148, 20 March 1915; *Bericht des Berliner Polizeipräsidenten*, 43, 2398/3, Bl. 188, 10 July 1915.
68 Hanssen, *Diary of a Dying Empire*, entry for 11 January 1916, p 122. Cf. Gertrude Baumer's (Head of German Women's Association) moving account of the burial of dead soldiers in Stuttgart in the weeks leading up to Christmas 1915. Baumer, *Heimatchronik wahrend des Weltkriegs* (Berlin, 1930), pp. 35–6, entry for 17 December 1915. Jurgen Kocka maintains that the annexationist propaganda contributed to a longing for peace on the part of the working class which eventually turned into a socially critical attitude towards 'those up there'. Kocka, *Facing Total War*, p 56.

4 THE CRUCIBLE OF WAR

1 G.D. Feldman, *Army, Industry, and Labour in Germany 1914–18* (Princeton, 1966).
2 The figures quoted are from *Dresdner Bank Report* (Berlin, 1917), p 45, deposited in MAS, M 1/3 (*Kriegsministerium*), 499. An interesting discussion of these financial problems can be found in Mendelssohn-Bartholdy, *The War and German Society*, pp 44–58.
3 Cited in Wehler, *German Empire*, p 201.
4 As a result, the *Frankfurter Zeitung* urged the government to undertake a vigorous propaganda campaign in the countryside. For a detailed account of how the first war loan was raised see, PRO/FO, 371, 1991, 1914.
5 Helfferich (formerly director of the Deutsche Bank), like so many German leaders, believed that as in the war of 1870/1, Germany would be able to offset its war debt by charging her defeated enemies. Explaining this to the Reichstag he claimed: 'we can cling to the hope that, once peace has been concluded, we can present our enemies with the bill for this war which has been forced upon us'. Quoted in Wehler, *The German Empire*, p 202.

6 The British Foreign Office monitored German war loans very carefully throughout the war, for they were convinced that they represented a reliable barometer of German public opinion. Cf. FO Economic Report on Fifth War Loan, PRO/FO 371, 2680, 1916.

7 Bayerisches Hauptstaatsarchiv, Munich Abteilung Kriegsarchiv (hereafter BHStA, Abt. IV), *'Zusammenstellungen der Monats-Berichte der stellvertretenden Generalkommandos'* (hereafter MB), 14 October 1916. The secret monthly 'Summaries of the Regional Command reports on the mood of the population' were used by the Prussian War Ministry until September 1916 when the reports are signed by the head of the War Office (*Kriegsamt*). The War Office distributed an edited version ('Summaries of the monthly reports of the Regional Command') from the 15 April 1916 to 3 October 1918. The Regional Commands sent off their reports on the 15th of each month allowing for compilation to take place in the middle of the report month. Initially the summaries from the previous month's reports were made according the the particular Regional Command, later they were compiled according to the subject. Not surprisingly, questions of the food supply and its distribution dominate these reports. As the MB got bigger (in March 1916, the MB consisted of 27 typed pages – by October 1918 it had risen to 85), so did the number of copies distributed. According the War Office's distribution list, 84 reports were sent out in September 1916 and by August 1917 the number had increased to 244. From April 1917, the Kaiser regularly received a copy of these reports. The *Monatsberichte* (MB) were secret and continuous and provide a fascinating and generally realistic picture of the mood and attitudes of the civil population. Although the reports cannot be divorced from the attitudes of their authors and need to be used critically, the MB remain a rich source of evidence.

In a letter of 21 March 1916 the Ministry of War asked for reports to be arranged under the following headings: (a) mood of civil population, (b) food production, (c) preparation of food, (d) distribution and sharing of food. See note 7 above. Cf. MAF, RM3, Bd 4, *10297*, Letter from the Ministry of War to Ministry of Interior and to those concerned with 'spiritual' and educational affairs, 21 March 1916.

8 MAF, RM5, Bd 2, 3754, Ludendorff to Army High Command, 18 October 1916.

9 Cf. Wehler, *German Empire*, p 202; and Mendelssohn-Bartholdy, *The War and German Society*, p 44. See also, M. Lanter, *Die Finanzierung des kriegs* (Lucerne, 1950); H. Homburg, *Industrie und Inflation 1916–1923* (Hamburg, 1977); R. Andexel, *Imperialismus-Staatsfinanzen-Rüstung-Krieg* (Berlin, 1968); F. Neumark, *Wirtschafts und Finanzprobleme des Interventionsstaats* (Tübingen, 1961).

10 Much of the material relating to the setting up of the KRA is taken from an address Rathenau gave to the German Society entitled, 'Germany's Provisions for Raw Materials', quoted in Lutz, (ed.), *Fall of the German Empire*, II, pp 77–91. On the supply of raw materials see O. Goebbel, *Deutsche Rohstoffwirtschaft im Weltkrieg* (Stuttgart, 1930). For the wider implications of the KRA see, A. Schröter, *Krieg, Staat, Monopol 1914–1918* (Berlin, 1965).

11 Interestingly enough this second measure was deleted from the first printed edition of Rathenau's speech by the military censor.
12 The situation was eventually improved when a Bundesrat decree officially centralized control of raw materials in the War Ministry on 24 July 1915.
13 Rathenau, *Politische Briefe*, pp 37–8. Rathenau's successor at the KRA was Major Josef Koeth, a military technocrat who ran the section with considerable skill until 1918.
14 *Vorwärts*, 1 August 1915.
15 Mendelssohn-Bartholdy, *The War and German Society*, p 224.
16 In the case of Hugenberg this not only allowed him to increase the power of his own party in domestic policy, but also to influence the case for more annexations in foreign policy.
17 Feldman tends to underestimate the extent of the 'corporatist' elements within the OHL at this time. For a discussion of these points see Kitchen, *The Silent Dictatorship*, pp 67–9.
18 *Kölnische Volkszeitung*, 23 November 1915.
19 Hugo Stinnes in fact had been in close touch with Ludendorff since 1915 pressing for controls that would favour heavy industry. Cf. Schröter, *Krieg, Staat, Monopol 1914–1918*, pp 94–7.
20 For a detailed discussion of the events leading up to the appointment of Hindenburg and Ludendorff as Chiefs of General Staff see K.H. Janssen, *Der Kanzler und der General* (Berlin, 1967), pp 230–52; Kitchen, *The Silent Dictatorship*, pp 25–41; Feldman, *Army, Industry, and Labour*, pp 135–45.
21 MAS, M77/1, Bu. 60, *Büro für Sozialpolitik*, 24 October 1916.
22 For an analysis of Hindenburg see J.W. Wheeler-Bennett, *Hindenburg, The Wooden Titan* (London, 1936).
23 K. Helfferich, *Der Weltkrieg* (Karlsruhe, 1919), p 279.
24 The letter is discussed in E. Ludendorff, *Urkunden der OHL*, pp 63–5. Ludendorff makes the point that the letter, which was drafted by Bauer, was written for Falkenhayn but signed by Hindenburg.
25 For the establishment of the Ministry of Munitions and its impact on British society see, A. Marwick, *The Deluge: British Society and the First World War* (London, 1965), pp 151–86, 246–54.
26 The draft of the memorandum was again written by Bauer and can be found in Ludendorff, *Urkunden der OHL*, pp 65–7.
27 BA Koblenz, *Nachlass Bauer*, Bd. 2, also quoted in Kitchen, *The Silent Dictatorship*, p 70.
28 Helfferich's memorandum can be found in DZA Potsdam, Kriegsakten 1, Bd. 8, see also, G. Ritter, *Staatskunst und Kriegshandwerk*, Band 3 (Munich, 1964), p 423; Feldman, *Army, Industry, and Labour*, pp 174–6.
29 For the most celebrated article see the report of Gustav Stresemann's speech, *Vossische Zeitung*, 1 October 1916.
30 Ludendorff, *Urkunden der OHL*, pp 68–9.
31 WUMBA was officially established on 30 September 1916.

32 The protocol of the meeting can be found in Deist, *Militär und Innenpolitik*, vol 1, p 486.
33 Much of the material relating to Wild's attitude is taken from MAF, *Nachlass Wild*, N442/2.
34 W. Groener, *Lebenserinnerungen, Jugend, Generalstab, Weltkrieg* (ed.), F. Freiherr von Gärtringen, (Göttingen, 1957), p 553. See Groener's notes in MAF, *Nachlass Groener*, N46/113.
35 MAF, *Nachlass Wild*, entry 14 October 1916; see also Feldman, *Army, Industry, and Labour*, pp 183–4.
36 Bethmann to Hindenburg, 15 October 1916 quoted in Groener, *Lebenserinnerungen*, p 554.
37 ibid, p 554.
38 MAF, *Nachlass Wild*, entry 29 October 1916.
39 H. Herwig, *The First World War. Germany and Austria–Hungary 1914–1918* (London, 1997), p 263. The material was only made available to historians in the West in 1990 and was not included in the official history of the war that was compiled by the Reichsarchiv team in the 1920s. From the documentary evidence now available it is clear that the War Office had already raised production quotas in many areas of armaments and therefore the Hindenburg Programme was not as ambitious as the OHL claimed at the time. By the autumn of 1917 the real problem was not a shortage of armaments but an acute shortage of soldiers to make use of them (see Note 60). The recently released documents are now deposited in MAF, W. 10/50397, (*Hindenburgprogramm und Hilfsdienstgesetz*). For a discussion of the number of closures and their effects see, Kocka, *Facing Total War*, pp 36–7.
40 A brief but interesting discussion of the ramifications of the SPD's response to these changes can be found in G. Eley, 'The SPD in War and Revolution, 1914–1919' in R. Fletcher (ed.), *Bernstein to Brandt: A Short History of German Social Democracy* (London, 1987), pp 65–74.
41 The phrase was coined by Feldman in *Army, Industry, and Labour*, Ch IV, 'The Auxiliary Service Bill and the Triumph of Labour'. Cf. also Ritter, *Staatskunst und Kriegshandwerk*, vol 3, pp 429–31.
42 MAF, *Nachlass Groener*, N46/113, the account of Groener's discussion with Ludendorff is recorded in his letter to Reichsarchiv, 9 April 1923. See also Deist, *Militär und Innenpolitik*, vol 1, p 502. The text of the Auxiliary Service Law is printed in, P. Umbreit and Ch. Lorenz, *Der Krieg und die Arbeitsverhältnisse* (Stuttgart, 1928), pp 239–45.
43 The plan of the new proposals can be found in Deist, *Militär und Innenpolitik*, vol 1, p 506.
44 The letter to Groener is quoted in Ludendorff, *Urkunden*, p 81.
45 Ibid, p 82.
46 Examples of protest against the law can be found in Weber, *Ludendorff und die Monopole*, pp 54–5.
47 Feldman, *Army, Industry, and Labour*, pp 204–6.

48 The protocol of the meeting can be found in Deist, *Militär und Innenpolitik*, vol 1, p 511.
49 Quoted in Feldman, *Army, Industry, and Labour*, p 215.
50 The immediate events leading up to the passing of the bill can be found in MAS, M 1/3, Bu. 493.
51 The *Kriegsamt* had the right to make final decisions in cases that could not be resolved by the arbitration committees. The full text of the law in German, *Reichsgesetzblatt 1916*, pp 1333–9, In English see, Lutz, *Fall of the German Empire*, II, pp 99–103, and Feldman, *Army, Industry, and Labour*, pp 535–41.
52 *Vorwärts*, 3, 12, 1916. This is a report of the 'critical' vote of 2 December when the PASL was passed by the Reichstag with a vote of 235 against 19 with 8 abstaining.
53 *Vorwärts*, 2, 12, 1916.
54 The resolution was unanimously adopted by the 500 delegates, see Mendelssohn-Bartholdy, *The War and German Society*, p 83.
55 The 'embourgeoisement' of organized labour is the central argument of G. Roth, *The Social Democrats in Imperial Germany. A Study in Working Class Isolation and National Integration* (Totowa, NJ, 1963). For a persuasive refutation of this concept see, D. Geary, 'Radicalism and the German Worker', in R. Evans (ed.), *Politics and Society in Wilhelmine Germany* (London, 1978), pp 267–86 and 'Revolutionary Berlin' in C. Wrigley (ed.), *Challenges of Labour. Central and Western Europe 1917–1920* (London, 1993) pp 24–50. Geary stresses the radical continuity and makes the point that often the best paid workers were the most radical. For an important regional study see, G. Mai, *Württemberg, Kriegswirtschaft und Arbeiterbewegung in Württemberg 1914–1918* (Stuttgart, 1983).
56 See G. Bry, *Wages in Germany 1870–1945* (Princeton, 1960).
57 The figures cited are taken from D. Geary, 'The German Labour Movement 1848–1918' *European Studies Review* (1976), vol 6, No. 3, pp 297–330 and *European Labour Protest 1848–1939* (London, 1981), pp 137–43. Also, Bry, *Wages in Germany*, pp 200–11.
58 For the number of lock-outs see, J. Kucynski, *Die Geschichte der Lage der Arbeiter unter dem Kapitalismus*, Part I, vol 4, Darstellung der Lange der Arbeiter in Deutschland von 1900 bis 1917/18 (Berlin, 1967), p 143.
59 Kocka, *Facing Total War*, p 18. For a detailed analysis of the women workers during the war see; A. Seidel, *Frauenarbeit in Ersten Weltkrieg als Problem der staatlichen Sozialpolitik. Dargestellt am Beispiel Bayerns* (Frankfurt, 1979); C. Lorenz, 'Die gewerbliche Frauenarbeit während des Krieges' in P. Umbriet & C. Lorenz, *Der Krieg und die Arbeitsverhältnisse* (Stuttgart, 1928); U. von Gersdorff, *Frauen im Kriegsdienst 1914–1945* (Stuttgart, 1969). The influx of women thrown into the factories led to a sense of alienation. Partly because women had not been trained and partly because they were viewed as a 'temporary' workforce, such women often felt detached from the industrial environment. Karl Retzlaw described conditions in a Berlin munitions factory:

> The working conditions were like they must have been under early capitalism. There was always 'something wrong'. Especially during the night shift. Never

a night passed without one or more of the women collapsing at their machines from exhaustion, hunger, illness... On many days in winter there was no heating, the workers stood around in groups, they could not and would not work.... In the canteen there were almost daily screaming fits by women, sometimes even depressing fights between them, because they claimed 'the ladle had not been filled'.

K. Retzlaw, *Spartakus. Aufstieg und Niedergang. Erinnerungen eines Parteiarbeiters* (Frankfurt, 1971), p 72; cited in V. Ulrich, 'Everyday Life of the German Working Class, 1914–18' in R. Fletcher (ed.) *Bernstein to Brandt*, p 59.

60 Bry, *Wages in Germany*, pp 193–4, Kocka, *Facing Total War*, p 18.
61 M. Geyer, *Deutsche Rüstungspolitik 1860–1980* (Frankfurt, 1984), pp 90–106. See also Herwigs's excellent synthesis (which I have unashamedly exploited!), *The First World War*, pp 264–6. On the question of post-war implications, compare the very interesting analysis by H.-J. Bieber, 'The Socialist Trade Unions in War and Revolution' in Fletcher (ed.), *Bernstein to Brandt*, pp 74–85.
62 MAF, *Nachlass Groener* N46/113. Heavy industry was particularly critical of the arbitration committees.
63 Ludendorff, *My War Memories*, p 333. See also Ludendorff, *Urkunden*, pp 136–7.
64 Feldman, *Army, Industry, and Labour*, p 327.
65 Groener had stated from the outset that the entrepreneurs were more afraid of the PASL than the workers. See, Deist, *Militär und Innenpolitik*, I, p 541.
66 For a fuller discussion see the excellent essay by D. Geary, 'Radicalism and the Worker: Metalworkers and the Revolution 1914–23', in R. Evans (ed.), *Society and Politics in Wilhelmine Germany* (London, 1978), pp 267–86. The theory that workers could be divided into two groups, the 'contented', well-fed, armaments workers and the 'discontented' and therefore more radical non-armaments workers, has been challenged by Volker Ulrich. According to Ulrich, the improvements in the position of armaments workers that were promoted by the military and employers, did not necessarily reduce industrial conflict. On the contrary, it strengthened their self-confidence and allowed such workers to assert their interests militantly. Ulrich, 'Everyday Life and the German Working Class', p 58. Cf. E. Tobin, 'War and the Working Class: The Case of Düsseldorf 1914–1918', *Central European History*, 18 (1985), pp 257–99.
67 The person in question was Dr von Gontardt the Director of the German Weapons and Munitions Factories in Berlin, who on 1 March 1917, had already asked General von Kessel, the High Commander in the Marks, to place workers under military surveillance and imprison any worker who refused to work. Feldman, *Army, Industry, and Labour*, pp 328–9.
68 The letter is reprinted in full in Ludendorff, *Urkunden*, pp 136–7.
69 Ludendorff, *My War Memories*, pp 333–4.
70 See Helfferich's reply to Ludendorff of 13.3. 1917, reprinted in Ludendorff, *Urkunden*, pp 87–8.
71 Quoted in Kitchen, *The Silent Dictatorship*, p 82. In August 1917, Groener was eventually dismissed for being too conciliatory towards labour. See, MAF,

Nachlass Groener, N46/112–117. The *Büro für Sozialpolitik* pointed out that his dismissal had unsettled the workforce who viewed it as a confirmation 'of their worse fears'. MAS, MI/11, Bd. 1082, *Büro für Sozialpolitik*, 15 September 1917. See biography of Groener written by his daughter, D. Groener-Geyer, *General Groener, Soldat und Staatsmann* (Frankfurt am Main, 1954).

72 A brief, but perceptive analysis of the government's policy of food rationing can be found in U. Daniel, 'The Politics of Rationing versus the Politics of Subsistence: Working-Class Women in Germany, 1914–1918', in R. Fletcher (ed.), *Bernstein to Brandt*, pp 89–95.

73 Official figures for food production and consumption until the beginning of 1916 can be found in HSS, E 130a, 87, 30.1.1916.

74 Sackett, *Popular Entertainment*, p 82.

75 *Reichsgesetzblatt*, 23 November 1914. The maximum price set varied from one part of the Reich to another.

76 *Reichsgesetzblatt*, 25 January 1915. For an English translation of the document, see Lutz, *Fall of the German Empire*, pp 143–53.

77 *Vossische Zeitung*, 11 Febuary 1915. The 'Ten Food Commandments' made up the central prong of a wider propaganda campaign against waste and indicated that, despite official denials, food shortages were already severe.

78 Feldman, *Army, Industry and Labour*, pp 102–4.

79 *Vorwärts*, 16 October 1915.

80 *Vorwärts*, 19 October 1915.

81 *Vorwärts*, 22 October 1915.

82 The Bundesrat had decreed that for two days of the week the delivery of meat would be suspended and on two other days shops and restaurants were forbidden to serve meat.

83 *Leipziger Neuste Nachrichten*, 23 October 1915.

84 *Vorwärts* 4 November 1915. Cf. also *Vorwärts*, 6 November 1915.

85 *Kölnischer Volkszeitung*, 23 November 1915.

86 *Berliner Tageblatt*, 20 November 1915.

87 Cf. *Deutsche Tageszeitung*, 24 November 1915.

88 *Berliner Tageblatt*, 27 November 1915. Cf. also *Frankfurter Zeitung* of 24 November 1915 that contains the original statement by Dr Wendorff-Toitz citing his experiences gained in the Grand Duchy of Hessen.

89 Letter from the Prussian War Ministry to the Acting General Command of VIII Army Corps, 25 November 1915. The Ministry of the Interior had written to all the Prussian Ministries of State on 12 November 1915, calling on their support for its plan to coordinate the press.

90 MAF, RM3 Bd 4, 10306, 27 December 1915.

91 Princess Evelyn Blücher, *An English Wife in Berlin* (New York, 1920), p 95. Formerly Evelyn Stapleton-Bretherton, she married Prince Blücher in 1907. Her husband's nationality forced her to go to Germany at the outbreak of hostilities. She spent the remainder of the war either on the ancestral estate of Krieblowitz in Silesia or in the Esplanade Hotel in Berlin. The diary provides a revealing

account of life in Germany viewed through (privileged) British eyes. As such, it needs to be read critically.
92 Gerard, *My Four Years*, p 298. For an analysis of the managerial problems supplying food in Berlin, see G.L. Yaney, *The World of the Manager: Food Administration in Berlin During World War I* (New York, 1994).
93 Figures taken from J. Kuczynski, *Die Geschichte der Lage der Arbeiter unter dem Kapitalismus* Band 4 (Berlin [GDR], 1967), p 249. See also table of strikes in Ch 6, n. 1.
94 *Vossische Zeitung*, 2 February 1916. From a letter sent by the OZS on 12 February 1916, the guidelines issued on 27 December 1915 had not been known to everyone in the press. MAF, RM3 Bd 2, 10307, 12 February 1916. On the city/country tensions see, BHStA,/Kr, Mkr, *12842* MB des Stellv. Gen. kdo's I, Bayerisches AK München für Oktober 1916.
95 Cf Report of Bavarian War Ministry to the Bavarian Minister of State on morale in army and home front, 1 February 1916, quoted in Deist, *Militär und Innenpolitik*, I, pp 294–9.
96 Blücher, *An English Wife*, pp 122, 135.
97 Decree from Bavarian Ministry of War to High Commander of the Bavarian Contingents, 1 February 1916. Quoted in Deist, *Militär und Innenpolitik*, I, pp 300–2.
98 MAF, RM3 Bd 4, 10297, 2 March 1916.
99 *Berliner Lokal-Anzeiger*, 20 April 1916.
100 Cf reports in *Frankfurter Zeitung*, 23 April 1916, *Berliner Tageblatt*, 22 April 1916; *Kölnischer Zeitung*, 29 April 1916. As the control of food was left in the hands of regional governments, the result was suspicion that some states were better off than others. Accusations often took the form of a North/South divide. While it is true that some states had more food than others, each state blamed the other for scarcity. In the Bavarian Landtag, Deputy Schlittenbauer attacked the North German Agrarians for not being able to provide Berlin with diary produce and reproaching Bavaria for not coming to the rescue. The Bavarian's attributed Berlin's plight to its pre-war policy of importing produce from Denmark in preference to Bavaria. Schlittenbauer's speech of 8 May 1916 is reprinted in, Bruntz, *Allied Propaganda*, pp 122–3.
101 *Müncher Neuester Nachrichten*, 24 May 1916. See also *Leipziger Volkszeitung*, 23 May 1916.
102 *Leipziger Neuester Nachrichten*, 26 May 1916.
103 Quoted in Feldman, *Army, Industry and Labour*, p 114.
104 Cf. A. Skalweit, *Die Deutsche Kriegsernährungswirtschaft* (Berlin, 1927) p 179ff. See also Groener, *Lebenserinnerungen*, pp 333ff, 549ff. Writing some years later, Ludendorff recorded:

> 'I had many intimate discussions with both presidents of our War Food Office, von Batocki and von Waldow. Different as they were, they both displayed stern devotion to duty and deep love of the Fatherland... It was with a heavy heart that

G.H.Q. had often temporarily to reduce the rations of meat, bread, potatoes and fats, and also of oats and hay. This was done to help the people at home and keep up the war spirit. The War Food Office, however, thoroughly understood the army's needs, and especially the fact that the men in the front line were deserving of the greatest consideration'. *My War Memoirs*, p 352

105 Generallandesarchiv Karlsruhe (hereafter, GLK), *Monatsberichte (MB)*, Abt 456, Bd. 70, 3 June 1916. Cf. also, BHStA, *MB*, IV M.Kr 12851, 15 July 1916, *MB*, 13878, 17 November 1916, *MB*, 12851, 16, December 1916.
106 Decree of 8 May 1916, cited in Deist, *Militär und Innepolitik*, I, pp 306–8.
107 BHStA, *MB*. IV, MKr 12851, 15 July 1916.
108 MAF, RM3 Bd 4, 10277, 9 June 1916. Writing in the 1920s, Georg Michaelis talked of his time in the Imperial Grain Office and his memories of the frustrations of women queuing outside empty shops: 'This was where housewives and mothers got the poison and the bile, with which, together with low-quality food substitutes, they cooked meals for their husbands and children'. Michaelis, *Für Staat und Volk. Eine Lebensgeschichte* (Berlin, 1922), p 288; cited in Daniel, *The War from Within*, p 264.
109 Cf GLK, *MB*, Abt. 456, Bd. 70, 3 July 1916. For an example of anti-monarchist propaganda see, Deist, *Militär und Innenpolitik*, vol II, pp 813–14.
110 MAF, RM5 Bd 2, 3740, 31 August 1916.
111 GLA Karlsruhe, *MB*, Abt 456, Bd 70, 3 September 1916. Also, MAF, RM5, Bd 2, 3740, *MB*, 4 September 1916. Reports from the Deputy Commanding Generals for June 1916 had already identified the failure of trade unions to pacify non-union workers, particularly women who 'constantly agitate and stir things up'. MAF, RM3, Bd. 4, 4670, *MB*, 13 June 1916.
112 Blücher, *An English Wife*, p 137.
113 O. Appel, *Die Kartoffellagerung unter Kreigsverhältnissen* (Berlin, 1920). *Monatsberichte* for April noted that bread rations and indigestible *Kriegsbrot* had lowered morale and was seen as the 'greatest test since the outbreak of war'. BHStA, *MB*, IV, MKr, 12851, 3 April 1917.
114 See A. Offer, *The First World War. An Agrarian Interpretation* (Oxford, 1989), p 62. A perceptive synthesis of this debate can be found in N.P. Howard 'The Social and Political Consequences of the Allied Food Blockade of Germany, 1918–19' *German History*, vol 11, no. 2, (1993) pp 161–88. Variations in food consumption is also examined in, A. Triebel, 'Variations in Patterns of Consumption in Germany in the Period of the First World War,' in R. Wall and J. Winter (eds), *The Upheaval of War: Family, Work and Welfare in Europe, 1914–1918* (Cambridge, 1988), pp 159–96.
115 R. Lutz (ed.), *Causes of the German Collapse in 1918* (New York, 1969), p 183.
116 Blücher, *An English Wife*, p 183.
117 P. Struve, *The Exhaustion of Germany's Food and Fodder Supply* (Petrograd, 1917). Mimeographed copy in PRO, FO 382: 1312 no. 93695.
118 Gerard, *My Four Years*, p 298.

119 Much of this information is taken from C.P. Vincent, *The Politics of Hunger. The Allied Blockade of Germany, 1915–1919* (Ohio University Press, 1985), pp 127–8. See also A.P. McDougall, *Memoranda on Agricultural Conditions in Germany* (London, HMSO, 1919).
120 M.E. McAuley, *Germany in War Time* (Chicago, 1917), p 59.
121 Blücher, *An English Wife*, p 225.
122 Quoted in Sackett, *Popular Entertainment*, p 82. On the food crisis in Munich see K.L. Ay, *Die Enstehung einer Revolution. Die Volksstimmung in Bayern während des 1. Weltkrieges* (Berlin, 1966), pp 29–33.
123 Kuczynski, *Die Geschichte*, p 351.
124 J. Flemming, *Landwirtschaftliche Interessen und Democratie* (Bonn, 1978), p 88.
125 O.M. Graf, *Prisoners All!* trans. M. Green (New York, 1928), p 258.
126 MAF, RM3, Bd. 2, 5183, Prussian War Ministry to Vice President, Prussian Minister of State, 2 February 1915. It was also hoped that such training would prove attractive to youth to reduce the influence of the Social Democratic youth organizations. Statistics of adolescent criminality during the war can be found in, M. Liepmann, *Krieg und Kriminalität in Deutschland* (Stuttgart, 1930), p 98. Cf. also, K.P. Müller, *Politik und Gesellschaft: Der Legitimitätsverlust des badischen Staates 1914–1918* (Stuttgart, 1988).
127 *Bremer Bürger-Zeitung*, 3 May 1916. The article also provides a breakdown of ages and convictions among juveniles (i.e. under 18 years old) for the first year of the war.
128 U. Daniel, 'The Politics of Rationing versus the Politics of Subsistence: Working-Class Women in Germany, 1914–1918' in R. Fletcher (ed.), *Bernstein to Brandt*, p 92. There existed a widespread belief that the authorities pursued and seized 'squirrel booty' on behalf of the well-to-do and/or local officials. One woman from Silesia wrote to a prisoner of war in February 1917:

> And then I travel for two days together with two or three women and one goes from house to house and one still has to properly plead for money before one gets anything to buy that's how it looks like beggars the women go around. Then you know that with [food] coupons there's too little to live on and too much to die.... But that's not all. Us poor women what shall we say when we come home from the [train] station with the goods then sometimes one or two gendarmes come and take the goods from the women don't pay for it they only write a ticket then comes wailing and complaining looks like the first day of the war is that justice in the world.

BHStA/*Kr, Stellv. Gen.kdo. I. Bayerisches AK München*. Letter from a Silesian to a prisoner of war, 20 February 1917; cited in Daniel, *The War from Within*, p 205. The war also transformed women in the urban conurbations into powerful consumers, feared by public officials. For an interesting discussion of this phenomenon see, B. Davis, 'Food Scarcity and the Empowerment of the Female Consumer in World War I Berlin', in V. de Grazia and E. Furlought (eds), *The Sex of Things: Gender and Consumption in Historical Perspective* (Berkeley, 1996), pp 287–310.

129 E. Gläser, *Class 1902* (London, 1929), pp 270, 271. A popular song with children went as follows: 'England knows no hunger yet, France still bakes fresh rolls, Russia still has pig's feet, Germany only has jam and kohlrabi!' MAF, RM3, Bd. 2, 4670, *MB*, 3 January 1917.

130 Flemming, *Landwirtschaftliche*, p 87, taken from R. Berthold, *Einige Bemerkungen über den Entwicklungsstand des bäuerlichen Ackerbus von den Agrarreformen des 19. Jahrhunderts* (Berlin, 1962), p 109; cited in Howard 'Allied Food Blockade', p 164.

131 G.E. Schreiner, *The Iron Ration* (London, 1918), p 239.

132 Quoted in W.A. Pelz, *The Spartakusbund and the German Working Class Movement 1914–19* (Lewiston, New York, 1987), p 89. 'Manslaughter' quote, cited in V. Moyer, *Victory Must Be Ours. Germany in the Great War 1914–1918* (New York, 1995), p 262.

133 Figures taken from R. Lindau, *Revolutionäre Kämpfe, 1918–1919* (Berlin [GDR], 1960), p 209.

134 ibid, p 209. In terms of births per 1,000 of the population, the figure fell from 27.5 in 1913 to 14.5 in 1918. As late as 1924 the German birth rate was still 23.9 per cent below the 1914 figure. Between 1915 to 1918, 365,581 children aged from 1 to 5 died, representing a child mortality rate among this group of 86 per 1,000.

135 Figures cited in Howard, 'Allied Food Blockade', p 168. For further discussion see W. Thönnessen, *The Emancipation of Women; Germany 1863–1933* (Frankfurt-am-Main, 1969; transl., London, 1973).

136 In recent years the conventional historical explanation for the increase in mortality is attributed more to the effects of the influenza epidemic and less to hunger. The Reich Health Office (RHO) claimed that 763,000 deaths were attributable to the food blockade. In 1928, Dr Franz Bumm, ex-President of the RHO reduced the figure to 424,000. See F. Bumm (ed.), *Deutschlands Gesundheitsverhältnisse unter dem Einfluss des Weltkrieges*. 2 vols. (Stuttgart, 1928). This revised figure was accepted by Bernhard Menne, *Armistice and Germany's Food Supply, 1918–19* (London, 1944). For further discussion see Vincent, *Politics of Hunger*, pp 136–42.

137 Hanssen, *Diary of a Dying Empire*, p 179. Princess Blücher recorded in her diary:

> We are all growing thinner every day, and the rounded contours of the German nation have become a legend of the past. We are all gaunt and bony now, and have dark shadows round our eyes, and our thoughts are chiefly taken up with wondering what our next meal will be, and dreaming of all the good things that once existed.

Blücher, *An English Wife in Berlin*, p 158, diary entry for January 1917.

138 In January 1917 the 5th Army Corps reported the increasing frustrations felt by small farmers in the Posen region against the large landowners who, they claimed, received preferential treatment. GLA Karlsruhe, *MB*, Abt 456, Bd 70, 3 February 1917. In May, *Monatsberichte* from Saarbrücken recorded the local farmer's resentment of the large landowners in the East who they believed

produced less but were allowed to sell their produce at higher prices. MAF, RM3, Bd. 2, *MB*, 4670, 3 May 1917.
139 Gläser, *Class 1902*, p 289.
140 For the relationship between the state and the powerful agrarian interests see, M. Schumacher, *Land und Politik: Eine Untersuchung über politische Parteien und agrarische Interessen 1914–1923* (Düsseldorf, 1978). For a brief discussion of the concerns of agricultural producers, see Kocka, *Facing Total War*, pp 118, 155–6. Cf. also, R.G. Moeller, 'Dimensions of Social Conflict in the Great War: The View from the German Countryside,' *Central European History*, 14, (1981), pp 142–68.
141 Reichsarchiv, *Der Weltkrieg 1914 bis 1918* (Berlin, 1938). Also quoted in Hanssen, *Diary of a Dying Empire*, pp 195–6.
142 MAF, RM3, Bd. 4, 10306, Letter for Supreme Censorship Office, 29 November 1916.
143 The report from Nuremberg is cited in K.D. Schwarz, *Weltkrieg und Revolution in Nürnberg: Ein Beitrag zur Geschichte der deutschen Arbeiterbewegung* (Stuttgart, 1971), p 153. For Ludendorff quote see, Ludendorff, *My War Memories*, p 349.
144 The 'turnip winter' miraculously brought out the population's sense of humour. In Hamburg, for example, a leaflet entitled

> 'The German Confession of Faith' commented sarcastically on the fact that turnips were now added to everything: 'I believe in the turnip, the general feeder of the German people, and in the jam, its comradely relation, conceived by the urban distribution centre, through which all my hopes of getting potatoes are dead and buried... resurrected as fruit, from which it will be made into breadspread for Germany's heroic sons. I believe in the holy war... the community of hoarders, higher taxes, cuts in the bread ration, and the eternal life of the bread coupon. Amen!': cited in Carsten, *War Against War*, p 147.

145 Quoted in Hanssen, *Diary of a Dying Empire*, p 162.
146 Ibid, p 167.
147 See Vincent, *Politics of Hunger*, p 47.
148 Reichsarchiv, *Der Weltkrieg 1914 bis 1918*, vol 13, p 326: cited in H. Herwig, *The First World War*, p 393. The statement was made by General von Kuhl.
149 Hanssen, *Diary of a Dying Empire*, p 170.

5 DISSENTING VOICES: PACIFISM, FEMINIST FERMENT, AND THE WOMEN'S MOVEMENT

1 Nolan, *Social Democracy and Society*, p 247.
2 J. Shand, 'Doves Among the Eagle: German Pacifists and their Government during World War I', *JCH*, 10.1, (January 1975) p 95.
3 For the background to the pacifist movement in the First World War, see R. Barkeley, *Die deutsche Friedensbewegung (1870 bis 1933)* (Hamburg, 1948); R. Chickering, *Imperial Germany and a World without War: The Peace Movement and*

Germany, 1892–1914 (Princeton, NJ, 1975). An interesting and informative history of the German Peace Society can be found in, F-K. Scheer, Die *Deutsche Friedensgesellschaft 1892–1933: Organisation, Ideologie, politische Ziele: Ein Beitrag zur Geschichte des Pazifismus in Deutschland* (Frankfurt am Main, 1983). See also, W. Eisenbeiss, *Die bürgerliche Friedensbewegung in Deutschland während des Ersten Weltkrieges: Organisation, Selbstverständnis und politische Praxis 1913/14–1919* (Frankfurt am Main, 1980). For a wider historical analysis see, D. Riesenberger, *Die Geschichte der Friedensbewegung in Deutschland. Von Anfängen bis 1933* (Göttingen, 1985) and K. Holl, *Pazifismus in Deutschland* (Frankfurt am Main, 1988). For a profile of Schücking see, D. Acker, *Walther Schücking* (Münster, 1970).

4 For further details see, A. H. Fried, *Mein Kriegs-Tagebuch*, an unpublished manuscript version is in the Hoover Library, Stanford.

5 *Berliner Volkszeitung*, 4 August 1914, BAK. *Nachlass Quidde*, Nr 96. Also quoted in Carsten, *War Against War*, p 18.

6 See Ludwig Quidde's statement, 'Der Pazifismus angesichts des Krieges,' *Völker-Friede* (1914), p 129. For Quidde see, B. Goldstein, 'Ludwig Quidde and the Struggle for Democratic Pacifism in Germany 1914–1930' (Unpublished doctoral dissertation, New York University, 1984); U.F. Taube, *Ludwig Quidde. Ein Beitrag zur Geschichte des demokratischen Gedanken in Deutschland* (Kallmünz, 1963); R. Rürup, 'Ludwig Quidde', Deutsche Historiker (ed.) H.U. Wehler, vol 3, (Göttingen, 1972); H.U. Wehler (ed.), *Ludwig Quidde: Caligula: Schriften über Militarismus und Pazifismus* (Frankfurt am Main, 1977). In 1894, while secretary of the Prussian Historical Institute in Rome, Quidde published *Caligula: Eine Studie über römischen Cäsarenwahnsinn* (Caligula: A Study on Roman Caesarian Megalomania), a thinly disguised satirical critique of Wilhelm II and his blindly subordinate imperial court.

7 Quoted in R. Evans, *The Feminist Movement in Germany, 1894–1933* (London, 1976), p 215. Heymann had already incurred displeasure and opposition from bourgeois women's groups by calling for the abolition of Paragraph 218 of the Criminal Code, which punished abortion. See, D. Beavan and B. Faber, *'Wir wollen unser Teil förden . . . ': Interessenvertretung und Organisationsformen der bürgerlichen und proletarischen Frauenbewegungim deutschen Kaiserreich* (Cologne, 1987).

8 For Stöcker see, C. Wickert, *Helen Stöcker, 1869–1943: Frauenrechtlerin, Sexualreformerin, und Pazifistin: Eine Biographie* (Bonn, 1991). On motherhood see, B. Nowacki, *Der Bund für Mutterschutz* (Husum, 1983) and A. Allen, *Feminism and Motherhood in Germany 1800–1914* (New Brunswick, 1991).

9 L. Gustava Heymann, *Völkerversöhnende Frauenarbeit während des Weltkrieges* (Munich, 1920).

10 Evans, *The Feminist Movement in Germany*, p 217.

11 Shand, p 97. The full programme can be found in E. Gülzow, 'Bund Neues Vaterland' in D. Fricke (ed.), *Die bürgerlichen Parteien in Deutschland* (Leipzig, 1968), I, pp 179–83.

12 For detailed background information to The Hague Congress see, G. Bussey and M. Tims, *Women's International League for Peace and Freedom 1915–16: A Record of Fifty Years' Work* (London, 1965). It is claimed that 28 German women managed to attend the Congress.

13 Quoted in Evans, *The Feminist Movement in Germany*, p 221. *Die Frauenbewegung* (Women's Movement) was conceived by Minna Cauer in Berlin in 1894 as a mouthpiece for the radical wing of the bourgeois women's movement demanding equal rights to political assembly. Cauer retained tight editorial control until it was discontinued in 1918. Although Cauer was committed to an international women's movement, she initially supported the war. From 1915, however, she adopted a pacifist stance. See, G. Naumann, *Minna Cauer: Eine Kämpferin für Frieden, Demokratie und Emanzipation* (Berlin, 1988) and E. Lüders, *Minna Cauer: Leben und Werk* (Gotha, 1925).

14 Quoted in Ay, *Die Entstehung einer Revolution*, p 49. In Munich, according to Ay, the first anti-war leaflet campaign of any significance took place at Christmas 1915, ibid, p 50.

15 *Vorwärts*, 12 June 1915. For background details of events in 1915 see, Shand, *Doves Among Eagles*, pp 97–8; Carsten, *War Against War*, pp 50–1. The Supreme Censorship Office issued its ban on the reporting of criminal procedures against pacifists in Stuttgart on 28 August 1915. See, Lutz, *Fall of the German Empire*, p 185.

16 MAF, RM3 Bd 4 10296, Prussian War Ministry to the Deputy General Commanders re: guidelines for measures to be taken against the pacifist movement, 7 November 1915.

17 Although the War Ministry did not specify, presumably when they referred to 'left-wing international groups of feminists' they had in mind the International Woman Suffrage Alliance. The Bavarian War Ministry's report is dated 2 November 1915, *Bayerisches Hauptsarchiv*, M Inn 66132, No. 101948, also cited in Ay, *Die Ensteung einer Revolution*, p 45, Shand, *Doves Among the Eagles*, p 107, Evans, *The Feminist Movement in Germany*, p 218.

18 Proclamation of 31 July 1914 was signed by von Kessel and is cited in Deist, *Militär und Innenpolitik*, I, p 263.

19 L. Quidde, *Der deutsche Pazifismus während des Weltkrieges 1914–1918* (Boppard, 1979). See also, Shand, *Doves Among the Eagle*, p 101, Carsten, *War Against War*, p 51. Quidde and Walther Schücking continued to work for *Völkerrechtspazifismus* (international pacifism) in the Weimar Republic. Quidde received the Nobel Peace Prize in 1927. In 1933 he emigrated to Switzerland.

20 MAF, RM3, Bd. 4, 10297, Prussian War Ministry to Prussian Ministry of Interior, 2 March 1916.

21 Ay, *Die Entstehung einer Revolution*, p 48, Evans, *The Feminist Movement in Germany*, pp 221–2.

22 Quoted in Ay, *Die Entstehung einer Revolution*, p 48.

23 Ibid, p 48.

24 Ibid, p 49. The military authorities were also having to contend with an increasing number of pacifist leaflets and books entering the Munich region from Switzerland. In a report from the Stellv. GK I, Bayerische AK to the War Ministry, concern was expressed of the likely affect of such pacifist literature on the women's peace movement. MAF, RM5/v, 3797, 20 April 1916.

25 Heymann & Augspurg, *Erlebtes-Erschautes. Deutsche Frauen kämpfen für Freiheit, Recht und Frieden, 1850–1940*, pp 142–5. Heymann claimed that she remained in Anita Augspurg's home in Isartal.

26 Carston, *War Against War*, p 90.

27 *BHStA IV Munich BM Berlin, B. Kriegsakten*, 16 Bd. 8, Extracts from the Bavarian War Ministry to the Bavarian Minister of State Concerning the Morale of the Army and the home front, 1 February 1916: Deist, *Militär und Innenpolitik*, I, pp 294–9. The report also provided a survey of foreign news agencies and the manner in which they were 'exaggerating' the extent and size of food and peace demonstrations in Germany. For example, it was reported that on 11 December 1915 an estimated 10,000 demonstrators chanting 'We Want Peace' marched on the Royal Palace and Reichstag buildings. The example cited in the text had already been taken up by the English newspapers. Princess Blücher alluded to this in her diary and attempted to place the rumour in some sort of context:

> This morning the English papers are full of the butter riots in Berlin. The accounts are, of course, exaggerated. There is absolutely no question of '200 people dead'; one or two slightly hurt is all that can be faithfully reported. Absolute silence on the subject is imposed here, and not a word is allowed to slip into the daily papers. I suppose they think this is the best way to suppress further disturbance. What really happened was the following. About 200 women trooped down the Linden, calling out 'Frieden, Frieden' (peace), and at once 150 mounted police appeared on the scene with drawn swords to disperse the crowd. This they soon succeeded in doing, though they are supposed to have said themselves that they hated such drastic measures towards women, and a common soldier on leave said that if the infantry at the front were to hear that their wives were being treated thus in their absence, whether they demanded butter or anything else, they would refuse to continue fighting. Blücher, *An English Wife*, pp 90–1.

28 Ay, *Die Entstehung einer Revolution*, p 47.

29 *Vorwärts*, 11 August 1916.

30 Deutscher Kinematek Berlin, *Richard Oswald* (Berlin, 1970), pp 43–4. For details of film censorship during the war see, H. Birett, *Verzeichnis in Deutschland gelaufeuer Filme. Entscheidungen der Filmzensur, 1911–1920* (Berlin et al., 1980).

31 *MAF*, RM3 Bd 2, 4655. Letter from the Military High Command to Deputy Commanding Generals re: the Pacifist Movement, 10 January 1918. Stein issued this recommendation after consultations had taken place between the Prussian War Ministry and the Ministry of the Interior. See letter from War Ministry dated 30 November 1917. *MAF*, RM3 Bd 2, 4655. In his letter of 10 January, Stein referred specifically to the international pacifist organization 'World

Freedom Work of the White Cross' (*Weltfriedenswerk vom Weissen Kreuz*) which was based in Graz and whose activities were obviously giving the OHL some concern.

32 MAF, RM5, Bd 2, 3828. Letter from Military High Command to the Deputy Commanding Generals Re: the German Peace Society, 8 July 1918.
33 Shand, *Doves Among the Eagle*, p 104.
34 Although pacifists were often accused by patriots of being defeatist, this was an accusation that was bitterly resented by pacifists and vehemently denied. There were very few 'authentic defeatist' voices in Germany – even in the pacifist camp. Some Germans did call for an end to the war with 'neither conquerors not conquered'. Indeed the Socialist Deputy, Stadthagen, use this phrase in a Reichstag debate on 30 May 1916. But this is a far cry from postulating a defeatist standpoint. The most notorious 'defeatist' was Hermann Fernau who wrote a pamphlet, *Das Königtum ist der Krieg* in which he blamed Germany for starting the war and hoped for an enemy victory in order to bring about the Kaiser's fall.
35 The following discussion of the women's movement focuses on the bourgeois, middle class movement that pressed for various forms of emancipation. For a detailed analysis of working class women see, Ute Daniel's excellent *The War From Within. German Working-Class Women in the First World War* (Oxford, 1997). See also, D. Bevan and B. Faber, *'Wir wollen under Teil fördern . . .'*: *Interressenvertretung und Organisationsformen der bürgerlichen und proletarischen Frauenbewegung in deutsche Kaiserreich* (Cologne, 1987). For an account of the role played by the middle-class women's movement in social affairs and in the labour market see, C.E. Boyd, *Nationaler Frauendienst: German Middle Class Women in Service to the Fatherland, 1914–18* (Athens, GA, 1979). See also, C. Sachsse, *Mütterlichkeit als Beruf. Sozialarbeit, Sozialreform und Frauenbewegung 1871–1929* (Frankfurt/M, 1986); B. Guttmann, *Weibliche Heimarmee. Frauen in Deutschland 1914–1918* (Weinheim, 1989); S. Hering, Die *Kriegsgewinnlerinnen. Praxis und Ideologie der deutschen Frauengewegung im Ersten Weltkrieg* (Pfaffenweiler, 1990). For an analysis of motherhood and feminism see, A. T. Allen, *Feminism and Motherhood in Germany* (New Brunswick, NJ, 1991).
36 Evans, *The Feminist Movement in Germany*, p 100.
37 Augspurg and Heymann were joined two years later by Minna Cauer. It has been estimated that in 1914 the Suffrage Union had approximately 9,000 members compared to the Alliance with 3,000 and the League which had 2,000. Figures quoted in Evans, *The Feminist Movement in Germany*, p 107.
38 Until 1908, women had been forbidden to join political parties.
39 Evans, *The Feminist Movement in Germany*, p 108.
40 Ibid, p 230.
41 For a corrective to the traditional view that the introduction of women's suffrage in Germany can be understood as a reward for female participation in the war, see Barbara Greven-Aschoff, *Die bürgerliche Frauenbewegung in Deutschland 1894–1933* (Göttingen, 1981); H.U. Bussemer, *Frauenemanzipation und Bildungsbürgertum: Sozialgeschichte der Frauenbewegung in der Reichsgründungszeit* (Weinheim, 1985); B. Clemens, *Menschenrechte haben kein Geschlecht: Zum*

Politverständnis der bürgerlichen Frauenbewegung (Pfaffenweiler, 1988). Cf. earlier works that tend to stress the positive link between women's participation and political emancipation: U. von Gersdorff, *Frauen im Kriegsdienst 1914–1945* (Stuttgart, 1969); S. Baujohr, *Die Hälfe der Fabrik: Geschichte der Frauenarbeit in Deutschland 1914–1945* (Marburg, 1979). See also, A. Marwick, *War and Social Change in the Twentieth Century: A Comparative Study of Britain, France, Germany, Russia and the United States* (London, 1974). Marwick argues that a number of processes take place in 'society at war' which do not take place in 'society not at war' and that these *together* can result in such developments as votes for women. Somehow, after the war, it became a European norm for women to have the vote, as it most certainly had not been before 1914. Spain and Switzerland, having been outside the war, stay out of what is now the mainstream. There is a brief exposition of this in Marwick's new Introduction for *The Deluge: British Society and the First World War* (London, 1996).

42 Williams, *The Home Fronts*, p 152. This, nevertheless, remains a readable, comparative account.

43 See Daniel, *The War From Within*, particularly Summary and Conclusion. For the manner in which women's suffrage was introduced in the last days of Wilhelmine Germany see, R. Patemann, *Der Kampf um die preussische Wahlreform im Ersten Weltkrieg. Beiträge zur Geschichte des Parlamentarismus und der politischen Parteien 26* (Düsseldorf, 1964); R.J. Evans, 'German Social Democracy and Women's Suffrage, 1891–1918,' *JCH* 15 (1980), 533–57.

44 This figure is now considered to be an overestimate. A figure of just under 300,000 is more realistic.

45 By 1908, the German Evangelical Women's League was equivalent in size to the Suffrage League with approximately 9,000 members. See, J.C. Kaiser, *Frauen in der Kirche: Evangelische Frauenverbände im Spannungsfeld von Kirche und Gesellschaft 1890–1945: Quellen und Materialen* (Düsseldorf, 1985).

46 Quoted in Evans, *The Feminist Movement in Germany*, p 198.

47 ZSta Potsdam, 61 Re. 1/7966, 74, 2 August 1914, quoted in Daniel, *The War from Within*, p 22.

48 In 1916, for example, the Patriotic Women's Associations distributed 1.6 million field postcards 'Christmas Greetings' to soldiers serving at the front, reminding them that they were not forgotten and that women at home were thinking about them. MAF, RM5, Bd. 2, 3754, War Press Office to Admiral Staff of Navy, 18 March 1917.

49 G. Bäumer, *Jahrbuch der Frauenbewegung* (1916); cited in Evans *The Feminist Movement in Germany*, pp 208–9. See also, Bäumer, *Heimatchronik während des Weltkriegs*, Erster Teil: 1 August 1914–29 December 1916; Zweiter Teil: 1 January 1917–30 September 1918 (Berlin, 1930); and an 'official' pamphlet setting out the achievements of the women's movement and particularly the Women's Home Army, F. Kaufman, *Das Heimatheer Deutscher Frauen* (Berlin, 1918).

50 G. Bäumer, *Lebensweg durch eine Zeitenwende* (Tübingen, 1933): cited in Daniel, *The War from Within*, p. 74. See also, M.-E. Lüders, 'Die volkswirtschaftliche

Bedeutung der qualifizierten Frauenarbeit für die gewerblichen Berufe', in *Frauenberufsfrage und Bevölkerungspolitik Jarhbuch des BDF, 1917* (Berlin and Leipzig, 1917).

51 Gerard, *My Four Years*, p 218. For examples of the range of work undertaken by women see files in, MAS, MI/3, Bü. 566, 'Frauenarbeit'.

52 Heymann, *Völkerversöhnende Frauernarbeit*, pp 14–15.

53 Bavarian War Ministry's report of 2 November 1915, see above, Note 17.

54 Ludendorff, *Urkunden der OHL*, pp 77–8. In a revealing letter to Bethmann Hollweg of 23 October 1916 Hindenburg wrote that compulsory labour for women was inappropriate because 'after the war we will need women as spouse and mother'. For this reason, continued Hindenburg, vigorous measures need to be taken now to extinguish feminist ferment that only 'serves to disrupt the family'. Hindenburg demanded once again that secondary schools and universities should not remain open only for women. The scholarly gain was 'minimal', it disrupted family life and promoted an injustice to young men 'giving their all for the Fatherland'. The letter is reproduced in Daniel, *War From Within*, pp 68–9. For further discussion, see, Ch 4.

55 MAS, 77/1, 62, Report of *Büro für Sozialpolitik*, 20 March 1916.

56 In certain industries, notably transport, employers practised employing wives in the same position as their conscripted husbands. This included not only manual labour but also skilled work. See, H. Fürth, *Die deustche Frau im Kriege* (Tübingen, 1917).

57 M.-E. Lüders, *Das unbekannte Heer. Frauen kämpfen für Deutschland 1914–1918* (Berlin, 1937), p 119.

58 Although Groener had promised all the necessary support, this was not forthcoming and Lüders resigned from the War Office shortly after Groener's departure in December 1917. Groener had been dismissed in August and given command of the 33rd Army Corp. See section on 'the Auxiliary Service Law and the German Labour Movement' in Ch 4. An excellent discussion of the various women's organizations within the War Office can be found in Daniel, *The War from Within*, pp 75–80. For the social policy dimension of female labour mobilization see, Lüders, *Volksdienst der Frau* (Berlin, 1937). For an in-depth analysis of Bremen see, E. Meyer-Renschhausen, *Weibliche Kultur und soziale Arbeit: Eine geschichte der Frauenbewegung am Beispiel Bremens 1810–1927* (Cologne, 1989).

59 Elizabeth Altmann-Gottheiner's lecture was published in the *Münchener-Neueste Nachrichten*, 30 January 1916, cited in Daniel, *The War from Within*, p 75.

60 For a more detailed discussion see, R. Bridenthal and C. Koonz, 'Beyond *Kinder, Küche, Kirche:* Weimar Women in Politics and Work,' in R. Bridenthal *et al.*, (eds), *When Biology Became Destiny: Women in Weimar and Nazi Germany* (New York, 1984). The two major occupational censuses that were taken in this period, in 1910 and 1925, reveal a shift in women's professions, but prove inconclusive as to whether this change was mainly due to the specific historical period itself, the wartime experience or the post-war inflation. In all probability it is a combination of all three.

61 Further examples of women's support for the war and the methods employed by the authorities to encourage them to continue to support the war effort can be found in, MAS, M1/4, No. 1727 and MAS, M77/1, Bü. 64.

62 The full verse reads as follows:

> They organized the field and made the bread in wartime
> and sowed good seeds.
> Plough and scythe were their weapons.
> They formed the home front,
> and the Homeland remains spared.
> Hail to our Women!
> Hail to our German Women!
>
> They have replaced the father,
> taught the girls and the lads,
> and taken care that they have never
> suffered shortages.
> Borne all the hard sorrow
> in calm and humility.
> Hail to our Women!
> Hail to our German Women!

The verse was composed by a man(!), D. Würth and a copy of the 'Hymne' can be found in, *MAS*, M 77/1, Bü. 64. In April 1918, the OHL created the Women's Home Army (*Heimatsheer der Frauen*) with the aim of combating 'defeatism'. For a brief discussion, see Ch 8.

63 Hindenburg to Bäumer, 27 September 1917; cited in Evans, *The Feminist Movement in Germany*, p 11. Following the Allies rejection of the German peace proposal, Bertrude Bäumer recorded a conversation she overheard between two women discussing the issue of peace. The first woman observed that: 'Yes, they should put an end to the war,' The other replied: 'To end it in a manner in which we would lose will simply not do'. Bäumer claimed that this reply reflected the 'unquenchable superiority of idealism' that she claimed characterized the nation's attitude towards the peace initiative. Bäumer, *Heimatchronik während des Weltkriegs*, II, p 80.

64 In 1918, Sebastian Schlittenbauer, the Centre Party's representative in the Bavarian Landtag and the General Secretary of the Bavarian Christian Farmers' Association (*Bayerischer christlicher Bauernverein*), argued that German women lacked a political consciousness and only the introduction of women's right to vote would lead to greater identification with the workings of the state:

> it will no longer do that we exclude women so totally from political life. How shall the woman have an understanding of state emergencies in the hour of danger if, in the hour of peace, she is never trusted with the spirit and essence of state. I emphatically support the right of women to vote... It is deeply rooted in the welfare of the state itself.'

Quoted in Daniel, *War from Within*, pp 237–8.

65 See *Confidential Supplement to the Daily Review of the Foreign Press* for April 1917, specifically, nos 140, 141, 148, 149. A few months later in Cologne there were serious riots, not only on account of food shortages, but also when troops were ordered to the front. Women threw themselves in front of the engine of the troop train, and had to be beaten off by police and troops. *Confidential Supplement of the Daily Review of the Foreign Press*, no. 149, 30 July 1917, p 5. These stories are substantiated by the monthly reports compiled by the Deputy Commanding Generals.

66 To place this decision in historical context: Finland had given women the vote in 1907, Norway in 1913, Denmark and Iceland in 1915, followed by Holland in 1917 and Russia after the Revolution in 1917. Hungary, Sweden and Britain introduced female suffrage by the beginning of 1918. See also, Note 41 above.

67 W. Schumann, 'Die Lage der deutschen und polnischen Arbeiter in Oberschlesien im Kampf gegen den deutschen Imperialismus in Jahren 1917 und 1918', *Zeitschrift für Geschichtswissenschaft*, iv, (1956), pp 484–5; also cited in Carsten, *War Against War*, p 165. The number of women convicted of public order violations increased during the war. In 1913 there were 273 recorded convictions for such offences, 187 were women, 77 were men and 9 were adolescents. In 1917 the number of women convicted had risen to 1,028 – the majority of whom were involved in food riots. As a rule, the authorities were reluctant to prosecute women for fear of the damaging political ramifications. See, S. von Koppenfels, *Die Kriminalität der Frau im Krieg* (Leipzig, 1926), p 23; M. Liepmann, *Krieg und Kriminalität in Deutschland* (Stuttgart *et al.*, 1930), p 24; Daniel, *War From Within*, p 250.

68 Ute Daniel's claim in her article on the politics of subsistence and working-class women that the spontaneous riots turned German towns after 1916 'into theatres of civil war' exaggerates the generally sound point about civil unrest. See, Daniel, 'The Politics of Rationing versus the Politics of Subsistence: Working Class Women in Germany, 1914–1918' in Fletcher (ed.), *Bernstein to Brandt*, p 94. For a discussion of the 'empowering' nature of women's consumerism see, B. Davis, 'Food Scarcity and the Empowerment of the Female Consumer', in V. de Grazia *et al.* (eds), *The Sex of Things. Gender and Consumption in Historical Perspective* (Berkeley, 1996), pp 287–310.

69 For examples of letters of complaints about intimidation and loss of Family Allowances sent by 'war wives' to husbands at the front see, *BHStA*, MB. IV, MKr 12851, 3 August 1917. The Military Commanders were concerned at the increasing number of 'letters of suffering' reaching soldiers, but were loathe to censor letters from wives punitively. Instead, a propaganda campaign was launched intended to persuade the home front, and particularly women, to keep their worries and their hardships to themselves. See Ch 6 for further discussion. The authorities did, however, take a stern line on so-called 'secret prostitution' between German women and prisoners of war.

70 The Social Democrats saw themselves very much as the custodians of welfare provision in the face of hostile military commanders. See Ch 6.

6 WAR AIMS AGAIN

1 Strikes and lock-outs in Germany 1913–19 (based on Reich statistics):

Year	No. of strikes and lock-outs	No. of employees (000s)	Working days lost (000s)
1913	2,464	323,4	11,761,0
1915	141	15,2	46,0
1916	240	128,9	245,0
1917	562	668,0	1,862,0
1918	532	391,6	1,453,0
1919	3,719	2,132,5	33,083,0

Source: V.R. Berghahn, *Modern Germany. Society, Economy and Politics in the Twentieth Century* (Cambridge, 1983) p 286. Figures on the number of strikes vary, but the figures above appear to be as accurate and correspond closely to those cited in Reichsstatistik. Kocka, for example, cites the following (strikes in brackets): 1915 (137); 1916 (240); 1917 (561); 1918 (531). Kocka, *Facing Total War*, p 61.

2 E.D. Bullitt, *An Uncensored Diary from the Central Empires* (London, 1918) p 273.
3 Extract from the Bavarian War Ministry to the Bavarian Minister of State on the Morale in the Army and at Home, 1 February 1916. Deist, *Militär und Innenpolitik*, 1, pp 294–9. For examples of reported worsening state of civilian morale, Cf. Deputy Commanding Generals Monthly Reports (*Monatsberichen*) for 3 March 1916, 3 June 1916, 3 October 1916, 3 December 1916, BHStA IV, MKr, 12851.
4 The issue of the demoralizing effects of letters to soldiers describing the hardships encountered by the home front, remained a major concern for the military authorities. Cf. the statement issued by the War Press Office on 29 December 1915 (cited by the Bavarian War Ministry in their report of 1 February 1916, above, Note 3):

> Such letter have a far worse effect than all the news which the enemy spreads, for soldiers recognise that the enemy disseminates lies in order to undermine morale. News from home, however, is received much less critically. People who have come to bear suffering and danger with intrepid fortitude, hardly reckon with the possibility that there are those who make unwarranted complaints about conditions at home simply to lighten their own burdens.
>
> See also guidelines set out by the Supreme Censorship Office of 26 January 1916:
>
> We owe it to our troops, who in the present war are meeting demands such as no army has ever faced in the history of the world, that no sickly sentimental or malicious complaints be sent to the army in the field, causing worry and anxiety among soldiers when the actual conditions at home do not justify it.
>
> Quoted in Lutz, *Fall of the German Empire*, p 191 For similar complaints see also, MAF, MB, RM3, Bd. 4, 10313, 4 April 1917.)

5 It was written by H. Priebe and its full title was *Kriegerfrauen! Helft euren Männern den Sieg gewinnen. Sieben ernste Bitten an die Frauen und Mütter unserer tapferen Feldgrauen* (Berlin, 1916).
6 This idea of a concerted propaganda campaign along 'patriotic' lines was the forerunner of a much larger campaign instigated by Ludendorff in July 1917 under the title *Vaterländische Unterricht* (Patriotic Instructions). This campaign forms the basis of Chapter 7.
7 BHStA *IV* BM Berlin. B. Kriegsakten, 16, Bb. 8, Decree of Bavarian War Ministry, 1 February 1916. Also cited in Deist, *Militär und Innenpolitik*, I, pp 300–2. On the question of the morale of soldiers at the front see, L. Scholz, *Seelenleben des Soldaten an der Front. Hinterlassene Aufzeichnungen des im Kriege gefallenen Nervenarztes* (Tübingen, 1920).
8 It was an issue taken up by General Ludendorff in October 1916. He complained that soldiers in their letters home and on leave were spreading false rumours about Germany's economic position undermining confidence in all sections of the population. MAF, RM5, Bd. 2, 3754, Order from the Chief of General Staff to the Army High Command, 18 October 1916.
9 MAF, RM3, Bd. 4, 10297, Letter from the Prussian War Ministry to the Prussian Minister of the Interior and of Spiritual and Educational Affairs. Recommendation of Measures to Counteract Worsening of the Mood at Home, 2 March 1916. The youth policy pursued by civilian and military authorities was markedly different. The civilian authorities favoured establishing Youth Offices (*Jugendämter*) in administrative districts and placing largely working-class male adolescents in youth-welfare schemes. The military attempted to inculcate military values of discipline and obedience by means of the Youth Army (*Jugendwehr*), a paramilitary organization that had been set up before the war. After the outbreak of war membership increased to 600,000 voluntary recruits in 1915, but during 1916 participation fell dramatically. Hence the concern in the Prussian War Ministry's report. For further details see, G. Fiedler, *Jugend in Krieg. Bürgerliche Jugendbewegung, Erster Weltkrieg und Sozialer Wandel, 1914–1923* (Köln, 1989). An interesting brief discussion can also be found in Daniel, *The War from Within*, pp 165–7.
10 HSS, E 150 (*Ministerium des Innen*) *IV*, Decree from the Württemberg Ministry of the Interior to the Higher Services re: Supporting Church and School Officials in their Efforts towards Keeping the Population Informed, 8 May 1916.
11 MAF, RM3, Bd. 4, *10277*. Meeting of Prussian War Ministry with Representatives of the Deputy Commanding Generals, 9 June 1916.
12 Colonel von Wrisberg, Director of the General War Departments in the Prussian War Ministry, agreed with Magirus and informed the meeting that his idea of creating a single organization had already been taken up by the War Press Office.
13 MAF, RM5, Bd. 2, 3722, Minutes of Meeting between *Kultur-Bund* and Representatives of the Deputy Commanding Generals re: Tasks of the Propaganda Organization to be Established, 24 June 1916. The executive board of the *Kultur-Bund* was made up of President Prof. Dr Waldeyer, Vice President Hermann

Sudermann and Dr Walter Rathenau, Rudolf Presber, Ludwig Fulda, Prof. Dr Plank and Leo Frobenius.
14. A preliminary meeting had taken place between Sudermann of the *Kultur-Bund* and Major Nicolai on 1 June 1916.
15. Representatives of the *Kultur-Bund* who attended the meeting stressed that the new organization should not be perceived as a mechanism for the dissemination of official propaganda. All those working for the Bund must feel that they were doing so of their own free will. MAF, RM5, Bd. 2, 3722, meeting of 24 June 1916.
16. Ludendorff to the Imperial Chancellor, 17 December 1916. The documented is reprinted in *The General Staff and its Problems*, vol II. Translated by F.A. Holt, (London, 1921), pp 401–3. To support his claim for a central authority, Ludendorff cited the poor handling of the so-called 'Polish Manifesto' and the belated instructions received by the military press departments of the German peace offer of 7 December. See also, Ludendorff, *My War Memories*, pp 373–4.
17. Cf. Kitchen, *Silent Dictatorship*, p 57.
18. BHStA IV, MKr, 12851, Note from Head of Press Section of Bavarian War Ministry, 5 December 1916; Deist, *Militär und Innenpolitik*, I, p 339. The hostility to Prussia was borne out in the interviews conducted by the Americans with German POWs. They discovered that 'political dissent' within Bavaria units arose primarily from dissatisfaction with Prussians who, they believed, were 'using' them. Bruntz, *Allied Propaganda*, p 191. The *Monatsberichte* also recorded Bavarians referring to Prussians as 'them' and viewing the continuation of the war in terms of forcing 'them' (meaning Prussians) to make peace. Carsten, *War Against War*, p 166. n. 37.
19. Cf. Monthly Report of 8 September 1916, BHStA MB, IV, MKr, 12851.
20. A. Rosenberg, *The Birth of the German Republic* (London, 1931) p 91.
21. *Confidential Supplement to the Daily Review of the Foreign Press*, No. 55, 31 May 1916, p 2. The letter was written on 30 April 1916.
22. Blücher, *An English Wife*, p 135, entry for May 1916. BHStA MB, IV, MKr, 2331, Minister of the Interior to Bavarian War Ministry, 8 November 1916; Carsten, *War Against War, p. 78*.
23. BHStA, MB, IV, MKr, 12851, Report to the Bavarian War Ministry, 31 August 1916.
24. MAF, RM5, Bd. 2, 3740, Minutes of Press Section of Admiralty in Conversation with Reich Chancellery Concerning Propaganda Questions, 31 August 1916. In fact this notion of distinguishing between the 'educated' middle class and the 'baser' working class was a recurring motif in the reports of the Regional Army Commands. Cf. BHStA, MB, IV, MKr, 12845, Reports for October 1917.
25. MAS, 77/1 (*Stellvertretendes Generalkommando XIII*), Bü. 64. On 30 December 1915 the Prussian War Ministry received a report from the *Büro für Sozialpolitik* which quoted a reliable SPD source suggesting that lifting the tax on sugar and salt might improve morale. MAS, M 1/3 495 (*Büros für Socialpolitik*),

30 December 1915. The folder contains reports for 1917, but inexplicably has two reports from 1915 (August and December).
26. *Verhandlungen des Reichstags*, 5 April 1916, p 853. Haase's speech, 6 April 1916, pp 881–9.
27. In the first months of 1917 over 20 million leaflets were distributed to the home front. Titles such as 'Until the Final Battle' of which 9 million were 'given' to the homeland by the OHL. Other titles included 'To the German People' (10.1 million) and 'We Must Win' (2 million). GLA Karlsruhe, 456, Bd. 87, War Press Office to Deputy Commanding General XIV A.K., 13 February 1917. See also MAF, RM5, Bd. 2, 3754, War Press Office to Admiral Staff of Navy, 18 March 1917.
28. Further details of official propaganda to promote the war loans can be found in, MAF, RM3, 10323, 10324 (*Kriegsanleihe*) and MAF, RM3/v, Bd. 4, 10323, 10324 (*Propaganda für die Kriegsanleihe*).
29. GLA Karlsruhe, MB, Abt. 456, Bd. 70, Zusammenstellung der Monatsberichte der stellv. Generalkommandos vom 3 October 1916 and 14 October 1916. However, in December the Bavarian War Ministry reported that its campaign for the Fifth War Loan, launched by over 150,000 copies of the leaflet 'War, Need, Victory' (*Krieg-Not-Sieg*) had been well received. BHStA, IV, MKr, 12851, 5 December 1916. Cf. Deist, *Militär und Innenpolitik*, I, p 339.
30. GLA, Karlsruhe, MB, 456, Bd. 70, Deputy Commanding Generals to Prussian War Ministry, February 1917.
31. BHStA, Kr, *Stellvertretenden Generalkommandos*, Garnisonsältester Kaufbeuren, 16 November 1916; Daniel, *The War From Within*, p 259.
32. Ludendorff, *My War Memories*, p 331.
33. H. Trotnow, *Karl Liebknecht*, (Cologne, 1980) p 240. See also, K.W. Meyer, *Karl Liebknecht: Man Without a Country* (Washington, DC, 1957); K. Liebknecht, *The Future Belongs to the People* (New York, 1918) and *Gesammelte Reden und Schriften* 9 vols, (Berlin, 1958–74). The SPD's decision in August 1914 to vote for war credits and support the 'political truce' also shocked Bolshevik leaders in Russia. Leon Trotsky later wrote: 'The telegram telling of the capitulation of the German Social Democracy shocked me even more than the declaration of war, in spite of the fact that I was far from a naive idealizing of German socialism.' L. Trotsky, *My Life* (New York, 1960), p 236.
34. W. Kruse, *Krieg und Integration. Eine Neuinterpretation des sozialdemokratischen Burgfriedensschluss 1914–1915* (Essen, 1993). See also Kruse's essay in Kruse (ed.), *Eine Welt von Frieden: Der grosse Kriege 1914–18* (Frankfurt am Main, 1997), pp 159–66.
35. G. Eley, 'The SPD in War and Revolution, 1914–19', in Fletcher (ed), *Bernstein to Brandt*, p 65.
36. For a brief perceptive analysis of the background and significance of the Zimmerwald Conference see, Carsten, *War Against War*, pp 36–42. For more detailed information see, H. Lademacher (ed.), *Die Zimmerwald Bewegung – Protokolle und Korrespondenz*, 2 vols, (Hague–Paris, 1967); A. Balabanoff, *Die Zimmerwalder Bewegung 1914–1919* (Leipzig, 1928 reprint 1969).

37 *The Crisis in German Social Democracy* (*The Junius Pamphlet*, New York, 1915) p 124, quoted in Bruntz, *Allied Propaganda*, p 173.
38 Liebknecht's speech was published in leaflet form and circulated throughout Germany. E. Meyer (ed.), *Spartakus im Kriege; die illegalen Flugblätter des Spartakusbundes im Kriege* (Berlin, 1927), Document No. 3, cited in Bruntz, *Allied Propaganda*, p 173.
39 For the article in full see, *Documente und Materialien zur Geschichte*, I, Nr. 57, pp 135–7.
40 Carsten, *War Against War*, p 47. The full speech in leaflet form is printed in, *Dokumente und Materialen zur Geschichte*, I, pp 162–6.
41 For a more detailed discussion see Chapter 3.
42 *Vorwärts*, 12 January 1916, also cited in Carsten, *War Against War*, p 82.
43 Hanssen, *Dairy of a Dying Empire*, p 134, entry for 24 March 1916.
44 General histories of the USPD can be found in, H. Krause, USPD: *zur Geschichte der Unabhängigen Sozialdemokratischen Partei Deutschlands* (Frankfurt, 1975) and D.W. Morgan, *A History of the German Independent Party 1911–22* (Ithaca, NY, 1976). For a perceptive discussion of the founding of the USPD, see, S. Miller, *Burgfrieden und Klassenkampf. Die deutsche Sozialdemokratie im Ersten Weltkrieg* (Düsseldorf, 1974) pp 156–177. For an interesting discussion on whether the USPD represented a continuum with the pre-1914 SPD, or a protest at the SPD's support for the government's war aims as well as its desire for an immediate negotiated peace, see, E. Kolb, *Die Arbeiterräte in der deutschen Innenpolitik 1918/19* (Frankfurt, 1978) pp 35–46.
45 For a history of the Spartacus League see, W. Pelz, *The Spartakusbund and the German Working Class Movement, 1914–1919* (New York, 1987).
46 MAF, RM3, Bd. 3, 10296; Prussian War Ministry to Deputy Commanding Generals, 18 August 1915.
47 MAF, RM3, Bd. 4, 10296, Pussian War Ministry to Deputy Commanding Generals on Measures Against Distribution of Party Political Printed Matter and Leaflets, 27 August 1915. In July, the War Ministry singled out a number of pamphlets for special mention: '*An den Vorstand der sozialdemokratischen Partei Deutschland!*', '*Frauen des arbeitenden Volkes! Wo sind eure Männer usw?*' and a speech by Liebknecht: '*Die Wahlrechtsfrage in der Kriegszeit*'. MAF, RM3, Bd. 4, 10296, 'Prussian War Ministry to Deputy Commanding Generals', 9 July 1915.
48 MAF, RM3 Bd. 4, 10298, Supreme Command to Deputy Commanding Generals, 26 June 1917. For censorship of USPD's manifesto; MAF, RM3, Bd. 4, 10297, Prussian Minister of war to Deputy Commanding Generals, 14 June 1917. For further examples of censorship of the publications, speeches, meetings, etc. of the far left see, MAS, 77/1, Bü. 62 (*Diensteelen und Zensur, 1915–18*).
49 *Fliegerabwurf-Schriften*, No. 5, undated, cited in Bruntz, *Allied Propaganda and the German Empire*, p 166.
50 H. Trotnow, *Karl Liebknecht*, pp 247–8; Carsten, *War Against War*, p 83.

51 Meyer, *Dokumente des Kommunismus*, p 22. In Stuttgart, the workers were joined by the *Frei Jugendorganization* but the demonstration was quickly dissolved by the 13th Army Corps. See folder in Stuttgart/Ludwigsburg, E150–153, Nr. 2048.
52 S.E. Bronner (ed.), *The Letters of Rosa Luxemburg* (Bolder, Colorado, 1978) p 167. See also, Pelz, *The Spartakusbund*, p 101.
53 Lutz, *Fall of the German Empire*, p 168.
54 For an example of how the Supreme Censorship Office attempted to control the reporting of Liebknecht's speeches in the Reichstag, see, MAF, RM3, Bd. 4, 10297, Telegram from the Supreme Censorship Office to the News Bureau of the Reich Naval Office on the Reporting of Liebknecht's Behaviour in the Reichstag to the Press, 8 April 1916).
55 IWM, *Weekly Reports on the German and Austrian Newspapers*, 2 June 1916.
56 *Vorwärts*, 18 January 1917.
57 MAF, RM3, Bd. 4, 10296, Telegram from Supreme Censorship Office re: Measures to be Taken Against the SPD's Guiding Principles on War Aims Questions, 21 August 1915.
58 GLA Karlsruhe, MB, Abt. 456, Bd. 70, 3 June 1916.
59 Hanssen, *Diary of a Dying Empire*, p 143.
60 GLA Karlsruhe, MB, Abt. 456, Bd. 704, Extract from Monthly Reports of the Deputy Commanding Generals to the Prussian War Ministry, re: the General Mood of the Country, 3 July 1916. See Ch 4 for a more detailed analysis of the propaganda that accompanied unrestricted submarine warfare.
61 GLA Karlsruhe, Abt. 456, Bd. 704, Extract from Monthly Reports of the Deputy Commanding Generals to the Prussian War Ministry, 3 August 1916.
62 Ibid.
63 MAF, RM3, Bd. 4, 10298, Letter from Supreme Censorship Office to all Regional Censorship Offices, 29 November 1916.
64 See above, Note 57.
65 Hanssen, *Diary of a Dying Empire*, entry for 31 March 1916, p 141.
66 MAF, RM3, Bd. 4, 10297, Telegram from the Supreme Censorship Office to the News Bureau of the Reich Naval Office on Directions for the Discussion of Speech by the Reichs Chancellor, 5 April 1916. The press were informed that they could report the Chancellor's speech in its broadest terms but criticism or analysis was forbidden.
67 *Verhandlungen des Reichstags*, 5 April 1916, p 853.
68 Ebert, speaking for the SPD, protested against the annexationist interpretation of the Chancellor's vague statement on Belgium. *Vorwärts*, 6 April 1916.
69 *Verhandlungen des Reichstags*, 6 April 1916, pp 866–70.
70 *Verhandlungen des Reichstags*, 9 December 1915, p 436.
71 Dahlin, *French and German Public Opinion*, p 67. My remarks on the question of the divisions within the annexationists' camp owe much to an excellent analysis by Dahlin, ibid, pp 65–9.

72 A typical outline of the Pan German Union's position can be found in *Berliner Tageblatt*, 20 December 1916. Articles against the annexation of Belgium see *Berliner Tageblatt*, 6 and 7 April 1916.
73 *Vorwärts*, 25 August 1916, cited in Dahlin, *French and German Public Opinion*, p 260.
74 *Germania*, 6 April 1916; *Kölnische Volkszeitung*, 6 April 1916.
75 Erzberger suggested to the Chancellor that he should set in motion a propaganda campaign aimed at unifying public opinion. Erzberger memorandum on the necessity of a Centralized Direction of the War Aims Discussion, date 15 April 1916, *Erzberger Papers*, File 4, cited in Epstein, *Matthias Erzberger*, p 111.
76 *Vorwärts*, 28 July 1916.
77 GLA Karlsruhe, MB, Abt 456, Bd 70, 3 August 1916. The monthly report refers to the petition being submitted on 19 July 1916.
78 *Vorwärts*, 11 August 1916, p 1.
79 MAF, RM3, Bd. 4, 10298, Telegram from War Press Office, re: Guidelines for Release of Statement of War Aims to the Public, 28 October 1916.
80 Statement from Press Office of the Admiralty re: Position of Head of the Admiralty and of the Secretary of State of the Imperial Naval Office on the Question of the Discussion of War Aims in Public, 7 November 1916: Deist, *Militär und Innenpolitik*, I, pp 446–7.
81 MAF, RM3, Bd. 4, 10280, Letter from Chancellor to Secretary of State and Prussian State Minister on the Public Release of Discussion of War Aims, 23 November 1916.
82 MAF, RM3, Bd. 4, 10280, Minutes of Talks Between Central Military and Civil Authorities at the War Press Office on Maintaining the Confident Mood of the People, 20 November 1916. More will be said about the significance of this important meeting in the final chapter.
83 MAF, RM3, Bd. 4, 10298, Supreme Censorship Office to Press on Question of War Aims, 27, November 1916.
84 MAF RM3, Bd. 4, 10298, Supreme Censorship Office to all censorship Offices on the Release of War Aims Discussion to the Public, 25 November 1916. The letter from the OZS ended with the warning to the press that it would suppress 'all self-seeking and base comments and comments of an unnecessary political nature intended to inflame social, class, or religious tension.' The version given to the press was almost identical and came into effect on 28 November 1916. The new definition of the *Burgfrieden* was issued again on 11 December 1916. See also, Nicolai, *Nachrichtendienst*, p 184.
85 Cf. Kitchen, *The Silent Dictatorship*, p 113.
86 Ludendorff claimed that:

> So far as he permitted, I co-operated with the Chancellor in the matter. In order to avoid giving the enemy the false impression that weakness was our motive for the proposal, I asked that it should not be carried out until the campaign in Rumania had been brought to a conclusion. Bucharest fell on the 6 December,

and with that I regarded the military position so secure that I had no objection to the publication of the Peace Note.

Ludendorff, *My War Memories*, pp 309–10.
87 *Verhandlungen des Reichstags*, 12 December 1916, p 2332. The peace proposal was made on behalf of the Kaiser and began:

> In a deep moral and religious sense of duty towards the nation, and beyond it towards humanity, the Emperor now considers that the moment has come for official action towards peace. His Majesty, therefore, in complete harmony and in common with our Allies, decided to propose to the hostile Powers to enter peace negotiations.

At the same time that the Reichstag was hearing Bethmann Hollweg read out the peace proposal, the Kaiser sent a message to his Generals: 'Soldiers, in an agreement with the Sovereigns of my Allies, and with the consciousness of victory, I have made an offer of peace to the enemy. Whether it will be accepted is still uncertain. Until that moment arrives you will fight on.' Gerard, *My Four Years*, p 257.

88 Erzberger, *Erlebnisse*, pp 219–20.
89 The Note was dated 18 December and addressed by the Secretary of State to American Ambassadors at the capitals of the belligerent powers. The Note referred to suggestions that the President 'had long had in mind to offer'. It also referred to his 'embarrassment'; 'because it may now seem to have been prompted by a desire to play a part in connections with the recent overtures of the Central Powers.' Gerard, *My Four Years*, p 256.
90 For the French position see, Dahlin, *French and German Public Opinion*, pp 250–3. The Entente's reply also claimed that the German peace move was a propaganda manoeuvre designed to mislead neutrals and cover up German crimes such as submarine warfare, the deportation of workers to Germany, and the forced conscription of nationals to fight against their own countries.
91 Mayor of Berlin's New year Message; *Berliner Tageblatt*, 31 December 1916. Gerard, *Kaiserism*, p 123.
92 Gerard, *My Four Years*, p 268. It was a claim that Bethmann repeated to the Commission of Inquiry in 1919. German animosity to Wilson, fuelled by his attitude on submarine warfare and the perception that he favoured the Allies, was too great to make him a suitable mediator. *Die deutsche Nationalversammlung*, 1919, pp 600–2.
93 Gerard, *My Four Years*, p 260. In fact, Hindenburg and Ludendorff threatened to resign (on more than one occasion) if the politicians did not agree to resuming unrestricted submarine warfare as soon as possible. Instead of informing the Supreme Command to mind their own business, Bethmann and Zimmermann (Foreign Office) begged them to await the Entente's reply before insisting on submarine warfare. See, Ludendorff, *Urkunden der OHL*, pp 312–16.
94 *Verhandlungen des Reichstags*, 27 February 1917, p 2377.

95 Hanssen, *Diary of a Dying Empire*, p 145, entry for 5 June 1916.
96 Kitchen, *The Silent Dictatorship*, pp 119–20.
97 Ex-Kaiser William II, *My Memoirs: 1878–1918* (London, 1922) p, 128. An insight into Bethmann's thinking at the time which also highlights the distance between the Chancellor and the Napoleonic ambitions of the OHL, can be gleaned from his statement to a committee of the Bundesrat towards the end of October 1916. Bethmann had soberly explained to the committee that survival was in itself a victory. 'If we survive this superior force and come out capable of negotiation', he said, 'then we have won.' Bethmann Hollweg to Bundesrat, 30/31 October 1916, cited in G. Ritter, *Staatskunst und Kriegshandwerk. Das Problem des 'Militarismus' in Deutschland*, vol 3: *Die Tragödie der Staatskunst. Bethmann Hollweg als Kriegskanzler (1914–17)* (Munich, 1964) p 336. For one of the more recent biographies of Bethmann Hollweg see, G. Wollstein, *Theobald von Bethmann Hollweg: Letzter Erbe Bismarcks, Erstes Opfer der Dolchstosslegende* (Göttingen and Cologne, 1990).
98 T. Curtin, *The Land of Deepening Shadow: Germany 1916* (London, 1917), p 352, quoted in Williams, *The Home Fronts*, p 224.
99 Blücher, *An English Wife*, p 162.
100 BHStA, MB, IV 155/85 MKr, 12851, 2 April 1917. Also cited in Kocka, *Facing Total War*, p 57.
101 Reichstag Deputies were shown pamphlets exhorting the strikers to end the war: 'When you stop work, no weapons are produced. Without weapons the war cannot be waged. When war can no longer be waged peace comes of itself. All wheels stand still when Your (God's) strong arm wills it.' Hanssen, *Diary of a Dying Empire*, pp 185–6.
102 Eley, 'The SPD in War and Revolution, 1914–1919' in Fletcher (ed.), *Bernstein to Brandt*. p.68.
103 In early 1915, for example, the SPD leadership informed the government that it was not prepared to preserve the *Burgfrieden* unless the rising price of basic foodstuffs was kept in check. Feldmann, *Army, Industry and Labour*, p 101.
104 GLA Karlsruhe, MB, Abt. 456, Bd. 70, 3 August 1916.
105 The membership of the SPD fell from 1,086,000 in 1914 to 586,000 in 1915, 433,000 in 1916 and 243,000 in 1917 – a figure which remained unchanged up to the Revolution. The figures, including the estimates made by the USPD leaders of their own gains, are taken from Kocka, *Facing Total War*, p 61.
106 This was certainly the position of the SPD in Nuremburg, see, K.D. Schwarz, *Weltkrieg u. Nürnberg* (Stuttgart, 1971). The USPD claimed that they had gained 100,000 members by the time of the Revolution.
107 Nolan, *Social Democracy and Society*, p 255.
108 The three constitutional organs consisting of the King, the Upper Chamber (*Herrenhaus*) and the Lower Chamber (*Landtag*). For reform of the Prussian franchise see, L. Bergstrasser, *Die preussische Wahlrechtsfrage und die Entstehung der Osterbotschaft 1917* (Tübingen, 1929); R. Patemann, *Der Kampf um die preussische Wahlreform im Ersten Weltkrieg* (Düsseldorf, 1964).

109 *Vorwärts* suggested that broad sections of the community regarded reform of the Prussian franchise as the most pressing internal problem facing the country. *Vorwärts* (8 January 1916). By the time the Kaiser made his speech it had been whittled down by conservatives who feared that concessions had already been made and that to promise immediate electoral reform risked 'undermining the patriotic will of the nation'. Cf. minutes of meeting to discuss the content of the Kaiser's speech at the Prussian Ministry of State, 3 January 1916; cited in Deist, *Militär und Innenpolitik*, I, pp 355–57.
110 Memorandum form Wild von Hohenborn re: Plan for an Audience with the Kaiser,9 March 1916; Deist, I, *Militär und Innenpolitik*, pp 357–9 The Conservative Party opposed electoral reform, preferring instead to talk of 'organic development' of the Prussian electoral system. For a succinct outline of the Conservative Party's position see, *Neue Preussische Zeitung*, 13 April 1917.
111 Quoted in *Vorwärts*, 3 February 1917.
112 *Stenographische Berichte über die Verhandlungen des Preussischen Hauses der Abgeordneten*, 14 March 1917, p 5255.
113 Kitchen, *The Silent Dictatorship*, 129.
114 Deist, *Militär und Innenpolitik*, I, p 448.
115 This was spelt out in a War Press Office directive of 26 January 1916 that spoke of the need for free expression 'restricted only by observing the *Burgfrieden* and by considering the effect that public criticism might have on the enemy'. MAF, RM3,Bd. 4, 10297, Directive from War Press Office re: the Discussion of War Aims, 26 January 1916.
116 MAF, RM3, Bd. 4, 10298, 5 February 1917. See also, Lutz, *Fall of the German Empire*, p 194.
117 *Verhandlungen des Reichstags*, 29 March 1917, p 2856. Scheidemann compared the government's decision to defer political reforms to the policy of the Tsarist government. The result was revolution and thus Scheidemann called for 'decisive action' to prevent similar events occurring in Germany. Scheidemann, *Zusammenbruch*, pp 41–2, from the original article published in *Vorwärts*.
118 Bethmann Hollweg, *Betrachtungen zum Weltkrieg*, II, p 174.
119 Quoted in the semi-official organ of the German government, *Norddeutsche Allgemeine Zeitung*, 8 April 1917. See also, Lutz, *Fall of the German Empire*, pp 423–4. On 5 March the Finance Committee of the Reichstag discussed Secretary of State Zimmermann's report on the publication of his sensational note, which had been intercepted both by the British and by the Americans, proposing a German–Mexican alliance against the United States. Gothein, the Progressive Party Leader stood up and asked: 'How shall we make peace with America?'. Hanssen, *Diary of a Dying Empire*, p 158.
120 In his memoirs, the ex-Kaiser criticized Bethmann's handling of the Prussian franchise and claimed the credit for initiating the reforms. Wilhelm II wrote that Loebbel had submitted proposals for reforms in the winter of 1914/15 which he approved and sent to the Chancellor with instructions that the draft proposals should be discussed by all his Ministers. According to the Kaiser, Bethmann

'vacillated' and as a result the reforms were not introduced until after the conclusion of peace. Ex-Kaiser William II, *My Memoirs*, pp 131–4.
121 BAK, *Nachlass Bauer*, Band 17. Kitchen, *The Silent Dictatorship*, 132, Ludendorff, *My War Memories*, pp 447–9. A number of strikes began in the munitions factories in Berlin on 14 April 1917 on the heels of the announcement by the government of further reductions in the food rations which were to come into effect on 16 April. Cf. also, Ludendorff's telegram of 24 April 1917 to Bethmann on how the strikes should be handled in the light of the Russian Revolution. Deist, *Militär und Innenpolitik*, II, pp 722–3.
122 In fact the first reading of the bill introducing suffrage reform did not take place until December 1917. Patemann, *Der Kampf um die Preussische Wahlreform*, pp 122–4. Support for 'moderate' political reforms came also from the *Büro für Sozialpolitik*. See report of 21 July 1917, MAS, MI/3, 495.
123 *Verhandlungen des Reichstags*, 15 May 1917, p 3398.
124 Princess Blücher noted in her diary:

> The interest awakened by hopes of the Chancellor's speech was somewhat disappointed. He was so excessively cautious. No new disclosures were made, no declarations offered as to the German war aims, and no new loopholes opened out for peace feelers, excepting the reserved hint of a possible separate understanding with Russia, which however cheers some people up wonderfully.' Blücher, *An English Wife*, p 169.

In fact in his speech of 15 May, Bethmann actually conceded that the government's peace plans leaned neither to the annexationist right not to the antiannexationist Left! *Verhandlungen des Reichstags*, 15 May 1917, p 3395.
125 The Majority Socialists made their famous proclamation 'peace without annexations and indemnities' on 20 April 1917. For the response of the proannexationist Independent Committee for a German Peace, see, *Neue Preussische Zeitung*, 23 April 1917 quoted in Lutz, *Fall of the German Empire*, p 353.
126 In the Reichstag debate of 3 July the government was seeking approval for a new war credit of 15 billion marks. Roedern informed the House that credits agreed so far amounted to 79 billion marks, combined with the regular peacetime war tax and other war funds, totalled 89 billion 900 million marks. Figures quoted in Hanssen, *Diary of a Dying Empire*, p 195.
127 See Kitchen's excellent account of the 'July crisis', *The Silent Dictatorship*, pp 127–51.
128 The letter is dated 27 June 1917 and is quoted in Ludendorff, *My War Memories*, p 451. Ludendorff claimed that Bethmann's reply of 25 June 'revealed extraordinary depression... He could find no way out of the situation, and still less could he summon up the energy to act'. Ibid, p 450.
129 A fascinating account of the intrigues leading to Bethmann's dismissal can be found in R. Valentini, *Kaiser und Kabinettschef. Nach eigenen Aufzeichnungen und dem Briefwechsel des wirklichen Geheimen Rats Rudolf von Valentini dargestellt von*

Bernhard Schwertfeger (Oldenburg, 1931), pp 154–64. Valentini was the Chief of the Civil Cabinet.
130   Hanssen recorded as early as 3 May that rumours were already circulating that Bethmann was about to resign and be replaced by General Hermann von Stein, the Minister of War, *Diary of a Dying Empire*, p. 193.
131   Quoted in Bruntz, *Allied Propaganda*, p 160.
132   The text of the speech can be found in Hanssen, *Diary of a Dying Empire*, pp 201–7. See also Erzberger's account, *Meine Erlebnisse im Weltkreige*, pp 254–6.
133   Ludendorff claimed that the OHL was 'utterly surprised' by Erzberger's speech, *My War Memories*, p 451. Conrad Haussmann, who had played a major role in discrediting the 'Adlon Group' recorded a conversation that took place between Mueller-Fulda (Centre) and Erzberger on 2 July:

> I met Erzberger in the Reichstag and discussed with him the dangerous feeling which had been aroused in many places because of the food shortage. He told me that Germany would have a peace if she were really in earnest about it. He mentioned the proposed attempts at mediation on the part of the Pope, and said that it was now a case of backing it up by a demonstration on the part of the Reichstag for a peace without annexations.

Haussmann, *Schlaglichter. Reichstagsbriefe und Aufzeichnungen* (Frankfurt, 1924) p 384.
134   On 29 June, Mgr Pacelli, the Apostolic Nuncio, delivered to the Kaiser a personal letter from the Pope calling on all belligerent states to end the war. In the course of the conversation with Pacelli, the Kaiser apparently welcomed any intervention from the Papacy that might secure peace. For the Kaiser's account of the meeting, see, Ex-Kaiser, *My Memoirs*, pp 258–65. See also Bethmann Hollweg, *Betrachtungen zum Weltkriege*, vol II, p 211. For the Vatican's role in the peace negotiations see, W. Steglich (ed.), *Die Friedensappel Papst Benedikts XV vom 1 August und die Mittelmächte* (Stuttgart, 1970). The wider implications are tackled in, Steglich (ed.), *Die Friedensversuche der Kriegführenden Mächte im Sommer und Herbst 1917* (Stuttgart, 1984).
135   Valentini, *Kaiser und Kabinettschef*, p 159, Kitchen, *Silent Dictatorship*, p 133.
136   Hanssen, *Diary of a Dying Empire*, p 224.
137   For different perspectives of the meeting see, Bethmann Hollweg, *Betrachtungen zum Weltkriege*, vol II, p 234; Ludendorff, *Urkunden der OHL*, p 408; Erzberger, *Erlebnisse im Weltkrieg*, p 262; F. von Payer, *Von Bethmann Hollweg bis Ebert. Erinnerungen und Bilder* (Frankfurt, 1923) pp 34–6.
138   Valentini, *Kaiser und Kabinettschef*, p 162, Kitchen, *Silent Dictatorship*, p 133. In his memoirs, the Kaiser maintained that although Bethmann made 'mistake after mistake' he continued to support him because he was 'loth to deprive the working classes, who behaved in an exemplary manner in 1914, of the statesman whom, I was told, they trusted.' Ex-Kaiser, *My Memoirs*, pp 129–30.
139   Ludendorff, *My War Memories*, pp 454–6.

140 An excellent account of the events can be found in Valentini, *Kaiser und Kabinettschef*, pp 166–7. According to Hanssen, Conrad Haussmann best expressed the general opinion in these words: 'We have lost a statesman and have secured a functionary in his place.' *Diary of a Dying Empire*, p 231.
141 The OHL preferred Prince Bülow but the Kaiser vetoed this, on account of the *Daily Telegraph* affair. Count Hertling had refused on the grounds that he could not work with the OHL.
142 Scheidemann's profession of 'innocence' can be found in Scheidemann, *Der Zusammenbruch*, pp 95–6.
143 *Verhandlungen des Reichstags*, 19 July 1917, p 3573.
144 *Verhandlungen des Reichstags*, 19 July 1917, p 3571.
145 Ludendorff, *Urkunden der OHL*, p 186; Rosenberg, *The Birth of the German Republic*, p 176.
146 Erzberger, for example, recognized that the vagueness of the resolution was intended to work to Germany's advantage. Prince Max von Baden recalled a conversation on the subject in which Erzberger explained: 'You see, Your Majesty, this way I get Longwy-Briey by negotiation!' Baden, *Erinnerungen*, p 114.

7 CIVILIANS 'FALL-IN'

1 Kitchen, *Silent Dictatorship*, p 22.
2 Kocka, *Facing Total War*, p 131.
3 K. Tschuppik, *Ludendorff. Die Tragödie des Fachmanns* (Vienna, 1931). See also his (second) wife's account in M. Ludendorff, *Als ich Ludendorff's Frau war* (Munich, 1929). Ludendorff met Mathilde von Kemnitz (nee Ludendorff), an eccentric religious philosopher in 1923, and together they founded the Tannenberg Bund in 1925 which propagated 'German religion' and was vehemently anti-Semitic. Brief, perceptive comments on Ludendorff can be found in Epstein, *Erzberger*, pp 157–8. For an analysis of Ludendorff's military conduct during the war see, R. Asprey, *The German High Command at War: Hindenburg and Ludendorff Conduct World War I* (New York, 1991).
4 Cf. Riezler's diary entry: 'The rising talents in the war, such as Ludendorff... immense energy, gross philistinism... ultimately an Americanised type-.... Hindenburg (by contrast)... completely a representative of Prussian particularism'. Riezler, *Tagebücher*, cited in Kocka, *Facing Total War*, p 134.
5 In his memoirs, Ludendorff equated Prussian militarism with 'unselfish loyalty to the conception of the State' and argued that it had been responsible for 'Germany's brilliant development'. However, during the war:

> People mistook externals for the substance of militarism, and failed to realize the national strength that issued from it. It should not have been resisted, but encouraged. Even high officials of the Government used the word reproachfully to me during the war, so that one can hardly blame the many who thought they were acting wisely in turning against 'militarism', even though they could not say

exactly what it meant. True, many of them knew perfectly well what they were after in this struggle. Authority was at stake!.
Ludendorff, *War Memories*, pp 447, 362.
6 Ibid, p 360.
7 MAF, RM3 Bd. 4, 10280, Minutes of talks between the Central Military and Civil Authorities, 20 November 1916.
8 Garnich included in this material: suitable war literature; books put together for this instructive purpose; suitable newspaper cuttings; and material from the *Deutschen Kriegsnachrichten* (DK) and leaflets from the state archives. Urged on by Deutelmoser at the Foreign Office, that DK should aim at the widest possible distribution, a number of representatives asked at the meeting for copies of the *Kriegsnachrichten* to be distributed in larger number to their sections for distribution. The meeting was much taken with shortening enemy army reports. Captain Bloem of the Field Press Office (*Feldpressstelle*) provided a summary of its activity and stressed that articles in the domestic press on all political and economic events had a restraining influence on the morale of the troops and called on the press to be more sensitive towards the fact that the mood at the Front is positively influenced by confident, up-beat articles – whereas reports on domestic conflict have a negative effect.
9 For an analysis of the strained relations between the OHL and civilian authorities on the question of propaganda see, D. Stegmann, 'Die deutsche Inlandspropaganda 1917/18. Zum innepolitischen Machtkampf zwischen OHL und ziviler Reichsleitung in der Endphase des Kaiserreichs', *Militärgeschichtliche Mitteilungen*, 12, (1972), pp 75–116.
10 Ludendorff, *Urkunden der OHL*, p 428.
11 The phrase was coined by the Berlin representative of the *Münchener Neueste Nachrichten* after the announcement of his appointment to the Chancellorship. *Münchener Neueste Nachrichten*, 15 July 1917.
12 The circular is dated 11 June 1917. Carsten, *War Against War*, p 152.
13 Blücher, *An English Wife*, p 179. There are isolated examples of resistance on the part of the clergy to German jingoism. For example in May 1916, clerics rejected the call from Württemberg officials to 'whip-up' renewed enthusiasm for the war, citing complaints from their parishioners that enlisted sons had received unequal treatment compared to the excessive privileges enjoyed by officers. Decree from the Württemberg Ministry of the Interior to Church and School Authorities and their roles in Enlightening the People, 8 May 1916: Deist, *Militär und Innenpolitik*, I, pp 306–7. For a dated but still important collection of essays see, O. Baumgarten *et al.*, *Geistige u. Sittliche Wandlungen des Krieges in Deutschland* (Stuttgart, 1927). See in particular, E. Forster, 'Die Stellung der evangelischen Kirche', pp 89–148. For more recent studies that analyse the churches in the wider propaganda process see, W. Pressel, *Die Kriegspredigt 1914 bis 1918 evangelischen Kirche Deutschlands* (Göttingen, 1967); H. Missalla, *Gott mit uns. Die deutsche Katholische Kriegspredigt 1914–18* (Munich 1968); G. Brakelmann, *Protestantische Kriegstheologie im Ersten*

Weltkreig: Reinhold Seeberg als Theologe des deutschen Imperialismus (Bielefeld, 1974); K. Meier, 'Evangelische Kirche und Erste Weltkrieg,' in W Michalka (ed.), *Der Erste Weltkrieg: Wirkung, Wahrnehmung, Analyse* (Munich and Zurich, 1994).

14 Michaelis was addressing the Main Committee of the Reichstag to outline the current military situation and to provide a 'gloss' on German war aims. The speech is reported in full in *Norddeutsche Allgemeine Zeitung*, 22 August 1917.

15 Wehler, *The German Empire* p 216. Tirpitz had resigned over Bethmann Hollweg's handling of unrestricted submarine warfare and spent the rest of the war campaigning vigorously for the annexationist and reactionary programme of the *Vaterlandspartei*.

16 The manifesto is printed in full in *Norddeutsche Allgemeine Zeitung*, 12 September 1917. See also Lutz, *Fall of the German Empire*, pp 368–70. Fascinating material on the founding of the *Vaterlandspartei* can be found in HSS, *Nachlass Haussmann*.

17 On the Fatherland Party see the recent monograph, H. Hagenlücke, *Deutsche Vaterlandspartei: Die nationale Rechte am Ende des Kaiserreiches* (Düsseldorf, 1997). On the politics of the right see, G. Eley, *Reshaping the German Right: Radical Nationalism and Political Change after Bismarck* (Ann Arbor, MI, 1991); J. Retallack, Notables of the Right: The Conservative Party and Political Mobilization in Germany, 1876–1918 (Boston, 1988); D. Stegmann, *Die Erben Bismarcks: Parteien und Verbände in der Spätphase des Wilhelminischen Deutschlands: Sammlungspolitik 1871–1918* (Cologne, 1970).

18 In April 1918, Princess Blücher cited a particularly poignant example of the power of the *Vaterlandspartei* and ruthlessness of its propaganda tactics. Secretary of State Richard von Kühlmann had just returned from Bucharest where he had been conducting peace negotiations. On his return to Berlin reports were already circulating throughout Germany that while in Bucharest he had inaugurated 'wild orgies' with smart Romanian ladies who were trying to influence him to make a weak peace for Germany. *An English Wife*, pp 214–15.

19 A sensitive synopsis of this debate can be found in Richard Evans, 'From Hitler to Bismarck: Third Reich and Kaiserreich in Recent Historiography' in Evans, *Rethinking German History*, (London, 1987), pp 55–92.

20 See, E.G. Reichmann, *Hostages of Civilisation* (Boston, 1951).

21 For an excellent account of the rise of anti-Semitism during the war see, W. Jochmann, 'Die Ausbreitung des Antisemitismus' in W.E. Mosse (ed.), *Deutsches Judentum in Krieg und Revolution 1916–1923* (Tübingen, 1971) pp 424–42. See also E. Zechlin, *Die deutsche Politik und die Juden im Ersten Weltkrieg* (Göttingen, 1969). Two more recent analyses can be found in, C. Picht, 'Zwischen Vaterland und Volk: Das deutsche Judentum im Ersten Weltkrieg,' in W Michalka (ed.), *Der Erste Weltkrieg: Wirkung, Wahrnehmung, Analyse* (Munich and Zurich, 1994) and C. Hoffmann, 'Between Integration and Rejection: The Jewish Community in Germany, 1914–1918,' in J. Horne (ed.), *State, Society and Mobilisation in Europe during the First World War* (Cambridge, 1997), pp 89–104.

22 Jochmann, 'Die Ausbreitung des Antisemitismus', pp 435–8; cited in Kocka. *Facing Total War*, p 124. In the end, however, the ministry decided against publishing its findings in order to keep the results of the Jew count (*'Judenzählung'*) from the public.
23 This was an outrageous suggestion but regional commanders failed to refute such allegations in their summaries of the reports. Even more alarming was the failure of the officials in the War Office to excise such comments from the edited accounts that were distributed to leading civil and military authorities. No doubt they reflected the attitudes and prejudices of staff within the War Office. Anti-Semitic comments become ever more virulent, especially towards the end of 1916. Cf *Monatsberichten* for September, November and December 1916 and February and March 1917. BHStA, MB, IV 155/85 Mkr, 12851.
24 Cf. the reaction to Haase's speech of 24 March 1916, cited in Ch 6, see Note 43.
25 Quoted in Wehler, *The German Empire*, p 219. For an example of anti-Semitic literature written by Class in 1912 see, Welch, *Modern European History*, pp 10–12.
26 Berghahn, *Modern Germany*, p 56. The *Vaterlandspartei* disappeared in the chaos of the revolution of 1918 and the trauma of military defeat, and disbanded on 10 December 1918.
27 F. Meinecke, *Autobiographische Schriften*, p 354, quoted in Wehler, *The German Empire*, p 218.
28 Blücher, *An English Wife*, p 182, entry for October 1917.
29 This evocative phrase is used by Philip Taylor in his introductory history to political propaganda. See, P.M. Taylor, *Munitions of the Mind. A History of Propaganda From the Ancient World to the Present Day* (Manchester, 1995).
30 Discussion between Central Military and Civilian Authorities in the Prussian War Ministry over Measures Taken to Counter Enemy Anti-Monarchy Propaganda, 25/26 May 1917, Deist, *Militär und Innenpolitik*, II, pp 824–34.
31 See Ch 6, Note 16.
32 Nicolai, *Nachrichtendienst*, p 119 ff. See the review of 1916 carried out by the War Press Office that hints at the ongoing conflict between military and civilian censorship agencies. MAS, M77/1 Bü. 60, Memorandum of 23 January 1917.
33 The government was particularly concerned to persuade SPD politicians that whenever they made speeches or wrote articles that they did so in the 'spirit of August 1914'.
34 Major Stotten reported that over 1,000 associations were helping the KPA in the campaign.
35 It was reported at the meeting that the President of the Reichstag had been instructed to counter a recent anti-monarchy statement made by Wilson in Congress with a strong supportive speech of his own. According to the minutes of the meeting he agreed to this 'willingly'.
36 Telegram from Legation Secretary Freiherr von Lersner to Secretary of State Zimmermann. General Ludendorff on How to Combat Anti-Monarchist

Propaganda, 29 April 1917, Deist, *Militär und Innenpolitik*, II, pp 813–14. The impossibility of a peace so long as the Kaiser remained in power in Germany was continually drawn to the attention of the German people. For an analysis of antimonarchist propaganda employed by the Allies see, Bruntz, *Allied Propaganda*, pp 130–41. See also Ch 8. Interestingly enough, the Allies employed similar tactics in the Second World War by attempting to convince the population that they were not at war with the German people, rather Hitler and Nazism. See, D. Welch, *The Third Reich. Politics and Propaganda* (London, 1995).

37 In 1987 a colloquium was held in Munich to define the place of Wilhelm II in German history. Sixteen papers were presented by distinguished historians of late nineteenth- and early twentieth-century German history. The essays were edited by John C. Röhl (ed.), *Der Ort Kaiser Wilhelms II in der deutschen Geschichte* (Munich: Oldenburg, 1991). A more convincing confirmation of continuities between Wilhelmine Germany and the Nazis can be found not in a biography of the Kaiser but of August von Mackensen. See, T. Schwartzmüller, *Zwischen Kaiser und 'Führer'. Generalfeldmarschall August von Mackensen* (Paderborn, 1995).

38 John Röhl has recently compiled a number of his essays that attempt to analyse the nature of power in Wilhelmine Germany, including a new essay on the Kaiser's anti-Semitism. Röhl, *The Kaiser and his Court. Wilhelm II and the Government of Germany* (Cambridge, 1995). See also, W Gutsche, *Wilhelm II: Der letzte Kaiser des Deutschen Reiches* (Berlin, 1991); L. Cecil, *William II: Emperor and Exile, 1900–1941* (Chapel Hill, NC, 1996).

39 Marwick first constructed the 'four-tier model' some years ago as a framework for analysing the impact of war on different societies. A. Marwick, *War and Social Change in the Twentieth Century. A Comparative Study of Britain, France, Germany, Russia and the United States* (London, 1974). Interestingly enough, the *Büro für Sozialpolitik* claimed in July 1917 that the Kaiser still retained the support of large sections of the community. MAS, MI/3, 495, *Büro für Sozialpolitik*, 21 July 1917.

40 BHStA, MB, IV 155/85 Mkr, 12851, July 1917. At the end of June a half-hearted 'assassination' attempt was censored by the War Press Office. Apparently a drunkard had thrown an object against the Kaiser's car and damaged a headlight. BHStA, MB, IV 155/85 Mkr, 12851, 14 July 1917; Daniel, *War from Within*, p 245.

41 Blücher, *An English Wife*, entry for June/July 1917, p 176. By the January 1918, Blücher was moved to write:

> 'The feeling towards the Kaiser is steadily diminishing in loyalty and respect, and some people who greeted him so warmly a short time ago with 'Ave, Caesar!' are now distributing leaflets in the back streets of Berlin proclaiming, 'Down with the Kaiser, down with the Government,' and the police, when called upon to suppress the evil-doers, refuse to act, and are more than suspected of being behind the movement themselves,

Ibid, entry for January 1918, p 190.

42 Quoted by Hanssen, *Diary of a Dying Empire*, entry for 10 July 1917, p 226.
43 The Sixth War Loan period of subscription was 15 March to 16 April. For details of the advertising campaign see, MAF, RM3/v, 10323 (*Propaganda für die Kreigsanleihe*).
44 The Erler poster was produced in three different sizes and also as a postcard. For brief descriptions of these and other German posters see, J. Darracott and B. Loftus, *First World War Posters* (London, IWM, 1972) and P. Paret, B. Irwin Lewis and P. Paret, *Persuasive Images. Posters of War and Revolution* (Princeton, 1992).
45 MAF, RM3/v, 10324, 21 March 1917.
46 A new feature associated with the Sixth War Loan was the national coalition of theatres who gave receipts for one day to the appeal. *Continental Times*, 16 April 1917. Copies of the paper can be found in MAF, RM 5/V, 3770 (*Propaganda Allgemeines*).
47 For a brief, but perceptive discussion of this 'resistance' see, Daniel, *War From Within*, pp 253–5.
48 MAS, M77/1, Bü. 60, Memorandum from War Press Office to Military Office in the Homeland, 13 January 1917.
49 Cf. report from OHL to the War Ministry, BHStA, Kr, MKr, 11484, 5 June 1917. For an example of how rumours of alleged increased food provision in certain parts of the country could 'trigger' civil disturbances in regions who felt that they were being deprived see, MAF, MB. RM3, Bd. 2, 4670, 3 April 1917.
50 MAF, RM5, Bd. 2, 3820, Order of the Chief of the General Staff of the Field Army to the Highest Commanding Authorities of the Field Army. Guiding Principles for the Patriotic Education for the Troops, 29 July 1917. The following information is taken from this document. In his memoirs, Ludendorff wrote that the original proposal had come from Nicolai, Ludendorff, *My War Memories*, p 460.
51 MAS, 77/1, 63, Order of the Chief of the General Staff of the Field Army to the High Command of the Army Groups about the Arrangements for an educational organization for the Field Army, 17 July 1917.
52 At this stage, Ludendorff used the terms 'patriotic instructions' and 'patriotic education' as interchangeable. This would change after 15 September 1917 when 'education' was substituted for 'propaganda'. See below, Note 76.
53 See memorandum of 25 July 1917, signed by Quartermaster-General, Hahndorff, MAS, M77/1, Bü. 63. See also, Ludendorff, *The General Staff and Its Problems*, II, pp, 392–3. One of its recommendations was that Commanding Generals should use the powers bestowed to them by the Chief of the General Staff to censor letters 'creatively' in order to gain an insight into the 'currents of opinion among troops'.
54 For 'official' German responses to the torrent of Allied propaganda see files in the Military Archive, Freiburg, MAF, RM5 (*Admiralstab der Marine*) V, 3769–3771.
55 The War Press Office acted as a conduit, receiving information and forwarding it via five channels: (a) the organs of the War Press Office (*Deutsche*

Wochenschau and *Deutsche Kriegsnachrichten;* (b) pamphlets; (c) The Field Press Office at Charleville, for articles and information from the occupied areas in the west; (d) photographs and posters 'such as the troops are likely to understand'; (e) leaflets from aircraft. The 'directors of propaganda' were instructed to keep the War Press Office informed of their experiences and for its part the War Press Office collated this information and circulated 'Hints on Patriotic Propaganda' to all units.

56 It was stipulated that for propaganda among the troops the material was disseminated by: (a) lectures, evening talks, field cinemas and theatrical performances, for which the Military Department of the Foreign Office provided material through the War Press Office; (b) the chaplains; (c) Army newspapers, particularly the *Mitteilungen für den vaterländischen Unterricht* a broadsheet specifically designed to disseminate 'patriotic instructions' and distributed to troops at the front and the homeland. A detailed analysis of this publication warrants further study as it covered every conceivable topic and provides an extraordinary insight into the military mind. A collection of the *Mitteilungen* can be found in, MAS, M77/1, Bü. 63. For interesting related material, see MAS, Ml/3, Bü. 501/561; (d) Field libraries; (e) Field bookstalls under the direction the education officer.

57 See memorandum of 25 July 1917, signed by Quartermaster-General, Hahndorff, MAS, M77/1, Bü. 63. See also, Ludendorff, *The General Staff and Its Problems*, II, pp, 392–3.

58 Cf. the similarities between these ideas and Hitler's thinking on propaganda which he outlined in two chapters in *Mein Kampf*. For an analysis of Hitlerite principles of propaganda see, Welch, *The Third Reich*, pp 10–13.

59 The letter, headed 'personal' is dated 31 July 1917 and was sent to all commanding officers and senior Divisional General Staff officers. Ludendorff, *Urkunden*, pp 278–9; Ludendorff, *The General Staff*, pp 398–9; Deist, *Militär und Innenpolitik*, I, pp 332–4.

60 MAS, M I/3, 1001, Directives for 'Patriotic Instruction' in the area for the Deputy Commanding General of 14th Army Corps, 15 December 1917.

61 MAS, M I/3, 498–500, contains numerous examples of such material. Two examples of recommended reading provide a flavour of the jingoistic literature; H. Beier *Vom Bismarck zum Weltkrieg* and K. Dietrich, *Wir wollen sein ein einzig Volk und Brüdern*. On the home front, librarians were recording that the public were no longer reading books on the war, but were much more interested in books on gardening! Moyer, *Victory Must Be Ours*, p 222. See also MAS, MI/II (*Kriegsarchiv*), 1084, *Volksaufklärung während des Weltkriegs 1914/18* which contains a wealth of material relating to *Vaterländische Unterrichts*. One of the criticisms levelled at the alleged failure of German propaganda in World War I was that military and civil authorities failed to invest enough money in the propaganda campaigns. A recurring theme in the *Kriegsarchiv* (1084) folder is how little speakers were paid and the bureaucratic zeal, with which officials attempted to recover the smallest of sums. All this at a vital stage in the war!

62 StA.P., *Bericht des Berliner Polizeipräsidenten*, 85, 2398/10, 18 June 1917.

63 G. Grosz, *Ein kleines Ja und ein grosses Nein. Sein Leben vom ihm selbst erzählt* (Reinbek, 1974), p 101; cited in Daniel, *The War From Within*, p 233. The War Ministry was particularly concerned during this period at the anti-war activities of the German Socialist Youth Movement. Not only was this radical youth group distributing anti-war pamphlets urging 'German youth, men and women' to undertake direct action and become 'Soldiers of the Revolution' but it was also planning a demonstration against the war on 2 and 3 September 1917. See surveillance details outlined in MAS, M 1/3, War Ministry to Commander-in-Chief in the Marks and all Authorities, 23 August 1917.

64 MAF, RM5, Bd. 2, 3722, Extract from the Minutes of the War Press Office concerning the Discussion between Military and Civilian Authorities and the 'Education Officer' for the Deputy General Command re: Propaganda Questions', 7–10 August, 1917. See also, Lutz, *Fall of the German Empire*, pp 120–31. In September Ludendorff confirmed that encouragement to invest in war loans should be included among the aims of patriotic education: 'Patriotic instruction and war-loan propaganda are working for the same end. Unity of aim and a tendency to supplement each other's efforts will be the natural result'. MAF, RM5, Bd. 2,3820, Chief of General Staff to the Highest Commanding Authorities of the Field Army. Re; the organization of 'Patriotic Instruction', 15 September 1917.

65 Hindenburg was used in ephemeral material for the Seventh War Loan. Postcards of the Field Marshal were bought for 10 pfg and posters and picture memories (*Errinerungsblatt*) for 50 pfg. For examples see, MAS, M77/1, Bü. 63, 2 October 1917 – the day of Hindenburg's birthday. For an analysis of German postcards as propaganda and the role of advertising see, R. Lebeck and M. Schütte, *Propagandapostkarten* (Dortmund, 1980).

66 Examples taken from, HSS, M 704 (*Archiv-Verzeichnis der Licht- und Frontbildersammlung*.

67 For reviews of the films see, *Kinematograph*, 561, 26 September 1917; *Der Film*, 29 September 1917. In fact the film was so successful that it was re-released in 1918 to promote the Ninth War Loan. Porten together with other movie stars, such as Asta Nielson and Paul Wegener, would frequently appear in public to promote war loans.

68 For an illuminating account of changing sexual conduct during the war see, Daniel, *The War From Within*, pp 138–57. For the relationship between German women and prisoners of war see, Chr, Beck (ed.) *Die Frau und die Kriegsgefangenen*, vol I pt 2: Die deutsche Frau und die fremden Kriegsgefangenen (Nürnberg, 1919).

69 Examples of all the incidents cited can be found of all MAS, MI/II (*Kriegsarchiv*), 1084, *Volksaufklärung während des Weltkriegs 1914/18*. See also below Note 89.

70 MAF, RM3, Bd. 4, 9901, Record of the Meeting Concerning the Foundation of *Universum-Film-Aktiengesellschaft* (Ufa), 30 January 1918.

71 Cf. account of the foundation of Ufa in *Vössische Zeitung*, 31 December 1917.

72 Major van den Bergh of the Prussian war Ministry set out these tasks as follows: (1) to remove foreign influence, so that the needs of the German film market

are covered mainly by the German film industry; (2) the dissemination of propaganda at home and abroad for the OHL and the political authorities; (3) the raising of the whole German film industry on to a higher level and in connection with this the implementation of national educational and ethical exercises. The record of the meeting is published in full in, D. Welch, 'A Medium for the Masses: Ufa and Imperial German film Propaganda during the First World War', *Historical Journal of Film, Radio and Television*, vol. 6, no. 1 (1986) pp 85–91.

73 See Ch 2 for further discussion of Deulig and Bufa.
74 The state was not a direct shareholder but three banks were put forward to act as a front on its behalf. The interests of the state were safeguarded by its influence over the compilation of the management committee and the board of directors and by establishing its right to intervene in matters it chose. Interestingly enough, Goebbels employed similar tactics when the Nazis took over the film industry in the 1940s. See, Welch, *Propaganda and the German Cinema, 1933–1945* (Oxford, 1983).
75 For the history of Ufa see, K. Kreimeier, *The Ufa Story. A History of Germany's Greatest Film Company 1918–1945* (New York, 1996).
76 MAF, RM5, Bd. 2, 3820, Chief of General Staff to the Highest Commanding Authorities of the Field Army. Re; the organization of 'Patriotic Instruction', 15 September 1917.
77 *Verhandlungen der Württembergischen Zweiten Kammer*, 22 June 1917, p 4440 in Dahlin, *French and German Public Opinion*, p 290.
78 See speech by Keil (SPD), ibid, p 4447. See also debate in the Bavarian Landtag, *Verhandlungen der Kammer der Abgeordneten des bayerischen Landtags*, 25 October 1917.
79 For the debate, see *Verhandlungen des Reichstags*, 6 October 1917, pp 3713–3765.
80 For Landsberg's speech, see *Verhandlungen des Reichstags*, 6 October pp 3714–23; see also, Lutz, *Fall of the German Empire*, pp 132–8.
81 *Verhandlungen des Reichstags*, 9 October 1917, pp 3813 ff.
82 See H. Herwig, *The German Naval Officer Corps: A Social and Political History 1890–1918* (Oxford, 1973). See also, Deist, *Militär und Innenpolitik*, II, pp 996 ff.
83 In fact Hertling had been suggested as the successor to Bethmann Hollweg in July. See, E. Deuerlein (ed.), *Briefwechsel Hertling-Lerchenfeld*, 2 vols (Boppard, 1973).
84 War Press Office to Bavarian War Ministry, 19 September 1917, BHStA, Kr, MKr 2335; Daniel, *The War From Within*, p 252.
85 MAF, MB. RM3, Bd. 2, 3 August 1917. The report claimed that women and adolescents in particular were impervious to the government's attempts at manipulation.
86 Ludendorff drew attention to this 'syllabus' in a memorandum of 14 November 1917, Ludendorff, *The General Staff*, p 397. For the 'syllabus' itself see minutes of the meetings which runs to 55 pages!, MAF, RM5/v, Bd. 2, 3821. The meeting of 4 November 1917 took place at Charleville and moved the following day to

GHQ. See also the new directives for the 'patriotic instruction', 15 December 1917, Deist, *Militär und Innenpolitik*, II, pp 889–93.
87 MAS, M I/3, 498, War Press Office to the Württemberg War Ministry, 30 May 1917.
88 Atrocity stories committed against German POW's was intended to 'stiffen' morale. For an example of suffering German officers in a French POW camp see, MAS, M I/3, *498*, undated drawings. Further examples can be found in, MAS, MI/II (*Kriegsarchiv*), 1084, *Volksaufklärung während des Weltkriegs 1914/18*.
89 L. Lewinsohn, *Die Revolution an der Westfront* (Charlottenburg, 1919), Forward. For examples of complaints to various aspects of 'patriotic instruction' see, MAS, M I/3, 561, Chief of the General Staff re: 'Patriotic Instruction', 7 October 1918.
90 For Ludendorff's generally favourable verdict of the War Press Office see, Ludendorff, *War Memories*, pp 375–6. Ludendorff was also favourably disposed to the work of the Deputy Commanding Generals but accused the civilian government of failing to support 'patriotic instruction' by remaining 'absolutely aloof' from the programme, p 464.
91 In his memoirs Ludendorff claimed that 'patriotic instruction' was the OHL's attempt to repair the damage caused by weak Chancellors who failed to provide leadership. According to Ludendorff, as the 'soul of the nation' was bereft of political leadership the military's patriotic instruction campaigns were 'mere crumbs to the hungry'. Ludendorff, *War Memories*, p 371.

8 DEFEAT AND REVOLUTION

1 Complaints about the patriotic instruction programme were numerous. They covered everything from lack of suitable speakers, not enough talks on patriotic themes or venues, and lack of sufficient funding. See, MAS, M I/3, 561 which contains files of complaints up to October 1918.
2 See, Carsten, *War Against War*, pp 143–166.
3 *Berliner Tageblatt*, 25 December 1917, in Moyer, *Victory Must be Ours*, p 228.
4 Erich Volkmann, quoted in A. Niemann, *Revolution von Oben, Umsturz von Unden* (Berlin, 1927) p 54. Niemann was quoting from Volkmann's study, *Der Marxism und das deutsche Heer im Weltkrieg*. See also, Bruntz, *Allied Propaganda*, p 187.
5 For background information see, Epstein, *Matthias Erzberger*, pp 233–5.
6 Fischer, *Griff nach der Weltmacht*, p 671.
7 The final settlement at Brest-Litovsk removed Russia from the war, thereby fulfilling one of Lenin's promises to the Russian people when the Bolsheviks seized power in the October Revolution of 1917. However, the price that Lenin was forced to pay by the OHL was high. Under the terms of the Treaty of Brest-Litovsk Russia agreed: (1) to give up Poland, Courland and Lithuania, and to let Germany and Austria determine the future status of these territories under the principle of self-determination; (2) to evacuate Livonia, Estonia, Finland and the

Asland Islands; (3) to evacuate Ukraine and to recognize the treaty signed by the Ukrainian People's Republic and the Central Powers; (4) to surrender to Turkey Ardahan, Kars and Batum; (5) to discontinue all Bolshevik propaganda in the territory of the Central Powers and in the territories ceded by the treaty. Bilateral supplementary treaties concluded in August detached Estonia and Livonia from Russia, which was to pay 6 billion marks in reparations. See, J. Wheeler-Bennett, *Brest Litovsk. The Forgotten Peace*, (London, 1938); W. Hahlweg (ed.), *Lenins Rückkehr nach Russland 1917, Die deutschen Akten* (Leiden, 1957); W. Baumgart, *Deutsche Ostpolitik 1918. Von Brest-Litovsk bis zum Ende des Ersten Weltkrieges* (Vienna, Munich, 1966); W. Baumgart (ed.), *Brest-Litovsk: Ausgewählt und eingeleitet von Winfried Baumgart und Konrad Repgen* (Göttingen, 1969); H.E. Volkmann, *Die deutsche Baltikumpolitik zwischen Brest-Litovsk und Compiègne: Ein Beitrag zur 'Kriegszieldiskussion'* (Cologne, 1970).
8 Blücher, *An English Wife*, p 185.
9 *Verhandlungen des Reichstags*, 20 February 1918, pp 4034–8 and 27 February 1918, pp 4208–12. The debate of 20 February was ostensibly to discuss the Ukrainian peace and dealings that had taken place between the Ukrainians and the Bolsheviks.
10 For an excellent discussion of the internal differences between the OHL and the civilian government see, Kitchen, *Silent Dictatorship*, pp 157–84.
11 Hanssen, *Diary of a Dying Empire*, pp 247–8. For an example of how the press were to report the negotiations at Brest-Litovsk see, Instructions from the War Press Office, 18 January 1918: Deist, *Militär und Innenpolitik*, II, pp 1129–30.
12 Russia lost 50 per cent of its industry and 90 per cent of its coal mines. Under a separate treaty signed in February, Austria–Hungary received 50 per cent, Germany 30 per cent and Bulgaria and Turkey 20 per cent of Ukraine's grain reserves.
13 Quoted in H. Herwig, *The First World War*, p 382.
14 On 7 May, the Treaty of Bucharest was signed that effectively reduced Romania to a German vassal state.
15 The speech is published in full and analysed in D. Welch, *Modern European History. A Documentary Reader, 1871–2000* (London, 1999), pp 81–87.
16 The ex-Kaiser's concern was that the Treaties of Brest-Litovsk and Bucharest should not be compared to the Treaty of Versailles:

> They were concluded in the very midst of war and had to include conditions which would guarantee our safety until the end of the war. Had it come to a general peace, the treaty made by us in the East would have had a far different aspect; had we won the war, we should ourselves have revised it. At the time when it was made it was necessary to give preference to military requirements.'
> Ex-Kaiser William II, *My Memoirs*, p 328.

17 A.J.P. Taylor, *The First World War: An Illustrated History* (London/New York), p 214. Before the war, Karl Radek had been actively engaged in Bremen's radical Social Democratic faction and later for Lenin's Swiss–internationalist exile

group. See, K. Radek, *In den Reihen der deutschen Revolution 1909–1919* (Munich, 1921).

18   In Bavaria a *Monatsberichte* claimed that large sections of the community in Bavaria held the Pan-Germans and the *Vaterlandspartei* responsible for the breakdown of peace negotiations. Ay, *Entstehung*, p 132.

19   *Verhandlungen des Reichstags*, 27 February 1918, p 4216.

20   The Berlin shop stewards were no doubt influenced by the wave of strikes that had recently taken place in Vienna and Budapest forcing a war-weary Austria–Hungary government to agree to the worker's peace programme and to concede to their other demands. See also F. Opel, *Der deutsche Metallarbeitverband* (Hanover, 1957).

21   The leaflet was printed in large quantities and distributed throughout Germany. L. Stern (ed.), *Die Auswirkungen der grossen sozialistischen Oktoberrevolution auf Deutschland*, (Berlin, 1959), vol 4/III, No. 334, p 953.

22   Berlin remained very much the centre for the strike movement, although strikes occurred in a number of cities including Hamburg, Nürnberg, Mannheim, Danzig, Breslau, Dortmund, Magdeburg and Ludwigshaven. The Berlin police reports can be found in, *Dokumente aus geheimen Archiven 4: Bericht des Berliner Polizeipräsidenten zur Stimmung und Lage der Bevölkerung in Berlin 1914–18*, eds I. Materna and H.-J. Schreckenbach (Weimar, 1987), pp 242–65 ff.

23   This estimate was for the 28 January. *Vorwärts* claimed that 250,000 workers were on strike in the afternoon and they were joined by a further 50,000 from the night shift. The paper also produced a breakdown of the factories affected. Especially hard hit were the Schwartzkopf, the General Electric Company, Goerz, Daimler and Auer. *Vorwärts*, 29 January 1918, p 1.

24   *Vorwärts*, 29 January 1918. The following day the Hamburg shipyard workers (not all of whom were on strike) put forward demands for improved food and working conditions. See, *Vossische Zeitung*, 2 February 1918.

25   Hanssen, *Diary of a Dying Empire*, p 259. For an example of an appeal on behalf of the National Workers' and Professional Union see, Bruntz, *Allied Propaganda*, pp 182–3.

26   Klein put the average caloric intake for 1918 lower at 1,100 calories, largely as a result of the absence of fats. Klein, *Deutschland im Ersten Weltkrieg*, 2, pp 633–4. Hanssen, *Diary of a Dying Empire*, pp 258–9.

27   Haase, Ledebour and Dittmann joined from the USPD and somewhat reluctantly Ebert, Scheidemann and Braun for the SPD. The fact that both parties delegated such important political figures testifies to the importance they attached to the strike. Hertling agreed to meet with trade union leaders provided that none of them were strikers.

28   Cf. statement of the executive committee of the SPD, *Vorwärts*, 2 February 1918.

29   *Berliner Lokalanzeiger*, 1 February 1918.

30   *Norddeutscher Allgemeine Zeitung*, 2 February 1918.

31   The Prussian Minister of War to the Kaiser, 5 February 1918: Deist, *Militär und Innenpolitik*, II, p 1157–63.

32 Commander-in-Chief in the Marks to the Kaiser, 6 February 1918: Deist, *Militär und Innenpolitik*, II, pp 1164–6.
33 Dittmann had been speaking to the strikers in one of Berlin's parks. As he was caught *in flagranti* he was not covered by his parliamentary immunity. For the background to Dittmann's arrest see, Carsten, *War Against War*, p 135.
34 Letter from the Deputy Commanding General of 3rd Army Corps to 14th Army Corps, 6 February 1918: Deist, *Militär und Innenpolitik*, II, pp 1169–70. According to E. Barth, *Aus der Werkstatt der deutschen Revolution* (Berlin, 1919) p 23, 40–50,000 strikers were called up in Berlin alone. In their military records, they were classified simply as 'Berlin 1918'. See S. Bailey, 'The Berlin Strike of January 1918,' *Central European History*, 13 (1980), pp 158–74. For a discussion of the wider ramifications of the January strikes and the labour movement in Berlin see, D. Geary, 'Revolutionary Berlin 1917–20' in C. Wrigley (ed.), *Challenges of Labour. Central and Western Europe 1917–1920* (London, 1993) pp 24–50. See also, W. Kruse, 'Sozialismus, Antikriegsbewegungen, Revolutionen,' in Kruse, (ed.), *Eine Welt von Feinden*, pp 196–226.
35 Letter from the Deputy Commanding General of 3rd Army Corps to 14th AK Unit, 6 February 1918: Deist, *Militär und Innenpolitik*, II, pp 1169–70.
36 Examples can be found in MAF, RM3, Bd. 4, 10317 (*Kriegspressamt*) and RM3, Bd. 4, *10325 (Kriegsaufklärung)*. For examples of the anti-strike propaganda used in the army see, Statement of Bavarian War Ministry, 24/30 March 1918: Deist, *Militär und Innenpolitik*, pp II, 932–5.
37 *Vorwärts*, 16 February 1918. Hanssen noted in his diary that rumours circulating in Stuttgart suggested that 16 workers had been killed and 60 wounded! *Diary of a Dying Empire*, p 260.
38 Pertinent documents can be found in MAF, RM5, Bd. 2, 3833–4 (*Volksaufklarung: Vorbeugung von Streiks*) Cf. also the the important discussion that took place between civilian and military representatives on 18 February and the reports of the War Ministries of 19 February 1918 which set out how the strikes and ring-leaders were to be 'sloganised' in all official statements. MAF, *RM3, Bd. 4, 4655*. It was reported that on one occasion the police had been forced by left-wing demonstrators to close down a meeting of the *Vaterlandspartei*. See also Deist, *Militär und Innenpolitik*, pp II, 1139 ff.
39 *Verhandlungen des Reichstages*, 26 February, pp 4162–71.
40 *Verhandlungen des Reichstages*, 26 February, pp 4171–5.
41 The military continued to use their powers under the 'state of siege' to suppress workers. In March, for example, the Berlin Metal Workers' Union was forbidden to hold a ballot to call for an extraordinary general meeting. Commander-in-Chief of the Marks to Director of Berlin Police, 9 March 1918, MAS, M 77/1, Bu. 64. See also, Deist, *Militär und Innenpolitik*, II, p 1202.
42 Although over 1 million soldiers remained in the East to police the occupied territories.
43 In 1937 the Nazis eulogized the military offensive in one of their most famous feature films *Unternehmen Michael* (Operation Michael). In the film a Commanding General remarks to a major in charge of a doomed assault unit: 'Posterity

will remember us not only by the greatness of our victory but by the measure of our sacrifice!'. See, D. Welch, *Propaganda and the German Cinema 1933–1945* (Oxford, 1983), p 189.

44 Herwig, *The First World War*, p 392. A number of Commanding Generals had serious reservations that Germany could sustain such an offensive including Colonel von Thaer who referred to it as 'the last card'. See, A. von Thaer, *Generalstabsdienst an der Front und in der OHL. Aus Breifen und Tagebuchaufzeichnungen*, ed. S. Kaehler (Göttingen, 1958), p 169. For the morale of the soldiers see, R. Hoffmann, (ed.) *Der deutsche Soldat: Briefe aus dem Weltkrieg: Vermächtnis* (Munich, 1937).

45 Riezler, *Tagebücher*, p 459–60, entry dated 15 April 1918. Nevertheless, just before the offensive began soldiers were showered with leaflets reassuring them that the Kaiser was 'at the scene of operations'.

46 BAK, *Nachlass Bauer*, quoted in Herwig, *The First World War*, p 381.

47 M. Middlebrook, *The Kaiser's Battle: 21 March 1918: The First Day of the German Spring Offensive* (London, 1978) p 349. To commemorate the early advances the Kaiser presented Hindenburg with the Iron Cross with Golden Rays, a decoration last given to General Blücher for ridding Prussia of Napoleon I. The Allies responded with a leaflet campaign that asked the German troops:

> What has he given you? Suffering, poverty, hunger for women and children, misery, pestilence and tomorrow the grave! They say you are fighting for the Fatherland – but what is your Fatherland? Is it Hindenburg, who with Ludendorff is many kilometers behind the front lines, making more plans to give the English more cannon-fodder?. Bruntz, *Allied Propaganda*, p 138.

48 Cf. the headlines in *Berliner Lokal-Anzeiger* and *Norddeutsche Allgemeine Zeitung* for 25 March 1918. Blücher recorded in her diary: 'The great offensive has begun, and the newspaper headings all speak of a great German victory. The whole town (Berlin) is being flagged and the bells are ringing'. Blücher, *An English Wife*, p 207.

49 W. Görlitz, (ed.) *The Kaiser and His Court: The Dairies, Note Books, and Letters of Admiral Georg Alexander von Müller Chief of the Naval Cabinet, 1914–1918* (New York, 1961) pp 344–5, entries for 25 and 26 March 1918.

50 Baumgart, *Deutsche Ostpolitik 1918*, p 132; Kitchen, *Silent Dictatorship*, p 199; Herwig, *The First World War*, p 384.

51 Both Ludendorff's letter and von Haeften's draft proposal can be found in, Ludendorff, *The General Staff*, pp 403–10.

52 Cited in D. Grosser, *Die monarchischen Konstitutionalismus zur parlamentarischen Demokratie. Die Verfassungspolitik der deutschen Parteien im letzten Jahrzehn des Kaiserreiches* (The Hague, 1970) pp 00–00 Ludendorff claimed that he 'begged' Hertling to create a Propaganda Ministry arguing that:

> Lord Northcliffe was not wrong when he claimed that the speech of an English stateman was worth £20,000; if it was copied in the German Press it was worth £50,000; if the Germans did not reply to it it was worth £100,000. We made no effective reply to the barrage of speeches from enemy statesmen, still less did

we think of repressing them. The campaign against these speeches could not be organized by the military branch of the Foreign Office, nor could it be done by any body, save an imperial department possessing special powers.

Ludendorff, *My War Memories*, pp 382–3.

53 Hertling's reply to Haeften, 26 March 1918: Ludendorff, *The General Staff*, pp 410–11. According to Ludendorff, the Foreign Office had continually blocked OHL's requests for a strong propaganda organization. Cf. Ludendorff, *My War Memories*, p 380. Although Haeften's MAA (Military Liaison Office to the Foreign Office) was notionally still under the ambit of the Foreign Office, it had, since January 1917, come under the control of the OHL. In July 1918 its title changed to *Auslandsabteilung den Obersten Heerslietung* (OHLA).

54 Cf. Ludendorff, *My War Memories*, p 464. When the *Vaterländischen Unterricht* programme was being established, the OHL placed considerable faith in the power of soldiers to encourage the home front to 'hold out'. So much so that the 'more educated' soldiers were selected to take special leave to spread the gospel of *Durchhalten* (holding out). Mai, 'Aufklärung', p 215; Daniel, *War From Within*, p 254.

55 Bavaria was the exception to the rule having established in 1916 its own propaganda organization within the Bavarian Ministry of the Interior largely independent of the Deputy Commanding Generals. Not surprisingly, this arrangement remained a source of some friction with Section IIIb of the OHL. See, Nicolai, *Nachrichtendienst*, pp 113–35; Ay, *Entstehung*, pp 61–5.

56 Taken from a forward to one of the first editions in May 1918: cited in Bruntz, *Allied Propaganda*, p 199.

57 *Verhandlungen des Reichstages*, 26 February 1918, pp 4172–3.

58 For a detailed analysis of British anti-German propaganda see, M. Sanders and P.M. Taylor, *British Propaganda During the First World War, 1914–18* (London, 1982), pp 134–6, 214–45. This work remains unsuperseded in its analysis of British organization and propaganda content. For examples of revolutionary agitation in Germany see, E. Drahn and S. Leonhard, *Unterirdisches Literatur im revolutionären Deutschland während des Weltkreiges* (Berlin, 1920).

59 Leaflet A.P. 18, Bruntz, *Allied Propaganda*, p 133. The British and French also exacerbated tensions that existed between Bavarians and Prussians by suggesting that Bavarians were simply prolonging the war to serve Prussian militarists and Junkers. See, Lutz, *Fall of the German Empire*, p 159.

60 General Order of 18th Army Corps from von Hurtier, 29 August 1918: Lutz, *Fall of the German Empire*, pp 162–3.

61 *Norddeutsche Allgemeine Zeitung*, 5 September 1918, p 1. Hindenburg made this claim in his Manifesto to the German People, which is discussed below. However, the number of leaflets handed in were but a fraction of those distributed by the Allies. For example, the number of leaflets dropped over and behind German lines by balloon totalled 1,689,457 in June and 2,172,794 in July. This figure rose to 5,360,000 in October. After the war the British government claimed that unrest in Germany was caused by British Propaganda: 'this propaganda used as

ammunition... not lies but solely the truth'. CAB 24/75, GT 6839: Sanders and Taylor, *British Propaganda*, p 237.
62 *Leipziger Volkszeitung*, 23 February 1918.
63 *Vorwärts*, 9 May 1918.
64 For examples see, Bruntz, *Allied Propaganda*, pp 85–129; for an analysis of the strategy that lay behind the propaganda campaigns aimed at Germany see, Sanders and Taylor, *British Propaganda*, pp 208–45.
65 K. von Vetter, *Der Zusammenbruch der Westfront. Ludendorff ist schuld! Die Anklage der Feldgrauen* (Berlin, 1919) p 8.
66 'Wir kämpfen nicht für Deutschlands Ehr – Wir kämpfen für die Millionare', cited in Bruntz, *Allied Propaganda*, p 204.
67 Cf BHStA, MB, IV, MKr, IV, 155/85, 12853, Reports for April 1918.
68 See *Mittielungen für den vaterländischen Unterrricht*, No. 11, 6 March 1918.
69 Princess Blücher noted that 'the so-called victories have been painted in glowing colours, for "dressing-up" the war loan'. Blücher, *An English Wife*, p 211, entry for April 1918.
70 One of the features of life in Berlin during this period was the sight of pale faces collecting outside the War Ministry in the Dorotheaen Strasse to glimpse the fresh list of casualty figures that were posted daily. See, Blücher, *An English Wife*, p 209.
71 Thaer, *Generalstabsdienst an der Front*, p 188. Entry for 2 May 1918. Cf. also the highly critical comments to be found in, General von Kuhl, MAF, *Kriegstagebuch v. Kuhl;* Kronprinz Rupprecht von Bayern, *Mein Kriegstagebuch*, (ed.) E. v. Frauenholz (3 vols. Berlin, 1929) especially vol 3. Ludendorff continued to defend his tactics to the official historians in the inter-war years. Cf. *Der Weltkrieg 1914 bis 1918*, 14, p 679.
72 Hanssen, *Diary of a Dying Empire*, pp 274–5, entry for 21 April 1918.
73 *Vorwärts*, 19 September 1918.
74 E. Tobin, 'War and the Working Class', p 287. For estimates of the scale of black markets operating in the summer of 1918 see, R. Meerwarth *et al., Die Einwirkung des Krieges auf Bevölkerungsbewegung, Einkommen und Lebenshaltung in Deutschland* (Stuttgart, 1932), pp 440–2.
75 Klein, *Deutschland im Ersten Weltkrieg*, 3, p 493; cited in Moyer, *Victory Must Be Ours*, p 290.
76 Kocka, *Facing Total War*, pp 99, 83. See also the report sent by the Police President of Berlin to the Kaiser on 29 October 1918. Oppen to Wilhelm II, 29 October 1918. Materna and Schreckenbach (eds), *Dokumente aus geheimen Archiven*. 4, pp 297–303.
77 For a revealing account of the declining morale of the *Mittelstand* see, MB for 3 May 1918, MAF, MB, RM3/7795. Cf. F. Winters, *Die Deutsche Beamtenfrage*, Berlin, 1920 and F. Falkenberg, *Die Deutsche Beamtenbewegung nach der Revolution* (Berlin, 1920. See also, Kocka, *Facing Total War*, pp 98–101.
78 Blücher, *An English Wife*, p 225.
79 Materna and Schreckenbach (eds), *Dokumente aus geheimen Archiven 4*, pp 277–8.

80 *Verhandlungen des Reichstages*, 24 June 1918, pp 5607–12. The text of the speech can also be found in *Berliner Tageblatt*, 25 June 1918.
81 *Verhandlungen des Reichstages*, 24 June 1918, pp 5635–7. For public reaction to Kühlmann's two speeches see, BHStA, MB, IV, MKr, IV, 155/85, 12853, Reports for 3 July 1918. Hans Peter Hanssen recorded: '...Dr Wiesener of the *Frankfurter Zeitung* said that the Secretary of State had stayed with the truth, but that his speech certainly would cause a loss of morale throughout the land. This was the general opinion'. Hanssen, *Diary of a Dying Empire*, p 287, entry for 24 June 1918.
82 *Verhandlungen des Reichstages*, 25 June 1918, pp 5640–2.
83 *Vorwärts*, 25 June 1918.
84 Helfferich, *Der Weltkrieg*, p 631.
85 Chancellor von Hertling's speech in the Prussian Abgeordnetenhaus on the Prussian Franchise, 30 April 1918, *Verhandlungen des Preussischen Hause der Abgeordneten*, No. 138, pp 9286–7; Lutz, *Fall of the German Empire*, pp 434–6. The proposal was rejected by 235 votes to 183.
86 Cf. *Neue Preussische Zeitung*, 1 May 1918.
87 Klein, *Deutschland im Ersten Weltkrieg*, vol 3, p 279; Moyer, *Victory Must be Our*, p 268.
88 *Vorwärts*, 5 July, 1918, p 1: Lutz, *Fall of the German Empire*, pp 446–8.
89 Hanssen, *Diary of a Dying Empire*, p 306.
90 *Die Ursachen des Deutschen Zusammenbruchs im Jahre 1918*, vol. l, p 23. On 18 June in a memorandum to the Chancellor, Hindenburg had demanded that all workers should be placed under military rule as wages were so high that there was no longer any incentive to work and produce the desperately required munitions. See BA, *Nachlass Bauer*, Band 11. See also Ludendorff, *Urkunden der OHL*, p 107.
91 Herwig, *The First World War*, p 420. For an illuminating analysis of the nature of the fighting during this stage of the conflict see, W Deist, 'Verdeckter Militärstreik im Kriegsjahr 1918?' in W. Wette (ed.), *Der Krieg des kleinen Mannes. Eine Militärgeschichte von unten* (Munich and Zurich, 1992) pp 146–67.
92 MAF, RM5/v, Bd. 2, 3770, Report on Enemy Propaganda from Colonel von Haeften, 17 July 1918. On the question of finance, Haeften claimed with some justification that his outfit employed only two officers with a monthly fund that 'the enemy would be ashamed to offer a journalist they were hoping to bribe'. The lack of financial resources allocated to domestic and foreign propaganda was a recurring complaint by both Nicolai and Haeften. See, MAF, *Nachlass Haeften*, N 35/4.
93 *Berliner Tageblatt*, 1 August 1918.
94 Cf. MB report from 2nd Army Corps in Stettin complaining of collapse of law and order and disintegration of public morality. BHStA, MB, IV, MKr, IV, 155/85, 12853,3 October 1918.
95 MAF, RM5/v, Bd. 2, 3771, The Imperial Chancellor to all Government Departments, 29 August 1918. See also, Ludendorff, *The General Staff*, pp 411–13.

96 MAF, *Nachlass Haeften*, N35/5, p 31 ff. The challenge confronting Deutelmoser and Haeften was awesome. On 19 August 1918 Deutelmoser is quoted as stating 'the authorities are not believed anymore – especially when they are attempting to raise morale'. Cited in Michaelis and Schraepler (eds), *Ursachen und Folgen*, vol 2, p 287.
97 Ludendorff, *My War Memories*, p 701.
98 *Der Weltkrieg 1914 bis 1918* vol 14, p 445.
99 Cf. F. von Lossberg, *Meine Tätigkeit im Weltkrieg 1914–18* (Berlin, 1939).
100 Cf. Ludendorff's dismissive rejection of American military power during the debate on unrestricted submarine warfare in January 1917. See section on unrestricted submarine warfare in Ch 4.
101 BHStA, MB, IV, MKr, IV, 155/85, 12853, Reports for September 1918.
102 MAS, MI/II, Bd. 1082, *Büro für Sozialpolitik*, 21 August 1918. The report was directed at the triumphalist propaganda of Pan-Germans and the *Vaterlandspartei*.
103 Facsimiles of the hand-posters of 'Hindenburg Speaks', 2 September 1918, can be found in MAS, M 1/3, Bü. 565. The tenor of the address was highly defensive. Referring to enemy propaganda Hindenburg wrote; 'He wants to deprive us of our belief, confidence, will, and strength'. The Field Marshal grandiosely claimed in the light of draconian censorship regulations: 'It is our strength, but also our weakness, that even in war we allow free expression to every opinion'.
104 See in particular the report of the 14th Army Corps for September: BHStA, MB, IV, MKr, IV, 155/85, 12853. The report pointed out that this perception was held even by 'people with intelligence'.
105 Cf. accounts from the following staunchly Pan-German papers: *Tägliche Rundschau*, 5 September 1918; *Hamburger Nachrichten*, 5 September 1918; *Deutsche Tageszeitung*, 6 September 1918.
106 *Correspondenzblatt der Generalkommission des Gewerkschaften Deutschlands*, 21 September 1918: quoted in Dahlin, *French and German Public Opinion*, p 146. By September 1918 the rising price of clothes and shoes had become a major issue. The Police President of Berlin commented that although the population had managed during the summer, the authorities could not alow the shortage of clothes to continue into the winter. The 1st Army Corps reported that the inadequate provision of clothes and shoes was impeding work in the countryside. BHStA, MB, IV, MKr, IV, 155/85, 12853, Reports for September 1918.
107 Reported in *Vorwärts*, 5 September 1918.
108 Blücher, *An English Wife*, p 249.
109 The transcription from the *Kölnische Zeitung* is taken from the Foreign Office Review of the German Press, FO, 395, 245/240504, September 1918.
110 For details leading up to the Armistice see, Kitchen, *The Silent Dictatorship*, pp 255–67. In 1919, Hindenburg addressed the *Untersuchungsausschusses* (parliamentary committee of investigation) and reaffirmed that the Germany army had 'been stabbed in the back'. A. Dorpalen, *Hindenburg and the Weimar Republic* (Princeton, 1964), pp 51–2.

111 Extracts of Meetings with Press Representatives. Protests by Press Representatives Against the Information Politics of the Authorities, 4 October 1918: Deist, *Militär und Innenpolitik*, II, pp 1300–5. The following day, however, the *Berliner Tageblatt* led with the optimistic headline: 'Successful Counter Attack on the West Front'. *Berliner Tageblatt*, 4 October 1918.

112 Hanssen, *Diary of a Dying Empire*, pp 332–3, entry for 8 October 1918.

113 Rathenau's call took the form of an article entitled 'A Dark Day' in the *Vossische Zeitung*, 7 October 1918. The article is reprinted in Prince Max von Baden, *Memoirs*, vol 2, p 55.

114 Ibid, p 66. See also, G. Hecker, *Walther Rathenau und sein Verhältnis zu Militär und Krieg* (Boppard, 1983).

115 Wilson had been placed under pressure by the German torpedoeing of the British packet liner, the *Leinster*, in which 450 passengers, including women and children, had been drowned.

116 Quoted in Ritter, *Staatskunst und Kriegshandwerk*, 4, p 441.

117 Ludendorff, *Urkunden der OHL*, p 407.

118 A.S. Link (ed.), *The Papers of Woodrow Wilson*, 40, pp 417–19, cited in Herwig, *The First World War*, p 427.

119 Ludendorff, *Urkunden der OHL*, pp 577–8.

120 According to Haeften, a shocked Ludendorff said that 'nothing surprises me anymore'. The Kaiser, who the previous day had been 'still very gracious' towards Ludendorff, behaved on 26 October 'very ungraciously'. He made pointed suggestions to Ludendorff during the course of the audience that he had lost faith in the General Staff and that he had decided to work with the Social Democrats in future. When Hindenburg asked permission to leave, the Kaiser said 'Stay!' Hindenburg bowed in acquiescence. Afterwards he justified his actions by the needs of the Fatherland. MAF, *Haeften Nachlass*, N35/7, p 15 ff. There have been a number of military biographies of Ludendorff that include: W. Venohr, *Ludendorff: Legende und Wirklichkeit* (Berlin, 1993); R. Parkinson, *Tormented Warrior – Ludendorff and the Supreme Command* (London, 1978); and D.J. Goodspeed, *Ludendorff: Genius of World War I* (Boston, 1966).

121 Cf. similar leader comments in *Berliner Tageblatt and Vorwärts*, both 27 October 1918.

122 Although the red banner of revolt had been hoisted on a number of dreadnoughts, few sailors were attempting a Bolshevik style revolution. Most would have considered their action a protest at the failure of the government to end the war. Wilson quote: Moyer, *Victory Must Be Ours*, p 292.

123 Hanssen, *Diary of a Dying Empire*, p 339, entry for 2 November 1918.

124 See MB Reports from Koblenz, Stettin and Frankfurt for 3 October 1918, BHStA, MB, IV, MKr, IV, 155/85, 12853.

125 Cited in Deist, *Militär und Innenpolitik*, II, p 1329, n. 5.

126 Ritter, *Staatskunst und Kriegshandwerk*, 4, p 458; Herwig, *The First World War*, p 443.

127 MAF, *Nachlass Groener*, N46/63.

128 Scheidemann was, of course, attempting to marginalize the proclamation of a socialist republic by Liebknecht and other radical socialists elsewhere in Berlin. In his address Scheidemann claimed that the 'German *Volk* has won a complete victory. The old decadence has collapsed; militarism is ended. The Hohenzollerns have abdicated. Long live the Republic...', cited in G. Ritter and S. Miller (eds), *Die deutsche Revolution 1918–19, Dokumente* (Hamburg, 1975), p 77.
129 During the war, Germany mobilized over 13 million men – virtually all males born between 1870 and 1899 served in one form or another. The Great War proved to be a demographic disaster. The scale of the carnage was staggering: 2,300,000 soldiers were killed, 2,700,000 permanently disabled. Its victims also included 530,000 widows and 1,192,000 orphans. Figures taken from R. Weldon Whalen, *Bitter Wounds: German Victims of the Great War, 1914–39* (Ithaca and London, 1984).
130 Klein estimates that over 20,000 turned up to greet Liebknecht. Klein, *Deutschland im Ersten Krieg*, 3, p 499.
131 Riezler, *Tagebücher*, p 480, entry for 1 October 1918 cited in Wehler, *The German Empire*, p 218.
132 Blücher, *An English Wife in Berlin*, p 253.

CONCLUSION: 'THE SINS OF OMISSION'

1 Cf. statements by the Prussian Minister of War on 5 February 1918 and by Von Kessel on 6 February 1918. See Ch 8, n. 31, 35.
2 Blücher, *An English Wife*, p 302, entry for December 1918.
3 I am most grateful to Jeffrey Verhey for drawing this phrase to my attention. Correspondence with author, 26 November 1991.
4 DZA Potsdam Reichskanzlei, Allgemeines 2398/11; Kitchen, *Silent Dictatorship*, p 249.
5 Ludendorff, *My War Memories*, p 368.
6 Ibid, p 361.
7 Ex-Kaiser William II, *Memoirs*, pp 282–3. For a penetrating analysis of how William II behaved in exile, his anti-Semitism and his flirtation with fascism see, W. Gutsche, *Eine Kaiser im Exil: Der Letzte deutsche Kaiser Wilhelm II in Holland. Eine kritische Biographie* (Marburg, 1991). See also, L. Cecil, *William II: Emperor and Exile 1900–1941* vol 2 (University of North Carolina Press, 1996). On the immediate aftermath of war see, R. Bessel, *Germany after the First World War* (Oxford, 1993).
8 Carsten, *War Against War*, see particularly Ch XII.
9 A. Hitler, *Mein Kampf* (London, 1939) p 169. For an analysis of Hitler's views on propaganda see, Welch, *The Third Reich*, pp 10–13, 17–20; and Welch, *Hitler* (London, 1998), pp 26–9.
10 Ludendorff contested this and in his memoirs claimed the credit for establishing a German propaganda organization. *My War Memories*, p 380.

11 Cf memo from the War Press Office to leaders of 'Patriotic Instruction', 26 October 1917. BHStA, Kr, MKr, 2336.
12 Epsten, *Matthias Erzberger*, p 263. Ludendorff wrote: 'I will say nothing of the Erzberger Bureau, as I have no knowledge of its activities. It was given up later'. *War Memories*, p 380. For further details of Erzberger's *Zentralstelle für Auslandsdienst* see Ch 2, 'the Organization of Official Propaganda'.
13 H. Wanderscheck, *Weltkrieg und Propaganda* (Berlin, 1936) p 5.

Bibliography

Unpublished primary sources

Politisches Archiv des Auswartigen Amts, Bonn, Akten der Politischen Abteilung
Gr. Hauptquartier
    28 Presse Band 1 und 2
    42 U-Bootkrieg Band 3
    232 Kriegsziele 16a Band 1
    237 Personalien Nr 25 Band 1
    247 Reichskanzler 29 Band 1
    248 Reichskanzler 29 Band 2

Staatsarchiv, Bremen
4, 14/1 Kr.A. Polizeidirektion (Kriegsakten)

Institut für den Wissenschaftlichen Film, Göttingen
Miscellaneous film material

Generallandesarchiv, Karlsruhe (GLA)
Abt. 456. Bd. 70 Zusammensstellungen der Monatsberichte der stellvertretenden Generalkommano des XIV. Armeekorps

Deutsches Zentralarchiv Abteilung 1, Potsdam
Reichsamt des Innern: Kriegszustand: 12217, 12255, 12260
Reichsamt des Innern: Presse: 12271, 12272, 12273
Reichskanzlei: Allgemeines 2398/6, 2398/7, 2398/8, 2398/9, 2398/10. 2398/11, 2398/12, 2398/13
Reichskanzlei: England: 2404112, 2407, 2408, 2409, 240911, 240912, 240913
Reichskanzlei: Presse: 2437/11, 2438, 2439, 2439/1. Reichskanzlei: Runidnien: 245813
Reichskanzlei: Reichskanzler und Gr. Hauptquartier: 2403/5
Stellvertreter des Reichskanzlers: 48, 53, 67(Juden), 72(Weltkrieg), 73 (Weltkrieg), 111(Presse)
69213: Friede Band 3. 69256: Schwarzes Meer Band 1. 69257: Schwarzes Meer Band 2

Bundesarchiv, Koblenz (BAK)
Miscellaneous collection of German films of World War One
Nachlass Bauer
Nachlass Berg
Nachlass Bulow
Nachlass Hertling
N 96 Nachlass Ludwig Quidde
P 135 Preussischen Justizministerium
R. 109 I (Ufa-Akten)

Hauptstaatsarchiv Stuttgart (HSS)
E 49 Ministerium der Auswärtigen Angelegenheiten. IV
E 130 a Akten des Württembergischen Staatsministerium I Bü (1876–1935)
E 130 b Akten des Württembergischen Staatsministerium II Bü (1876–1945)
E 150 IV Akten des Ministerium des Innen (1870–1920)
E 151 a Abt. I Kanzleidirektion; b Abt II Kanzleidirektion; c Abt III Polizei und Verfassungsschulz, ziviler Bevölkerungsschutz; d Abt IV Kommunalangelegenheiten
E 741 BGY 170 Vaterländische Hilfsdienste
J 150 Flugschriftensammlung
Q I/2 Nachlass Conrad Haussmann

Hauptsaatsarchiv Stuttgart, Militärarchiv (MAS)
M/11, Kriegsarchiv
M 1/3, Kriegsministerium
M77/1 Stellvertredendes Generalkommando XIII. AK B 60–71
M77/2 Denkschriftensammlung des Stellvertretenden Generalkommandos
M 704 Archiv-Verszeichnis der Licht- und Frontbildersammlung
M 705 Lichtbildsammlung verzeichnis der Konigsbilder
M 730 Denkschriften-Sammlung Bd. 405–7
M 731 Druckschriften- und Zeitungsausschnitt-Sammlung des Kriegsministeriums Bd. 149–163

Staatsarchiv Ludwigsburg
E 130 Akten des Koniglichen Staatsministeriums: Massnahmen des Württembergischen. Zivilverwaltung

Bundesarchiv Militärarchiv, Freiburg (MAF)
N 35 Nachlass von Haeften
N 44 Nachlass Wild von Hohenborn
N 46 Nachlass Groener
RM 2 Kaiserliches Marine-Kabinett
RM 3 Akten des Reichsmarineamtes
RM 5 Admiralsstab der Marine
RM 28 Oberbefehlshaber der Ostseestreitkräfte

RM 31 Akten der Marinestation der Ostsee
RM 33 Akten der Marinestation der Nordsee
RM 47 Kommando der Hochseestreitkräfte

Staatsarchiv, Potsdam (StA.P)
Pr. Br. Rep. 30 C, 84/560, Polizeipräsidium, Berlin

Bayerisches Hauptstaatsarchiv Abteilung IV, Kriegsarchiv (BHStA)
MKr 12842–12853, Monatsberichte über Volksstimmung und Volksernährung, Bayerische stellvertretende Generalkommandos, 9 Bde., 1916–18.
MKr 14029, Berichte des Büros für Sozialpolitik
M. Kr. 1830 Berichte des Militärischen Bevollmächtigten im Grossen Hauptquartier 1916
M. Kr. 1831 ditto 1917. M. Kr. 1832 ditto 1918

Imperial War Museum, London (IWM)
Collection of films, leaflets, photographs and pamphlets from 1914–18
Daily Review of the Foreign Press
Lee Collection (material relating to propaganda leaflets)
Weekly Reports on German and Austrian Papers (Foreign Office)

Public Records Office, Kew (PRO)
FO Foreign Office News Department, 1916–1919
INF Ministry of Information (War of 1914–18)

Published primary sources

Deist, Wilhelm, *Militär und Innenpolitik im Weltkrieg 1914–1918*, 2 vols (Düsseldorf, 1970).
Huber, E.R., *Dokumente zur Deutschen Verfassungsgeschichte*, Band 2 (Stuttgart, 1964).
Institute for Marxistmus-leninismus Beim ZK der SED, *Dokumente und Materialien zur Geschichte der deutschen Arbeiterbewegung*, Reihe 11, Band 1 und 2 (Berlin 1957–8).
Materna, Ingo and H.J. Schreckenbach, (eds), *Dokumente aus geheimen Archiven. 4: Berichte des Berliner Polizeipräsidenten zur Stimmung und Lage der Bevölkerung in Berlin 1914–1918* (Weimar, 1987).
Michaelis, Herbert, Schraepler, Ernst, *Ursachen und Folgen. Vom deutschen 7usammenbruch 1918 und 1945 bis zum staatlichen Neuordnung Deutschlands in der Gegenwart*, Band 1–3 (Berlin, 1958).
Ministerium für auswärtige angelegenheiten der UDSSR und Ministerium für auswärtige angelegenheiten der DDR, *Verhandlungen des Reichstags. XII, XIII. Legislaturperiode. II. Session. Stenographische Berichte* (Berlin, 1914–18).
―――― *Deutsch-Sowjetische Beziehungen von den Verhandlungen in Brest-Litovsk bis zum Abschluss des Rapallovertrages*, Band 1 (Berlin, 1967).

——— *Amtliche Urkunden zur Vorgeschichte des Waffenstillstandes 1918* (Berlin, 1967).
Reichsarchiv, *Schlachten des Weltkrieges in Einzeldarstellungen*, 37 vols (Oldenburg and Berlin, 1921–30).
——— *Der Weltkrieg 1914 bis 1918. Kriegsrüstung und Kriegswirtschaft*, 2 vols (Berlin, 1930).
——— *Der Weltkrieg 1914–1918. Die militärischen Operationen zu Lande* 14 vols (Berlin, 1925–44).
Stem, Leo, (ed.), *Das Werk des Untersuchungsausschusses der Verfassungsgebenden. Deutschen Nationalversammlung und des Deutschen Reichstages. IV Relhe: Die Ursachen des Deutschen Zusammenbruches.* Band 1–12 (Berlin, 1919–29).
——— *Spartakusbriefe* (Berlin, 1958).
——— *Archivalische Forschungen zur Geschichte der deutschen Arbeiterbewegung*, Band 4/11 bis IV (Berlin, 1959).

Newspapers
Berlin Newspapers
Berliner Lokal-Anzeiger
Berliner Neueste Nachrichten
Berliner Tageblatt
Deutsche Tageszeitung
Kreuzzeitung
Norddeutsche Allgemeine Zeitung
Täglische Rundschau
Vorwärts
Vossische Zeitung

Regional Newspapers
Frankfurter Zeitung
Hamburger Nachrichten
Kölnische Volkszeitung
Kölnische Zeitung
Leipziger Neueste Nachrichten
Münchner Neueste Nachrichten
Rheinisch-Westfälische Zeitung

Memoirs, diaries, etc.
Bauer, Max, *Der Grosse Krieg in Feld und Heimat Erinnerungen und Betrachtungen*, (Tübingen, 1921).
Baumer, Gertrude, *Heimatchronik Wahrend des Weltkriegs* (Berlin, 1930).
Bethmann Hollweg, Th. Von, *Kriegsreden*, hrsg. von F. Thimme (Stuttgart, 1919).
——— *Reflections on the World War* (London, 1920).
——— *Betrachtungen zum Weltkrilege*, 2 vols (Berlin, 1919, 1922).
Binding, R., *A Fatalist at War*, trans. I.F.D. Morrow (London, 1929).

Bibliography

Blücher, Evelyn Princess, *An English Wife in Berlin: A Private Matter* (London, 1920).
Braun, Magnus Freiherr von, *Von Ostpreussen bis Texas. Erlehnisse und Zeitgeschichtliche Betrachrungen ernes Ostdeutschen* (Stollhamm, 1955).
Bülow, Prince von, *Memoirs, 1909–1919* (London, 1932).
Cramon, A. von, *Unser österreich-ungarischer Bundesgenosse im Weltkriege* (Berlin, 1920).
Czernin, Ottokar, *Im Weltkriege* (Berlin, Vienna, 1919).
David, Eduard, *Das Kriegstagebuch des Reichstagsabgeordneten Eduard David 1914–1918*, hrsg. von E. Matthias and S. Miller (Düsseldorf, 1966).
Eisenhart Rothe, Ernst von, *Im Banne der Persönlichkeit. Aus den Lebensetinnerungen des Generals der Infanterie Emst von Eisenhart Rothe* (Berlin, 1931).
Erzberger, Matthias, *Erlebnisse im Weltkrieg* (Stuttgart, 1920).
Falkenhayn, Erich von, *Die Oberste Heeresleitung 1914–1916 in ihren wichtigsten Entscheidungen* (Berlin, 1920).
Goltz, Rildiger Graf von der, *Meine Sendung in Finnland und im Baltikum* (Leipzig, 1920).
Groener, Wilhelm, *Lebenserinnerungen. Jugend, Generalstab, Weltkrieg*, hrsg. von Friedrich Freiherr von Gärtringen (Göttingen, 1957).
Hanssen, Hans Peter, trans. Oscar Osburn Winther, *Diary of a Dying Empire* (Bloomington, 1955).
Haussmann, Conrad, *Schlaglichter. Reichstagsbriefe und Aufzeichnungen*, hrsg. von U. Zeller (Frankfurt, 1924).
Helfferich, Karl, *Der Weltkrieg* (Karlsruhe, 1919).
Hertling, K. Graf von, *Ein Jahr in der Reichskanziei. Erinnerungen and die Kanzierschaft meines Vaters* (Freiburg im Breisgau, 1919).
Hindenburg, Generalfeldmarschall, Paul von, *Aus meinem Leben* (Leipzig, 1927).
Hoffmann, Max, *Die Aufzeichnungen des Generalmajors Max Hoffmann*, hrsg. von Karl Friedrich Nowak, 2 vols (Berlin, 1929).
Hutten-Czapski, Bogdan Graf, *Sechzig Jahre Gesellschaft und Politik*, Band 2 (Berlin, 1936).
Kühlmann, Richard von, *Erinnerungen* (Heidelberg, 1948).
Lancken Wakenitz, O. Freiherr von der, *Meine 30 Dienstjahre 1888–1918* (Potsdam, 1931).
Lloyd George, David, *War Memoirs of David Lloyd George, 1914–1918*, 6 vols (London, 1933–6).
Lossberg, F. von, *Meine Tätigkeit im Weltkrieg 1914–1918* (Berlin, 1939).
Ludendorff, Erich, *Meine Kriegserinnerungen 1914–1918* (Berlin, 1919).
―――― *Urkunden der Obersten Heeresleitung über ihrer Tätigkeit 1916–18* (Berlin, 1920).
―――― *The General Staff and its Problems*, 2 vols, trans. by F.A. Holt (London, 1921).
―――― *Kreigführung und Politik* (Berlin, 1921).
Mannerheim, G., *Erinnerungen* (Zurich, 1952).
Matthias, E. and Morsey, R., *Der Interfraktionelle Ausschuss*, 2 vols (Düsseldorf, 1959).
―――― *Die Regierung des Prinzen Max von Baden* (Düsseldorf, 1962).
Max von Baden, Prinz, *Erinnerungen und Dokumente* (Berlin, 1927).

Merton, Richard, *Erinnernswertes aus meinem Leben* (Frankfurt, 1955).
Messter, Oskar, *Mein Weg mit dem Film* (Berlin, 1936).
Michaelis, Georg, *Für Staat und Volk* (Berlin, 1922).
Moltke, H. von, *Erinnerungen, Briefe, Dokumente 1877–1916*, hrsg. von E. von Moltke (Stuttgart, 1922).
Müller, Georg Alexander von, *Regierte der Kaiser? Kriegstagebücher Aufzeichnungen und Briefe des Chefs des Marine-Kabinetts Admiral Georg von Müller 1914–1918*, hrsg. Walter Görlitz (Göttingen, 1959).
Nadolny, Rudolf, *Mein Beitrag* (Wiesbaden, 195).
Nicolai, Walter, *Nachrichtendienst, Presse und Volksstimmung im Weltkrieg* (Berlin, 1920).
―――― *The German Secret Service* (London, 1924).
Payer, Friedrich von, *Von Bethmann Hollweg bis Ebert. Erinnerungen und Bilder* (Frankfurt, 1923).
Pogge von Strandmann, Hartmut (ed.), *Walther Rathenau: Industrialist, Banker, Intellectual, and Politician. Notes and Diaries 1907–1922* (Oxford, 1985).
Rathenau, Walter, *Politische Briefe* (Dresden, 1929).
Rupprecht von Bayern, Kronprinz, *Mein Kriegstagebuch*, hrsg. von Eugen Frauenholz, 3 Vols., (Berlin, 1929).
Scheidemann, Philipp, *Der Zusammenbruch* (Berlin, 1921).
―――― *Memoiren eines Sozialdemokraten*, 2 vols (Dresden, 1928).
Seeckt, Hans von, *Aus meinem Leben 1866 bis 1917*, hrsg. von Fr. von Rabenau (Leipzig, 1938).
Seldte, F., *Through a Lens Darkly* (London, 1933).
Stein, Dr von, *Erlebnisse und Betrachtungen aus der Zeit des Weltkrieges* (Leipzig, 1919).
Stürgkh, Josef Graf, *Im deutschen Grossen Hauptquartier* (Leipzig, 1921).
Thaer, Albrecht von, *Generalstabsdienst and der Front und in der OHL. Aus Briefen und Tagebuchaufzeichnungen 1915–1919*, hrsg. von Siegfried A. Kachier (Göttingen, 1958). Tirpitz, A. von, *Erinnerungen* (Leipzig, 1919).
Valentini, Rudolf von, *Kaiser und Kabinettschef Nach eigenen Aufzeichnungen und dem Briefwechsel des wirklichen Geheimen Rats Rudolf von Valentini dargestellt von Bernhard Schwertfeger* (Oldenburg, 1931).
Westarp, Kuno Graf von, *Konservative Politik im Letzten Jahzehnt des Kaiserreiches*, Band 2 (Berlin, 1935).
Wilhelm, Kronprinz, *Erinnerungen*, hrsg, von K. Rosner (Stuttgart, 1922).
William II, Ex-Kaiser, *My Memoirs: 1878–1918* (London, 1922).
Wrisberg, Ermt von, *Erinnerungen an die Kriegsjahre im Königlich Preussischen Kriegsministerium*, Band 1–3 (Leipzig, 1921–2).

Secondary sources

Adam, B. *Arbeitsbeziehungen in der bayerischen Grossstadtmetallindustrie von 1914 bis 1932* (Munich, 1983).
Adams, M.C.C. *The Great Adventure. Male Desire and the Coming of World War I* (Bloomington and Indianapolis, 1990).

Adler, G., *Die imperialistische Sozialpolitik* (Tübingen, 1897).
Afflerbach, Holger, *Falkenhayn, Politisches Denken und Handeln im Kaiserreich* (Munich, 1994).
Anderson, P.R., *The Background of Anti-English Feeling in Germany 1890–1902*, (Washington, 1939).
Armeson, R.B., *Total Warfare and Compulsory Labour. A Study of the Military–Industrial Complex in Germany during World War I* (The Hague, 1964).
Asprey, Robert, *The German High Command at War: Hindenburg and Ludendorff and the First World War* (London, 1991).
August 1914: Ein Volk zieht in den Krieg. Berliner Geschichtswerkstatt (Berlin, 1989).
Ay, K.L., *Die Entstehung einer Revolution. Die Volksstimmung in Bayern während des Ersten Weltkriegs* (Berlin, 1968).
Bailey, S. 'The Berlin Strike of January 1918', *Central European History*, 13 (1980), 158–74.
Barkhausen, H., *Filmpropaganda für Deutschland im Ersten und Zweiten Weltkrieg* (Hildesheim *et al.*, 1982).
Barnett, Correlli, The *Swordbearers: Studies in Supreme Command in the First World War* (London, 1963).
Basler, W., *Deutschlands Annexionspolitik in Polen und im Baltikum 1914–1918* (Berlin, 1962).
Baumgart, W., *Deutsche Ostpolitik 1918. Von Brest-Litovsk bis zum Ende des Weltkrieges* (Vienna and Munich, 1966).
_____ 'Ludendorff und das auswärtige Amt, zur Besetzung der Krim 1918', *Jahrbuch für die Geschichte Osteuropas*, 14, 1966.
_____ 'Neue Quellen zur Beurteilung Ludendorffs. Der Konflikt niit dem Admiralstabschef über die deutsche Schwarzmeerpolitik im Sommer 1918', *Militärgeschichtliche Mitteilungen*, 1970.
Bechtel, H., *Wirtschaftsgeschichte Deutschlands* (Munich, 1956).
Beckett, I., *The Making of the First World War* (London, 2012).
Berghahn, Volker, 'Zu den Zielen des deutschen Flottenbaus unter Wilhelm 11', *Historische Zeitschrift*, Band 210, 1970.
_____ *Der Tirpitz-Plan Genesis und Verfall einen innenpolitischen Krisenstrategie unter Wilhelm II* (Düsseldorf, 1971).
_____ *Germany and the Approach of War in 1914* (London, 1973).
Bergsträsser, L., *Die preussische Wahlrechtsfrage im Kriege und die Entstehung der Osterbotschaft 1917* (Tübingen, 1924).
Bessel, Richard, *Germany After the First World War* (Oxford, 1993).
Beyer, Hans, 'Die Mittelmächte und die Ukraine 1918,' *Jahrbuch für die Geschichte Ost Europas*, Beiheft 2, Munich, 1956.
Bieber, H-J., *Gewerkschaften in Krieg und Revolution. Arbeiterbewegung, Industrie, Staat und Militär in Deutschland 1914–1920*, 2 vols (Hamburg, 1981).
Birett, Herbert, *Verzeichnis in Deutschland gelaufener Filme*, Entscheidungen der Filmzensur 1911–20 (Berlin *et al.*, 1980).
Birnbaum, K.E., *Peace Moves and U-Boat Warfare, A Study of Imperial Germany's Policy Towards the United States April 18, 1916 – January 9, 1917* (Stockholm, 1958).

Bloch, Ernst, 'Der Faschismus als Erscheinungsform der Ungleichzeitigkeit', in *Erbschaft dieser Zeit* (Frankfurt, 1962).
Blücher, W. von, *Deutschlands Weg nach Rapallo* (Wiesbaden, 1951).
Böhme, H., *Deutschlands Weg zur Grossmacht* (Cologne, 1966).
────── *Prolegomena zu einer Sozial- und Wirtschaftsgeschichte Deutschlands in 19 und 20. Jahrhundert* (Frankfurt, 1968).
Boldt, H., *Rechtsstaat und Ausnahmezustand* (Berlin, 1967).
Boll, Friedhelm, *Massenbewegung in Niedersachsen 1906–1920. Eine sozialgeschichtliche Untersuchung zu den unerschiedlichen Entwicklungstypen Braunschweig und Hannover* (Bonn, 1981).
Born, K.E., 'Die soziale und wirtschaftliche Strukturwandel Deutschlands am Ende des 19. Jahrhunderts', *Vierteljahrsschrift für Sozial- und Wirtschaftsgeschichte*, Band 50, 1963.
Borowsky, Peter, *Deutsche Ukrainepolitik 1918* (Lübeck and Hamburg, 1970).
Bott, J.P., 'The German Food Crisis of World War I. The Cases of Coblenz and Cologne', Diss., University of Missouri-Columbia, 1981.
Boyd, C.E., *Nationaler Frauendienst: German Middle Class Women in Service to the Fatherland, 1914–1918* (Athens, GA, 1979).
Breucker, W., *Die Tragik Ludendorffs* (Oldenburg, 1953).
Bridgewater, Patrick, *German Poets of the First World War* (London, 1985).
Brown, M., *The Imperial War Museum Book of 1918* (London, 1998).
Bruntz, G.B., *Allied Propaganda and the Collapse of the German Empire in 1918* (Stanford, 1938).
Bry, G. *Wages in Germany, 1871–1945* (Princeton, 1960).
Bub, Gertraude, *Der deutsche Film im Weltkrieg uns sein publizistischer Einsatz* (Berlin, 1938).
Bucholz, Arden, *Moltke, Schlieffen, and Prussian War Planning* (New York and Oxford, 1991).
Buitenhuis, P., *The Great War of Words: Literature as Propaganda, 1914–18 and After* (London, 1989).
Bunyan, J. and Fisher, H.H., *The Bolshevik Revolution 1917–1918* (New York, 1961).
Burchardt, L., 'The Impact of the War Economy on the Civilian Population of Germany during the First and Second World War,' in W. Deist, (ed.), *The Germany Military in the Age of Total War* (Leamington, 1985), 40–70.
Carr, E.H., *The Bolshevik Revolution, 1917–1923*, 3 vols (London, 1951–3).
Carsten, Francis, *War Against War. British and German Radical Movements in the First World War* (London, 1982).
Cecil, Hugh and Liddle, Peter H. (eds), *Facing Armageddon: The First World War Experienced* (London, 1996).
Cecil, Lamar, *William II: Emperor and Exile, 1900–1941* (Chapel Hill, NC, 1996).
Chickering, Roger, *We Men Who Feel Most German. A Cultural Study of the Pan-German League 1886–1914* (London, 1984).
────── (ed.), *Imperial Germany: A Historiographical Companion* (Westport, CT. 1996).
────── *Imperial Germany and the Great War, 1914–1918* (Cambridge, 1998).

Clarke, C., *Kaiser Wilhelm II: A Life in Power* (London, 2009).
_____ *The Sleepwalkers. How Europe Went to War in 1914* (London, 2013).
Condell, D.J.L., *Working For Victory? Images of Women in the First World War, 1914–1918* (London, 1987).
Conze, W., *Polnische Nation und deutsche Politik im ersten Weltkrieg* (Cologne, Graz, 1958).
Craig, Gordon, 'Military Diplomats in the Prussian and German Service: The Attachés 1816–1914,' *Political Science Quarterly*, 64, 1949.
_____ *The Politics of the Prussian Army 1640–1945* (Oxford, 1955).
_____ 'The World War I Alliance of the Central Powers in Retrospect: The Military Cohesion of the Alliance', *Journal of Modern History*, 37, 1965.
Creutz, M., *Die Presspolitik der kaiserlichen Regierung während des Ersten Weltkriegs* (Frankfurt/M., 1996).
Cron, H., *Die Organisation des deutschen Heeres im Weltkrieg* (Berlin, 1923).
Crone, Wilhelm, *Achtung! Hier Grosses Hauptquartier* (Lübeck, 1934).
Dahlin, Ebba, *French and German Public Opinion on Declared War Aims 1914–18* (Stanford, 1933).
Daniel, Ute, 'The Politics of Rationing, Versus the Politics of Subsistence: Working-Class Women in Germany, 1914–1918,' in R. Fletcher (ed.), *Bernstein to Brandt: A Short History of German Social Democracy* (London, 1987), 89–95.
_____ *Arbeiterfrauen in der Kriegsgesellschaft. Beruf, Familie und Politik im Ersten Weltkrieg* (Göttingen, 1989). English tr.: *The War from Within. German Working-Class Women in the First World War* (Oxford, 1997).
Darracott, Joseph and Loftus, Belinda, *The First World War Posters* (London, IWM, 1974).
Davis, Belinda, 'Food Scarcity and the Empowerment of the Female Consumer in World War I Berlin,' in V. de Grazia et al. (eds), *The Sex of Things. Gender and Consumption in Historical Perspective* (Berkeley, 1996), 287–310.
Deist, Wilhelm, 'Zur Institution des Miltilärbefehlshabers und Obermilitärbefehlshabers im Ersten Weltkrieg,' *Jahrbuch für die Geschichte Mittel- und Ostdeutschlands*, Band 13114, Berlin, 1965.
_____ 'Zensur und Propaganda in Deutschland während des Ersten Weltkrieges,' in Deist (ed.), *Militär, Staat und Gesellschaft: Studien zur preussisch-deutschen Militärgeschichte* (Munich, 1991).
Denham, Scott, *Visions of War: Ideologies and Images of War in German Literature before and after the Great War* (Berne, 1992).
Deuerlein, E., 'Zur Friedensaktion Benedikts XV', *Stimmen der Zeit*, 80, 1954–5.
Deutschland im Ersten Weltkrieg, 3 vols (Berlin, 1968–9).
Deutelmoser, E., 'Die amtliche Einwirkung auf die deutsche Öffentlichkeit im Kriege,' *Die deutsche Nation* 10 (1919), 18–22.
Domelier, Henri, *Behind the Scenes at German Headquarters* (London, 1921).
Dorpalen, Andreas, 'Empress Auguste Victoria and the Fall of the German Empire', *American Historical Review*, 1952.
Edwards, Marvin, *Stresemann and the Greater Germany* (New York, 1963).

Eksteins, Modris, *Rites of Spring: The Great War and the Birth of the Modern Age* (Boston, 1989).
Eley, G., *Reshaping the German Right. Radical Nationalism and Political Change after Bismarck* (New Haven, 1980).
Engelberg, E., 'Zur Entstehung und historischen Stellung des preussisch-deutschen Bonapartismus', *Beiträge zum neuen Geschichtsbild*, hrsg. von F. Klein und J. Streisand (Berlin, 1956).
Epstein, Klaus, 'The Development of German-Austrian War Aims in the Spring of 1917', *Journal of Central European Affairs*, vol XVII, April 1957.
―――― *Matthias Erzberger and the Dilemma of German Democracy* (Princeton, 1959).
Evans, R.J., *The Feminist Movement in Germany, 1894–1933* (London, 1976).
―――― *Sozialdemokratie und Frauenemanzipation im deutschen Kaiserreich* (Berlin and Bonn, 1979).
―――― 'German Social Democracy and Women's Suffrage, 1891–1918,' *Journal of Contemporary History* 15 (1980), 533–57.
Faust, M., *Sozialer Burgfrieden im Ersten Weltkrieg. Christliche und sozialistische Arbeiterbewegung in Köln* (Essen, 1992).
Feldman, G.D., *Army, Industry and Labor in Germany, 1914–1918* (Princeton, 1966).
Ferguson, Niall, *The Pity of War* (London, 1998).
Fischer, Fritz, *Griff nach der Weltmacht. Die kriegszielpolitik des kaiserlichen Deutschlan 1914–18* (Düsseldorf, 1961).
―――― *Krieg der Illusionen. Die duetsche Politik von 1911 bis 1914* (Düsseldorf, 1969).
Fischer, Hans-Dietrich (ed.), *Pressekonzentration und Zensurpraxis im Ersten Weltkrieg: Text und Quellen* (Berlin, 1973).
Foerster, W., *Der Feldherr Ludendorff in Unglück. Eine Studie über seine seelische Haltung in der Endphase des Ersten Weltkrieges* (Wiesbadon, 1952).
Fricke, Dieter, 'Der Reichsverband gegen die Sozialdemokratie', *Zeitschrift für Geschichtswissenschaft*, Heft 7, 1959.
Fröhlich, Paul, *Rosa Luxemburg: Her Life and Work* (London, 1972).
Fussel, P., *The Great War and Modern Memory* (London, 1975).
Galos, A., Gentzen, F.H. and Jakobezyk, W., *Die Hakatisten. Der deutsche Ostmarkenverein 1894–1934* (Berlin, 1966).
Gatzke, H.W., *Germany's Drive to the West. A Study in Germany's Western War Aims During the First World War* (Baltimore, 1950).
―――― 'Zu den deutsch-russischen Beziehungen im Sommer 1918' *Vierteljahrshefte für Zeitgeschichte*, Heft 3, 1955.
Geary, Dick, *European Labour Protests, 1848–1939* (London, 1981).
―――― 'Revolutionary Berlin 1917–20,' in C. Wrigley (ed.), *Challenges of Labour. Central and Western Europe 1917–1920* (London, 1993), 24–50.
Geiss, Imanuel, *Der poinische Grenzstreifen 1914–1918* (Lübeck and Hamburg, 1960).
―――― *Das Deutsche Reich und der Erste Weltkrieg* (Munich, 1985).
Genno, C.N. and Wetzel, H. (eds), *The First World War in German Narrative Prose* (Toronto, 1980).

Gerschenkron, H., *Bread and Democracy in Germany* (Berkeley, 1943).
Giese, Hans-Joachim, *Die Film Wochenschau im Dienste der Politik* (Dresden, 1940).
Gläser, Ernst, *Jahrgang 1902* (Berlin, 1931).
Goodspeed, D.J., *Ludendorff: Genius of World War I* (Boston, 1966).
Groener-Geyer, Dorothea, *General Groener, Soldat und Staatsmann* (Frankfurt am Main, 1954).
Gutsche, Willibald, 'Bethmann Hollweg und die Politik der 'Neuorientierung'. Zur innenpolitischen Strategie und Taktik der deutschen Reichsregierung während des Ersten Weltkrieges', *Zeitschrift für Geschichtswissenschaft*, Heft 17, 1965.
_____ *Wilhelm II: Der Letzte Kaiser des Deutschen Reiches* (Berlin, 1991).
Guttmann, B., *Weibliche Heimarmee. Frauen in Deutschland 1914–1918* (Weinheim, 1989).
Hagenlücke, Heinz, *Deutsche Vaterlandspartei: Dienationale Rechte am Ende des Kaiserreiches* (Düsseldorf, 1997).
Hager, P. E. and Taylor, D., *The Novels of World War I. An Annotated Bibliography* (New York, 1981).
Hahlweg, W. (ed.), *Lenins Rückkehr nach Russland 1917, Die deutschen Akten* (Leiden, 1957).
_____ 'Lenins reise durch Deutschland', *Vierteljahrshefte für Zeitgeschichte*, Heft 5, 1957.
_____ *Der Diktatffieden von Brest-Litovsk 1918 und die bolschewistische Weltrevolution* (Münster, 1960).
Hallgarten, G.W.P., *Imperialismus vor 1914*, 2 vols (Munich, 1963).
Hamerow, T.S., *Restoration, Revolution, Reaction, Economics and Politics in Germany* (Princeton, 1958).
Hammer, K., *Deutsche Kriegstheologie 1870–1918* (Munich, 1974).
Hardach, K.W., *Die Bedeutung wirtschaftlicher Faktoren bei der Wedereinführung der Eisen- und Getreidezö11e in Deutschland* (Berlin, 1967).
Hardie, Martin and Sabin, Arthur, *War Posters. Issued by the Beligerent and Neutral Nations 1914–19* (London, 1920).
Hecker, Gerhard, *Walther Rathenau und sein Verhältnis zu Militär und Krieg* (Boppard, 1983).
Heffter, H., 'Bismarcks Sozialpolitik', *Archiv fir Sozialforschung*, 3, 1963.
Hegemann, M., 'Der deutsch-rumänische Friedensvertrag im Mai 1918 – ein Vorstoss der imperialistischen Reaktion gegen die junge Sowjetmacht', *Zeitschrift für Geschichtswissenschaft*, Heft 5, 1957.
Hellwig, A., *Die Krieg und die Kriminalität der jungenlichen* (Halle and Salle, 1916).
Henning, Heinz, *Die Situation der deutschen Kriegswirtschaft im Sommer 1918 und ihre Beurteilung durch Heeresleitung, Reichsführung und Bevö1kerung*, phil. Diss. (Hamburg, 1957).
Hering, S., *Die Kriegsgewinnlerinnen. Praxis und Ideologie der deutschen Frauenbewegung im Ersten Weltkrieg* (Pfaffenweiler, 1990).
Herwig, Holger, *The German Naval Officer Corps: A Social and Political History, 1890–1918* (Oxford, 1973).
_____ *The First World War. Germany and Austria–Hungary 1914–1918* (London, 1997).

Herzfeld, Hans, *Die deutsche Sozialdemokratie und die Auflösung der nationalen Einheitsfront im Weltkrieg* (Leipzig, 1928).

―――― *Der Erste Weltkrieg* (Munich, 1968).

Hiden, J.W., 'The Baltic Germans and German Policy towards Latvia after 1918,' *Historical Journal*, vol. XIII, 1970, no. 2.

Hirschfeld, Gerhard, Krumeich Gerd and Renz, Irina (eds), *Keiner fühlt sich mehr als Mensch. . . . Erlebnis und Wirkung des Ersten Weltkriegs* (Essen, 1993).

Hirschfeld *et al.* (eds), *Kriegserfahrungen. Studien zur Sozial- und Mentalitätsgeschichte des Ersten Weltkriegs* (Essen, 1997).

Hoffmann, W.G., 'The Take-off in Germany', in *The Economics of Take-off into Sustained Growth*, ed. W.W. Rostow (London, 1963).

―――― *Das Wachstum der deutschen Wirtschaft seit der Mitte des 19. Jahrhunderts* (Heidelberg, 1965).

Horkheimer, Max, 'Die Juden und Europa', *Zeitschrift für Sozialforschung*, Jahrgang 8, 1939, Heft 1 und 2.

Horn, Daniel, *The German Naval Mutinies of World War I* (New Brunswick, NJ, 1969).

Horne, Alistair, *The Price of Glory, Verdun 1916* (London, 1962).

Horneffer, Ernst, *Soldaten-Erziehung. Eine Ergänzung zum allgemeine Wehrpflicht* (Munich, 1918).

Hubatsch, Walter, 'Grosses Hauptquartier 1914–1918. Zur Geschichte einer deutschen Führungseinrichtung', *Ostdeutsche Wissenschaft*, Band 5, Munich, 1959.

Jaeger, H., *Unternehmer in der deutschen Politik (1890–1914)* (Bonn, 1967).

Jäger, W., *Historische Forschung und politische Kultur in Deutschland. Die Debatte 1914–1980 über den Ausbruch des Ersten Weltkriegs* (Göttingen, 1984).

Janssen, K-H., 'Der Wechsel in der OHL 1916', *Vierteljahreshefte für Zeitgeschichte*, Heft 7, 1959.

―――― *Macht und Verblendung, Kriegszielpolitik der Bundesstaaten 1914–1918* (Göttingen, 1963).

―――― *Der Kanzler und der General Die Führungskrise um Bethmann Hollweg und Falkenhayn* (Göttingen, 1966).

Jarausch, Konrad, *The Enigmatic Chancellor: Bethmann Hollweg and the Hubris of Imperial Germany* (London, New Haven, 1973).

Joll, James, *The Unspoken Assumptions* (London, 1968).

Kaeble, H., *Industrielle Interessenpolitik in der wilheiminischen Gesellschaft* (Berlin, 1967).

Kaehler, S.A., *Vier quellenkritische Untersuchungen zum Kriegsende 1918* (Göttingen, 1960).

―――― *Zur Beurteilung Ludendorffs im Sommer 1918*, Studien zur deutschen Geschichte des 19 und 20 Jahrhunderts (Göttingen, 1961).

Keegan, John, *The First World War* (London, 1998).

Kehr, Eckart, *Schlachtflottenbau und Parteipolitik 1894–1901* (Berlin, 1931).

―――― *Primat der Innenpolitik*, hrsg. von H.-U. Wehler (Berlin, 1965).

Kennan, George F., *Soviet–American Relations 1917–1920. Russia Leaves the War* (Princeton, 1956).

Kirimal, E., *Die nationals Kampf der Krimtürken mit besondere Berücksichtigung der Jahre 1917–1918* (Emsdetten, 1952).

Bibliography

Kitchen, Martin, *The German Officer Corps 1890–1914* (Oxford, 1968).

―――― *The Silent Dictatorship* (London, 1976).

Klein, Fritz (ed.), *Politik im Krieg 1914–1918. Studien zur Politik der herrschenden Klassen im Ersten Weltktieg* (Berlin, 1964).

―――― *Deutschland im Ersten Weltkrieg*, 3 vols (East Berlin, 1968–9).

Knesebeck, L., *Die Wahrheit über den Propagandafeldzug und Deutschlands Zusammenbruch. Der Kampf um die Publizistik im Weltkriege* (Munich, 1927).

Koschnitzke, R., *Die Innenpolitik des Reichskanzlers Bethmann Hollweg in Weltkrieg*, Diss. phil. (Kiel, 1952).

Koszyk, K., *Deutsche Pressepolitik im Ersten Weltkrieg* (Düsseldorf, 1968).

Kremeier, Klaus, *The Ufa Story: A History of Germany's Greatest Film Company, 1918–1945* (New York, 1996).

Kruck, A., *Geschichte des Alldeutschen Verbandes 1890–1939* (Wiesbaden, 1954).

Kruse, Wolfgang, *Krieg und nationale Integration. Eine neuinterpretation des sozialdemokratischen Burgfriedensschlussess 1914–15* (Essen, 1993).

―――― 'Krieg und Klassenheer: Zur Revolutionierung der deutschen Armee im Ersten Weltkrieg,' *Geschichte und Gesellschaft* 22 (1996), 530–61.

―――― (ed.), *Eine Welt von Feinden: Der grosse Krieg 1914–1918* (Frankfurt am Main, 1997).

Kuczynskj, J., 'Die Barbarei', *Zeitschrift für Geschichtswissenschaft 1*, Heft 7, 1961.

―――― *Die Geschichte der Lage der Arbeiter unter dem Kapitalismus*, Band 4 (Berlin, 1967), Band 5 (Berlin, 1966).

Kundrus, B., *Kriegerfrauen. Familie, Politik und Geschlechterverhältnisse im Ersten und Zweiten Weltkrieg* (Hamburg, 1995).

Lasswell, Harold, *Propaganda Techniques in the World War* (New York, 1927, reprinted 1970).

Lebeck, R. and Schütte, M., *Propagandapostkarten I* (Dortmund, 1980).

Lenin, V.I., *Selected Works* (Moscow, 1970).

Lewerenz, L., Die *deutsche Politik im Baltikum 1914–1918*, Diss. (Hamburg, 1958).

Lewinsohn, Ludwig, *Die revolution an der Westfront* (Charlottenburg, 1919).

Linde, Gerd, *Die deutsche Politik in Litauen im Ersten Weltkrieg* (Wiesbaden, 1965).

Loth, W., *Katholiken im Kaiserreich. Der politische Katholizismus in der krise des wilhelminischen Deutschlands* (Düsseldorf, 1984).

Ludendorff, E., *Kriegführung und Politik* (Berlin, 1922).

―――― *Der Totale Krieg* (Berlin, 1935).

Lüdtke, A. (ed.), *Alltagsgeschichte. Zur Rekonstriktion historischer Erfahrungen und Lebensweisen* (Frankfurt, 1989).

Lütge, L., 'Die Grundprinzipien der Bismarckschen Sozialpolitik, *Jahrbücher für Nationalökonomie und Statistik*, 134, 1931.

Lutz, Ralph Haswell (ed.), *The Fall of the German Empire, 1914–1918*, 2 vols (Stanford, 1932).

Mai, Günter, 'Burgfrieden und Sozialpolitik in Deutschland in der Anfangsphase des Ersten Weltkriegs (1914–15),' *Militärgeschichtliche Mitteilungen* 20 (1976), 21–50.

―――― '"Aufklärung der bevölkerung" und "Väterlandischer Unterricht" in Württemberg 1914–18,' *Zeitschrift für Württembergische Landesgeschichte* 36 (1977), 199–235.

―――― *Kriegswirtschaft und Arbeiterbewegung in Württemberg 1914–1918* (Stuttgart, 1983).

―――― (ed.), *Arbeiterschaft in Deutschland 1914–1918: Studien zu Arbeitskampf und Arbeitsmarkt im Ersten Weltkrieg* (Düsseldorf, 1985).

Manes, A., 'Arbeiterversicherung in Deutschland', *Handwörterbuch für Staatswissenschaften*, Band 1.

Mann, Bernhard, *Die baltischen Länder in der deutschen Kriegs publizistik 1914–18* (Tübingen, 1965).

Marquis, A.G., 'Words as Weapons: Propaganda in Britain and Germany during the First World War,' *Journal of Contemporary History* 13 (1978), 467–498.

Marwick, Arthur, *War and Social Change in the Twentieth Century. A Comparative Study of Britain, France, Germany, Russia and the United States* (London, 1974).

―――― *The Deluge* (London, 1970) (revised edn, 1996).

Marx–Engels, Werke (Berlin, 1957).

Maser, Werner, *Hindenburg: Eine politische Biographie* (Rastatt, 1989).

Massing, P.W., *Vorgeschichte des politischen Antisemitismus* (Frankfurt, 1959).

May, E.R., *The World War and American Isolation 1914–17* (Cambridge, Mass., 1959).

Meinecke, F., *Kühlmann und die päpstliche Friedensaktion von 1917* (Berlin, 1928).

Mendelssohn-Bartholdy, A. von *The War and German Society. The Testament of a Liberal* (New Haven, 1937).

Meyer, H.C., *Mitteleuropa in German Thought and Action 1815–1945* (The Hague, 1955).

Michaelis, W., 'Der Reichskanzler Michaelis und die päpstliche Friedensaktion 1917', *Geschichte in Wissenschaft und Unterricht*, Heft 7, 1956.

―――― 'Der Relchskanzler Michaelis und die päpstliche Friedensaktion 1917. Neue Dokumente', *Geschichte in Wissenschaft und Unterricht*, 12, 1961.

―――― 'Zum Problem des Königstodes am Ende der Hohehzollern-monarchie', *Geschichte in Wissenschaft und Unterricht*, 1962.

Michalka, Wolfgang (ed.), *Der Erste Weltkrieg: Wirkung, Wahrnehmung, Analyse* (Munich and Zurich, 1994).

Michelson, Andreas, *Der U-Bootkrieg 1914–1918* (Leipzig, 1925).

Mockelmann, Jürgen, *Das Deutschlandbild in den USA 1914 bis 1918 und die Kriegszielpolitik Wilsons*, phil. Diss. (Hamburg, 1964).

Mommsen, Wolfgang, 'Die Regierung Bethmann Hollweg und die öffentliche Meinung 1914–1917,' *Vierteljahrshefte für Zeitgeschichte* 17 (1969), 117–55.

―――― *Bürgerstolz und Weltmachtstreben: Deutschland unter Willhelm II 1890 bis 1918* (Berlin, 1995).

―――― 'German Artists, Writers and Intellectuals and the Meaning of War, 1914–1918,' in J. Horne (ed.), *State, Society and Mobilization in Europe during the First World War* (Cambridge, 1997), 21–38.

Morgan, David, *The Socialist Left and the German Revolution: A History of the German Independent Social Democratic Party, 1917–1922* (London, 1975).
Moser, Otto von, *Die obersten Gewulten im Weltkrieg* (Stuttgart, 1931).
Mosse, George, 'The Jews and the German War Experience 1914–18,' The Leo Baeck Memorial Lecture, 21 (New York, 1977).
_____ *Fallen Soldiers: Reshaping the Memory of the World Wars* (Oxford, 1990).
Moyer, Laurence, *Victory Must Be Ours: Germany in the Great War 1914–1918* (New York, 1995).
Müffelmann, Leo, *Die Wirtschaftliche Verbände* (Leipzig, 1912).
Mühlmann, C., *Oberste Heeresleitung und Balken im Weltkrieg 1914–1918* (Berlin, 1942).
Müller, K.-P., *Politik und Gesellschaft im Krieg. Der Legitimitätsverlust des badischen Staates, 1914–1918* (Stuttgart, 1988).
Nettl, J.P., *Rosa Luxemburg*, 2 vols (Oxford, 1966).
Niemann, A., *Kaiser und Revolution. Die entscheidenden Ereignisse im Grossen Hauptquartier im Herbst 1918* (Berlin, 1922).
_____ *Kaiser und Heer. Das Wesen der Kommandogewalt und ihre Ausübung durch Kaiser Wilhelm II* (Berlin, 1929).
Nolan, Mary, *Social Democracy and Society: Working-Class Radicalism in Düsseldorf, 1890–1920* (Cambridge, 1981).
Noske, G., *Von Kiel bis Kapp. Zur Geschichte der deutschen Revolution* (Berlin, 1920).
Nussbaum, H., *Unternehmer gegen Monopole* (Berlin, 1966).
Offer, Avner, *The First World War: An Agrarian Interpretation* (Oxford, 1989).
Oppeland, Torsten, *Reichstag und Aussenpolitik im Ersten Weltkrieg: Die deutschen Parteien und die Politik der USA 1914–1918* (Düsseldorf, 1995).
Parkinson, Roger, *Tormented Warrior – Ludendorf and the Supreme Command* (London, 1978).
Patemann, R., *Der Kampf um die preussische Wahlrechtsreform im Ersten Weltkrieg* (Düsseldorf, 1964).
Petzold, J., 'Ludendorff oder Kühlmann? Die Meinungswershiedenheiten zwischen OHL und Reichsregierung zur Zeit der Friedensverhandlungen in Brest-Litovsk', *Zeitschrift für Geschichtswissenschaft*, Heft 12, 1964.
_____ 'Die Entscheidung von 29 September 1918', *Zeitschrift für Militärgeschichte*, 1965.
Pohle, H.-J., *Agrarische Interessenpolitik und preussischer Konservatismus im wilheiminischen Reich* (Hanover, 1966).
Ponsonby, Lord, *Falsehood in Wartime* (London, 1927).
Quidde, Ludwig, *Der deutsche Pazifismus während des Weltkrieges 1914–1918*, hrsg. K. Holl (Boppard, 1979).
Rakenius, Gerhard, *Wilhelm Groener als erster Generalquartiermeister. Die Politik der Obersten Heeresleitung 1918–19* (Boppard, 1977).
Reichsarchiv, *Der Weltkrieg 1914–1918* (Berlin, 1929).
Retallack, James, *Germany in the Age of Kaiser Wilhelm* (New York, 1996).
Ritter, Gerhard, *The Schlieffen Plan: A Critque of a Myth* (New York, 1958).

——— *Staatskunst und Kriegshandwerk*, Band 3 (Munich, 1964), Band 4 (Munich, 1968).

Roerkohl, Anne, *Hungerblockade und Heimatfront: Die kommunale Lebensmittelversorgung in Westfalen während des Ersten Weltkrieges* (Stuttgart, 1991).

Roetter, Charles, *Psychological Warfare* (London, 1974).

Röhl, J.C.G., *Germany without Bismarck* (London, 1967).

——— 'Staatsstreich oder Staatsstreichbereitschaft?', *Historische Zeitschrift*, Band 209, 1969.

——— (ed.), *Der ort Kaiser Wihelms II in der deutschen Geschichte* (Munich, Oldenburg, 1991).

——— *The Kaiser and his Court. Wilhelm II and the Government of Germany* (Cambridge, 1995).

——— *Young Wilhelm. The Kaiser's Early Life, 1859–1888* (Cambridge, 1998).

——— *Wilhelm II: Into the Abyss of War and Exile, 1900–1941* (Cambridge, 2014).

Rosenfeld, Günter, *Sowjetrussland und Deutschland 1917–1922* (Berlin, 1960).

Roshwald, Aviel and Stites, Richard (eds), *European Culture in the Great War. The Arts, Entertainment and Propaganda, 1914–1918* (Cambridge, 1999).

Sackett, Robert, *Popular Entertainment, Class, and Politics in Munich, 1900–1923* (Cambridge, MA, 1982).

Sanders, Michael and Taylor, Philip, *British Propaganda During the First World War* (London, 1982).

Saul, K., 'Der Deutsche Kriegerbund. Zur innenpolitischen Funktion eines nationalen Verbandes im kaiserlichen Deutschland', *Militärgeschichtliche Mitteilungen*, Heft 2, 1969.

Scharlau, W.B. and Zeman, Z.A., *Freibeuter der Revolution. Parvus Helphand* (Cologne, 1964).

Scheck, Raffael, *Alfred von Tirpitz and German Right-Wing Politics, 1914–1930* (Atlantic Highlands, NJ, 1997).

Schellenberg, Johanna, 'Die Herausbildung der Militärdiktatur in den ersten Jahren des Krieges', in *Politik in Krieg 1914–1918* (Berlin, 1964).

Schmidt-Reichberg, W. and Matuschka, E. Graf von, *Handbuch der deutschen Militärgeschichte*, Band 3 (Frankfurt, 1967).

Schöne, Siegfried, *Von der Reichskanzlei zum Bundeskanzleramt* (Berlin, 1968).

Schröter, A., *Krieg-Staat-Monopol 1914–1918. Die Zusammenhänge von imperialistischer Kriegswirtschaft Militarisierung der Volkswirtschaft und Staatsmonopolistischem Kapitalismus in Deutschland während des Ersten Weltkrieges* (Berlin, 1965).

Schulte, B.F., *Die verfälschung der Riezler-Tagebücher. Ein beitrag zur Wissenschaftsgeschichte der 50er und 60er Jahre* (Frankfurt am Main, 1985).

Schulze, W. (ed.), *Sozialgeschichte, Alltagsgeschichte, Mikro-Historie* (Göttingen, 1994).

Schwartzmüller, T. *Zwischen Kaiser und' Fuhrer'. Generalfeldmarschall August von Mackensen* (Paderborn, 1995).

Schweke, Hans-Jürgen, *U-Bootkrieg und Friedenspolitik*, phil. Diss. (Heidelberg, 1952).

Shand, James, 'Doves among the Eagles: German Pacifists and Their Government during World War I,' *Journal of Contemporary History* 10 (1975), 95–108.

Sichler, R. and Tiburtius, J., *Die Arbeiterfrage, eine Kernfrage des Weltkrieges* (Berlin, 1925).
Skalweit, A., *Die deutsche Kriegsernährungswirtschaft* (Berlin, 1927).
Spindler, A., *Wie es zu dem Entschluss zum uneingeschränkten U-Boot- Krieg 1917 gekommen ist* (Göttingen, 1961).
Stanley, Peter, (ed.), *What Did You Do in the War, Daddy? A Visual History of Propaganda Posters* (Oxford, 1984).
Stark, G.D. 'Cinema, Society, and the State: Policing the Film Industry in Imperial Germany,' in G.D. Stark and B.K. Lackner (eds), *Essays on Culture and Society in Modern Germany* (Arlington, Tx, 1982), 122–66.
———— 'All Quiet on the Home Front: Popular Entertainments, Censorship and Civilian Morale in Germany, 1914–1918,' in Coetzee, F. and Shevin-Coetzee (eds), *Authority, Identity and the Social History of the Great War* (Oxford, 1995), 57–80.
Steglich, W., *Die Friedenspolitik der Mittelmächte 1917–18*, Band 1 (Wiesbaden, 1964).
Stegmann, Dirk, 'Die deutsche Inlandspropaganda 1917–18: Zum innenpolitischen Machtkampf zwischen OHL und ziviler Reichsleitung in der Endphase des Kaiserreiches,' *Militärgeschichtliche Mitteilungen*, No. 2 (1972), 75–116
Stern, Fritz, *Bethmann Hollweg und der Krieg. Die Grenzen der Verantwortung* (Tülbingen, 1968).
Sternsdord-Hauck, Ch., *Brotmarken undrote Fahnen. Frauen in der bayerischen Revolution und Räterepublik 1918–19* (Frankfurt am Main, 1989).
Stevenson, D., *1914–1918: The History of the First World War* (London 2004).
Stöcker, M., *Das Augusterlebnis 1914 in Darmstadt. Legend und Wirklichkeit* (Darmstadt, 1994).
Strachan, Hugh (ed.), *The Oxford Illustrated History of the First World War* (Oxford, 1998).
Taylor, Philip, *Munitions of the Mind. A History of Propaganda from the Ancient World to the Present Era* (Manchester, 1995).
Terveen, Fritz, 'Die Anfange der deutschen Film-Kriegsberichterstaltung in den Jahren 1914–1916,' *Wehrwissenschaftliche Rundschau*, Heft 6 (1956), 318–28.
Thieme, H., *Nationalliberalismus in der Krise. Die nationalliberalen Fraktion des preussischen Abgeordnetenhauses 1914–1918* (Boppard, 1963).
Thimme, Annelise, *Flucht in den Mythos. Die Deutschnationale Volkspartei und die Niederlage von 1918* (Göttingen, 1969).
Thimme, Hans, *Weltkrieg ohne Waffen. Die Propaganda der Westmächte gegen Deutschland, ihre Wirkung und ihre Abwehr* (Berlin, 1932).
Tobin, E.H., 'War and the Working Class; The Case of Düsseldorf 1914–1918', *Central European History* 18 (1985), 257–98.
Travers, M., *German Novels on the First World War and their Ideological Implication; 1918–1933* (Stuttgart, 1982).
Trotnow, Hartmut, *Karl Liebknecht (1871–1919): A Political Biography* (Hamden, CT, 1984).
Tuchmann, B.W., *The Zimmermann Telegram* (London, 1959).

Tucker, Spencer, *The Great War 1914–18* (London, 1997).
Ulrich, B. and Ziemann, B. (eds), *Frontalltag im Ersten Weltkrieg* (Frankfurt am Main, 1994).
Ulrich, Volker, *Die Hamburger Arbeiterbewegung vom Vorabend des Ersten Weltkrieges bis zur Revolution 1918–19* (Hamburg, 1976).
Umbreit, P., 'Gemeinsame Arbeit der Behörden und der Gewerkschaften', *SozialistischeMonatshefte*, 26, 1916.
—— *Die deutschen Gewerkschaften im Kriege* (Stuttgart, 1928).
Ungern-Sternberg von Pürkel, J. and Ungern-Sternberg, W. von, *Der Aufruf andie Kulturwelt: Das Manifest der 93 und die Anfänge der Kriegspropaganda im Ersten Weltkrieg* (Stuttgart, 1996).
Varain, H.J., *Freie Gewerkschaften, Sozialdemokratie und Staat. Die Politik der Generalkommission unter der Führung Carl Legiens (1890–1928)* (Düsseldorf, 1958).
Venohr, Wolfgang, *Ludendorff: Legende und Wirklichkeit* (Berlin, 1993).
Verhey, Jeffrey, 'The Spirit of 1914". The Myth of Enthusiasm and the Rhetoric of Unity in World War I Germany', PhD Diss. (Berkeley, University of California, 1991).
—— 'Krieg und geistige Mobilmachung: Die Kriegspropaganda', in W. Kruse (ed.), *Eine Welt von Feinden: Der grosse Krieg 1914–1918* (Frankfurt am Main, 1997), 176–82.
—— *The Spirit of 1914. Militarism, Myth and Mobilization* (Cambridge, 2000).
Vincent, C. Paul, *The Politics of Hunger: The Allied Blockade of Germany, 1915–1919* (Athens, OH, 1985).
Volkmann, E. O., *Der Marxismus und das deutsche Heer im Weltkrieg* (Berlin, 1925).
Wall, R. and Winter, J. (eds), *The Upheaval of War: Family, Work and Welfare in Europe, 1914–1918* (Cambridge, 1988).
Waschnek, E., *Weltkrieg und Propaganda* (Berlin, 1936).
Watson, A., *Ring of Steel: Germany and Austria-Hungary at War, 1914–1918* (London, 2014).
Weber, H., *Ludendorff und die Monopole* (Berlin, 1966).
Wehler, Hans-Ulrich, *Bismarck und der Imperialismus* (Cologne, 1969).
—— *The German Empire, 1871–1918* (Leamington Spa, 1985).
Weitz, Eric, *Creating German Communism, 1890–1990: From Popular Protest to Socialist State* (Princeton, 1997).
Welch, David, *Hitler* (London, 1998).
—— 'August 1914: Public Opinion and the Crisis', in G. Martel (ed), *A Companion to Europe 1900–1945* (London, 2011), 197–212.
—— 'War Aims and the "Big Ideas" of 1914', in D. Welch and J. Fox (eds), *Justifying War. Propaganda, Politics and the Modern Age* (Basingstoke, 2012), 71–94.
—— 'Images of the Hun: The Portrayal of the German Enemy in British Propaganda in World War I' in D. Welch (ed.), *Propaganda, Power and Persuasion. From World War I to WikiLeaks* (London, 2013), 37–61.
Wendt, Hermann, *Verdun 1916. Die angriffe Falkenhayns im Maasgebiet mit Richtung auf Verdun* (Berlin, 1936).

Wertheimer, M.S., *The Pan-German League 1890–1914* (New York, 1924).
Westarp, Kuno Graf von, *Das Ende der Monarchie am 9 November 1918* (Berlin, 1952).
Whalen, Robert Weldon, *Bitter Wounds: German Victims of the Great War, 1914–1939* (London, 1984).
Wheeler, Robert, *USPD und Internationale: Sozialistiscner Internationalismus in der Zeit der Revolution* (Frankfurt, 1975).
Wheeler-Bennett, J., *Hindenburg, the Wooden Titan* (London, 1936).
_____ *Brest-Litovsk, the Forgotten Peace, March 1918* (London, 1938).
Williams, John, *The Home Fronts: Britain, France and Germany 1914–18* (London, 1972).
Winkler, Erwin, *Die Bewegung der Berliner Revolutionäiren Obleute in Ersten Weltkrieg*, phil. Diss. (Berlin, 1964).
Winter, J. and Jean-Louis Robert (eds) *Capital Cities at War: Volume 2, A Cultural History: Paris, London, Berlin 1914–1919* (Cambridge, 2012).
Wohl, Robert, *The Generation of 1914* (Cambridge, MA, 1979).
Wollstein, Günter, *Theobald von Bethmann Hollweg: Letzter Erbe Bismarcks, Erstes Opfer der Dolchstosslegende* (Göttingen, 1990).
Wrisberg, Ernst von, *Heer und Heimat 1914–1918* (Leipzig, 1921).
Yaney, George, *The World of the Manager: Food Administration in Berlin during World War I* (New York, 1994).
Zechlin, E., *Die deutsche Politik und die Juden im Ersten Weltkrieg* (Göttingen, 1968).
Zeman, Z.A., *Germany and the Revolution in Russia 1915–1918* (London, 1950).
_____ *The Break-up of the Habsburg Empire. A Study in National and Social Revolution* (London, 1961).
Ziemann, B., *Front und Heimat. Ländliche Kriegserfahrungen im südlichen Bayern 1914–1923* (Essen, 1997).
Zuber, T., *The Real German War Plan, 1904–1914* (London, 2011).
Zwehl, H. von, *Erich von Falkenhayn General der Infanterie. Eine biographische Studie* (Dresden, 1926).

Index

Addams, Jane, 146
'Adlon Group', 196
Advisory Food Council, 117, 119
AEG, *see* General Electric Company
Africa, 66
agriculture, 109–10, 111, 112, 114, 132–3
Alldeutsche Verband, *see* Pan-German Association
Allied blockade, 7, 83, 88, 123, 126, 139, 169, 265
Altona, 165
Amiens, 252
annexations, 185–92, 202, 205, 227, 253
anti-Slav, 210
anti-Semitism, 12, 209–10, 324–5
anti-war, 16, 142, 146–7
Argentina, 56
Armistice, the, 253, 260, 263
Army League, 72, 208
Augspurg, Anita, 144–5, 146, 151, 153, 155
Austria-Hungary, 14, 24, 40, 56, 89, 175, 177, 233, 236
Auxiliary Service Cross, 108

Baden, Max von, Prince, 155, 168, 254–9
Balkans, 14, 56, 57, 76
Balkan-Orient GmbH, 57
Baralong incident, 67
Barmen, 46
Bassermann, Rudolf, 12
Batocki, Freiherr von, 96, 119, 120

Bauer, Max, 28, 88, 90, 96, 238, 249, 263
Bäumer, Gertrude, 157–9, 163, 290
Bavaria, 15, 46, 117, 145, 148, 150, 152, 158, 170, 174, 213
Beaverbrook, Lord, 239
Bebel, August, 12
Belgium, 3, 26, 61, 187, 207, 265
Benedict XV, Pope, 207
Berghahn, Volker, 210
Berlin, 16, 17, 20, 45, 96, 112, 128, 130, 132, 146, 148, 150, 152, 160, 169, 178, 182–3, 233, 235, 245, 246, 247, 249, 257, 259
Berliner Lokalanzeiger, 32, 52, 151
Berliner Morgenpost, 32
Berliner Tageblatt, 75, 113, 114, 231
Bernard, Lucien, 220
Bernhard, Georg, 40, 254
Bernstein, Eduard, 12, 73, 153, 179–80
Bethmann Hollweg, Theobald von, 13, 15, 18, 21, 23, 28, 35, 36, 42, 70, 72, 79, 90, 94, 96, 98, 99, 108, 135, 154, 169, 172, 178, 187, 191, 192, 194–8, 201, 204, 228, 262, 265
Bismarck, Otto von, 10, 12, 30, 133, 213, 256
Blücher, Princess, 17, 115, 117, 123, 125, 174, 193, 207, 232, 247, 253, 259, 261
Blunck, Andreas, Dr, 37
Bolsheviks, 109–10, 232–3, 235, 236, 237, 249, 254, 260, 263, 265; propaganda, 7, 240, 263
Bremen, 49

Bremer Arbeiterzeitung, 185
Bremer Bürgerzeitung, 185
Breslau, 152, 247
Brest-Litovsk, Treaty of, 4, 77–8, 202, 231–8, 265, 331
Briand, Aristide, 191
Britain, 3, 18, 41–2, 65, 188, 238, 238, 261
Brunswick, 46, 121, 171, 183
Brusilov Offensive, 89
Bryce Report, 66–7, 286
Bucharest, 129, 191, 239
Bulgaria, 26
Bull, John, 123, 220
Bullitt, Edward, 169
Bund der Landwirte, 132–3
Bund Deutscher Frauenvereine, see Federation of German Women's Associations (BDF)
Bund neues Vaterland, 73, 146, 148, 151
Bundesrat, 11, 97, 99, 101, 111, 113
Burgfrieden, 2, 3, 14, 18, 26, 27, 29, 30, 32, 35, 60, 61, 68, , 70, 79, 80, 111, 134, 141, 147, 149, 150, 153, 155, 159, 166, 175, 176, 184, 186, 191, 194, 195, 204, 206, 261, 262, 265, 266
Büro für Sozialpolitik, 6, 89, 161–2, 252

Cappelle, Eduard von, 135, 136, 136
Carr, E.H., 3
Carsten, Francis, 263
casualties, 169, 189
Catholic Centre Party (*Zentrum Partei*), 24, 49, 88, 113, 164, 188, 199, 229
Catholicism, 17, 66, 189, 207, 229
Cauer, Minna, 144, 149
censorship, 30–9, 60, 69, 182–4, 233, 253; pre-censorship (*Präventivzzensur*), 38
Central Office for the Foreign Service (*Zentralstelle für Auslandsdienst*), 24, 44
chemical industries, 209

child mortality, 131
church, 66, 170, 171
cinema, 4, 43–60, 154, 170, 221, 228; attendance, 43–4; numbers, 59; *Reichslichtspielgesetz*, 46
Class, Heinrich, 210
Cologne, 33, 62, 112, 142
Colonial Office, 41
Colonial Society, 72, 188
Committee of Christian National Workers, 188
Compiègne, 259
constitution, imperial Germany, 10–11, 15
Continental Korrespondenz, 25
Continental Times, 215
Council of War (1912), 13
Counter Intelligence Department, 173
'counter public' (*Gegenöffentlichkeit*), 215, 253
Courland, 92
crime: adolescents, 49–50, 128–9, 236, 237; women, 128–9, 309

Dahlin, Ebba, 188
Darmstadt, 15
Darwinism, 145
David, Eduard, 136, 156, 179–80, 233
Delbrück, Clemens Dr, 37, 110–12
'Demand of the Hour', 73–4, 178–9
Deputy Commanding Generals, 4, 22, 35, 42, 85, 118, 120, 121, 122, 134, 147, 152, 154, 161, 170, 171, 175, 181, 213, 216, 246, 252, 257, 264
Deutelmoser, Erhard, Major, 39, 41, 42, 122, 161–2, 172, 212, 239, 250
Deutsche Kriegsnachrichten, 40, 206
Deutsche Lichtbild Gesellschaft (Deulig), 57, 224
Deutsche Tageszeitung, 114
Deutsche Zeitung, 25
diet, see food
Dittmann, Wilhelm, 20, 180, 236
Ditz, Walter, 251

Dolchstoss, see 'stab in the back'
Dortmund, 20
Dresden, 127
Drexler, Anton, 210
Duhr, Reverend Bernhard, 66
Duisberg, 89
Duisberg, Carl, 196
Durchhalten ('holding out'), 27, 35, 61, 78, 150, 173–5
Dürer League, 45
Düsseldorf, 106, 143, 179, 185

Ebert, Friedrich, 72, 133, 233, 237, 260
Eckert, Paul, 235
economy, 80; black market, 127, 130, 231, 246; finance, 80–3; savings, 81; scientific management, 88
Eiko-Woche, 52
Eiserne Kruez, Das (The Iron Cross, 1915), 154
Eley, Geoff, 177, 194
Elias, Norbert, 213
'emergency materials' (*zwangsläufig materiale*), 85
Enabling Act (August 1914), 4, 19, 99
Engelhard, F.K., 220
'enlightenment' (*aufklärung*), 190, 206, 215
Erdt, Hans Rudi, 90, 135–6
Erler, Fritz, 214–5, 219
Erzberger, Matthias, 24, 189, 199, 201, 229, 266
Erzberger Office, 24, 266
Essen, 107, 117, 183, 185
Evangelical Women's League (DEF), 157, 164–5
Evans, Richard, 156
Exceptional Laws, the, 18, 274

Falkenhayn, Erich von, 28, 34, 70, 84, 88, 89
famine, 109–34
families, 80, 118, 128, 131, 165, 223

Federation of German Women's Associations (BDF), 146, 155, 158–61, 163, 166, 170
Feldman, Gerald, 70, 80
feminists, 144–7, 152–4, 156, 157, 176
Fieldkinos, 57, 58
film, *see* cinema
Film Censorship Office (*Filmprüfungsamt*), 46
Fischer, Edmund, 77
Fischer, Fritz, 13, 61, 69
Fischer, Richard, 35
Flottenverein, see Navy League
Foch, Ferdinand, 244, 256
food, 109–34, 175, 182, 231, 265, 291, 297; prices, 110, 112, 116, 246; production, 116, 125–7; rationing, 111–3, 117–34, 235; riots, 117, 128,182; 'self-help', 119, 121; substitutes, 117, 125, 126, 130, 221, 246
Foreign Office, 34, 44, 212, 253
'Fourteen Points', 234, 254, 255
France, 19, 26, 30, 41–2, 48, 59, 68, 188, 238; army mutinies (1917), 232
Francis Ferdinand, Austrian Archduke, 13
Frankfurt Parliament, 9
Frankfurter Zeitung, 32, 66, 77, 118
Frauenbewegung, Die, 147, 151
Frederick the Great, 85, 215, 257
Free Trade Union, 235
Friedensturm ('assault to peace'), 238
French Revolution, 254
Fried, Alfred, 143–4
Friedenswarte, Die, 143

Geldkrieg, 210
Generalanzeiger, 31–2
General Electric Company (AEG), 84, 254
General Staff, 33, 36, 41, 42, 70, 89, 96
General Workers Union, 179

Gerard, James, 16, 62, 115, 127, 160, 192
German Army League, 9
German Communist Party, 181
German Employer Organizations, 105
German Fatherland Party, 6, 186, 195, 208–10, 227, 241, 262
Germania, 25, 188
German Peace Society, 144, 148, 151, 153
German Publishers' Association (*Verein Deutscher Zeitungsverleger*), 36
'German socialism', 42
German National Women's Committee for a Lasting Peace, 146–7, 151
Gläser, Ernst, 129, 133
Gleichheit, Die, 147, 158, 161
Goethe, J.W., 2, 22, 199
Golem Der (1915), 48
Graf, Oskar Maria, 128,
Grey, Edward Sir, 56, 62–3
Gröber, Adolf, 37
Groener, General Wilhelm, 96–7, 100–101, 105–6, 119–20, 162, 256–7
Group International, 178
Gruner, Eric, 227
Gunsser, Hermann, 213

Haase, Hugo, 19, 35, 37, 74, 75, 175, 178–80, 227, 233–4
Habsburg Monarchy, *see* Austria-Hungary
Haeften, Lt-Colonel von, 206, 239, 250
Hague Congress, The, 146
Hamburg, 122, 145, 146, 148, 152, 165
Hamburger Fremdenblatt, 25
Hamburger Nachrichten, 25
'hamster trains', 128
Hann, Hein und Henny (1917), 220
Hanssen, Peter, 17, 35, 79, 179, 187, 235, 249, 256
Hauptmann, Gerhart, 66
Health Office (Reich), 130, 300, *see* food

Hearst newspapers, 32
Heine, Wolfgang, 71, 178
Helfferich, Karl, 82, 90, 94, 99–100, 135, 246
Hertling, Georg von, 229, 233, 236, 247, 250–51, 254
Herwig, Holger, 97
Heymann, Lida Gustava, 144–6, 151–2, 155, 161
Hindenburg, Paul von, 2, 39, 69, 89, 92, 93, 96, 161, 163, 172, 192, 198–201, 204–5, 220, 233, 235, 240, 241, 252, 255, 260
Hindenburg line, *see* Siegfried Line
Hindenburg Programme, 4, 57, 88–97, 293
Hitler, Adolf, 1, 16, 212, 261, 264, 266; *Mein Kampf*, 1, 264, 328
Hoch, Gustav, 199, 203
Hohenzollerns, 10, 92, 212, 256
Hohlwein, Ludwig, 250
Holland, 152, 259
home front, the, 95, 170, 196, 206, 218
Homunculus (1916), 48
Horrmeyer, Ferdy, 243
Hötzendorff, Conrad von, 89
Hugenberg, Alfred, 57, 88, 209
humour, 301
Hungary, 236, *see also* Austria-Hungary
Hutier, General von, 240–41

'ideas of, 1914', *see* 'Spirit of 1914'
Imperial Distribution Office, 111
Imperial Naval Office, 36, 190
Imperial Office for Potato Supplies, 112
Imperial Price Examination Agency, 112
Imperial War Grain Board, 111
Independent Committee for a German Peace, 188
Independent German Social Democratic Party (USPD), 101, 108, 168, 180, 181, 194, 216, 227, 229, 233–6, 241, *see also* Social Democratic Party

Index

industry, 94, 95, 97, 99, 202
inflation, 83–4
influenza, 126, 132, 252
internal reforms, 60, 253
Isonzo Front, 89

Jagow, Gottlieb von, 36, 68
Jahrgang 1902, see Ernst Gläser
Jesuits, 17, 37, 274
Jews, 17, 83, 84, 254, 263, see anti-Semitism
Junkers, 6, 133
Jutland, Battle of, 185
juveniles, 49

Kaiser, The, see Wilhelm II
Kaiserin, The, 20, 81, 212; see also Wilhelm, Augusta Princess
Kaiserreich, 259, 263
Kaiserschlacht ('Kaiser's battle'), 238
Kapp, Wolfgang, 208
Kautsky, Karl, 73, 74
Kerensky, Alexander, 232
Kessel, Gustav von, 34, 47, 236–7
Kiel, 234, 255, 256, 260
Kinematograph, 52, 53, 54
Kinoreformbewegung, 45
Kirdorf, Emil, 209
Kitchen, Martin, 204
Kladderadatsch, 65
Knute entflohen, Der (Escaping from Tyranny), (1917), 228
Koblenz, 35
Kocka, Jürgen, 44, 205
Kolb, Wilhelm, 74
Kölnische Volkszeitung, 88, 113, 189
Kölnische Zeitung, 61, 62, 75, 77, 253
König, Max, 20
Königsberg, 121, 246
Kopp, Martin, 52
Kriegsamt, see Supreme War Office
Kriegsanleihen, see war loans
Kriegsbier, 125
Kriegsbrot, 124

Kriegsernährungsamt, see War Food Office
Kriegsgefahrzustand, 15
Kriegspresseamt (KPA), see War Press Office
Kriegsrohstoffabteilung (KRA), see War Raw Materials Office
Kriegsrohstoffgesellschaften, see War Raw Materials Corporations
Krupp AG, 57, 89, 107, 117
Kruse, Wolfgang, 177
Kuhl, General von, 249
Kühlmann, Richard von, 228–9, 232, 247, 324

labour movement, 80, 94, 96, 101, 103, 245, 249; changing perception of women, 80, 106, 161; juvenile workforce, 93, 244, 249; mobilization of women, 93, 104, 106, 157, 160, 162, 294
Lamprecht, Karl, 66
Landsberg, Otto, 228
Law of Siege, Prussian, 2, 22, 23, 27–8, 85, 108
League for a New Fatherland, see *Bund neues Vaterland*
League for the Protection of Mothers, 145
League of German Farmers, 110
League of German Scholars and Artists, 171–2
League of Progressive Women's Associations, 157
Ledebour, Georg, 76, 178
Lederer, Emil, 18
Leipzig, 16, 112
Leipziger Neuste Nachrichten, 113
Leipziger Volkszeitung, 73, 182, 241, 274
Lenin, V.I., 232–3
Leuna works, 107
Lewinsohn, Ludwig, 230
Liebknecht, Karl, 72, 75, 76, 147, 168, 169, 177–9, 181–3, 259
Limburg, Bishop of, 207

Lissauer, Ernst, 62
Lithuania, 188, 331
Lloyd George, David, 191, 237,
Loebbel, Friedrich Wilhelm von, 38, 49, 78, 200
Longwy-Briey, 53, 322
Ludendorff, Erich von, 2, 4, 39, 42, 59, 70, 83, 96, 108, 168, 172, 176, 192, 196–201, 204–7, 215–8, 222, 226–30, 232–3, 138–9, 254–6, 260, 261, 263, 266; resignation, 255
Ludendorff Fund, 250
Ludendorff Offensive, 238–40, 243
Lüders, Marie-Elisabeth, 162
Lusitania, 67
Luxemburg, Rosa, 69, 147, 165, 168, 178, 183
Lyncker, General von, 200

Mackensen, Field Marshal, 239
Mainz, 106
Majority Socialists, 199
Mannheim, 43
Marburg, 292
Marie Therese of Bavaria, 158
Marx, Karl, 12
Marxism, 80, 155
Mehring, Franz, 178
Meinecke, Friedrich, 196, 210
Mendelssohn-Bartholdy, A. von, 87–8
Messter, Oskar, 51–4
Messter Woche, 52–6;
  Sascha-Messter-Woche, 56
Metal Workers Union (*Metallarbeiterverband*), 99, 108, 234
Michaelis, Georg, 168, 201–2, 207, 228–9, 298
Miquel, Johann, 12
Militärische Stelle des Auswärtiges Amts (MAA), 44, 57, 206
militarism, 2, 42, 63, 79, 196
military districts (*Wehrkreise*), 21
Ministry of Agriculture, 114
Ministry of Finance, 110
Ministry of Information (British), 7, 239
Ministry of the Interior, 46, 110, 114, 159
Ministry for Popular Enlightenment and Propaganda, 8
Ministry of Propaganda, *see* propaganda
Ministry of War, *see* War Ministry
Mittel-Europa, 188
Mittlestand, 246, 262
Moltke, Hellmuth von, 29, 33, 38
Mommsen, Wolfgang, 13
Monatsberichten, 4, 118, 121, 122, 134, 149, 152, 169, 170, 171, 172, 185, 185, 190, 192, 213, 216, 223, 229, 236, 237, 240, 246, 247, 252, 254, 257
morale, 122, 204–6, 218, 230, 246, 249, 263–4, 291
Morality Associations, 157
Mosse, Rudolf, 32
MSPD, *see* Majority Social Democratic Party Munich
Müller, August, 119
Müller, Karl Alexander von
Müller, Richard, 234–5
Müller-Meiningen, Dr, 37
Mumm, Schwartzenstein von, 37, 49
Münchener Neueste Nachrichten, 65
Munich, 16, 19, 22, 57, 110, 146, 148, 149, 151, 152, 169, 170, 251
Munitions of War Act (1915), 91

Nachrichtungabteilung (News Section), 28
National Liberal Party, 51, 164, 188, 196, 197, 233
National Socialism (NSDAP), 209, 210, 261, 267
National Women's Service, 159
Nauen (transmitter), 24–5
Naval Office, imperial, 36, 235
navy, German, 41, 255
Navy League, 12, 72, 208; 'mutinies', 229, 256, 260
Neuorientierung, 37
New Fatherland Alliance, *see Bund Neues Vaterland*

Newspapers, *see* press
Nibelungen, legend, 223
Nicolai, Walter, 28, 33, 189, 190, 206, 211–2, 216, 252
Norddeutsche Allgemeine Zeitung, 32, 62, 65 , 66
Northcliffe, Lord, 26, 32, 239, 240
Noske, Gustav, 51
Nuremberg, 134, 145

Oberzensurstelle, see Supreme Censorship Office
Obermilitärbefehlshaber (Supreme Military Commander)
Oberste Heeresleitung – OHL, see Supreme Command of the Army
Oncken, Hermann, 77
Oppenheim, Louis, 90, 220
Oswald, Richard, 154

Paasche, Dr, 72
Pacelli, Papal Nuncio, 207
pacifism, 140, 141–55, 161, 166–7, 176, 207, 254; 'defeatists', 305
Pan German, 79, 186, 188, 204, 208–9, 226–8, 252, 254
Pan-German League, 12, 19, 188, 208
Pan-Slavism, 70
Papal peace initiative, 207, 229
Paul, Bruno, 90, 93, 213
Paul, Gerd, 220, 225
Patriotic Auxiliary Service Law, 4, 28, 98–109
Patriotic Instruction, 4, 140, 203, 211–30, 240, 262, 330–31; organization, 217
Patriotic Women's Associations, 159
Peace movement, *see* pacifism
Peace Resolution, 105, 154, 168, 201–2, 205–8, 228–9, 234
People's League for Freedom and Fatherland, 186
Perlen, Frida, 145
Photographic and Film Office (Bufa), 51, 57, 224–5

Planck, Max, 66
Plank, Mathilde, 145
poetry, 280
Poland, 76, 188, 205
political reforms, 187, 188, 192–203
Polte, Oswald, 163
Pomerania, 113
Porten, Henny, 220
press, the, 30–43, 114, 121–2, 171, 238, 253, 254
Press Bureau, 33
Prinzregent Luitpold, 229
prisoners of war, 166, 221
profit-mongering, 112, 122
Progressive People's Party, 168, 199, 227
propaganda, 4, 7, 106, 107, 151, 163, 169, 170, 173, 204–6, 211–2, 213, 215, 219–22, 226, 229–30, 239, 249–53, 259, 6, 263, 264, 265, 266; anti-British, 61–3, 66, 67, 70, 115, 123, 135–6; anti-French, 19, 70, 115; anti-Russian, 19, 70; British, 7, 174, 240–42, 250; 'directors of', 218; hate, 61–7; images of women, 142–3, 164, 163, 223, 226, 227, 243–5; leaflets, 240; Ministry of Propaganda, 7, 42, 206, 239, 250, 266, 335; organization, 23–43, 217; postcards, 63, 65, 81, 115, 125, 240, 241; posters, 48, 50, 86, 87, 93, 106, 115, 124, 126, 137, 138, 139, 163, 164, 170, 174, 214–5, 218–23, 248, 250, 251; problems of, 230
Protestantism, 207,
Prussia, 5–6, 9, 249, 249; parliament, 10, 247
Prussian Landtag, 11
Prussian Law of Siege (1851), 15
public opinion, 3, 4, 7, 23, 169–76, 192–203, 204–6, 241, 246, 254, 263, 265, 266

Quidde, Ludwig, 143, 146–8, 150, 153

Radek, Karl, 234
Radel, Frieda, 144–5
Rathenau, Walter, 84–8, 95, 254
rationing, *see* food
Reichsbank, 111
Reichs Press Office, 230
Reichstag, 6, 10, 19, 34, 40, 49, 63, 72, 78, 102, 119, 136, 163, 168, 198, 199, 232, 233, 259, 266; budget committee, 100–101, 119
Reinhardt, Max, 66
Reuters, 24, 31, 277
revolution (1918), 254, 256–8, 260, 261
Rhine Metal Works, Düsseldorf, 246
Riezler, Kurt, 21, 238, 259, 260
Roedern, Graf, 198
Röhl, John, 13
Romania, 56, 89, 239
Ruhr, 205
rumours, 64, 218, 253
Russia, 13, 16, 16, 6470, 89, 115, 155, 232, 233; Revolution, 141, 169, 193–4, 197, 205, 232–4
Russo-Japanese War (1905), 29

Sailer, Josef Benno, 127
Sammlaungspolitik, 209
Sarajevo, 13
Scandinavia, 24
Scheidemann, Philipp, 73, 79, 189, 201, 237, 239, 246, 249, 259
Scherl, August, 32
Scheüch, Colonel, 84
Schiffer, Eugen, 72
Schirmacher, Käthe, 144
Schleswig-Holstein, 17
Schlicke, Alexander, 99
Schlieffen Plan, 3, 5, 129
schools, 171, 238
Schorlemer, von, 111
Schreiner, George, 130
Schücking, Walter, 143, 153
Schundfilme, 45
Schweitzer, Major, 40
Second World War, 261

Sedan, Day of (1917), 208
shop stewards, 234–6
Siegfried Line, 249, 261
Siegfrieden, 2, 186, 208, 209, 210, 226, 252
Siemens AG, 209
Sigrist, Karl, 243
Silesia, Upper, 165
Simplicissimus, 65, 259
Six Economic Associations, 72, 148, 288
Social Democratic Party (SPD), 12, 15, 19, 35, 51, 71–3, 80, 101, 112, 141–3, 147, 166 168, 169, 176–81, 185, 194, 199, 233, 235–7, 259, 260; 'Minority Socialists', 101
Socialist opposition to war, 168, 176–8, 184, 193
Social Democratic Labour Association, 184
Social Democratic Working Group, 180
Socialist International, 159, 164
Somme, Battle of the, 89, 90, 91, 169
Sonderweg, 212
Sonnemann, Leopold, 32
Sozialdentokratische Arbeizsgenieinschaft, *see* Social Democratic Working Group
Spain, 56, 191
Spartacists, 165, 178, 231, 263
Spartacus League, 147, 180, 183, 185, 194
'*Spartacus Letters*', 180, 183
SPD, *see* Social Democratic Party
'Spirit of 1914', 2, 14–21, 181, 232
spy scares, 63–4
Staats-Zeitung, 25
'stab in the back' legend, 7, 134254, 262–4
State of Siege, The Law of, 6, 15, 28, 33, 143–4, 149, 253, 265
Stegerwald, Adam, 119
Stein, Hermann von, 29, 154, 236
Stöcker, Helene, 145, 156
Stotten, Major, 42, 172, 219

Stinnes, Hugo, 89, 209
Stresemann, Dr Gustav, 51, 187, 197, 200, 233, 247
strikes, 103, 115, 169, 181, 182, 193, 231, 234–8, 261, 310
Stuttgart, 49, 71, 145, 152, 183, 246
Submarine warfare (unrestricted), 135–40, 192, 208, 255
suffrage, 12, 151, *see* women, women's movement
Supreme Censorship Office (OZS), 36–9, 44, 114, 134, 184, 184–6, 187
Supreme Command of the Army (OHL), 28, 26, 41, 42, 52–4, 57–9, 68, 90, 91, 96–7, 97, 104, 105, 107, 140, 154, 168, 169, 189, 192, 196, 198, 202, 211, 227–30; Third, 2, 89, 205, 223, 224, 254–6, 260, 262, 264, 266
Supreme War Office (*Kriegsamt*), 83, 96, 97
Suttner, Bertha von, 143
Sweden, 56, 256
Switzerland, 143, 178, 191

tanks, 249
Tannenberg, Battle of, 90, 205, 252
Third Reich, *see* National Socialism
Thaer, General von, 244
Tirpitz, Alfred von, 12, 158, 208, 210
Tönnies, Ferdinand, 18
'total war', 67, 175, 204–5
trade unions, 98, 99, 100, 102, 102, 103, 112, 235–7, 253, *see also* labour movement
Trotsky, Leon, 284
Tsar, 14, 20
Turkey, 26, 56
'Turnip winter', 109, 120, 132, 139

Überseedienst Transozean GmbH, 25
U-boats, *see* submarine warfare
Ukraine, 233
Ullstein, Leopold, 32
Ullstein Publishing Company, 32

United States of America, 25, 56, 191, 226, 227, 238, 252; entry into war, 135–8
Universum-Film-Aktengesellschaft (Ufa), 51, 59, 222–6
universities, 94, 161
USPD, *see* Independent Social Democratic Party

Valentini, Rudolf von, 200
Vaterländischer Hilfsdienst (PASL), *see* Patriotic Auxiliary Service Law
Vaterländischen Unterrecht, *see* Patriotic Instruction
Vaterlandspartei, *see* German Fatherland Party
Vatican, 207
Verdun, Battle of, 89, 169, 175
Völker-Friede, 143, 144
völkisch, 262
Volksbund für Freiheit und Vaterland, 186
Volksgemeinschaft, 14, 19, 21, 185, 262
Volkskaiser, 266
Volksstaat, 14, 20
Volkssturm, 254
Vollmar, Georg von, 12
Vorwärts, 14, 32, 34, 34, 71, 74, 87, 112, 148, 179, 180, 184, 189, 201, 235, 236, 242, 246, 247, 258
Vossische Zeitung, 40, 73, 94, 254.

wages, 103, 129
Wallruf, Minister of Interior, 237
Wandel, Franz von, 170–1
Wanderkinos, 43, 58
war aims, 60, 61–79, 168–76, 179, 181–92, 262
War Boards (*Kriegsgesellschaften*), 111–2
war corporations, 86–8, 115
War Food Office (KEA), 96, 119–20, 298,
war loans (bonds) (*Kriegsanleiehen*), 82–3, 90, 175, 213–6, 219–23, 227, 243–4; '*Kriegsanliehe-Filme*', 221

War Ministry, 22, 28, 48, 51, 59, 88, 89, 90, 96–7, 118, 145, 151, 175, 211, 223, 229
War Press Office (KPA), 39–3, 44, 51, 57, 122, 161, 172, 184, 206, 211, 216, 217, 229–30, 253, 265
War Production Law (1872), 91
War Raw Materials Corporations, 85
War Raw Materials Office (KRA), 83–8, 96
'war socialism', 102
Weapons and Munitions Procurement Office (WUMBA), 95–6
Weber, Max, 2, 195
Wedekind, Frank, 19
Wehler, Hans-Ulrich, 208
Wehrkreise, *see* military districts
Weimar Republic, 165, 181, 262
Weltpolitik, 12, 266
Wendorff-Toitz, Dr, 113–4
Wernecke, Klaus, 13
Westarp, Graf von, 72, 247
Wild von Hohenborn, Adolf, General, 91, 94, 97, 196
Wilhelmshaven, 229, 256 , 260
Wilhelm, II, German Emperor (Kaiser), 1, 2, 10, 15, 18, 19, 28, 30, 37, 54, 54–5, 76, 82, 97, 101, 122, 138, 140, 141, 163, 166, 177, 192, 195–6, 197–9, 205, 209, 212–3, 227, 232, 238–41, 250, 255–7, 261, 262, 263, 266; abdication, 257, 258
Wilhelm, Augusta Princess, 53, 212, *see* Kaiserin, the

Wilhelm, Crown Prince, 200–2, 249
Wilson, Woodrow, 138, 163, 191, 224, 254–6, 257, *see also* Fourteen Points
Woche, Die, 52
Wolff's Telegraphisches Büro (WTB), 24, 30, 34, 40, 42
women, 80, 131, 141, 170, 221–2, 227; women's movement, 141, 155, 159, 161
Women's Home Army, 246
Women's League for Peace and Freedom
Women's Suffrage Alliance, 155
Women's Suffrage League, 142, 145, 151, 155
Women's Suffrage Union, 155
workers, 80, 181,264; standard of living, 80, 103; workers' councils, 101, 193, 235
Wrisberg, Colonel Ernst von, 171, 211
Württemberg, 121, 122, 154, 193, 213, 225–6

youth, 98, 171, 222, 244, 311

Zekin, Clara, 147, 155, 161, 178
Zietz, Luise, 147, 155
Zimmermann, Arthur, 212; telegram, 319
Zimmerwald, 178–80
Zivilversorgungsschein, 29
Zuckmayer, Carl, 273